THE GERMAN ECONOMY
1870 to the Present

THE GERMAN ECONOMY
1870 to the Present

by

GUSTAV STOLPER

KARL HÄUSER / KNUT BORCHARDT

translated by

TONI STOLPER

Harcourt, Brace & World, Inc.

New York, Chicago, San Francisco, Atlanta

to

ALBERT J. HETTINGER, Jr.

for decades of friendship

BIBLIOGRAPHICAL HISTORY

1. Gustav Stolper, *German Economy, 1870–1940: Issues and Trends* (New York: Reynal & Hitchcock, 1940; London: George Allen & Unwin, 1940).
2. Gustav Stolper, *Deutsche Wirtschaft 1870–1940: Kaiserreich, Republik, Drittes Reich,* translated into German by Dr. Toni Stolper (Stuttgart: Franz Mittelbach Verlag, 1950).
3. Gustav Stolper, continued by Karl Häuser and Knut Borchardt, *Deutsche Wirtschaft seit 1870* (Tübingen: J. C. B. Mohr [Paul Siebeck], 1964); 2. ergänzte Auflage, 1966.

Library of Congress Catalog Card Number: 67–13682

PRINTED IN THE UNITED STATES OF AMERICA

PREFACE

GUSTAV STOLPER'S *German Economy: 1870 to 1940* was first published in 1940 by Reynal & Hitchcock of New York. The author noted in his preface (reprinted here in the appendix) that, although history never ends, the tale he was telling had been provided with a dramatic conclusion—a "caesura" that future historians might choose to call the Second World War. Since that war, history has indeed continued along its involved path.

In time, the first English editions of Stolper's book in the United States and Britain and the translated edition of 1950 in Germany went out of print. Meanwhile, too many events of the greatest significance for German economic history had occurred to make republishing the original work meaningful. Thus it seemed that a valuable presentation of an important phase of history might be lost to students of these matters, which would be all the more regrettable in that no other comparable publication had appeared in the intervening years in the United States or Germany—or in the Spanish speaking countries, either, where a Spanish edition of Stolper's book had also enjoyed wide circulation.

With this in mind I felt it was my duty to find those experts in German economic history who would think as highly of the value of Stolper's book as I do and who would be stimulated by the assignment of following German economic history through several more of its turbulent phases. Professors Karl Häuser of Frankfurt University and Knut Borchardt of Wirtschaftshochschule Mannheim, as well as the publishing house of J. C. B. Mohr, Tübingen, rose to my challenge with enthusiasm. The outcome was a volume of about double the original size, published in 1964 with a title having a more flexible dateline, *Deutsche Wirtschaft seit 1870*. A Japanese edition of this book was quickly arranged. In 1966 a slightly expanded edition appeared in Germany.

After its revival in Germany had proved successful, a return of the enlarged *German Economy* to its first habitat, the English speaking countries, was the next logical step. The result is the present volume; its contents are virtually the same as those of the German edition of 1966, except that the bibliography has been extended to take in more recent studies by American as well as European scholars.

It has not been the aim of Professors Häuser and Borchardt nor my aim as editor and translator to create an illusion of continuing the original author's work in its personal style and form. Each part of the book stands on the studies and reflects the way of presenting facts, issues, and trends of the particular author who wrote it. However, a community of spirit in the approach to history and public affairs among the three authors may be noted, and I have always been conscious of the need to perform a unifying function.

Chapters I to IV are basically Stolper's, although a few changes have been made. Chapter V represents a combination of Stolper's original text and Häuser's contributions based on the inside materials and knowledge concerning the Hitler years that have become fully available after Hitler's downfall. Professor Häuser alone signs for Chapter VI, Professor Borchardt for Chapters VII and VIII.

It remains my grateful duty to acknowledge the help I received in preparing the present edition. Two of my sons, Professor Wolfgang F. Stolper of the University of Michigan, Ann Arbor, and Max A. Stolper of Deltec Corporation, Nassau, Bahamas, read my English manuscript in the true filial spirit of strict criticism. My thanks are also due Professor Karl Roskamp of Wayne State University, Detroit, for some helpful suggestions.

TONI STOLPER

New York
November 3, 1966

CONTENTS

CONTENTS

TABLES

THE GERMAN ECONOMY
1870 to the Present

I

INTRODUCTORY

THIS BOOK COVERS a historical span of about seventy years, the biblical life of man.* In the first forty-three of these years, the German nation, united for the first time in its history, enjoyed unparalleled prosperity, political power, and economic expansion. In the following twenty-five years it had to go through five catastrophes equally without parallel: those of 1914, 1918, 1923, 1933, and 1939. And the next, most dreadful, and possibly final catastrophe already looms on the horizon—defeat in the present war, which may once more mean the end of a united Germany.

No other nation's history displays such a sequence of rise and collapse. To the retrospective eye the years from 1870 to 1914 may appear as a unique episode. In almost two thousand years of European history there were German tribes and German states wielding various degrees of power and influence. But there never was a united Germany before 1871. German tribes overran the ancient Roman Empire and ruled over its dismembered parts. Emperors of the "Holy Roman Empire of the German Nation" were the masters of Europe in the Middle Ages. But not until 1871 was there a German nation that constituted an empire. In the centuries when England and France were laying the foundations on which the structures of their unified states were built, the German people were split into hundreds of principalities and free cities that fought and conquered one another according to the greater or

* This introductory chapter, written in May, 1940, has been left virtually unchanged.

lesser ability and ambition of their rulers. When in the sixteenth and seventeenth centuries the Reformation broke up the Catholic world, the religious wars of Europe were fought on German soil, by Germans against Germans, resulting in the complete exhaustion of the German people and their intellectual and economic life. After the thirty years' war Germany was a desert, depopulated and barbarized.

Germany never recovered from the effects of the thirty years' war. That war shaped the character of the German nation, determined its history, molded its subsequent political and social evolution. As a political power Germany was wiped out after 1600. As an economic power that had flowered in the member towns of the Hanseatic League and the wealthy commercial centers of western and southern Germany, it was annihilated. As an intellectual power, which, after all, had contributed Martin Luther and Albrecht Dürer to European civilization, it disappeared for almost one hundred years—a period, however, during which, miraculously enough, Johann Sebastian Bach and Gottfried Wilhelm Leibnitz were born. Between 1640 and 1740—a century of flourishing power and civilization in England, France, and Spain—the European map seems to show a blank where later modern Germany was to arise.

But the new Germany did not arise from this blank spot. What we understand as German history up to the seventeenth century has its scene of action predominantly west of the Elbe and south of the Main. Here lay the rich towns where commerce and the arts thrived; here were the great monuments of German history, the cathedrals and monasteries and castles and proud mansions of wealthy patrician families; here the battles were fought, the peace treaties signed; here the German princes convened in their Reichstags; here the German kings were chosen by the electoral princes to receive the Holy Imperial Crown from the hands of the pope in Rome.

After the end of the thirteenth century, rarely disputed leadership among the German princes was maintained by the Habsburg dynasty. Originally a penurious Swiss family of counts risen to power in one of the periods of chaos that seemed to be the ever recurring fate of that perennially amorphous part of Europe, the Habsburgs acquired and expanded as a family domain the poor Alpine provinces (much later to be known as Austria) in the southeastern corner of the Germanic territory and gradually extended it from the Danube down to the Adriatic Sea. The Habsburgs acquired but little land in Germany proper; their imperialist drive was directed east, south, and west of German soil. They did not conquer their power, they married it. Even Charles V, the Habsburg emperor who had to confront and to condemn Martin Luther and the Reformation, although German by blood (as far as the blood of any of the European dynasts can be ascertained), was a Spaniard by character and inclination. His residence was not in Vienna or any other German town but in Madrid, and it was from there that the Spanish expeditions were sent out over the oceans to open new worlds. Care of the Austrian provinces—and, a few years before he died (1558), the German affairs as well—he left to his brothers and their descendants.

In 1526 the Habsburgs, again by dint of a marriage contract, inherited the lands of the Bohemian and Hungarian crowns (or at least the disputed titles to them) when the thrones of Bohemia and Hungary became vacant through the death in action of the last king. By the middle of the sixteenth century the high point of Habsburg influence had been reached. Except for Poland the Habsburg sphere covered about the area that four centuries later the Austrian Adolf Hitler would proclaim to be German *Lebensraum* (living space)—including, by no means accidentally, Spain and Italy. But Germany proper, the country between the Rhine and the Elbe, between the North Sea and the Alps, lived her own life under her own princes, not much affected by the aspirations, successes, and failures of the Habsburgs.

The thirty years' war devastated the Habsburg provinces as much as the western parts of the Reich. It is to be remembered that this war originated in Prague and Vienna. Its fury raged in Bohemia and Austria as much as in the Palatinate, in Saxony, Bavaria, and Swabia.

Only a few decades after the termination of this fateful war, at the end of the seventeenth century, a new Germanic power arose in the east—the Prussian state built up by the Hohenzollern princes of the Mark of Brandenburg. The Hohenzollerns, like the Habsburgs, came from the south, close to the Swiss border; but as early as 1415 a Hohenzollern had been invested with the Mark of Brandenburg. When a century later (1525) the Hohenzollerns were made dukes of Prussia, they were under Polish overlordship. From then on, slowly but steadily and irresistibly, German history took more and more of its cues from the East. In 1640 the Great Elector Frederick William became Margrave of Brandenburg. He laid the foundation of Prussian power. He defeated Poland with the help of the Swedes, and Sweden with the help of the Poles, and thereby acquired the territory which in 1701 was elevated to the status of a kingdom under his son, Frederick I.

From that time German history was dominated by the struggle for hegemony of two peripheral powers, Prussia and Austria. The peoples over which the Habsburgs ruled were, and remained to the very end, predominantly non-German. Only very late did Prussia become a German state. Most of the population of its eastern provinces was undoubtedly of Slavic origin, and until late in the eighteenth century a large part of the working classes spoke a Slavic dialect. To this day Slavic tribes survive in the very neighborhood of Berlin, tenaciously preserving their language and their customs. Not until Frederick II, the Great, who ruled from 1740 to 1786, had wrested the province of Silesia from the Austrian Empress Maria Theresa did Prussia include a German majority. Frederick II himself—who was to be a canonized demigod of the Nazi interpretation of history—did not like to speak German and loved French; he wrote his books in French and despised the German language as rude, barbaric, inarticulate. In fact the great masters of German poetry, born in rapid succession from about the middle of the eighteenth century, had to create their language from the poor remnants that survived the thirty years' war. But they again, without exception, were not Prussian, any more than were the radiant stars that arose in the sky of music, the great gift of the German race to mankind. Bach and Handel were Saxons, Mozart and Haydn Austrians, Beethoven a Rhinelander. The early history of Prussia has little to do with the arts and sciences. It is a history of statecraft, administrative efficiency, and military organization. It contributed a peculiar feature to the European picture, a new sort of state, built up by means of a novel type of military organization and administrative machinery. This state was a creation of the dynasty, and the dynasty alone, out of a people that was uneducated, undifferentiated, and only recently colonized and Christianized.

From the very beginnings in Prussia the state was everything, not as a result of any preconceived philosophy, but because of the lack of creative forces other than the state, which was itself the creature of an ambitious dynasty and its military exploits. The state was the source from which both material and spiritual life emanated. Let us remember that the eighteenth century in which Prussia grew into a great power saw the birth of the capitalist system, the origins of modern industrialism with all its social consequences. In France, too, Louis XIV could proclaim the principle *"L'état, c'est moi!"*; but the social stratification of the French people was variegated and complicated. France had its nobility, high and low, the hierarchy of the Catholic clergy, its bourgeoisie, its petite bourgeoisie, its peasantry, the beginnings of a pauperized proletariat. By the end of the eighteenth century the "third" and "fourth" estates, together with the peasants, had overthrown the ruling feudal upper classes of nobility and clergy. The French revolution had been preceded one hundred and fifty years before by the English revolution.

Prussia was free of social problems of this kind. In eighteenth-century Prussia there could be no class struggle, because there was only one class that mattered, the Junkers, who supplied the administration with civil servants and the army with officers. The Junkers were the state. Not until after the conquest of Silesia did any substantial towns exist in Prussia east of the Elbe where a modern industry could evolve from ancient crafts. In eighteenth-century Prussia industry was almost entirely a product of the government. It was the government that founded banks, long before private banks were known. From the very beginning the government displayed all the initiative in capitalist developments, while in the Western world private capitalists took the lead.

The historical reality of the omnipotent state dominated German philosophy; it was not German philosophy that created the omnipotent state. Fichte and Hegel had to deal with and to explain the accomplished facts. This was the world they lived in; it appeared as familiar and natural to them as the air they breathed. At the turn of the eighteenth century the spiritual and social problems of the Western world hardly existed to the Prussian mind. The attack of the French revolution was the attack of an enemy of the nation. Napoleon was not an apostle of revolutionary ideas, as he appeared to many in western and southern Germany, but the tyrannical destroyer of the Prussian principles of law and order and discipline under a respected dynasty that ruled by the grace of God.

With the defeat of Napoleon, Prussia definitely established its sway in western Germany also. From then on the fascinating process of Germany becoming a nation conscious of its destiny grew in scope and intensity. It was not Prussia that took the lead in this national emancipation and integration. Modern nationalism was a direct offspring of the French revolution, suspect to all autocratic rulers and particularly alien to Prussia. German nationalism in the first half of the nineteenth century was definitely liberal and democratic and therefore was suppressed as dangerous to the established order. Not until the failure of the revolution of 1848 was the later marriage of nineteenth-century nationalism and eighteenth-century Prussian absolutism prepared. When this marriage was consummated after the victories of the Prussian armies—in 1864 over Denmark, in 1866 over Austria, and finally in 1871 over France—the prestige of Prussianism reached its zenith. Prussian armies had realized the dream of national unification that the liberals had longed for in vain since the days of Napoleon. The German Reich of Otto von Bismarck was the offspring of that marriage.

What happened after 1870 was the inevitable outgrowth of the peculiar origin of the new Reich. German liberalism, never deeply rooted in the masses even in western and southern Germany and virtually unknown outside of a stratum of intellectuals in East Elbian Prussia, had sold its soul to the principles of Prussian state power. This was the price for the achievement of national glory by Prussia on the battlefields of France. What was left of independent thought, upright individualism, opposition to the deification of the state and the classes personifying the state was crushed or corrupted by the ruthless genius of Bismarck. He broke the backbone of those classes that everywhere else were most jealous of encroachments of the governments upon the lives of the people and were the most successful in preventing them.

Thus Germany acquired a strange cant that began to irritate and increasingly to terrify the world. Germany presented herself to the outside world as a great nation of rapidly growing wealth on the march to unlimited power, a nation successfully displaying all the resources dammed up by the adversities of centuries, a nation inspired by gifts and capacities that aroused the envy and the admiration of friend and foe. And yet, while the German leaders assured themselves loudly enough of steady and rapid progress in every direction, the country was not happy. There was something definitely unhealthy in the estrangement between the German government, holding all the concentrated power of the most powerful state, and the intellectuals of the nation, who never really felt at home in Bismarck's Reich. To be sure, we still speak of the nineteenth century as the era in which liberal principles held so strong a sway over the minds of Europe that even the autocratic leaders of the half-absolutist governments felt constrained to render them their respect. Measured by Hitlerian standards, the Germany of Bismarck and Wilhelm II was a free and liberal country. But measured by the standards of the Western world it was autocratic, authoritarian, unfree. The opposition was not arrested and sent to concentration camps, but it was subdued by more subtle means. The real power rested exclusively with the army and the bureaucracy, whose leading ranks were still recruited from, and dominated by, a few thousand Junker families. Whoever refused to sing their tune eliminated himself from any public career. The Junkers were still the state, and the state still refused to limit its power and pretensions.

It is futile to speculate about possibilities that might have existed had not the first world war interfered. There are many good reasons to believe that Germany was on the road to gradual democratization. The growing influence of the wealthy bourgeoisie, the intensified contacts with the world overseas, the definite change of the powerful Socialist Party from a suspect revolutionary gang into a reliable pillar of the existing order—all this and many other political and social forces tended toward a modernization of the entire setup of the state. Theobald von Bethmann Hollweg, Reich Chancellor after 1909, was a modern-minded man, a liberal conservative. The decisive issue prior to the war was the breaking up of the stronghold of feudalism in the Prussian Diet. This Diet was still elected on a franchise that secured its control by the landed aristocracy and their plutocratic allies. A second issue was a Reich government responsible to Parliament, not to the Emperor. But before these issues could be settled the world war engulfed the scene.

It is beyond the scope of this book to analyze the origins of the world war. Even today these origins are clouded by misconceptions spread by war propaganda. The war originated not in Germany but in Austria-Hungary. Whatever criminal blunders the Austrian statesmen might have committed, in the end the war became inevitable because the Habsburg monarchy was a living negation of the two principal forces of the nineteenth and twentieth centuries: national and social emancipation. The shots of the fanatical, twenty-year-old Serbian student who assassinated the Austrian Archduke in Sarajevo, Bosnia, on June 28, 1914, were only the challenging signal that the existing order of Austria-Hungary had become untenable. This old Habsburg monarchy, formed and expanded by dynastic marriages, was the giant stumbling block to the aspirations for national unity of too many races. Included among the Habsburg subjects were Poles, Ukrainians, Rumanians, Yugoslavs, and Italians, all ardent nationalists passionately desirous to join their brothers who lived outside the monarchy. Only the Czechs lived altogether within the Austrian state, but they too were denied complete independence or home rule. Any change of the status quo would have destroyed the precarious balance of the existing order.

Again we may wonder whether, over a period of time, the Dual Monarchy, dominated by the German and the Magyar elements, might have been gradually transformed into a supranational federation, perhaps on the pattern of Switzerland. It just did not happen. Both Germany and Austria-Hungary were too rigid structurally. They both failed to cope with the rising historical forces; they lacked the genius of constructive compromise that time and again had made the survival of the British Empire possible. The pressure was too strong; the explosion became inevitable. Austria-Hungary did not survive the war. The Monarchy had fallen to pieces several months before its disintegration was made official by the Paris peace treaties. When the statesmen of the Allied and Associated Powers met in Paris, the new successor states were already constituted in the area formerly ruled by the Habsburgs. Yet the order established by the Allies was to create more problems than it settled.

In Germany the world war had revolutionary effects. It intensified and magnified to the extreme the driving forces of German history. It made a nationalistic country even more nationalistic, a powerful government even more powerful. It merged the originally conflicting elements of German history into a new unity. By disrupting the continuity of life the war made a fundamentally conservative nation turn to revolution.

The old Prussia disappeared on August 4, 1914. The first world war soon proved to be different from Bismarck's short, glorious campaigns of 1864, 1866, and 1870. The whole nation, its entire manpower and material resources, had to be mobilized and organized in order to face the overwhelming pressure of a hostile world. The Socialist trade unions, which up to this date were so to speak outside the pale of respectable society and the state it represented, became overnight accepted instruments of the state machinery. Their official recognition implied their participation in political power. No constitutional changes occurred during the war, but it was no longer doubtful that these changes were bound to come after the war ended.

The Prussian state had a long and commendable tradition of social-mindedness that went back to the days of Frederick the Great, who had declared: "The King is the first servant of the state." This tradition found its expression in social security legislation passed under Bismarck, the earliest protective social laws in any great nation, exemplary for their time. It did not sound too far fetched when Oswald Spengler, the famous author of *The Decline of the West,* published a pamphlet on Prussian Socialism which propounded the thesis that Prussianism and Socialism were essentially the same—a point of view which made Spengler one of the many intellectual precursors of National Socialism. The war broke down whatever limitations the nineteenth century had built around state power. There was hardly anything that was not subject to government regulation and covered by government responsibility. The German people accepted this situation with unquestioning readiness as a matter of course, without noticing that it was also a matter of principle.

The catastrophe of 1918 caught the German people unawares. They had been deluded and had indulged in self-delusion about the realities. It was a terrific awakening. What happened in 1918 was not a revolution but a collapse. The Kaiser fled to Holland, the army was defeated and destroyed, the classes that had been responsible for German destiny for almost two centuries were annihilated or discredited. The defeat of 1918 left a vacuum. All true revolutions in history had been victories of preconceived ideologies influential in the preparatory organization of the revolutionary forces, but nothing of the sort existed in Germany. When the army collapsed and chaos became rampant, there was one task only, to restore order and survive as a nation. Under the circumstances this was a superhuman task. Whatever the merits or demerits of the Versailles treaty may have been, one fact should always be remembered: it created no peace. Large parts of German territory, among them some of the richest regions, remained occupied by foreign troops; important parts of the border in the west (the Saar region) and in the east (Upper Silesia) remained undefined; and above all, the grotesque reparations clauses made a restoration of orderly economic life utterly impossible. It is absurd to explain—as nationalistic and above all National Socialist propaganda did—all German postwar troubles as resulting from the Versailles treaty alone, not from the effects of the lost war. Nevertheless, even in the best of circumstances no German government would have been able to prevent the next catastrophe, that of 1923, which followed the French occupation of the Ruhr valley and the utter annihilation of the German currency through inflation. In the first five years after the war the authority of the German government was indeed reduced to a shadow, but no corresponding reduction in the scope of necessary government interference and organization occurred.

Once the mark had been stabilized at the end of 1923, and the Dawes Plan had been instituted in the spring of 1924, a phenomenal recovery set in. The framework within which this prosperity was built up was not the result of a revolutionary ideology, for with the default of its anticapitalist and antirepublican elements, Germany remained a capitalist republic. It was a sort of Directorate (in terms of the French revolution), or a sort of NEP (in terms of the Bolshevik revolution), not too much hampered by issues of principle.

The old ideologies had become meaningless and new ones had not appeared. Nobody had any program to offer. The Socialists were satisfied, the demands of their program having been realized up to the point from which they themselves shrank: the socialization of private industry. The Liberals had become conservative, and the Conservatives reactionary. Once more, as in the days of Wilhelm II, a general malaise spread over the German nation, which too easily begot disloyalty to the existing political order. As long as foreign troops stood on German soil and the Reparations Agent with his staff kept the Berlin government under tutelage, the stability of the Republic was not threatened. It was a tragic coincidence that in 1930, together with the last French contingents and the Reparations Agent, prosperity disappeared from Germany.

The hurricane that blew in from New York in the autumn of 1929 swept over Germany with deadly force. Once more Germany fell back into the restrictions of a war economy. In 1931 the German banks were taken over by the government; currency controls were reintroduced that were bound to result in a foreign trade monopoly. Government orders again became the backbone of what was left of private business. In May, 1930, the Republican constitution was irretrievably broken by Chancellor Heinrich Brüning's misuse of the emergency paragraph of the Weimar Constitution to carry on the affairs of government. The Reichstag was dissolved, and the elections in September, 1930, produced for the first time huge revolutionary parties, the National Socialists on the Right and the Communists on the Left. From then on, step by step, the constitutional guarantees of civil liberties were eliminated. With their legitimate authority steadily diminishing, the governments, which followed each other in rapid succession, constantly usurped larger prerogatives.

On January 30, 1933, when Adolf Hitler was appointed Reich Chancellor by a senile Reich President who had never understood his solemn oath to uphold the Weimar Constitution, there were in all Germany not a handful of men independent enough to be willing to resist. The machinery of the state, holding in its grip every individual citizen in every walk of life, had been perfected. Hitler needed only to press the button, and the machine sprang into action. His predecessors had done good work for him. The trend toward statism that had pervaded all Germany's history after she was resurrected under Prussian leadership had reached its climax. The state owned the banks, the banks owned and controlled business, business controlled the jobs, and the masses who wanted the jobs had been trained by Marxist and anti-Marxist leaders alike to look to the government for whatever they asked of life. Matters had gone full circle, and Hitler knew it. He promised the people what they wanted, and they did not care by what means he fulfilled his promises. He kept these promises, except one—that in making the German nation wealthy and dominant once more he would preserve the peace. Unless controlled by free citizens, a state is a Moloch that cannot stop devouring, in Germany just as in Russia or anywhere else. It feeds on its own children until it perishes.

II

TOWARD INDUSTRIAL POWER

1. Before Germany's Unification

IT IS A COMMON belief that Germany owed her rapid ascent to the rank of the foremost industrial power on the continent of Europe to the founding of the Reich in 1871. As a general proposition this is true. Yet it would be a misconception to believe that before the Reich was established Germany had been a poor agricultural country lagging far behind the rest of western Europe in her industrial development. To be sure, before 1870 the centers of European industrialization lay west of the Rhine, and from there, primarily from England, came the stimuli for Germany's own industrialization. But when Bismarck forged the Reich with "blood and iron," according to a remark John Maynard Keynes made in his *Economic Consequences of the Peace,* "coal and iron" were already busy building up the foundations for this new great power.

The chief advantage in industrialization that a big nation enjoys over a smaller one is its large area free of tariff barriers and other trade impediments. Until the Reich was founded, Germany (that is, its territory as of 1937) was politically divided into thirty loosely interconnected states. Before 1866 it was not even clear whether the Austro-Hungarian monarchy with all its territory—huge as compared with any single German state—would remain inside the German Confederacy, perhaps subsequently to become the nucleus for a new German empire. But while politically this paramount question was yet to be decided by the sword, economically the decision had been made more than a generation earlier.

The solution of the "Smaller German Reich"—which meant a German Empire under Prussian hegemony, excluding Austria-Hungary—was imposed politically by Prussia in her victories on the Bohemian (1866) and French (1870–71) battlefields, but it had been established in the economic sphere as early as 1833. In that year Prussia succeeded in uniting the most important of the future federal states in the framework of the German *Zollverein* (Customs Union). Other states joined in rapid succession, and after 1854 the Zollverein encompassed all the territory later to be included in the German Reich, with the exception of Mecklenburg, Hamburg, Bremen, and the territories annexed in the wars of 1864 to 1871—Schleswig-Holstein and Alsace-Lorraine.

The German Zollverein was a complete customs union. Commerce among the member states was free of any customs barriers. The only customs frontiers were those between the Zollverein states and the world outside, which in this respect included Austria-Hungary. For the time being, German unification did not go further than this. Among the member states there was neither a common currency nor freedom of movement or of settlement. And yet the Zollverein proved to be a powerful stimulant to economic growth. Many authors see in it the chief source of the economic expansion of Germany in the period that preceded the founding of the Reich, although factors outside Germany contributed also. Some of these factors were: the agrarian reforms of the Napoleonic era, influences from the French sway over western Germany, and the influx of British capital and British enterprise. But whatever its causes, in the 1840's the surging strength of the German economy began to be revealed.

Modern industries developed simultaneously from several centers, primarily in those areas where various kinds of local skills and crafts had enjoyed an old tradition. Agriculture, long dominant in Germany's economic life, underwent a process of modernization and intensification. The first modern credit banks began to do business, and between 1848 and 1857 Germany's first promoters' boom developed as the discovery of the California gold fields sent vigorous impulses through the entire American-European world. In Germany, these were the beginning days of rapidly expanding railroad construction, banking facilities, and heavy industries. This promoters' boom ended in the international economic crisis of 1857.

On the eve of the founding of the Reich, Germany was still what by present-day yardsticks would be called an agricultural country. In 1871, of a population of 41 million, 65 per cent lived in the open country or in communities with fewer than 2,000 inhabitants. By the standards of that time, however, the achievements of German industry were considerable. In 1871 in Germany, including Luxembourg, 29.4 million tons of coal and 8.5 million tons of lignite were mined. The output of iron ore was 4.4 million tons, the production of pig iron 1.6 million tons—compared with a British annual production of 6 to 7 million tons. Among other industries textiles were relatively well developed in some areas, whereas mechanical and chemical industries were still in their infancy. Several substantial enterprises were already in existence in the machine industry, among them that of Krupp in Essen, which by 1873 employed 16,000 persons, and that of Borsig in Berlin. The stage of economic development that Germany had reached in 1870 may be assessed by the fact that the railroad system had a mileage of 18,887 kilometers, roughly 11,500 miles, which compared with 52,922 miles in the United States.

2. *The Founding of the Reich*

WHEN AUSTRIA-HUNGARY and the German states allied with her were finally defeated in the brief war of 1866, and after Prussia had united the north German states in the North German Confederation, the founding of the "Smaller German Reich" under Prussian leadership could be a question of but a few years. The way this Reich was founded five years later remains a relevant historical fact. It happened after another victorious campaign in the heart of the defeated enemy country, France. Thus the economic effects of unification and of victory over a prosperous neighbor coincided and enhanced one another.

The Customs Union had prepared the ground, and now the nation derived further economic advantages from its newly won political unity. First of all, the unified legal codes were of immediate benefit. Some conformity had previously been enforced by the needs of business in the specific field of commercial law. In 1847 the first draft of a General German Negotiable Instruments Law (*Allgemeine deutsche Wechselordnung*) had been published; during the following years it was enacted by the various member states of the Zollverein. In 1861 the draft of a General German Commercial Code was completed; by 1865 it had been ratified by almost all the states, including Austria. Nevertheless, legal and administrative conditions for economic activity differed in the individual states in essential respects.

In the new Reich trade regulations could finally be unified for the entire territory. The tight restrictions on trade that had hitherto prevailed could now be relaxed in the spirit of liberalism that predominated during this period in Germany. For the first time complete freedom of movement for individuals and goods was secured all over the Reich. Weights and measures that varied widely in the several states were now everywhere based on the metric system. The post office became a Reich enterprise, except in Bavaria and Württemberg, where "postal sovereignty" was only relinquished when the Reich was remodeled in the years after the revolution of 1918.

But the postal sovereignty of the southern German states was not the only, nor was it the most important, relic that survived from the time of the many petty sovereignties and that lasted to the turn of the century. The federal states held fast to their traditional civil laws until the beginning of the twentieth century, when at last the Reich Civil Code (*Allgemeines Bürgerliches Gesetzbuch*) was enacted. Long after the railroads had been nationalized they remained the property of the various larger states (Prussia, Bavaria, Saxony, Baden, Württemberg, Oldenburg, Mecklenburg); they were only transferred to the Reich in the course of the reforms after the first world war. And, most important of all, the individual states retained virtual financial sovereignty, apart from a few tax privileges vested in the Reich.

THE FISCAL POWERS OF THE FEDERAL STATES

Like the United States of America, the German Reich began as a confederation of sovereign states, and this status survived until the revolution of 1918. As far as foreign and even many domestic affairs were concerned, Germany rapidly developed into a unified state; but financial and administrative powers remained chiefly with the individual states through all the decades up to the Weimar Constitution of 1919.

The Reich of 1871 had no administrative organs except the army, the navy, the foreign service, the customs administration, the post office, and, somewhat later, the colonial administration. The entire internal administration —police, judiciary, public finance, and education—remained in the hands of the federal states. Accordingly, the Reich was left with little freedom of action in the field of fiscal policy. It had inherited from the Zollverein control over customs revenues and over some excise taxes, which until the first world war were rather narrow in scope. Older even than these customs revenues was another peculiar Reich revenue, the so-called matricular contributions. Originally, these were payments the member states of the German Confederation—the *Bund,* formed in 1815 after Napoleon's collapse—made to the central authority to keep up its somewhat shadowy existence. These contributions were continued into the North German Confederation and into Bismarck's Reich. With all this, the Reich was largely dependent on the federal states. After 1880, when the states were awarded a share in certain indirect Reich taxes, this was a mere matter of form. The matricular contributions of the states to the Reich and the payments of the Reich to the states approximately canceled each other out.

The only new source of revenue of the North German Confederation and Bismarck's Reich was the revenue from the post and telegraph administration, to which was added in 1871 income from the management of the Alsace-Lorraine railroads. It is hardly surprising that in 1913, on the eve of the first world war, the Prussian revenue of 4.2 billion marks exceeded the ordinary and extraordinary Reich revenue by 100 million marks. In addition, the other federal states had revenues of a total of 2.5 billion marks. As of October 1, 1913, the Reich debt, 4.9 billion marks, was considerably below the Prussian debt of 9.9 billion marks and of the aggregate debt of the other states, 6.3 billion marks (figures for most of the states as of April 1, 1913). It should however be noted that the states' debt included their railroad bond indebtedness.

Before the Weimar Constitution, the entire field of direct taxation was a prerogative of the states, which also received considerable revenues from their railroads. The municipalities derived most of their income from real-estate taxes, but they also put surtaxes on some of the state taxes.

Only in the last years preceding the first world war did the Reich succeed in entering the field of direct taxation to some extent. In 1906 the Reich was allotted a share in the inheritance taxes, which previously had been reserved to the states. The states continued to administer these taxes, however, and the Reich share remained inconsiderable. The first really significant inroads into the traditional tax system were made under the shadow of the impending war. In 1913 the Reich imposed a capital levy combined with a surtax on higher incomes for the purpose expressed in its name: defense contribution (*Wehrbeitrag*). The revenue from this levy that reached the Treasury in 1914 and 1915 amounted to approximately one billion marks.

Thus, with respect to economics, the Reich was set up in three stages: the first was the Zollverein of 1833; the second the political founding of the Reich in 1871; the third the revolution of 1918. Undoubtedly, the second stage was by far the most important.

UNIFICATION OF THE CURRENCY

When the Reich was founded, Germany was still divided into seven separate currency areas. There were thirty-three banks of issue, totally unconnected with each other and carrying on their issuing activities under widely differing rules and regulations.

With such a chaotic currency system no monetary policy consistent with the needs of an industrialized country could be devised. The one feature common to these currencies was that silver was the legal tender, with the exception of the Bremen currency, which was based on gold. The states entered certain agreements as to the relative values of their respective currencies. In addition to silver, gold coins also circulated in all German states; the ratios between these coins and the legal silver currencies fluctuated, except in Prussia, where the ratio between gold and silver money was fixed by law.

The unified currency of the new Reich was based on the gold standard. The immediate adoption of the gold standard was a step of extraordinary significance at a time when no great country besides Britain had yet introduced it. When Germany reached this momentous decision, the great crisis of silver was already in the offing, and it could be foreseen that before long France and the United States would join the gold-standard countries. By taking the lead the young German Reich served the world economy well. It cleared the path toward a unified international currency based on gold and thus strongly encouraged rapid expansion of world trade in the decades preceding the first world war. Credit for this move is primarily due to the liberal statesman and economist Ludwig Bamberger, though some of the credit belongs to Bismarck himself and to his Secretary of State, Rudolf Delbrück, whose influence on German economic policy, up to his resignation in 1876, tended toward strengthening liberalism. For Germany herself the adoption of the gold standard expressed the ascendancy of the liberal "Western orientation" which in Bismarck's earlier years characterized his personal attitude.

The new currency system was set up in three stages. (1) In 1871 a law regulating the minting of gold coins was passed. The mark was adopted as the currency unit, its ratio to the values of the circulating silver coinage was defined, and the silver coins were withdrawn. (2) In 1873 the gold standard was established by law, and the use of silver was reduced to small coins. (3) In 1875 one of the thirty-three banks of issue, the Prussian Bank, was reorganized as the Reichsbank. The other banks of issue were left in a precarious situation, both in relation to the Reichsbank and to the private commercial banks. The plan was to induce them to relinquish voluntarily to the Reichsbank the rights which still belonged to them by law to issue fixed contingents of banknotes. By 1910, in fact, twenty-seven of them had yielded to this pressure; the rights of issue of the remaining five banks were canceled only as late as 1935. The note circulation of these "private issuing banks," as they were called after the Reichsbank had been organized, was so small and so strictly regulated that it counted for little in the new monetary setup.

THE FRUITS OF VICTORY

The unification of the Reich was of indubitable and permanent benefit to the German economic system. On the other hand, the benefits accruing from the victory over France were questionable, and they were certainly not permanent.

The annexation of Alsace and Lorraine, two of the most prosperous French provinces, undoubtedly proved a source of wealth for one and a half German generations. Aside from agriculture, the textile industry was the most highly developed among local industries of these provinces. In the new Reich Dominion (*Reichsland*) there were more than half as many cotton spindles and almost as many mechanical looms as in the rest of the Reich taken together. Germany was thus chiefly indebted to the new provinces for the prosperous growth of her textile business.

The abundant mineral wealth of Alsace-Lorraine was as yet almost untapped. Only after the process of iron ore treatment invented by the Englishmen Thomas and Gilchrist had been introduced into Germany in 1879 could the Lorraine ore mines be exploited. On this basis the German steel industry expanded to become one of the main factors in the rapid progress of Germany's industrial power. At the beginning of the twentieth century another Alsatian treasure was uncovered, potash. Added to the deposits in central Germany, the Alsatian mines gave Germany a virtual monopoly on the world potash market.

When Alsace-Lorraine was ceded to France by the Versailles treaty, Germany lost both the ore basis for her steel industry and half of her monopoly position in potash. The iron ore deposits of Lorraine were estimated at 700 million tons of metallic iron; after the Versailles treaty, Germany retained only 300 million tons. As for potash, a few years after the war the German and French potash interests were pooled for concerted exploitation of foreign markets. Meanwhile, however, this monopoly had been considerably impaired by the discovery and development of potash deposits in the United States, Poland, Palestine, and elsewhere.

The war indemnity imposed on France in 1871 did not prove an unmitigated blessing for Germany. It is often asserted that Germany owed the secure foundation of her gold currency to this war contribution of five billion gold francs. Indeed, Germany used 273 million francs that France paid in gold to build up a gold reserve, and the balance of payments profited by the influx of the French billions. But it is also true that this sudden bounty started a tremendous business boom which went far beyond what mere enthusiasm over national unification could have explained. It is easy to imagine the change it must have meant on the very narrow German securities market when within a short period of time a major part of the public debt of the federal states was repaid from the proceeds of the war indemnity. What followed was a speculative boom of unprecedented intensity and scope.

Between 1826 and 1870 stock companies with an aggregate capital of only 3.1 billion marks had been founded in Prussia. Between 1870 and 1874, 857 new companies with a capital of 3.3 billion marks had been established. The speculative frenzy gained particular impetus in railroads and heavy industry.

In some ways, perhaps, German industry was permanently benefited by the boom. However, encouraged by the lack of any restraining regulations so characteristic of the era, all too many of the upstart enterprises were utterly reckless and fraudulent. The result was the crash of 1873–74, as unprecedented in its dimension as the boom. Of the 857 companies founded in the "promoters' years" no less than 123 were in liquidation and 37 in bankruptcy by December, 1874. The years 1873 and 1874 were a sad time for all industrial countries of the world, and they marked but the beginning of a long-drawn-out period of depression.

3. Germany's Industrialization

ON THE EVE of the founding of the Reich, Germany's economic character was predominantly agricultural, but the process of industrialization had begun. The very existence of the Reich was the source of powerful impulses toward further industrial development, and within a few years Germany had joined the ranks of the leading industrial nations. In contrast to Britain, however, Germany did not sacrifice her agriculture to her industrial expansion. As will be shown more extensively later, the German government came to the aid of agriculture by means of a tariff as soon as the threat of American competition began to be felt on the grain market, the broad basis of German agriculture. This protection was given at the price of raising the cost of living for the urban population, but it enabled German agriculture to take advantage of new agricultural methods to continue its spectacular expansion during the era of rapid industrialization. Between the founding of the Reich and the first world war, German grain and potato production approximately doubled, partly from increased acreage but mainly as a result of improved yields per unit under cultivation. For example, a comparison of the yields of 1878–79 with the average yields of the decade 1901–10 shows that the average yield per hectare (2.47 acres) rose for wheat from 1.35 to 1.86 metric tons, for rye from 1.06 to 1.63 metric tons, for potatoes from 7.11 to 13.51 metric tons.

POPULATION GROWTH

Despite this favorable development, German agriculture was no longer able to satisfy the food requirements of the German population. Gradually the country was transformed from a grain exporter to an importer. The population increase was so dynamic and the standards of nutrition improved so drastically that even though grain production doubled it did not cover the demand. Along with industrial expansion the population grew steadily up to the first world war, in its turn furnishing the basis for further industrialization.

Actually, the natural increase in the population was even greater than shown in Table 1. Part of the increase was offset by emigration, which between the 1840's and the 1880's became a mighty stream. It was only at the end of the 1880's that German national wealth had increased sufficiently and German industry developed a large enough demand for labor to cause the economic motive for emigration practically to disappear. Between 1840 and the first world war five million Germans emigrated overseas, but most of this took place before 1890. After 1890 emigration petered out, as shown in Table 2.

From the beginning of the nineteenth century the country of destination

TABLE 1

Population Within the Territory of the Reich, 1816–1915

Year	Population (millions)	Increase during preceding decade (per cent)
1816	24.8	
1825	28.1	13.2
1835	30.8	9.6
1845	34.3	11.3
1855	36.1	5.4
1865	39.5	9.4
1875	42.5	7.5
1885	46.7	9.9
1895	52.0	11.3
1905	60.3	16.0
1915	67.9	12.5

SOURCES: *Statistisches Jahrbuch für die Bundesrepublik Deutschland 1965,* p. 31; *Statistisches Jahrbuch für das Deutsche Reich 1882,* p. 5.

TABLE 2

Overseas Emigration from Germany, 1821–1930

Years	Number of persons
1821–1830	8,500
1831–1840	167,700
1841–1850	469,300
1851–1860	1,075,000
1861–1870	832,700
1871–1880	626,000
1881–1890	1,342,400
1891–1900	529,900
1901–1910	279,600
1911–1920	91,000
1921–1930	567,300
TOTAL	5,989,400

SOURCE: Friedrich Burgdörfer, "Die Wanderungen über die Deutschen Reichsgrenzen im letzten Jahrhundert," *Allgemeines Statistisches Archiv* (1930), vol. 20, pp. 161 ff., 383 ff., 537 ff.

of the emigrants was almost exclusively the United States. Of the roughly six million Germans who emigrated overseas from 1821 to 1930, 5.3 million went to America.

Overseas emigration was partly balanced by immigration from other European countries, chiefly from Austria-Hungary, Italy, and the western parts of Russia, especially Russian Poland. This immigration increased steadily until in the last two decades preceding the first world war emigration was more than balanced by immigration. According to the figures on population movements, Germany had become an underpopulated country.

TRANSITION FROM AN AGRICULTURAL TO AN INDUSTRIAL SOCIETY

Despite the technical intensification of agriculture the rural sector absorbed but a negligible part of the population increase. As happened in other industrial societies rural life lost its attractions. A flight from the land began, and the natural population increase was drawn into the cities by the greater demand for labor there, by rising wages, and by the promise of the amenities of urban life. This shift is shown by Table 3.

TABLE 3

Gainfully Employed; Selected Years, 1882–1964 *

	1882	*1907*	*1925*	*1939*	*1950*	*1964*
Total gainfully employed (in millions)	17.0	25.4	32.3	35.7	20.4	27.0
Distribution by sectors (as per cent of total)						
Agriculture and forestry	42.2	33.9	30.3	25.0	24.6	11.4
Industry and crafts	35.6	39.9	42.3	40.8	42.7	48.3
Commerce, communications, other services	22.2	26.2	27.4	34.2	32.7	40.3

* Territories involved: 1882–1939, borders of 1937; 1950, Federal Republic without West Berlin and Saar; 1964, Federal Republic including West Berlin and Saar.

SOURCES: Statistisches Bundesamt Wiesbaden, *Bevölkerung und Wirtschaft. Langfristige Reihen 1871 bis 1957 für das Deutsche Reich und die Bundesrepublik Deutschland,* vol. 199, p. 30; *Statistisches Jahrbuch für die Bundesrepublik Deutschland 1965,* p. 151.

The trend from country to town between 1871 and 1882, for which period no detailed census is available, was no different. Thus it can almost be said that after the founding of the Reich agriculture and industry exchanged their relative importance in Germany's economic life.

The broad foundation for Germany's economic expansion was provided by the development of heavy industry. The German steel industry grew rapidly, as much because of progress in coal mining as because of the ore mines of Lorraine. In coal mining, Germany never quite caught up with her rival, Britain, but even so German coal mining expanded at a rate with which only that of the United States can compare. Coal production rose from an annual average of 34.5 million tons in the period 1871–75 to 191.5 million tons in 1913. The rich lignite mines were increasingly developed, and the production of lignite rose from 9.7 million to 87.5 million tons during the same period. In iron mining, ore production increased from an annual average of 5.3 million tons in the period 1871–75 to 28.7 million tons in 1913. These developments in coal and iron mining led to the growth of the steel industry. In 1871 pig iron output amounted to only 1.6 million tons; in 1910, 14.8 million tons were produced (Luxembourg's production included in both figures). As late as 1900 the British pig iron output of 9.1 million tons exceeded the German-Luxembourg production of 8.5 million tons, but in steel Germany had already outdistanced her British rival—7.4 million as against 6.0 million tons. In 1910 German production of 13.1 million tons of pig iron and 13.0 million tons of crude steel led that of all other European countries by a wide margin; Britain with 10.2 million tons of pig iron and 7.6 million tons of crude steel had been left far behind.

Germany utilized her heavy industries (1) to build up her railroad system—the mileage of which increased from 18,887 kilometers in 1870 to 60,521 kilometers in 1912; (2) to construct one of the mightiest merchant fleets in the world—steam-powered ships in the merchant marine increased from 147 units with a total of 81,994 gross register tons in 1871 to 2,098 units with 4,380,348 gross register tons in 1913; (3) to expand her machinery industry at a remarkable pace, making machinery one of the largest exports—51,000 workers were employed in 1861, 356,000 in 1882, and 1,120,000 in 1907. Within the machinery group the importance attained by the armament industry deserves attention. In 1912 the firm of Krupp in Essen employed 68,300 workers.

The special pride of Germany in this period was her electrical and chemical industries. As measured by number of persons employed, both industries were relatively small. Their significance, however, in the complex of German industrialization, for her foreign trade and for her prestige abroad was outstanding.

The development of the electrical industry is tied to the names of Werner von Siemens and Emil Rathenau. (Emil Rathenau was the father of Walter Rathenau, later Foreign Minister of the Weimar Republic, who in 1922 fell a victim to nationalistic fanatics.) Siemens was an ingenious inventor who as early as 1867 constructed a dynamo and in 1879 worked on the problem of electrical railroad traction. He was the founder of the *Siemens* concern, which together with Germany's General Electric Company (*Allgemeine Elektricitäts-Gesellschaft,* A.E.G.) was to dominate her electrical industry. In partnership with the firm of Siemens, Emil Rathenau founded in 1883 the German Edison Company for Applied Electricity (*Deutsche Edison Gesellschaft für angewandte Elektrizität*), which under his initiative soon broke away from Siemens to form the company which later became A.E.G. To both these groups belongs the credit for Germany's electrification, for the construction of the extensive trolley system and the municipal and overland power transmission systems, and in general for developing high- and low-voltage techniques.

The chemical industry did not have to start from scratch as did the electrical industry, since Germany already had a tradition of chemical experimentation. Justus von Liebig's momentous contribution to agricultural chemistry may be recalled. But the chemical industry underwent a decisive, steady expansion during the almost five decades of the Reich. The great chemical concerns which were later amalgamated in the German Dye Works (*I. G. Farbenindustrie*) date from this time. After the amalgamation, this company enjoyed almost a monopoly position within the German chemical industry. The worldwide reputation of German dyes, pharmaceuticals, and many other chemical products was firmly established in this period.

4. *The Role of the Banks*

NO ACCOUNT OF German industrialization would be complete without full consideration of the important function of the banks. The dynamics of economic development can be assessed only if due weight is given to the peculiar banking system, which, in contrast to what took place in Britain and America, gave a most powerful stimulus to industrialization. The difference between the German and Anglo-Saxon banking systems becomes apparent in the respective connotations attached to the term "bank" in German and

English. The German bank is a combination of commercial bank, investment bank, and investment trust—a combination which, as will be shown in detail, can function only with the backing of a central bank.

Before the first world war, only a minor part of the funds of a typical bank was invested in government securities—long-term bonds and treasury bills. Another part was invested in commercial bills, which could be rediscounted with the Reichsbank and were therefore regarded as a liquid reserve. But primarily bank funds were used for direct loans (mostly long term, partly secured and partly unsecured) to industrial and commercial enterprises, and for industrial promotion. Industrial promotions or capital issues were either made by one bank alone or, when large-scale enterprises were concerned, by a group of banks, the so-called consortiums or syndicates. The bank or group of banks would take over the stocks or bonds to be issued at a fixed price and then try to place them with the public. In consequence, the banks kept substantial holdings of stocks and bonds of commercial and industrial firms in their own portfolios. They also traded in stocks and bonds either to regulate the market or for speculation.

To shoulder the risks connected with such transactions, the banks needed a large capital of their own. As a rule, capital, reserves, and undistributed profits amounted to 25 per cent of their deposits and other liabilities. When later, as a result of the first world war and the subsequent inflation, the capital of the banks had melted away, this in itself inevitably led to a crisis of the entire banking system. The banks derived their deposits largely from the enterprises they financed, while the savings of the public at large went mainly into the savings banks, most of them municipal.

From their very inception, German banks were planned primarily as institutions for the financing of industry, not as sources of current business credits after the British and American pattern. According to Gerhart von Schulze-Gaevernitz (*The German Credit Banks*), the banks, after 1848, were founded in a revolutionary spirit as instruments of the industries for their financing needs in opposition to the private bankers, who represented *haute finance*. These bankers were at the time the almighty masters of the capital market, typified by the House of Rothschild, originally stemming from Frankfurt but now international in scope. It was not by mere chance that the first German banking company of the modern type, the *A. Schaaffhausensche Bankverein* in Cologne, was founded in a year of revolution, 1848. The first constitutional administration of Prussia granted this institution its charter, which included the privilege of issuing banknotes.

How revolutionary these ideas on the financing of industries appeared in those days becomes evident when it is recalled that it was also the time of Pierre Joseph Proudhon's schemes for organizing industrial banks in the interest of the workers, which left their characteristic imprint on the origin of the French *Crédit Mobilier*. Following the same principles, Gustav von Mevissen, founder of the Schaaffhausensche Bankverein, proclaimed the promotion of industries to be the paramount function of this first German bank. In 1849, Mevissen's bank helped form one of the first stock companies in German mining, the *Kölner Bergwerksverein,* and also, as stock companies, the first steel plant and the first machine works.

In view of this close interrelation between industry and banking, it seems only natural that the foundation of the leading banks coincides with the two important periods of industrial development before the first world war, the early 1850's and the early 1870's. In both periods a major part of the available promoters' capital went into new banks; almost all prominent German banks originated then. The Schaaffhausensche Bankverein of 1848 was followed by the *Disconto-Gesellschaft* in 1851, which in 1856 was developed into a regular bank; the *Darmstädter Bank,* which was organized in 1853; and the *Berliner Handelsgesellschaft* of 1856. In the second period, the *Deutsche Bank* was founded in 1870 and the *Dresdner Bank* in 1872.

THE INTERDEPENDENCE OF BANKING CAPITAL AND INDUSTRIAL CAPITAL

Up to the second world war, the German banks remained essentially true to their original pattern. This should not, however, be taken to imply that all industries were founded and permanently controlled by the banks. Frequently, perhaps even in the majority of cases, the initiative lay not with the banks but with individual industrial promoters. The importance of the original contribution of the banks, and accordingly of their lasting influence, varied widely with different industries and enterprises. But in one way or another the banks had their hands in almost all developing and promoting activities and remained financially interested in the industries concerned.

The influence of the banks on the industries they promoted was made permanent by voting practice in stockholders' meetings. The banks' voting powers were derived not only from their own stock holdings in these industrial companies but also from those of their customers. Possessed of such voting power and relying on their influence as underwriters, the banks themselves were active in industrial management, delegating their own officers to the boards of directors of industrial corporations. Conversely, the large industrial concerns were represented on the boards of the banks with which they had business connections.

In the heavy industries the large enterprises, such as Krupp's and Thyssen's, were originally independent, but gradually their relations to the banks became closer, and the leading banks started a keen competition among themselves for establishing intimate contacts with the major industries. In the end, every one of the large banks had its connections with at least some of the foremost groups of heavy industry.

The interrelations between banks and industries fostered the process of concentration in both fields. In the course of its rapid growth, industry shifted its weight more and more from the smaller and medium-sized companies to those firms which by their nature required huge capital investments, such as the heavy industries, the electrical industries, and shipbuilding. It became increasingly necessary that large, efficient, and rich banks exist to shoulder the task of industrial financing. Thus industrial concentration became a powerful incentive to banking concentration.

The Berlin banks spread out to the provinces by forming branches and by amalgamating small provincial banks—and later even larger ones. Thus, in 1897 the Deutsche Bank took over the *Hannoversche Bank* and, in 1903, the *Essener Creditanstalt,* both strong companies closely connected with flourishing industries. In 1895 the Disconto-Gesellschaft took over the *Norddeutsche Bank.*

Finally, the large banks themselves began to amalgamate. Before the outbreak of the first world war only one of these fusions was perfected. In 1914, just before the war began, the Schaaffhausensche Bankverein was merged with the Disconto-Gesellschaft. After Germany's defeat, this process of concentration was resumed with growing impetus. Most important were the amalgamation of the *Mitteldeutsche Privatbank* with the *Commerz und Discontbank* under the firm name of *Commerz und Privatbank* in 1920, and the merger of the Darmstädter Bank with the *Nationalbank für Deutschland* in 1921. The next phase, characterized by the amalgamation of the Deutsche Bank with the Disconto-Gesellschaft in 1929 and by the taking over of the Darmstädter Bank by the Dresdner Bank following the bank crash of 1931, resulted in a powerful concentration of banking facilities in the hands of fewer than half a dozen institutions.

The following figures illustrate how far concentration in banking had advanced before the first world war. At the end of 1910, 48.3 per cent of the deposits in all the commercial banks with at least one million marks share capital were held by the large Berlin banks (including the Darmstädter Bank and the Schaaffhausensche Bankverein); of these 40.2 per cent were held by the so-called D-Banks alone (Deutsche Bank, Disconto-Gesellschaft, Dresdner Bank, and Darmstädter Bank). In 1911, according to J. Riesser (*The German Great Banks and Their Concentration*), the share capital plus reserves of all commercial banks with at least one million marks share capital amounted to 3.7 billion marks; of this total, 2.7 billion were represented by the four D-Banks and the Schaaffhausensche Bankverein with their affiliates.

In turn the bank mergers accelerated concentration in industry. As the banking concentration progressed, more and more often the great banks took up an interest in several industries working in the same line, or in several branches of industry whose production was technically interconnected. This again favored the trend toward monopolies. The banks used their influence to help organize horizontal and vertical industrial combinations or cartels.

5. *The Expansion of Foreign Trade*

ANOTHER SIGNIFICANT FEATURE in German banking before the first world war was the leading role the banks played in Germany's economic and political expansion outside her frontiers. Her industrial development had raised Germany to the rank of Britain, the two now being the world's foremost exporters. In 1880 German foreign trade had ranked fourth among exporting nations, after Britain, France, and the United States. Before long Germany had moved to second place after the United States, a position which she maintained up to the first world war.

The growth of German foreign trade from the founding of the Reich to the war of 1914 indicates the headlong pace of German economic expansion, especially during the last two decades of this era. Table 4 shows a doubling of German exports in the twenty-eight years from 1872 to 1900, and more than a doubling again in the following thirteen years.

The composition of German foreign trade is another illustration of the rapid industrial development. The ratio of finished industrial products to total exports rose from 38 per cent in 1873 to 63 per cent in 1913. The industrial affluence and the exporting capacity of the country, however, were

TABLE 4

German Foreign Trade, Selected Years, 1872–1913
(without re-exports; in billions of marks)

Year	*Exports*	*Imports*
1872	2.5	3.5
1880	3.0	2.8
1890	3.4	4.3
1900	4.8	6.0
1910	7.5	8.9
1913	10.1	10.8

SOURCE: *Statistisches Jahrbuch für das Deutsche Reich,* 1880–1915.

closely dependent on imports of raw materials and foodstuffs, which exceeded industrial exports in value. Table 5 shows this to be true both for the earlier as well as for the later period.

TABLE 5

Composition of German Foreign Trade, 1890 and 1913
(in billions of marks)

	EXPORTS	IMPORTS	
YEAR	*Semifinished and finished products*	*Foodstuffs*	*Raw materials*
1890	2.1	1.4	1.8
1913	7.5	3.0	5.0

SOURCE: *Statistisches Jahrbuch für das Deutsche Reich 1900,* p. 82; *ibid., 1914,* p. 181.

THE ROLE OF THE BANKS IN FOREIGN TRADE AND CAPITAL EXPORT

Foreign trade of such dimensions required adequate financing facilities. As time went on German business inevitably strove to break loose from its dependence on the British banking system, which heretofore had practically held a monopoly position in international trade.

The determined efforts of the German banks to build international connections began with the founding of the Reich. But individual bankers had been cultivating foreign relations even before. Personal ties between the

Frankfurt and New York houses of Speyer were later extended to the London house. In 1871, one year after its foundation, the Deutsche Bank took an interest in a London bank, and two years later it started its own branch in London. Others followed suit. In 1871 German banks took an interest in Belgian banks. One of the few large banks in Italy, the Banca Commerciale Italiana, was founded in 1894 on the initiative and influence of German banking capital. In Austria the Mercur Bank was controlled by German banking. Connections with the United States were primarily under the care of private bankers who established themselves in New York, such as Hallgarten & Company and Ladenburg, Thalmann & Company. The most notable of these connections was that of the Hamburg house of M. M. Warburg & Company, founded in 1798, with the New York house of Kuhn, Loeb & Company.

The main function of these banking connections with the western European countries was to finance foreign trade. In contrast, the American connections were formed chiefly to direct German capital into investments in the United States. The same motive led to the making of banking connections with economically less developed countries. German investors acquired growing amounts of American securities, and in particular the expansion of American railroads was to a considerable extent financed by German capital.

The activity of German banks in establishing foreign branches to promote capital investment abroad centered mainly in three geographic areas: the Near East, Latin America, and the Far East. In the Near East the *Deutsche Orientbank*, founded in 1906 by German banks, deserves to be mentioned first. Before the first world war it had several branches in commercial centers of Turkey, as well as in Egypt and Morocco. Another field of banking activity opened up in Rumania, a country of particular interest because of its rich oil deposits. As early as 1890 the Darmstädter Bank acquired shares in the Banca Marmarosch, which was to become one of the leading Rumanian banks. The Disconto-Gesellschaft took a decisive hand in organizing the Banca Generala Romana in 1897.

In the Far East the main center of German banking influence was the *Deutsch-Asiatische Bank*, founded in 1889 by a group of German banks under the leadership of the Disconto-Gesellschaft. The bank was given the right of note issue for China, and its influence reached as far as Japan and India.

In Latin America, finally, two powerful banking organizations carried forward the influence of German capital: the *Deutsche Überseebank*, a subsidiary of the Deutsche Bank, founded in 1886; and the *Deutsch-Südamerikanische Bank,* founded in 1906 under the auspices of the Dresdner Bank. Both banks established far-flung networks of branch institutions, partly under their own firm name, partly under the name of subsidiaries, to work in almost every Latin American country.

GERMAN CAPITAL INVESTMENT ABROAD

The branching out of the German banking system to foreign countries reflected the broad outflow of German investment capital. In the 1880's Germany experienced the transition from a capital-importing to a capital-exporting country. This would also happen to the United States more than thirty years later, during the first world war, but several characteristic differences in the two cases may be noted. In the first place, capital imports into Germany had never been as considerable as those into the United States. Besides, the heavy capital influx into Germany in the 1870's was of purely political origin—the French war indemnities—although its effects on prices and the balance of payments were naturally similar to capital imports for economic reasons. Finally, Germany's transition from capital importer to capital exporter was not, as it was in the United States, caused by the proceeds of large exports of war supplies. It was, on the contrary, achieved at a time of substantial import surpluses. The explanation lies in the invisible items of the balance of payments, which were heavily in Germany's favor during her rapid industrialization prior to the first world war. Mainly responsible for this favorable balance were the proceeds of German shipping and railroads (Germany being geographically in the center of European railway traffic), the services of foreign banking, and the sale of German patents to other countries.

German capital investment abroad appeared under various headings. German firms founded foreign commercial and industrial companies; German capital participated in foreign firms and purchased foreign securities. Finally, after the 1880's, German banks began to underwrite foreign capital issues on the German market. At first these foreign issues were considerable, but they decreased with the growing capital needs of industry at home. Yet during this entire period foreign issues never amounted to less than 400 million marks a year. In all, between 1886 and 1912, 10.6 billion marks in foreign securities were placed in Germany.

For the last prewar year conservative estimates of German capital investments abroad give a total of approximately 30 billion marks, while about 5 billion marks of foreign capital were invested in Germany. It is safe to assume that German holdings of foreign securities reached about 20 billion marks, the balance of 10 billion consisting of private investments. These estimates are probably not too high, since the registration of foreign securities, imposed by law in 1916, revealed a sum of 16 billion marks. This leaves but a small margin for capital repatriated in the course of two war years, for capital that escaped abroad, and for capital that failed to register.

"DRANG NACH DEM OSTEN"

German exports of goods and capital played an important role in German expansion abroad which, by its main orientation, was bound to disturb the prevailing balance of power in Europe. In politically independent areas like Russia, North America, and Latin America, German capital did not gain much political influence. In capital-importing countries situated in geographically and politically more exposed areas of expansion, economic influences received political backing and aid. This is particularly true of southeastern Europe and Asia Minor, the regions traditionally in the line of the German *Drang nach dem Osten* (drive toward the East), where the chief goals of expansion were the Austro-Hungarian monarchy, Rumania, and Turkey. In contrast, the colonies offered only little scope to German capital.

In Austria-Hungary, Germany set the pace for this country's own industrialization. In Rumania and Galicia—an Austrian province later to become a part of Poland—German banks began from the turn of the century to develop their interest in opening up the oilfields. Soon after the Reich was founded Austria-Hungary became its closest political ally. Rumania was chiefly developed by German and Austrian capital and thereby drawn closely into the orbit of German power. Nevertheless in 1916 after some hesitation Rumania was to join the Allies against the Central Powers.

German expansion into Turkey approximately coincided with her expansion into Rumania; German efforts in Turkey were directed primarily toward railroad construction, which this poor country was unable to finance on its own. In 1899 the Deutsche Bank, in partnership with an Austrian bank, acquired an interest in the Operating Company for Oriental Railroads (*Betriebsgesellschaft für Orientalische Eisenbahnen*), which ran the Macedonian lines. In the same year the Deutsche Bank, jointly with the Dresdner Bank and other institutions, founded the Anatolian Railroad Company, which among others built the important line from Constantinople to Ankara. In the following year the Deutsche Bank cooperated in organizing the

Bank for Oriental Railways in Zürich to finance the construction of the Anatolian Railroad. Finally, in 1901 the Sultan granted the Anatolian Railroad Company the famous and controversial concession for the construction of a railroad to Baghdad and the Persian Gulf. To exploit this concession, the Anatolian Railroad Company founded the Imperial Ottoman Baghdad Railroad Company (*Kaiserlich Ottomanische Bagdad-Bahngesellschaft*).

In carrying her ventures into Asia Minor and threatening to extend them to the Persian Gulf, Germany made deep inroads into the sphere of interest of the British Empire. It is widely known how the expanding German Empire crossed British interests in various other ways, chiefly by developing a leading position in world trade and by building up a German navy. And yet all these trends furnish no factual evidence for the often-repeated theory that it was the economic rivalry between Germany and Britain that was in the last analysis to blame for bringing about the catastrophe of the first world war. Britain would very likely have tolerated German expansion into Asia Minor, merely counteracting it by increasing her own naval armament to keep abreast. Europe was to be thrown off its extremely precarious balance from another quarter.

6. *From Liberalism to Protectionism*

IT IS A well-known fact that Germany achieved her unification at a time when half-feudalistic and militaristic Prussia had established its sway over the entire nation. A contrasting fact should not be overlooked, however: at the same time, liberal forces were so powerful in Prussia—and even more so in other German states—that the dynasty never succeeded in eliminating them altogether. It would be a basic misconception to assume that the dominant economic creed at the birth of the Reich was nationalistic and in favor of autarky.

It has been noted above that the adoption of the gold standard reflected the "Western liberal orientation." This orientation pervaded economic policies in the early history of the Reich. Rudolf Delbrück, the minister who after the revolution of 1848 determined Prussian trade policy and after 1871 that of the Reich, was a liberal free-trader. All his policies were dominated by this spirit, which at the time had Bismarck's full endorsement. In the course of the 1860's and the early 1870's business was liberated from all sorts of legal and administrative shackles. In 1870 the licensing system for stock companies was abolished, at first without any obligatory regulations of their charters and bylaws being formulated to replace it.

After the establishment of the Zollverein in 1833, protectionist tendencies made themselves felt in German trade policy as a reaction to the devastating competition from the British textile industry and under the influence of the great German economist Friedrich List, who had been the principal champion of the Zollverein idea. In the 1840's a number of duties were in fact introduced. However, in the 1860's the general trend of European trade policies turned once more toward liberal concepts, moderate tariffs, and the most-favored-nation principle.

TOWARD FREE TRADE

The decisive turn was achieved in the famous Cobden Treaty signed in 1860 by Britain and France. Prussia at once followed along the same line by concluding in 1862 a trade pact with France that was also based on the most-favored-nation clause. This Prussian-French trade pact was destined to become exemplary. Adopted in 1865 by the Zollverein, it furnished the pattern for a number of treaties concluded about this time by the Zollverein with other important trading countries such as Britain, Austria, and Belgium. All these treaties contained the most-favored-nation clause and resulted in a long list of duty reductions and the elimination of all agricultural duties.

After the Reich was founded, the free-trade course was at first even strengthened. The trade treaty with France had been annulled by the war of 1870–71. In its place a remarkable paragraph was inserted in the Frankfurt Peace Treaty, which stipulated "eternal," irrevocable mutual most-favored-nation treatment without allowing any duties to be rigidly determined. This clause was to apply to all commercial treaties made by France or Germany with other countries. Two years later, in 1873, Germany abolished the duties on pig iron, scrap iron, and shipbuilding materials and lowered the duties on semifinished iron products and machinery with the proviso that the latter duties were to lapse entirely in 1877.

TOWARD PROTECTIONISM

Meanwhile, however, a fundamental change gradually emerged that was to exert a deep influence on German history. In 1873 the speculative boom exploded, and a heavy and persistent depression settled on German business.

This was the year in which the iron duties were abolished. But depression reigned in Britain also, and therefore the British iron industry, still superior to the German in technical skill, flooded the German market with products at prices that made it impossible for German heavy industry to compete. At the same time, German textiles were exposed to the superior competitive power of Alsace-Lorraine, against which there was now no protection. Finally, the turning point was near at hand for German agriculture, after which this traditionally exporting industry was to be transformed into a vulnerable industry open to imports and dependent on them. The turnabout in agricultural trade policies did not occur abruptly. In the years from 1876 to 1879 the German Agricultural Council (*Landwirtschaftsrat*) repeatedly pleaded for the preservation of free trade in agricultural products. These were, however, the very years when agriculture in western and central Europe decided to employ intensive cultivation methods, while simultaneously the rest of the world, notably America, turned to extensive agriculture. For over fifty years German agriculture had been making remarkable progress, aided by British experience and by the epoch-making research in soil chemistry of Justus von Liebig. From extensive triennial crop rotation, which left one third of the arable land fallow every year, German agriculture had moved on to intensive crop rotation with the use of fertilizers.

Intensive farming on soil kept under cultivation for generations caused higher costs per unit compared with those of the extensive methods traditional in eastern Europe, and even higher costs than those of extensive farming on the virgin soils overseas. The rising curve of agricultural production costs in Germany clashed with the opposite trend of decreasing costs in overseas countries, and in the 1870's these curves met and crossed. American grain now flooded the open German market, strongly favored as it was by the rapid development of railroad transportation on the North American continent and by the lively competition among transatlantic steamship lines. Germany, heretofore the classical grain exporter, found herself suddenly transformed into an import market. Thus, in 1879–80, 324,000 tons of wheat and 160,000 tons of corn were imported from the United States, and additional grain entered from Hungary and Russia.

All these changes—the strain of the worldwide depression, the reversals in international agriculture, and the inroads of British iron, which threatened to stifle the flourishing German iron industry—reinforced one another to uproot the German free-trade philosophy. It was not the triumph of Bismarck's Prussia over the rest of Germany that finally brought down the German free-trade policy, but rather this concentric pressure from many quarters. To emphasize this fact once more, Bismarck and his hereditary social caste, the Prussian Junkers, were free-traders originally and became protectionists in the 1870's only under the strains of altered conditions.

Things came to such a pass that in 1876 Rudolf Delbrück, then president of the Chancellor's office, resigned. His fall was not directly attributable to the free-trade crisis but to a controversy in railroad matters. Even so, his resignation signaled the incipient fundamental change in German economic policies and ideologies. The drive in favor of a radical break with free trade had begun to gain momentum, and only three years later was the break actually made. The new tariff bill, enacted in 1879–80, reintroduced duties for agricultural products, iron, and various industrial goods, and increased textile and other industrial duties.

These duties remained moderate, however, at least as measured by later standards. The duty on wheat and rye was only 10 marks per ton, not quite 5 per cent of the value. The iron duty was also 10 marks, amounting to a somewhat higher percentage of the price. Only when it had become evident over several years that the initial low tariff had failed to halt the decline of grain prices on the German market were these duties raised to a higher level. Wheat and rye duties gradually rose, reaching 50 marks per ton in 1887, but average grain prices still remained below what they had been before the duties were first introduced.

In reviewing the course of German tariff policies up to the first world war, it should be noted that the protectionist trend was not pursued without hesitation. Bismarck's dismissal in 1890 was once again indicative of a turn—although it proved only short-lived—toward liberalism in politics as well as in economics. Bismarck's successor was Georg von Caprivi. The Anti-Socialist Laws of 1878 lapsed, and the agricultural and several industrial duties were lowered in the hope of inducing other countries to reciprocate.

The Caprivi era was but a brief episode, however. In 1902, under Bernhard von Bülow's chancellorship, tariffs were once again raised. But even after this raise they remained moderate up to the first world war, compared with the levels reached after the war and compared with contemporaneous tariffs in the United States, France, Austria, and Russia—countries that were all more or less determined to build up their own industries. Even after 1879, when German trade policies veered toward protectionism, the country was neither in fact nor in ideology actuated by autarkic aspirations.

7. *The Colonial Era*

BISMARCK'S PRUSSIA was a military, not a naval state. Hamburg and Bremen, German outlets to the world at large, were not Prussian and did not even join the Zollverein. The Prussian ports of Danzig and Königsberg lay far back on the Baltic, which was obviously an inland sea, especially before the construction of the Kaiser Wilhelm Canal. Prussia's aspirations centered on continental Europe only, and Bismarck himself was originally a declared adversary of the "colonial idea." This is proved not only by his private correspondence from just before the Franco-Prussian war, but also by the fact that as late as 1874 Germany declined to consider an appeal for protection from the Sultan of Zanzibar, missing thereby a favorable opportunity to lay the foundation for a colonial empire in the very region where ten years later one of the foremost colonial ventures was to be initiated. After Germany had turned away from her liberal trade policies, however, Bismarck himself altered his approach to colonial matters, and the "colonial idea" began its ascendancy.

One may well argue that this alteration was only natural, the inevitable consequence of Germany's advancing industrialization and of the fact that the great ports, Hamburg and Bremen, had been incorporated into the Reich. One may also point out that for centuries past other European nations had hurried forward on the path to colonial empires, ahead of Germany and that precisely in the period following the Franco-Prussian war France as well as Belgium and Portugal were feverishly active in the colonial sphere. Finally, one could consider the massive German emigration which, as shown above, turned chiefly to the United States, where sooner or later the emigrants were lost to the German nation. Undoubtedly each of these facts had some influence on the adoption of the colonial idea; but it is also true that the German colonies never acquired much importance for the developing German industries, nor did they ever become outlets for German emigration.

As it happened, this emigration began to dwindle just at the time of Germany's colonial successes. But even under a different constellation the colonies would hardly have offered settlement opportunities for a large number of European emigrants. All Germany's African colonies had been acquired in 1884 and 1885. In 1897 the ninety-nine-year lease of Kiaochow from China was added, and in 1899 and 1900 the Carolines and half of Samoa in the Pacific were acquired. On the eve of the first world war the German colonies had an aggregate size of more than a million square miles with a population of more than 13 million. But, after thirty years of colonizing activity, the number of white inhabitants in all German colonies was only 23,952, of whom 5,764 were in military or police service.

How modest the value of Germany's colonies was for her economic life appears from the following facts: before the first world war, German capital at work in the colonies was a little over 500 million marks, that is, not quite 2 per cent of total German capital investment abroad. German capital in the colonies was primarily employed in building up a comparatively strong railroad system—a total of 3,350 miles in 1914—and also port facilities, plantations, and mines. The main export goods produced in the colonies were diamonds (Southwest Africa), rubber, and vegetable-oil products. All told, exports did not exceed 83.6 million marks in 1912. Hence, the colonies were hardly of any value for supplying German industry with raw materials, nor could they offer a sizable market for German exports. In 1913, of the total exports of 10,097 million marks, only 55 million went into Germany's own colonies (disregarding Kiaochow), that is, only one-half of 1 per cent.

In 1906 the banker Dr. Bernhard Dernburg was appointed chief of the colonial administration. He organized the Colonial Office, and, subsequently, increased efforts were devoted to the economic development of the colonies. The effect was inconspicuous, however, and it may be doubted that colonial administration could ever have improved very much, had German colonial power survived the first world war.

8. *Government in Business*

AS IN ALL other European countries, during the mercantilist era, government help and initiative in the development of industries were among the most potent driving forces in the history of German capitalism. Also as in other countries, state owned "factories" (*Manufakturen*) were established in Germany. Some of them remained state owned enterprises down to the second world war—for instance the Prussian and Saxon porcelain factories. The peculiar political conditions in Germany favored this kind of state ownership. The several dozens of princes reigning since feudal days owned domains, forests, and also some industrial enterprises that were in fact state property, although many were officially considered as the private property of the individual reigning houses.

Thus Germany entered the liberal era with a relatively large sector of the economy state controlled, and no purely ideological considerations could bring about the liquidation of such state properties. It was, however, of great significance for Germany's destiny that when she emerged from the liberal era there was an old mercantilist tradition to fall back upon and resume with growing impetus.

PUBLIC OWNERSHIP OF THE RAILROADS

The first and most important measure in this direction was the transfer of the railroads to public ownership. The first German railroad, connecting the neighboring towns of Nürnberg and Fürth, was built in 1835, and up to the first world war the tempo of development of the German railroad system must be considered as extraordinary when measured by European standards. As in other highly developed countries, the expansion of railroads stopped abruptly with the first world war. The pace of railroad construction is shown by Table 6.

TABLE 6

German Railroad Network, 1835–1915
(in kilometers)

Year	*Track in operation*	*Increase during preceding decade*
1835	6	
1845	2,300	2,300
1855	8,290	5,990
1865	14,690	6,400
1875	27,960	13,270
1885	37,650	9,690
1895	46,560	8,910
1905	56,980	10,420
1915	62,410	5,430

SOURCES: *Statistisches Jahrbuch für das Deutsche Reich,* 1880–1915; Hauptverwaltung der Deutschen Reichsbahn, *Hundert Jahre deutsche Eisenbahnen* (1935).

In some of the German states—Baden, Braunschweig, Oldenburg, Württemberg—railroad construction was from the very beginning carried on by the states themselves. In others—Saxony, Bavaria—only part of the railroad system was state owned or subsequently taken over by the state. In Prussia, initially (1838) the state only organized an extensive system for supervising private railroads, reserving the right to acquire them after thirty years. Construction remained a matter of private enterprise, and not until 1874 did the Prussian state begin to build railroads on its own. Through the annexation of Hanover and several other territories in 1866, Prussia acquired additional state lines. The Reich itself up to the Weimar Constitution owned only one line, the Alsace-Lorraine system that had become Reich property in 1871.

In 1875, on the eve of the period of comprehensive nationalization, approximately one-half of the railroad system was still in private hands. In fact, in the first half of the 1870's private railroad construction had shown its most rapid expansion, this being the preferred field for promoters' activity. Table 6 shows that in the decade from 1865 to 1875 the system almost doubled. Railroad shares were the main object of the speculative bubble, and accordingly, when the great crash came in 1873, countless bona fide shareholders found themselves robbed of the savings they had invested in railroad "securities."

It would certainly have been possible to prevent further promotional frauds, unsound business practices, and chaotic growth by methods short of outright nationalization. But noneconomic considerations, primarily military, played an important part in the discussion. Bismarck personally advocated nationalization, while his liberal minister Delbrück opposed it. As mentioned before, it was this difference of opinion that led to Delbrück's resignation in 1876. From then on the path lay open, and, characteristically, the railroad-nationalization scheme was adopted in the very year that witnessed the great turn toward protectionism in foreign trade.

Prussia was the first to carry out nationalization. As provided for in the original charters, the private roads were purchased by the states. The governments raised the money by issuing bonds, which they exchanged for the bonds of the private companies. In 1875, of a total system of 27,956 kilometers only 12,062 were state owned, another 3,253 were privately owned but under state management, and 12,641 were privately owned and operated. In 1912, of a total network of 60,521 kilometers, only 3,631 were privately owned, and of these only 277 involved main lines.

One of the advantages usually derived from nationalization, unification of management, could still not be completely realized in pre-Weimar Germany. Aside from the residual private roads, eight state owned systems remained in operation. The largest was jointly managed by Prussia and Hesse; six systems belonged to other federal states, and one belonged to the Reich. The constitution of the North German Confederation (founded in 1815) placed the federal government in supreme management control, and the same clause applied during Bismarck's Reich. After 1871, railroad services were unified as to many technical details. However, Bismarck's original plan of 1866 to unify all railroads under Reich ownership was defeated by opposing forces in the various states. As a result, the Reich's powers of control over the nationalized railroads were much weaker than those that the United States could exert through the Interstate Commerce Commission. The relationship among the eight public railroad systems was about what it would have been among private systems under loose state supervision.

The Weimar Constitution of 1919 at last achieved full unification by ordering all railroads to be transferred to the Reich. This was executed by contractual arrangements between the Reich and the railroad-owning states; the Reich thereby acquired a system (the *Reichsbahn*) of 53,000 kilometers.

HEAVY INDUSTRIES, PUBLIC UTILITIES, BANKS

After the railroads had been nationalized, state entrepreneurial activities in many other fields of business grew apace. The federal states as well as the municipalities participated most actively in the development of industries, chiefly state owned mines and ironworks. Thus, at the beginning of the first world war, the Prussian state owned some forty mines and twelve blast furnaces. The slogan of "municipal socialism" began to be widely discussed in the Imperial era, not waiting for the Weimar Republic. The rapidly growing cities "socialized" more and more waterworks, gasworks, power plants, public transport systems, and slaughterhouses, or erected new, publicly owned plants.

Apart from those under full public ownership, companies of a new type, the so-called "mixed-ownership" companies (*gemischt-wirtschaftliche Gesellschaften*), originated in the twentieth century. These companies were under the joint control of private capital and public authorities. This kind of organization was tried out chiefly for public utilities, such as power plants, gas- and waterworks, and municipal transport. As a rule the companies were formed by private initiative, and the municipalities, in exchange for franchises, acquired part of the stock. The most important example of this type was the *Rheinisch-Westfälische Elektrizitätswerke,* located in Germany's main industrial region and providing several industrial cities with electric light and power. This company was formed in 1905 by private enterprise; later, the consumer municipalities participated in its management. Local distribution was as a rule in the hands of municipal companies, which bought power wholesale and derived substantial profits from these transactions. This process came to be one of the most important sources of municipal revenue.

The Republic thus inherited from the Monarchy a peculiar economic system of mixed ownership in which, in the aggregate, the sector of public ownership did not rank far behind the private. On the eve of the first world war the following services were entirely state owned: the postal, telephone, and telegraph systems (with the exception of the overseas telegraph systems, which were in private hands), and the railroads. Almost fully under municipal or mixed ownership were the gasworks, waterworks, and transport systems. Power production was predominantly under state, municipal, or mixed ownership.

The state also played an important role in banking even apart from the central bank, which in the German economic system held a much stronger position than was true in this period of the central banks in the Anglo-Saxon countries. The Reichsbank stock was privately owned; however, its president and top officers were appointed by the Kaiser, and the stockholders had no say in management or policy. In addition to the Reichsbank there were several powerful state banks that together dominated the Berlin money market. The strongest among them was the Prussian State Bank (*Preussische Seehandlung*), founded in 1772. Practically the entire savings bank business was municipal, an important fact because the savings banks handled far greater funds than all the commercial banks taken together.

To round out the picture it should be noted that a very considerable proportion of the mines and other industries were state controlled, that state and municipal ownership was preponderant in forestry, and that even among the large-scale farms state owned units had some importance. Imperial Germany had gradually developed a system of partly private, partly public ownership. In this early period the groundwork had been prepared upon which the war economy, the Republican experiments, and the National Socialist system could proceed.

9. *Social Reforms*

THE PHILOSOPHY OF social reform originated in countries with older industrial traditions—particularly Britain—not in Germany. Social reforms were meant to brake the full power of capitalistic forces wherever they could breed, or had bred, obvious social defects. But in no other country had the idea of social reform taken hold of people's minds as thoroughly as in Germany, and nowhere else was it developed as comprehensively into a novel system of social thought. The movement conquered the universities, where it was represented by the so-called Professorial Socialism (*Kathedersozialismus*). So deeply rooted was its influence that the glamor of the renowned association of social scholars founded in 1872 under the name of Association for Social Policy (*Verein für Socialpolitik*) was still fresh when the National Socialist regime wiped it out. In the churches the Christian Socialist movement developed, its chief exponent the Roman Catholic Bishop Ketteler; it culminated in the formation of the Christian trade unions.

In Germany more than in any other country it was the state that first adopted the philosophy of social reform and became active in the field. Two distinct motives shaped the social program of the period: (1) the protectionist ideology prevalent since the second half of the 1870's and (2) the competition with the vigorously rising Socialist movement. It is significant that the entire social security system, which in one stroke placed Germany in the lead of social reform throughout the civilized world, was constructed in the era of the Anti-Socialist Laws.

By 1878 the reaction against the liberal era had advanced so far that Bismarck conceived the ill-fated plan of stifling the powerful upsurge of Socialism by emergency legislation. In that year two unsuccessful attempts on the life of the old Kaiser Wilhelm I had occurred. The perpetrators were proved to be clearly unconnected with the Socialist Party, yet the incidents were made the pretext for setting in force the Anti-Socialist Act, which enjoined the Socialist Party and its affiliated unions to cease every sort of activity. The Law Against the Security-Endangering Activities of the Social Democratic Party (*Gesetz gegen die gemeingefährlichen Bestrebungen der Sozialdemokratie*) went into effect on October 1, 1878. Under this act, Socialist associations were to be dissolved and their funds seized. Individuals who professionally propagated Socialist or Communist ideas could be restricted in their choice of domicile and deprived of free movement. The police authorities had the right to forbid or dissolve meetings and to confiscate or suppress printed materials. In perfect discipline the Social Democratic Party submitted to this law and reported to the police that it had dissolved its party organizations. However, before long the effects of the law, dubious from the outset, became wholly negative.

Only nine Socialist members were left in the Reichstag, but they formed the nucleus for future party reorganization. The party ran a publishing house in Zürich, Switzerland, which published an official newspaper, the

Sozialdemokrat, and forbidden pamphlets and books; the German Socialist leader Eduard Bernstein served as editor. The relatively liberal atmosphere of this period as compared with the oppressive methods of modern dictatorships is suggested by the fact that this newspaper and other publications were smuggled from Switzerland into Germany without much difficulty.

In the first two years of the law about a thousand persons were forcibly removed from a few big cities, while 150 periodicals and roughly a thousand books and pamphlets were suppressed. A few hundred individuals were sentenced to prison terms for lese majesty.

Despite these persecutions, at the Reichstag elections of 1881 the Socialist Party increased its representatives from nine to twelve, The Party had rebuilt itself in camouflaged organizations, such as glee clubs, bowling societies, and charity associations, which served the purpose. From London, Friedrich Engels sent money and thereby strengthened the influence of his more radical views. By the end of the 1880's the Hamburg organization alone numbered about 6,000 members. When, in the elections of 1890, the number of Socialist votes doubled and the number of deputies quadrupled as compared with 1878, the time seemed ripe for the young Kaiser Wilhelm II to let the Anti-Socialist Laws lapse. A few months before this Bismarck had been dismissed; an important point in his conflict with the Emperor was his insistence on keeping the Anti-Socialist Laws in force.

Five years after enactment of the Anti-Socialist Laws the first social-insurance law came into force. This compulsory health-insurance law of 1883 was based on older voluntary arrangements. In the next year a workmen's compensation scheme was instituted; it was followed in 1889 by old-age and disability insurance. This completed the basic structure of the plan as far as the imperial era was concerned.

Thus, German workers were the first among workers of all countries to be protected against the worst social dangers to which they were exposed—with the exception of unemployment, which, as Germany continued her spectacular economic progress, was not yet recognized as a common and alarming social evil. If a worker or his wife or child fell ill the health-insurance fund furnished adequate medical and financial aid, placed the patients in hospitals or rest homes, and provided for medication. Whenever a worker suffered an accident the compensation fund took care of all medical costs. If he became partly or totally disabled, or after he reached the age of 65, he was entitled to a pension that provided for his basic needs. If he died before reaching retirement age his widow and children would draw an annuity.

The costs of workmen's compensation were borne by the employer alone;

those of health insurance were shared by employers and the employed. In meeting the costs of old age and disability insurance the Reich was from the start the third participant. To the extent of their contributions employers and the employed participated in the autonomous management of the social-insurance institutions. Naturally, this feature disappeared under the National Socialist regime, together with all other forms of self-government.

Workers' protection was not confined to social insurance. In 1891, immediately following Bismarck's resignation, the first protective law for workers was enacted. It provided for a maximun working day of eleven hours for women and ten hours for children, and it prohibited night work for women and children and most kinds of employment for children under the age of fourteen years in any industry or trade. A free Sunday and various rules of hygiene were made obligatory. Other protective legislation followed.

Social reforms were not confined to the working class. Gradually it became evident that the industrial middle classes were also entitled to some protection. The old guilds had lost their legal standing in the liberal Trades Code of 1871, but after 1878 new regulations recognizing them were enacted. By a law of 1897 the guilds could ask the government to unite craftsmen in statutory guilds to regulate the training of apprentices. However, the majority of guilds remained voluntary associations.

10. The Organization of Business and Labor

THE COMPULSORY CRAFT guilds were, in a way, cartels of artisans instituted by law. When the guilds were first organized, industrial cartels were already in existence. But only after 1879 did the German cartels increase in number and scope to become a characteristic feature of German industrial organization. In fact, modern industrial cartels are of German origin. For an understanding of the peculiar development of Germany in political and economic affairs, the significance of the cartels needs to be clarified.

THE CARTELIZATION OF INDUSTRY

In every country two conflicting trends have determined the development of modern industrialism. One trend has been the liberation of the individual from the shackles and codes inherited from medieval times and the mercantilist era; the other trend has been toward integration on a more or less monopolistic basis. The entire Western world experienced this conflict. With the marked exception of Germany, the various industrial countries defended pluralistic tendencies, while monopolies were broken up or at least placed under strict restraints. The Anti-Trust Laws of the United States, steadily improved upon since first introduced with the Sherman Act of 1890, were the conspicuous expression of this individualistic philosophy. Free competition was the only admissible economic policy; infringement of free competition was made a criminal offense. The western European countries did not go quite so far, but Britain, France, Austria-Hungary, and, in their wake, the smaller industrial countries declared agreements in restraint of trade void and therefore not enforceable in the courts. In Germany alone cartel agreements had legal status and were treated by law in the same way as any other private contract. Any contravention of contractual obligations by a member of the cartel could be brought into court or penalized by the forfeiture of bonds provided for the purpose in the cartel agreement. Not until 1923, at the end of the inflation period, was a decree to regulate cartels enacted. This will be dealt with in a subsequent chapter.

The divergent treatment of cartels in Germany gives the clearest indication of how weak the roots of liberalism were in the German mind. Liberalism was never recognized as the basis of a free, capitalist system. As early as 1883 Professor Kleinwächter, an Austrian economist who wrote the first scholarly work on cartels, gave them his approval for being "the pathfinding pioneers for an economy guided by the state." Even in the liberal era the mercantilist spirit, which was later to merge all too readily with the collectivist spirit of the labor movement, remained strong. (When the two did unite, the ultimate result was Hitlerism.) In this brief liberal era the profit motive, which is fundamental to free competition, was never regarded, even by the ruling classes, as either desirable or honorable. The tone was set by the bureaucracy and the army; in their opinion the profit motive was something rather contemptible. The capitalist bourgeoisie regarded the way of life of the nonbusiness strata of society as an ideal to which they tried to conform.

The cartelization of German business did not progress along a steady line. Years of expansion of cartels were followed by setbacks. As a rule, cartels in Germany were an outgrowth of depressions. Whenever prices tended to drop below costs, cartels were organized in order to keep business "in the black." When prosperity returned the more successful entrepreneurs tired of the restrictions imposed upon them and tried to rid themselves of the cartels.

In the history of cartels, as in so many other respects, the year 1879—in which German trade policy veered toward protectionism—marked a turning point. Cartel agreements can only become effective behind a tariff wall, and only when competition among domestic producers of a commodity is eliminated can each producer exploit to the full the margin between domestic and foreign prices established by the tariff. The first cartels were formed for coke, pig iron, and steel sheets. The Potash Syndicate, probably the most interesting cartel theoretically, was founded in 1881. It was the earliest experiment in the exploitation of a basic raw material, and it concerned the one natural resource of which Germany possessed a virtual world monopoly up to the first world war. In 1910 the government made this cartel compulsory for the entire potash industry primarily in order to exploit the American market, where German potash was sold at a higher price than at home. Materially more important for Germany than potash was a combination of Ruhr coal-mining firms, organized in 1893 by the Rhenish-Westphalian Coal Syndicate. In the same period cartels were formed in various branches of the steel industry, a process that culminated in 1904 in the formation of the Steelmakers Association (*Stahlwerksverband*). German industries also very early played a leading role in international cartels. The first important one was the International Rail Makers Association, IRMA, founded in 1883 by British, German, and Belgian steel mills and later joined by the French. Its object was to distribute the world market among the various national producers of rails.

By the middle of the 1890's, aside from cartels in steel and coal, there were cartels in plate glass, cement, and certain chemicals. The era of almost total cartelization came only after the turn of the century. The attack on free individual competition was then launched both through comprehensive mergers —principally in the heavy industries—and through nationwide cartels. At the outbreak of the war in 1914 the structure of the German cartel system was virtually completed.

The term "cartel" actually covers a variety of trade combinations. The most stringent form provided for the sale of certain products by a centralized sales office, excluding any outside sales and purchases. Production was distributed by quotas among the member-producers, and the only entrepreneurial function left to individual firms was to ensure technical efficiency in order to reduce costs and raise the profit margin. In general such complete centralization was rather the exception; only in basic industries was it the rule. The thousands of cartels into which most German industry eventually became organized were much looser arrangements. Some of them fixed production quotas without centralizing sales; others assigned regional markets to the individual producers; still others only regulated business practices and terms of sale, for instance by listing conditions of credit or rules for the calculation of costs to prevent "cutthroat competition," and so forth.

The history of German cartels is one of continual internal struggles. At every renewal of an expiring cartel agreement fights flared up both against outsiders who had come up in the meantime and among the members themselves, who demanded higher quotas at the expense of their fellows. Time and again such struggles ended in disruption of the cartel and then led to price cutting and other practices, but in many cases, under the promptings of a benevolent government, a new agreement was established and peace returned. The experience of decades of cartel practice proved most helpful after 1914 when a war economy had to be improvised. Eventually, the totalitarian economic system of Hitler's Third Reich made good use of the cartel spirit for its own purposes.

THE FLOWERING OF TRADE UNIONS

As had been the case in Britain, the German workers were long hampered by anti–trade-union legislation in building up their unions. Only when the liberal era of the 1860's was well under way were most of the restrictions removed. First among the German federal states to repeal these antiorganization laws was highly industrialized Saxony, in 1861. In 1869 the new Trades Code of the North German Federation granted freedom of organization, at least to industrial workers. In 1871 this Code was adopted by the Reich.

Immediately after the legal barriers had fallen the first trade unions were formed: these were the national organizations of tobacco workers and of printers in 1865 and 1866. In marked contrast to the trade unions of Anglo-Saxon countries, the German unions were built up by central organizations decidedly political in character. As early as 1868 three separate attempts were made to organize a centralized union of unions. One of these experiments, at the time the most important of the three, was initiated by Johann von Schweitzer, leader of the group of unions originally formed by Ferdinand Lassalle. The second attempt, later to result in the dominant group, was made by August Bebel, leader of the Marxist International Workers' Association. The third effort came from two leaders of the Progressive party, Max Hirsch and Franz Duncker. All three attempts were at first surprisingly successful, but soon the Schweitzer unions began to disintegrate and, after the Lassalle and Marxist movements had merged, were taken over by the Marxist unions. The Hirsch-Duncker unions remained in existence to the end of the Weimar Republic, without ever gaining much importance. In 1899 a new group of unions became an active third factor, the Christian unions, a combination of scattered local unions formed in the 1890's by Roman Catholic workers' associations, later joined to a lesser degree by Protestant workers' groups.

Thus, from its beginnings to its dissolution in May, 1933, the German trade-union movement was politically oriented. The Free Unions, the name later adopted by the largest union body, were affiliated with the Social Democratic Party. The Christian unions, despite the denominational differences among their membership, were affiliated with the Catholic Center party, as were the Hirsch-Duncker unions with the liberal parties.

Later, especially in the period of the Anti-Socialist Laws, the contact between the Free Unions and the Social Democratic Party was temporarily somewhat loosened, since union as well as party activity had been declared illegal. Soon, however, organizations reappeared under the guise of nonpolitical professional associations, which in 1884 gained union status. Immediately after the end of the Anti-Socialist Laws in 1890, the Free Unions placed themselves under a General Commission, which they declared independent of the Social Democratic Party. This remained the central body of the Free Unions, changing only its name after the first world war to General German League of Unions (*Allgemeiner Deutscher Gewerkschaftsbund,* ADGB).

The lapse of the Anti-Socialist Laws opened the way to uninterrupted growth of the trade-union movement. In the period from 1890 to 1914 the Free Unions increased their membership from roughly 300,000 to 2,500,000, with the development of the other unions proportionate. Table 7 shows the total trade-union membership attained prior to the first world war.

TABLE 7

Membership of German Trade Unions, 1913
(thousands of members)

Free unions	2,525
Christian unions	342
Hirsch-Duncker unions	107
Independent unions	319
TOTAL	3,293

SOURCE: *Statistisches Jahrbuch für das Deutsche Reich 1915,* pp. 433 ff.

The unionization of the workers was paralleled by activities among the employers, who also formed centralized organizations. In the entire pre-1914 era relations between employers and the employed remained an autonomous affair of these groups. Government kept aloof except for the protection that civil law accorded to industrial agreements just as to any other contract. However, the industrial courts (*Gewerbegerichte*) formed in 1891 may be regarded as the first step in the direction of government regulation of employer-employee relationships. Beyond this, the relations of the employers and their associations with the unions were free of government interference. The technique of collective bargaining developed very slowly, and the number of collective agreements remained small. The rapid expansion of industry and the comparative mildness of cyclical business booms or setbacks in this period helped to promote industrial peace and to keep labor struggles within moderate limits as to the number of strikes and workers involved.

COOPERATIVE SOCIETIES

Parallel to the rise of cartels and trade unions, cooperative societies organized themselves in mighty associations, reviving a tradition dating in Germany from medieval times. Following the British example set by the Rochdale Pioneers in 1844, consumers' cooperatives were formed, which in membership and scope of activities—extending into the sphere of production—were second only to the British organizations of this type. For small tradesmen the ideas of Schulze-Delitzsch were decisive, for farmers those of Raiffeisen. These two main groups of the middle classes derived much economic support from the cooperative movement, primarily through cooperative credit organizations. Purchasing and marketing cooperatives were formed chiefly in the field of agriculture.

Thus during the last decades of Imperial Germany, long before the Weimar Republic and the National Socialist regime, an economic system had developed which in its basic features differed widely from the so-called classical liberalism attempted in the Bismarck era to conform with western European patterns. Even in its time of triumph German capitalism displayed a generous admixture of state and association control over business.

III

THE FIRST WORLD WAR

1. War Finances

GERMANY'S PHENOMENAL RISE to the rank of an industrial world power with a safe balance both at home and as a member of the economic world community ended in 1914 in sudden catastrophe. The first world war convulsed the entire globe; but in no other leading industrial country was the upheaval of the economic, social, and political structure as fundamental and as lasting as in Germany. To be sure, we see the actors who had dominated the public scene during the preceding forty years continue to perform throughout the four appalling war years. Indeed, as viewed from outside, these four years would even appear to carry the old system to its ultimate fulfillment and highest accomplishment. In reality, what was going on in Germany during the war constituted an entirely new departure, even though the threads that connected the present to the past seemed strong enough to make the change at least comprehensible.

Not only had Germany, and specifically the German economy, the tremendous task of providing alone, without outside economic or financial help, for all armament needs during the greatest war ever fought in history. Germany's fate was also decisively modified by the fact that, while the opposing industrial nations were able to call in the aid of the power with the greatest economic potential, the United States of America, Germany had to submit to a blockade of her shores. The blockade now imposed an involuntary but inexorable autarky. This happened to a country that previously had taken a larger share in world trade than any other except Britain. This experience of forced autarky never faded from the memory of the German people. Without it the economic policy of the Hitler regime cannot be understood.

When the first world war broke out on August 4, 1914 (hostilities between Austria-Hungary and Serbia had begun a week earlier), Germany was utterly unprepared economically for a war that was to expose her for many years to the bitter endurance test of economic and financial isolation. German statesmanship had obviously envisaged only a lightning campaign. Nothing had been planned for the eventuality of a struggle over a long period of time with adversaries of equal strength, nothing for the possibility or the consequences of the blockade. The first Battle of the Marne in September, 1914, ended the German dream of quick military victory; it also gave the signal for starting a war economy in Germany.

FINANCIAL MOBILIZATION

In one sphere of the economy alone had something in the way of a plan been prepared under which, in case of war, action was immediately possible: in the sphere of money and credit and of public finance. The authorities had not troubled their heads about the problem of how, should the dire necessity confront them, they would find bread for the German population and raw materials for army procurement. But they had taken well to heart the old and wise adage that to wage a modern war three things were indispensable: money, money, and again money. Soon it was to become apparent that this time the money that could be provided was not of much use.

On July 23, 1914, the Austro-Hungarian government had served a forty-eight-hour ultimatum on the Serbian government. In the following week, ending July 31, the Reichsbank lost more than 100 million marks in gold, the gold reserves decreasing from 1,357 to 1,253 million. Gold hoarding and the rush to change money from bank deposits into banknotes were clear evidence that the public had been gripped by the war scare. On that day of July 31, 1914, for the first time in its almost forty years of history, the Reichsbank discontinued redeeming banknotes in gold, in breach of its legal obligations. Note circulation was still 43 per cent covered by gold, banknotes plus demand deposits 30 per cent. (The statutory gold-coverage requirements of the Reichsbank, 33⅓ per cent, referred to banknotes alone, not to other demand liabilities. Therefore the public was not accustomed to regarding banknotes and other demand liabilities as essentially the same.)

In the memorable session for which the Reichstag assembled on August 4, 1914, it became evident that the suspension of gold payments was more than a precautionary measure to guard against the threat of a panic. It was, rather, the first step in the execution of a prepared plan. Several bills on public finance placed before the Reichstag that day were speedily enacted. One of them authorized the Reich government to borrow up to five billion marks for war expenditures. As is widely known, this was the formal act by which the Reichstag, including the Social Democratic deputies, sanctioned the war which had been decided upon over their heads on the monarch's prerogative.

The law on war credits was an enabling act such as is needed by any government in an emergency. The other financial laws enacted on August 4, 1914, were of greater immediate importance and more characteristic of the specifically German methods of war finance. They provided:

1. The obligation to redeem in gold the banknotes of the Reichsbank as well as of the private banks of issue was suspended, or rather the suspension ordered five days before was to be valid indefinitely.
2. The tax on all note circulation in excess of 550 million marks over and above the gold coverage was abolished.
3. Loan Banks (*Darlehenskassen*) were to be organized.
4. The Reichsbank was empowered to include in its note coverage the three-month treasury bills issued by the Reich, and in its "ready money coverage" (*Bardeckung*), the notes of the Loan Banks (*Darlehenskassenscheine*).

Of these four laws the first can be explained as a purely defensive measure against gold hoarding. In time of war a government is in such urgent need of keeping the centralized gold reserve intact that safeguards are imperative against its being scattered. By the three other laws the government was definitely, though at the time unconsciously, paving the way toward future inflation.

The Loan Banks were an emergency organization used for the first time during the Franco-Prussian war of 1870–71 to procure credits for business requirements. The Loan Banks of 1914 had the same task, for which they functioned up to the end of the inflation period in 1924. Apart from granting credit to business they served chiefly as supplementary agencies of the Reichsbank, in which function they profited from not being tied by various legal regulations that still hampered the Reichsbank itself. These banks were the first in a long line of auxiliary institutions of the Reichsbank, a feature that was to become characteristic of Germany's later monetary policy.

The Loan Banks were allowed to extend credit on collateral not qualifying for Reichsbank loans. They also gave credit to the federal states and municipalities and to the newly founded war corporations (*Kriegsgesellschaften*). Finally, it was their allotted task to advance money for the purpose of war bond subscriptions. The funds of the Loan Banks were simply provided by the printing presses. So-called Loan Bank notes (Darlehenskassenscheine) were issued to the full amount of the outstanding credits of the Loan Banks. These notes were regarded as legal tender and were in part taken up by the Reichsbank, in part put into immediate circulation.

The easiest opening for unrestrained inflation was created by the clause that allowed the Reichsbank to rediscount unlimited amounts of short-term Treasury bills against banknotes. The requirement of one-third gold coverage for note circulation might still have been a certain safeguard against inflation, had it not been rendered illusory by the fact that Loan Bank notes were included in the coverage; but later the gold-coverage requirement was formally repealed.

Thus, the government's financial war plans were as clear and simple as they were premeditated. The printing press had been chosen as the first and foremost resource both for the immediate war needs of the government and for the increased credit requirements of private business. It was planned that at some later time the credits for which the government had drawn on the Reichsbank would be refunded from the proceeds of war loans. But before 1916 it was not contemplated to finance war expenditures even in part by taxation.

THE COSTS OF THE FIRST WORLD WAR

War expenditures rapidly grew to a point where they could be expressed only in astronomical figures. In the last fiscal year preceding the war, 1913–14, Reich expenditures amounted to 3,848 million marks, to which must be added expenditures of the federal states of 8,507 million, forming a total of 12,355 million marks. Against this, the expenditures of the Reich "occasioned by the war" reached the figures given in Table 8, to which again substantial state and municipal expenditures must be added.

In assessing these figures it should be noted that in the course of the war years the purchasing power of the mark declined substantially. The simple summing up of war expenditures from year to year, based as it is on the

TABLE 8

German War Expenditures, First World War *

April 1 to March 31	*Millions of marks*
1914–15	6,936
1915–16	23,909
1916–17	24,739
1917–18	42,188
1918–19	33,928
ACCOUNTED AFTER 1918	32,599
TOTAL	164,300

* Extraordinary expenditures of the General Finance Administration.

SOURCE: *Statistisches Jahrbuch für das Deutsche Reich,* 1918 to 1921–22.

fictitious rule of "mark equals mark," fails to convey a true picture. The erratic rise of war expenditures from 1916 to 1917 and 1918 is due at least in some degree to the marked rise in prices. But even if a usable formula could be found to reflect the change in prices, war expenditures should probably be estimated at well above 100 billion prewar marks.

The public at large never was informed of the fact that at the beginning of the war Germany still hoped to receive some financial aid from abroad. A brief, inconspicuous report of the Reich Debt Commission indicates that on August 8, 1914, the Reich government printed Treasury certificates in the amount of 175 million dollars inscribed in English and sent them to the United States. The sum, after all, was almost 15 per cent of the first war-credit appropriations. In a later report the Reich Debt Commission drily remarks: "These Treasury certificates were never placed. They were cancelled in the Imperial Embassy in Washington and will be returned to the Control Bureau of State Securities (*Kontrolle der Staatspapiere*) as soon as traffic conditions permit sending them back from America."

Thus ended the first and most important attempt to raise war loans abroad. Similar efforts were later repeated on several occasions. Their success was never reported and can only have been paltry. The fate of these Treasury certificates sent to America in 1914 leaves no doubt on which side were the sympathies of the United States from the outset and how complete was Germany's isolation with respect to finance, as in every other way.

Thus Germany depended entirely on her own financial resources. Fortunately, the credit and currency systems of modern economies are sufficiently elastic to cope with even the most extreme strains to which they may be exposed, provided only that government authority remains intact. If the strain should eventually go beyond a nation's endurance, the final collapse need not unavoidably originate in the financial sphere. It may manifest itself as a purely physiological or psychological breakdown in the political or social sphere because of the utter exhaustion of the productive forces or of the human beings who must work with them.

WAR LOANS AND BANK ADVANCES

As in all other belligerent countries, war loans were the most important means of war financing in Germany. Their success was great beyond expectations, though this resulted in considerable degree from heavy moral and political pressures on the public. Increasingly, and with little camouflage toward the end, the war loans assumed the character of forced loans.

The war loans were issued mostly in the form of 5 per cent perpetual bonds. Only a small part was issued in 4.5 or 5 per cent Treasury certificates with varying maturities. War loans were regularly issued in half-yearly intervals, nine times altogether. The proceeds kept growing from the first to the eighth loan. The first war loan netted 4,492 million marks, the eighth 15,126 million, and only the proceeds of the last loan, issued a short time before the collapse, showed a decline to 10,570 million marks. In sum total the Reich procured through these loans 96,929 million marks, the aggregate par value amounting to 99,265 million marks.

Although the sums these war loans poured into the Treasury were enormous, they did not cover more than 60 per cent of war expenditures. Only two orthodox methods were available to take care of the rest: the more orthodox method of increased taxation, and the less orthodox method of short-term credits extended by institutions other than banks of issue. Actually, the credit banks eagerly accepted the Treasury bills. The inflationary Reichsbank policy had greatly increased the liquidity of the banks and a short-term, rediscountable investment regarded as absolutely secure and bearing interest at 4 or 4.5 per cent seemed highly desirable. Hence the amount of Treasury bills held outside the Reichsbank had increased to 29,300 million marks by the end of the war.

WAR INFLATION

Because most of the war loans had the character of compulsory loans, it should have been tempting to replace them by tax receipts and thereby save some of the rising expenditure for interest payments. Important psychological considerations should likewise have prompted a drastic increase in taxation, to make some concessions to the public's growing animosity against "war profiteers," the industrialists and tradesmen who as a result of the war boom enjoyed good business.

And yet, tax increases were resorted to only reluctantly and ineffectually. The Secretary of the Treasury, Karl Helfferich, before the war a director of the Deutsche Bank and the Anatolische Eisenbahngesellschaft, one of the most impressive figures among the civilian leaders of the war effort, and one of the few who continued to play an important role in postwar life (until his tragic death in a railroad accident in 1924), declared in open Reichstag session as late as March, 1915, that it was the intention of the Reich authorities to finance the war exclusively by borrowing.

Only slowly, under the combined pressure of public opinion and the political parties, were the methods of financing changed in some measure. Several tax laws were adopted, the first in June, 1916. Among the most important were a tax on war profits and a turnover tax, the latter at first at extremely low rates, one-tenth of 1 per cent on every subsequent turnover from producer to consumer. Both taxes were gradually increased, and others, primarily indirect taxes, were added, the most important of which were a coal tax and a transportation tax.

As a consequence of the new taxes, the revenues of the Reich did rise considerably. Net receipts (eliminating the budgets of Reich enterprises) increased from 2,357 million marks in 1914 to 7,830 million in 1917, followed by a slight decrease during the fiscal year 1918. However, this nominally large increase in revenues did not even suffice to balance the increase in ordinary expenditure that resulted from the depreciation of the currency and the inflated interest burden for the war debt. Reich expenditures, excluding direct war expenditures, amounted to a total of 26,449 million marks during the period 1914–18 as against only 20,740 million marks of revenue (excluding the proceeds of credits).

To explain the timidity of Germany's war fiscal policy it is usual to point primarily to constitutional difficulties. As noted in the preceding chapter, the

Reich had very limited fiscal powers. However, the war had placed such concentrated powers in the hands of the Reich administration that with better judgment it could undoubtedly have wielded as much authority over fiscal matters as it did over industry and commerce.

If one includes as legal money coins in circulation, banknotes, Loan Bank notes, and the daily maturing Reichsbank liabilities, it is fair to say that the circulation of government money increased during the war from 7,400 million to 44,400 million marks, that is, to six times the original amount. Bank money, consisting of deposits with the credit banks, increased somewhat less, from 4,900 million to 19,100 million marks. The total result is an increase in government plus bank money circulation from 12,500 million to 63,500 million marks, five times the prewar amount.

The "German inflation" is usually thought of as a postwar phenomenon. The above figures indicate that in fact the inflation began with the war, and that by its end was already in excess of anything ever before experienced. However, when the war ended Germany found herself in such generally extraordinary and unprecedented circumstances that the economic consequences of the war did not clearly emerge at once and were partly disguised by other factors.

The German stock exchanges remained closed for the full duration of the war, and no quotations of foreign exchanges were published. Thus, people were kept ignorant of the effects of inflation on security values and foreign exchange rates. However, the mark was being traded and quoted on the exchanges of neutral countries, and insiders were able to gauge by the continuously deteriorating mark values there what the effects of German inflation were. When the war was over, the mark had declined on neutral markets to about half its gold parity.

The effects of inflation on domestic prices were likewise obscured by the war economy measures. After the war the Reich Statistical Bureau computed that on the average the level of German wholesale prices had risen during the war years by 130 per cent. This only took account of the legal maximum and guideline prices, not of the prices actually paid by the public. As the importance of the black market (*Schleichhandel*) at far higher prices grew, the published indices became more and more fictitious. Only after the breakdown of the war economy with its framework of pervasive regulation did the full extent of economic dislocation and imbalance become discernible to all.

2. *War Socialism*

AT THE OUTBREAK of the first world war Germany was the greatest military land power in the world. But in one crucial respect, which was to become decisive after four years of war, she found herself at a disadvantage in comparison to the alliance of her adversaries: she was not mistress of the seas and was unable to fend off a blockade.

Germany and her allies were forced to construct an autarkic economic unit in central Europe. Within this region close market relations were built up. German industries exchanged their products for the (in fact very limited) products—of some raw materials and foodstuffs—of Germany's allies. By conquests in southern and eastern Europe these supplies could be somewhat increased—grain from the Ukraine, oil from Rumania—but throughout the war they remained totally insufficient. Trading continued to some extent with the adjacent neutral countries, primarily the Netherlands, Switzerland, Denmark, and Sweden. Germany and her allies were practically cut off from all other markets, and British ships were on the alert to prevent goods from outside countries from reaching Germany via the neutrals.

The effects of the blockade on the quality and quantity of available goods were to prove fatal in the long run. As to quality, the blockade denied Germany access to selected metals, rubber, oil, and certain other raw materials that are indispensable for armament production but which were not found, at least in sufficient quantities, within German territory. As to quantity, the blockade restricted Germany to her own economic resources, from which she was forced to supplement by various economic and financial expedients the even scarcer resources of her allies. The Allies, on the other hand, disposed not only of their own production but had free access to the surpluses of the entire world and, most importantly, to the growing output of the United States.

If the blockade succeeded in cutting off the Central Powers from all outside resources, it was bound to lead to Germany's downfall, provided only that the Allies could continue the war long enough. The end could be postponed, however, if, as in a beleaguered fortress, a commandeered economy were substituted for a market economy. Thus the war imposed upon Germany a basic change in her economic structure, and this new type of organization was to exert a deep influence on future developments.

When Germany entered the war her business setup was that of a basically free economy. Liberal capitalism was the prevalent mood, although government intervention was a stronger element than in the Western countries. When the war ended, German business was radically militarized. Half in jest, half in earnest, people talked about "war socialism."

Dire necessity, not a preconceived plan, had shaped this economic organization. Business was not methodically militarized at one stroke. As the war lengthened and scarcities made themselves felt in one field after another, business was gradually drawn into the military scheme.

For the purposes of this presentation it may suffice to sketch the basic organization of the three most important fields of the war economy: the administration of food, of raw materials, and of manpower.

FEEDING THE NATION

A highly industrialized country with a densely concentrated urban population such as Germany normally depends on the exchange of her own manufactured goods for the agricultural products of other countries. Before the war Germany had produced two-thirds of her food and fodder requirements, importing the other third. When a war cuts off such a country from its normal foodstuff resources it may draw for some time upon the abundant reserves usually accumulated in a free economy. All sorts of inducements to increase home production may follow, but their success will necessarily be limited at a time when the men to till the soil are progressively drawn into war service and the chemical plants must turn out gunpowder instead of fertilizer.

The German food administration resorted to every expedient available to a military system. Consumption was cut down with increasing ruthlessness, distribution was closely regulated by newly devised methods, and experiments were made in the field of production. Had this administration performed miracles of wisdom and foresight, had it succeeded in stopping every loophole through which consumers and producers struggled to evade the network of restrictions, after four and one-half years of deprivations it still could not have prevented the physiological and psychological collapse. Step by step food rationing was made more comprehensive and stringent, and the hapless consumer found himself shackled in his every move. In the beginning, aside from abolishing agricultural tariffs and prohibiting exports of foodstuffs, only a regulatory law providing for maximum prices was enacted; this empowered the individual states to set price limits on foodstuffs. At that time it was not contemplated to abolish the free market for food but only to provide safeguards against any incipient panic. Gradually a comprehensive system of maximum prices evolved which in the course of the war years came to cover every item of food throughout the country.

Maximum prices without a simultaneous regulation of consumption are like a knife without a handle or blade. At a moment of panic they may work for a short time, but they must necessarily fail as a lasting method of distribution. They cannot establish equality in distribution, which would be the main point under conditions of scarcity.

To make the food shortages more bearable the consumers were first told what to consume, or rather what not to consume. As early as October, 1914, the notorious K-bread (war bread) was introduced; for it grain had to be ground out to an abnormally high percentage and substitutes—consisting first of potatoes, later of turnips and even more objectionable substances—mixed in. A year later two meatless days per week were decreed on which meat was neither to be bought nor sold nor consumed in public eating places.

Finally, a more efficient method was found to regulate and restrict consumption: the rationing system. The first ration card was the bread card, introduced on January 25, 1915, which fixed the maximum amount of bread that could be purchased for every member of a household. Ration cards for other essential foods, such as fats, milk, meat, and butter, followed. The end result was an intricate system of consumption, differentiated as to physiological and social characteristics. A flexible factor was introduced by adjusting individual rations to harvests and imports, but the trend always remained downward. Physiological differentiation allowed rations to be adapted to the work load demanded of an individual (example qualifications being "hard labor" or "extremely hard labor") and also according to age and other criteria. Children and expectant mothers, for instance, received preferential milk rations; in the last war years milk in tiny rations was distributed to these two categories exclusively. The social differentiation favored two groups of citizens: the army, which was totally exempt from the rationing system, and the farmers, so-called self-providers, who were in theory allowed bigger rations than the rest of the population.

Under such a system all depends on the size of the ration. It varied in the course of the war years. For ordinary mortals who did not qualify in any one of the preferred categories the following rations may be regarded as typical, although not everyone was lucky enough to get full rations at all times: 225 grams of bread or 220 grams of flour per capita per day, and 56 to 68 grams of fat stuffs (butter, lard, oil, or margarine) per capita per week. Vegetables and fruit were usually available in more or less satisfactory quantities; in all other food stuffs—too often including the potato, a basic staple of German nutrition—distressing shortages prevailed despite the conspicuous emergence of *ersatz* products.

Agricultural production itself was drawn into a network of strict regulations, which failed to induce the individual farmer to increase his production and had very questionable results in the attempt to redirect production into desired channels.

As an illustration, one may cite the story of the notorious "hog massacre," which in later years was to loom large in the rising tide of National Socialist propaganda. It began with the authorities assuming that the pig was man's competitor for the limited food supply. They figured out exactly how much grain and potatoes the pig took away from human consumption and then declared a class war of the starving people against the greedy pigs. The theory was that in view of the scarce overall food resources the detour of foodstuffs through the pigs' stomachs was uneconomical. This theory, however, was not implemented in the one rational way, which would have been to regulate maximum prices so as to give the farmer an incentive to sell his grain and potatoes rather than feed them to his hogs before selling them in the market. Instead, the method of compulsion was chosen. In the autumn of 1914 the use of wheat and rye for animal fodder was prohibited and the amounts of oats and barley usable for this purpose were rationed. Finally, in the beginning of 1915, all municipalities were forced by decree to build up stocks of packed meat, for fear that the feeding restrictions were not being strictly observed and that a potato shortage might develop. This was the signal for the "hog massacre." After the forced slaughter had continued for some time it was discovered that the potato supply had been underestimated, and now the opposite danger arose: that there would be an insufficient number of pigs to eat the potatoes. Loud were the laments about the "St. Bartholomew's Day of the bristle bearers." The disturbance in regular food distribution as a consequence of the forced hog slaughter was a relatively minor incident and the matter is recorded here merely as a drastic example of the sort of error to which every planning system is likely to be exposed.

The regulation of agricultural production became more and more refined, but nothing could stop the gradual decay of farming that resulted from the growing deficiencies in farm hands, fertilizers, and implements. At the end of the war, not only had the livestock on German farms decreased to an alarming low but grain production also had decreased to less than half the prewar harvests, as far as official figures went. All of Germany had reached the end of the road, and German agriculture was no exception.

COMPULSION IN INDUSTRY

To a large extent modern war has become a function of industrial capacity. Under normal conditions the food needs of an army at war are not considerably in excess of what a standing army plus the active reserve needed before mobilization. What must rise sharply from the very first day of a war is the demand for certain industrial products. Hence, the serious character of the German emergency was recognized much earlier in the industrial field than in agriculture, and accordingly the first compulsory measures were decreed within two weeks of the start of the war.

It is the historic merit of Walter Rathenau—later the great Foreign Minister of the Weimar Republic, in 1914 head of the Allgemeine Elektricitäts-Gesellschaft, founded by his father Emil—to have realized the extent of the emergency before all others and to have dealt with it imaginatively and energetically. Though a leader in industry, Rathenau was a mere private citizen in the framework of the established system of public authority, and he needed courage to penetrate the hallowed precincts of the War Ministry to place before the appointed masters of Germany's destinies his plan for the management of the country's raw material resources. To appreciate his boldness one should recall what tremendous weight the military hierarchy had in Imperial Germany. The impression created by Rathenau's plan in August, 1914, was so deep that the Prussian war minister immediately appointed him chief of the War Raw Material Bureau (*Kriegsrohstoffabteilung,* K.R.A.), formed to implement the plan. In this capacity Rathenau laid the administrative foundation for the German war economy.

The so-called war companies (Kriegsgesellschaften) founded on Walter Rathenau's initiative had a certain kinship with the mixed-ownership companies developed in the prewar period. In their legal form as well as in their management the war companies were a peculiar mixture of private and public ownership elements. Usually they were formed as stock companies or limited-liability companies; however they differed from genuinely private organizations in the public function assigned to them. They had to administer the raw materials which the government was taking over and to act as the government's trustees. As it turned out, the companies were run jointly by the government and the former owners, producers, and processors of the sequestered raw materials. Where the war companies remained under the administration of private industrialists they acted as autonomous organs of the industry concerned, under public control and for the public benefit.

Necessarily, these war companies degenerated rapidly. On the one hand, they were blamed for allowing the industries under their control to garner excessive war profits, and it is true that they were unable to prevent profits from being accumulated by the affiliated plants although it was one of their assigned duties to keep profits within reasonable bounds. On the other hand, the principle of self-government had to be curtailed as shortages grew, and in the end the war companies were little more than bureaucratic government agencies.

Even so, Rathenau's creative idea provided one of the important guidelines for the subsequent development of a state economy in Germany. All later efforts of the Weimar Republic and, ironically enough, of Hitler's Third Reich to develop state economic agencies along nonbureaucratic lines and to create intermediary institutions between public and private business management must be traced back to Rathenau's organizing genius.

During the first two war years the government confined its interference in industrial matters to the following measures:

1. Raw materials, as they became scarce, were sequestrated and the producers were compelled to sell their products to the war companies.
2. Maximum prices were decreed.
3. Raw materials were resold to processors for prescribed purposes, and distribution to manufacturers was according to priorities assigned to their products.

Not before the end of 1916, in the so-called Hindenburg Program, was a transition made to all-out "war socialism." This, together with the unrestricted submarine war, was to be the nation's supreme effort. By mustering and mobilizing every last resource of the economy Germany tried to break through her enemies' strategy of exhaustion and despite all to force ultimate victory.

The framework for the Hindenburg Program was set by the law of December 5, 1916, which provided for the Patriotic Auxiliary Service (*Vaterländischer Hilfsdienst*). The economic life of the nation was now to be militarized to the utmost degree. The law required every male German citizen between the ages of seventeen and sixty, not on active service, to be drafted into the Auxiliary Service. Actually the law applied mainly to workers in shops directly or indirectly employed in the war industry or on farms, and the effect of it was that they were thereby deprived of their freedom of movement. They could change their place of employment only with the consent of the employer or of a committee. Where a war plant experienced difficulties in recruiting needed labor by voluntary means, workers could be conscripted for the jobs.

The compulsory service of the shops themselves consisted in the drafting of their products for military purposes. Industries not geared to the war effort were deprived of their workers and forced either to shut down or to amalgamate with war industries. State interference in industry went so far as to seize unused machinery and assign it to other plants. Finally, the law provided for the retraining of workers for munition jobs.

3. *Social Changes*

IN A PREVIOUS chapter it was shown how much power the German trade unions had accumulated and how closely they were woven into the texture of German economic life. Before 1914, however, this important factor in the industrial organization had lacked a well-defined legal status. Officially the unions were still regarded as revolutionary and consequently as illegitimate, although after the repeal of the Anti-Socialist Law no longer as illegal organizations. The Social Democratic Party, with which the Free Unions were connected, held fast to the pretense of being a revolutionary opposition party, even after it had become, under August Bebel's and Wilhelm Liebknecht's leadership, the largest political party in Germany.

By voting for the war credits on August 4, 1914, the Social Democrats abandoned this pretense, as other socialists did in the western and northern countries of Europe. Until this August day the Social Democrats had officially been a revolutionary party but in reality a party of loyal opposition. After August 4 they were officially a loyal opposition party but in reality a government party subject only to those actual limitations which the Bismarckian system of government imposed on all parliamentary parties. They were allowed to vote for the government but were not themselves called upon to form and administer the government.

This change of status and function was of great consequence to the unions, especially since at the same time the industrial war effort necessarily enhanced their influence. In their relations with employers they refrained from openly pressing their advantage. Politically, August 4 signified the formation of what was for practical purposes a national government including all parties; the Independent Social Democrats were to secede from the mother party only at a later stage of the war. Almost simultaneously in the economic field a kind of peace covenant (*Burgfrieden,* an expression going back to the medieval knights) was concluded. As in a beleaguered fortress all personal feuds were suspended until the enemy could be repulsed, the unions and employers agreed on August 2 to suspend all labor strife for the duration of the war.

As a natural consequence of the prevailing labor shortage, the real power of the unions was hardly curtailed by their official renunciation of the strike weapon. It became evident upon some critical occasions that the organized workers themselves, if not the unions as such, remained quite expert at handling this weapon.

WELFARE POLICIES IN WARTIME

The war stimulated the beginnings of unemployment relief in Germany. As early as August 4, 1914, certain payments were promised to destitute families of soldiers in war service, though not yet as part of a planned unemployment relief scheme. At this time it was still seriously believed that the war would cause mass unemployment. Somewhat later several municipalities began on their own account to dole out relief to their unemployed, and after January, 1915, the Reich provided the municipalities with funds for unemployment relief. The relief money was granted only after proof of genuine individual need, a system that remained in force until 1926.

Not all industries participated in the developing war boom. Understandably, consumer goods in general were in much less urgent demand than raw materials and durable goods. Of consumer-goods industries the textile industry was foremost among those which the war boom passed by, chiefly for lack of raw materials. Despite the draft of textile workers into war service there was unemployment, and textile wages were least adjusted to the rising cost of living.

This explains why the textile industry was the first to develop new principles of social reform that later, in Weimar Germany, were to become of basic importance. The state authorities assumed responsibility not only for procuring employment but for distributing the available opportunities as fairly as possible among the labor force. The employers were not allowed to discharge workers except in especially defined cases; also, in order to spread labor, working hours were curtailed by decree. On August 12, 1915, the Federal Council (*Bundesrat*) cut work in spinning and weaving plants to a maximum of five days a week, a ten-hour working day then being the rule. Finally, on November 18, 1915, general relief for textile workers was instituted, to be paid to needy workers even when employed.

CONCILIATION COMMITTEES AND SHOP COUNCILS

Despite statutory maximum prices and compulsory management of raw material resources the war years were a time of rising prices. Because this trend had its origin not in rising wages but in monetary conditions, wages tended to lag behind prices. In order to stop this source of social unrest the military authorities began to develop some interest in employer-employee relations. They were not only favorably inclined toward letting the unions negotiate with the employers but took the initiative toward such negotiations. Often they went so far as to make minimum wages a condition for awarding military orders to individual firms. Finally, in some places the military authorities set up conciliation committees with equal representation of employers and employees.

The decisive step was taken in the framework of the Hindenburg Program by the formation of workers' councils and conciliation committees. The shop councils resulted from a compromise between the government, the Social Democratic Party, and the unions. The Social Democrats gave their consent to the full militarization of the industrial labor force called for by the Hindenburg Program of December, 1916, in exchange for the concession that the workers' interests were to be safeguarded by workers' councils.

Accordingly, the Law on Patriotic Auxiliary Service ordered workers' committees to be set up. In every plant with more than fifty workers such committees were elected by secret ballot with proportional representation. These committees were the direct precursors of the shop council system inaugurated by the Weimar Republic, one of the prominent features of the new labor constitution. The Auxiliary Service Law also provided for conciliation committees formed of an equal number of employers and employees under the chairmanship of an impartial arbitrator. Their duty was to decide on all wage questions, and their decisions were binding.

4. *The End*

IN THE BITTER struggle between Republican Germany and her foes on the Right, which was to end in the defeat and destruction of the Republic, a legend played a major role: the so-called stab in the back. The nationalists contended that in 1918 Germany had not been defeated on the battlefield; the people at home had stabbed the fighting men in the back.

The military history of the first world war shows beyond a doubt which of the contending parties commanded the superior power in the last phase of the war. Slowly but surely, both at the front and in the hinterland, the limits of Germany's resources came in sight. In technical equipment the military machine of the Central Powers fell further and further behind those of their adversaries. The scales were weighted decisively in favor of those powers whose resources, superior from the beginning, at last became practically limitless by the accession of their new American ally, the world's foremost industrial power.

To be sure, in addition to the material factors there were, less visibly, factors of morale on either side of the trenches that in the end contributed to breaking the long deadlock. The self-confidence of the armies and of the hinterland took first place in this respect. Imagine the state of morale in a nation which for four years had been called upon to offer the utmost sacrifices of life and limb and wealth, which felt starvation drawing closer, and which finally could not but realize that its vaunted last card in the military game, unrestricted submarine war, was not trumps but, on the contrary, had summoned the fresh new armies of the mightiest western nation into the enemy camp.

These factors of morale were at work just as strongly at the fronts as at home. The troops therefore could not possibly have been dealt a "stab in the back." The only difference between the men in the field and the people at home was that at home the effects of moral disintegration were more generally visible because people were not subjected to the same degree of military discipline as in the trenches. In the economic sphere the most telling symptoms of disintegration were the black market and strikes.

At this point not even the most determined government action could have stemmed the tide of black market trading in all publicly administered commodities. Weakened public morale allowed law infringement to become a habit. In stressing the differences between the rich and the poor, the black market tended to destroy the spirit of solidarity. When the impression spreads that the upper classes are unwilling to bear the same heavy burdens as the rank and file, people begin to imagine that they are called upon to fight a "war for the rich" and their spirits sink to new lows. The black market demonstrated conclusively that the well-to-do no longer possessed the moral stamina to shoulder their proper share in the nation's effort. The decline in morale could not be attributed to the lower classes alone.

The second symptom of disintegration, the strike wave, assuredly had at least some direct connection with the Russian revolution which began in the spring of 1917 with the downfall of the Czarist regime and culminated in the Bolshevik Revolution in November. Not long before these events a political group openly opposed to the war had been formed in Germany; in 1916 the Independent Social Democratic Party broke away from the majority Social Democrats. After the Russian revolution a wave of excitement spread over Germany, and various opposition groups began partly legal, partly illegal political activities. Yet none of the large strikes of the last war years could be said to be genuinely revolutionary in character. They were sufficiently explained by the distressing food shortages, although the propaganda of radical socialist groups certainly helped to spread them.

On April 16, 1917, immediately after the collapse of Czarism in Russia, the Reich government was compelled to cut bread rations. This caused such exasperation among the workers that spontaneous strikes broke out in numerous munitions factories, particularly in the large cities and in the Ruhr district. After negotiations between the government and the central bodies of the Social Democratic Party and the trade unions, the old bread rations were restored pending the availability of sufficient ersatz foodstuffs. The strike wave receded, but from time to time labor unrest flared up in various localities. A second wave of scattered strikes, this one also of short duration, threatened the war industries in January, 1918.

In July, 1918, an unauthorized strike broke out in the Upper Silesian mining district with demands reflecting the state of food supplies. The strikers wanted their daily working hours cut to eight because, due to inadequate food, their physical strength could not carry them through longer working hours. It should be noted that miners, classified as "hardest workers," were entitled to the largest rations. The military authorities countered the strike by proclaiming a "major state of siege," placing all miners of the district under martial law. However, in August, 1918, while the strike movement was at its height, the changed situation on the war fronts brought the dictatorship of the Military High Command to a sudden halt. In October, 1918, the

Reichstag, now in fact in full charge of the government, voted a constitutional amendment curtailing the High Command's powers to proclaim martial law. Only a few days after this, the Military High Command requested that the government enter into armistice negotiations forthwith, as the fronts were breaking up.

This narrative of events shows two things: first, that the almost superhuman sacrifices imposed on the German people, in overstraining the nation's economic and military strength, had slowly but surely undermined its power of resistance; and, second, that the final collapse was caused by a combination of military, economic, and physiological—not political—processes. The stab in the back is nothing but a legend. The flames kindled by the Russian revolution may have encouraged the German workers to make use of the strike weapon in war time, yet the strikes themselves, indicative of fading endurance, were not widespread or persistent enough to justify the unexpected, abrupt cessation of the fighting.

At the moment of Germany's military collapse her economic and psychological forces were at last also about to give way in utter exhaustion. The collapse at the fronts had become inescapable with the arrival from America of fresh auxiliary troops for the Allies at the same time that German combat action was crippled by growing ammunition shortages. On the other hand, the hopelessness of the military situation, which had finally become common knowledge despite heavy censorship, precipitated the breakdown of German public morale.

IV

THE WEIMAR REPUBLIC

1. General Characterization

THE REVOLUTION THAT followed the military collapse altered Germany's political structure to its very foundations. The economic changes were far less revolutionary once several timid attempts at nationalizing the key industries had failed. And yet, Germany's economic structure in 1932 differed widely from what it had been in 1914.

When the first world war ended, conditions in Germany seemed to favor a socialist regime. The trend toward state penetration (*Durchstaatlichung*) of all economic relations had not originated in the revolution of 1918. This revolution merely hastened a development which, apart from the comparatively brief period of early Bismarckian liberalism, seems to be in tune with German historical tradition. This trend had grown progressively stronger during the last decades preceding the first world war; it became dominant during the war and because of it.

The Weimar Republic had a short but eventful life. From both the political and the economic points of view its span of fourteen years may be divided into three well-defined periods.

The first period lasted five years, from November, 1918, to November, 1923. Politically, this was the time of the worst disorders and of dangerous attempts directed against the very existence of the young Republic. Economically, the period was dominated by inflation. The era of political upheavals, of *putsches* and political mayhem ended on the day that inflation ended. Hitler's and Ludendorff's foolhardy Munich Putsch miscarried on November 9, 1923. On November 15 of the same year the currency was stabilized.

The second period lasted to the end of 1929. It was terminated with the death of Gustav Stresemann, the last Foreign Minister of the Weimar Republic to enjoy both national and international confidence and authority. Stresemann died in October, 1929, and at about the same time the great American economic boom collapsed. In politics as in economics this had been the period during which the Weimar Republic prospered. To all appearances German democracy was consolidated, and in the more peaceful political atmosphere an economic recovery of truly American proportions gained momentum.

The third period, which lasted to the end of 1932, was a time of crisis in industry, agriculture, and banking. Like the preceding boom the German depression can only be measured by American standards. There was one difference between the two countries, but it was a fundamental one: America's democracy was established beyond doubt. The economic crisis could therefore have no more tragic political consequence in the United States than to bring about the traditional replacement of the ruling party by the opposition. In contrast, the young German Republic was not as yet sufficiently sure of itself to withstand the shocks to its economic fabric.

2. *Inflation*

THE TREATY OF VERSAILLES

ON ENTERING THE Weimar period, first of inflation and then of reconstruction, Germany as a territorial unit was far different from the powerful prewar Reich. She had been deprived of all her colonies, whose value, as we noted, had been questionable. But the main body of the Reich, too, had lost 13.1 per cent of its prewar territory and 10 per cent of its 1910 population (if the Saar region, which remained separated from Germany up to 1935, is included in the losses). The territories lost permanently (or until 1935) in consequence of the Versailles treaty and the partition of Upper Silesia (1921) were particularly rich in agricultural and mineral resources. They comprised 14.6 per cent of the arable land, 74.5 per cent of the iron ore, 68.1 per cent of the zinc ore, 26 per cent of the coal production. Added to this was the breakup of the German potash monopoly by the loss of the Alsatian potash mines and the conversion of the Alsatian textile industry from one of the most prosperous parts of German textile manufacturing to its most dangerous competitor. Finally, the loss of Alsace-Lorraine and, even more, the loss of half of Upper Silesia, disrupted some of the most important connecting links in the industrial and transportation systems.

In fact, Germany had become very much poorer by these territorial changes. This loss was greatly intensified when the armistice and the peace treaty imposed on Germany huge deliveries in kind to her former adversaries. First, Germany had to deliver all armament materiel and her entire navy. In addition the deliveries included:

all merchant ships of more than 1,600 gross tons;
half of the merchant ships of 1,000 to 1,600 gross tons;
one-quarter of the fishing fleet;
one-fifth of the river and lake fleet;
5,000 locomotives, 150,000 railroad cars, 5,000 motor trucks;
the entire Alsace-Lorraine railroad system with all rolling stock;
all materiel left behind in the combat zones;
all public property in the ceded territories and colonies.

Furthermore, the Allies reserved the right to confiscate all German private property in their own countries and in the ceded territories, the German owners to be compensated by the Reich government. This threat was subsequently carried out in the Allied countries, though not in the ceded territories. The United States alone provided a notable exception by later returning the seized German properties.

All these deliveries were to be credited to the reparations account at wholly arbitrary valuations, a purely fictitious procedure. In view of the astronomical reparations figures, recording these credits amounted to pouring wine into a bottomless barrel.

The territorial losses and the deliveries in kind resulted in a dangerous deterioration in the German balance of payments. More foodstuffs had to be imported; minerals heretofore mined in Germany now had to be purchased abroad; exports of other raw materials had to be curtailed. The loss of the merchant fleet deprived the country of the foreign exchange paid by other countries for the fleet's services. The loss of capital invested abroad cut down the influx of profit and interest payments. Even without reparations obligations it would have been hard for Germany to re-establish a sound balance in her external exchange accounts unless foreign aid were forthcoming.

REPARATIONS

The reparations made the German situation hopeless in the years to come. When on October 3, 1918, Prince Max von Baden's government accepted Woodrow Wilson's Fourteen Points it thereby assumed the obligation to repair the devastated war zones. In his note of December 5 addressed to the German government, Secretary of State Robert Lansing defined the reparations obligation more precisely. Germany was to undertake reparation of all damage to private property of the Allies with the exception of Russia. "Compensation will be made by Germany for all damage done to the civilian population of the Allies and to their property by the aggression of Germany by land, sea, and from the air." Had there been any fair computation of these damages, the reparations debt would very probably have been balanced to a large extent by the deliveries in kind enumerated above. However, reparations as ultimately defined lost all relation to the original American definition.

The Versailles treaty obligated Germany to pay all costs of Allied occupation troops on German territory, this superimposed obligation not to be credited to the reparations account; the treaty also extended the definition of reparations to include all capitalized pension payments to Allied combatants. Thereby, reparations obligations were inflated beyond all bounds. However, the peace treaty stated no definite total for the reparations debt; it only stipulated that the German government was at once to issue and deliver bonds to the amount of 100 billion gold marks, of which 20 billion were to serve as security for the interim payments due prior to May 1, 1921. Interest on and amortization of the balance of 80 billion gold marks were to be paid over the following thirty years. This alone would have entailed reparations payments of one billion gold marks each year after 1921. The Reparations Commission provided for by the peace treaty was assigned the task of determining the definite amounts and modes of payments in a general reparations plan to be completed by May 1, 1921.

The Versailles treaty only came into force on January 10, 1920, but payments were to begin earlier and by May 1, 1921, were to amount to 20 billion gold marks. The value of the deliveries in kind was to be credited against this sum. Part of the balance of 80 billion marks was also to be paid in kind. On this account Germany was ordered to deliver annually during the following decade at least 38 million tons of coal and large quantities of chemicals and other goods. These deliveries actually began in August, 1919, that is, before the peace treaty was in force.

The following years, up to the time of the Dawes Plan of 1924, were filled with bitter and harmful wrangling over amounts and modes of reparations payment. At last, in January, 1921, the Paris Resolutions set up a payments plan which provided for payment of 2 billion gold marks in each of the next two years, 3 billion gold marks in each of the following three years, 4 billion for three years, 5 billion for three years, and finally 6 billion gold marks annually over the subsequent thirty-one years. In addition, 26 per cent of the proceeds of German exports were to be paid in each of these forty-two years. Since the reparations payments themselves forced Germany to increase her exports to a fantastic level, the 26 per cent export duty meant an additional burden that would rapidly rise to from 2 to 3 billion gold marks per year.

The Allies sought to force the German government to accept this preposterous plan by imposing "sanctions," as provided by the peace treaty. In March, 1921, several towns on the Rhine and in the Ruhr region were occupied, and the customs receipts in the occupied territories were impounded.

The "final" payments plan, known as the London Ultimatum, which the Reparations Commission worked out and the Allied governments presented to the German authorities in the first days of May, 1921, was hardly closer to reality than the Paris Resolutions. First, Germany's reparations debt was fixed at 132 billion gold marks, an amount which, according to the most eminent economic expert on the Allied side, John Maynard Keynes, was three times the maximum that Germany was able to pay. Second, the reparations debt was to bear 6 per cent annually in interest and amortization. For the moment, the Reparations Commission was to issue only 50 billion in gold mark bonds to be serviced by the reparations annuities. The balance of 82 billion was not to be issued until the Commission was satisfied that Germany would be able to bear the added burden.

The first reparations annuities were set at 2 billion gold marks plus the 26 per cent export duty, a sum virtually identical with that provided by the Paris Resolutions for the first year. As a down payment Germany was to deliver one billion gold marks over the next few months. The full receipts from German export duties, plus the 26 per cent special duty, plus several taxes were to serve as guarantees for this payment. A guarantee committee sitting in Berlin was to watch over the execution of the plan. The Reparations Commission was empowered to demand payment in kind for any part of reparations. The German government was obligated to let the British government cash in its share of the 26 per cent export tax through its own agents (British Recovery Act) while the German government had to compensate the German exporters.

This reparations plan was presented to Germany in the form of an ultimatum. Unless it were accepted within six days the Ruhr basin would be occupied. In the Reichstag a bare majority acceded. In the following months the plan was actually executed within the prescribed time limits, and even the one billion marks cash payment was delivered before the end of August, 1921. Only in December did the government ask for a reduction. In January, 1922, it was agreed that payments were to be reduced for that year to 2.17 billion marks, the additional payments for the armies of occupation to be canceled. Of the total, not more than 720 million marks were to be paid in cash, the rest in kind. This agreement was implemented up to July, 1922.

Meanwhile, Germany's situation had deteriorated to such a degree that the government begged for a moratorium on cash payments until the end of 1924, declaring itself ready to continue payments in kind to the agreed maximum of 1.45 billion marks. This request was turned down, but in September, 1922, an agreement was reached that allowed Germany to pay, in addition to the deliveries in kind, 270 million marks in the form of six-month treasury certificates.

THE STRUGGLE FOR THE RUHR

Thus to a large extent reparations payments had been converted into deliveries in kind, and it was in this field that the severe struggles of 1923 were carried on. The Poincaré government in France was convinced that Germany was evading her obligations in bad faith and that the only way to retrieve reparations was to go and get them. Consequently, Poincaré decided to occupy the Ruhr basin, center of Germany's iron and coal production. A minor conflict between Germany and France, or rather between Germany and the Reparations Commission, had arisen over the delivery of telegraph poles and a small deficiency in coal deliveries. This was used as a pretext by France and Belgium to order troops to march into the Ruhr region in January, 1923.

For the first time Germany went into open revolt against a measure taken by the victors. The moment the French and Belgian troops entered the Ruhr the German government stopped all reparations payments to these two countries and forbade all German officials, including Reichsbahn personnel, to take orders from the occupying authorities. These responded by evicting all German officials from the Ruhr district. They organized a civil and railroad administration of their own and cut off the Ruhr from economic communication with the rest of Germany. Funds of the banks and Reichsbank branches and inventories of mines and factories were seized. After passive resistance, which at first had been ordered for the civil servants only, had spread to the workers in mines and factories, the occupying authorities tried to keep up activities in the workshops partly by force, partly with their own men.

The Ruhr struggle plunged Germany into dire straits. She was now separated from her most essential raw material resources. Moreover, the government had to feed the workers and civil servants who had struck in the Ruhr territory or had been evicted from it, to maintain the families of thousands who had been jailed by the occupiers, and, on top of all this, to compensate industry heavily for the losses incurred in the conflict. And yet, reparations deliveries in kind to the Allies, except to France and Belgium, together with payments under the British Recovery Act, were kept up until August, 1923.

Add to this plight the mounting political chaos in consequence of the currency collapse, and it will be seen that ultimately resistance was bound to crumble. In August, 1923, the Cuno cabinet, which had carried through the Ruhr conflict, resigned. The new coalition government headed by Gustav Stresemann at once ordered passive resistance ended and payments to the resisting workers and officials stopped. In November, 1923, agreements were signed between the occupiers and representatives of industry, with the German government concurring, pursuant to which the companies were to pay taxes and deliver their products directly to the Allies. These agreements remained in force until the Dawes Plan was adopted in August, 1924.

Certainly not by mere chance, the end of the Ruhr conflict coincided with the end of the great inflation. The situation called for a thorough rehabilitation of German finances and currency on the one hand, and of the relations between Germany and the Allies on the other. Both had to be accomplished together or not at all.

FINANCIAL REFORMS

Despite all these tribulations the German government had made serious attempts from time to time, even prior to the Dawes Plan, to rid itself of budget deficits. The Reich Treasury was overburdened by reparations, the service of the huge war debts, and the relief for war victims. Decisive financial reforms were undertaken in 1920 but even before that several taxes, chiefly the turnover tax, had been increased and export duties had been introduced. In December, 1919, the Reichstag voted a capital levy, the Reich Emergency Levy (*Reichsnotopfer*); it was to take up to 65 per cent from the largest properties while also reaching down to the smallest, and it was expected to net not less than 80 billion marks; at the time the bill was passed this represented a sum equal in purchasing power to more than eight billion prewar marks.

Only too soon the intrinsic weakness of a financial policy that defined taxes in terms of nominal money values at a time of progressive currency depreciation was to become apparent. Necessarily, there are considerable delays between the assessment and the payment of a tax, and meanwhile actual revenue will shrink to a fraction of expected returns. This weakness was especially marked for the Emergency Levy because long-drawn-out installment payments had to be granted. The purchasing power of the mark did not vary much during 1920, but began to decline in 1921 and continued at such a rate that soon it was no longer worthwhile to enforce payment. Accordingly, installment payments on the levy were suspended in 1922 and replaced by a property tax.

The most comprehensive and systematic attempt to solve the financial problems was undertaken in Erzberger's fiscal reforms. The importance of these reforms transcends the mere restoration of a balanced budget. The novel theoretical concepts of the Weimar Constitution were now made a vivid reality in the field of public finance: Germany was transformed from a federated group of states into a federal state. While Bismarck's Reich could use only the few sources of taxation not pre-empted by the federal states, now the Reich was made the supreme bearer of financial sovereignty and the states were limited to those taxes not claimed by the Reich.

Despite the confusion incident to the inflation period, the Erzberger reforms initiated a system of taxation which, with relatively few changes, remained the basis of German fiscal affairs into the second world war. At the same time, the Reich organized a well-planned fiscal administration. It was the first comprehensive nonmilitary executive organ of the Reich, which until now had depended on the cooperation and goodwill of the states.

Matthias Erzberger should be given credit for other achievements beside those of a minister of finance. As a leader of the Center party during the war, he had been the foremost backer of the Reichstag's peace resolution of July, 1917. Representative of the new Germany, he was one of the main targets of the Rightist opposition, particularly after he had courageously attempted to tax property heavily. A campaign of vilification forced him to resign his office as finance minister. In August, 1921, he fell victim to nationalist assassins. His end paralleled the fate of another great leader of the young Republic, Walter Rathenau. After rising to power Hitler personally honored the murderers of both men by dedicating public monuments in their names.

Well thought out and efficient as Erzberger's reforms proved to be after the inflation had been stopped, they were bound to fail, as had all previous experiments, under the overwhelming impact of currency depreciation. When, during 1922, the momentum of the mark's decline had mounted, there was a renewed political struggle for a large-scale capital levy. The Socialist parties demanded it in the belief that the levy could be protected against depreciation by tapping so-called real property values (*Sachwerte*). This rather nebulous term was at the time meant to designate all property titles not immediately affected by money valuations, such as factories, stocks of commodities, and real estate. The "bourgeois" parties were opposed since they sensed the danger of a partial socialization of business under the guise of fiscal measures, which would nevertheless fail to solve the financial problems. The eventual compromise provided for a compulsory loan to the government of one billion gold marks, in the first three years bearing no interest, later 4 to 5 per cent. As this loan was written in "gold marks," the fictitious notion of "mark equals mark" was officially abandoned for the first time. Once more, however, depreciation between assessment and payment was so rapid that again the scheme remained largely on paper.

Thus all financial efforts had mostly negative results as long as the inflation proceeded. Tax increases, the emergency levy, and the forced loan notwithstanding, fiscal receipts dropped off hopelessly when the devaluation of the currency had become catastrophic.

Defining the "purchasing-power mark" as the paper mark divided by a cost-of-living index, the record of Reich income and expenditure may be computed as set out in Table 9.

The deficits were covered by "floating debts," in other words, by the printing press. As the table shows, the decisive turn for the worse occurred in 1923. This was the price Germany had to pay for fighting the Ruhr resistance.

TABLE 9

Reich Finances, 1920–23
*(in millions of "purchasing-power marks" *)*

April 1–March 31	*Income*	*Expenditure*	*Excess of expenditure over income*
1920–21	4,091	11,266	7,175
1921–22	5,236	11,964	6,728
1922–23	3,529	9,665	6,136
1923–24	2,913	14,963	12,050

* A "purchasing-power mark" is defined here as the actual "paper" mark divided by the cost of living index.

SOURCE: Statistisches Jahrbuch für das Deutsche Reich, 1924–25, p. 348.

CURRENCY IN DISTRESS

From May, 1919, when the peace conditions became known, to February, 1920, the dollar quotation (parity 4.20 marks) moved from 13.5 to 99 marks. This period was characterized, on the one hand, by the shock that followed the announcement of the terms of the peace treaty, and on the other hand, by the domestic turmoil which culminated in the Kapp putsch of March, 1920. After this putsch had been successfully put down in the same month, the dollar rate rapidly improved to 40 marks in June, 1920, and then oscillated between 60 and 70 marks for an entire year. This was a time of domestic consolidation in which the first deflationary effects of Erzberger's reforms and a breathing spell in reparations made themselves felt. Two events that deeply depressed the German people, the London Ultimatum of May, 1921, and the partition of Upper Silesia in October of the same year, sent the dollar quotation up to 270 marks in November, 1921. A short interval of receding foreign exchange rates followed when the German government was granted a partial moratorium on reparations payments. But in June, 1922, following large disbursements on reparations account and the assassination of Walter Rathenau amidst growing domestic tensions, the dollar rate resumed its upward surge. In July, 1922, the mark sank for the first time below 1 per cent of its original value; and when Raymond Poincaré's reparations policy was seen to drive straight toward conflict, the plunge became ruinous. By January, 1923, after the Ruhr adventure had begun, the dollar rate had reached 18,000 marks. Then, surprisingly, the exchange market quieted down somewhat. German strategy in the Ruhr conflict demanded that the currency be defended by all possible means. But after May, 1923, the economic consequences of the Ruhr resistance on finance and business became so catastrophic that support for the mark had to be discontinued. A new break followed, and now nothing could hold the downward race of the mark.

Disregarding intermediate fluctuations, Table 10 shows the dollar quotations on the Berlin exchange at regular intervals. They convey a graphic picture of a phenomenon not previously recorded in history. Reality was just as fantastic as the visual impression of the curving statistics. For several years the German people had to live through such chaos.

TABLE *10*

Dollar Quotations for the Mark; Selected Dates, 1914 and 1919–23
(*monthly averages*)

July, 1914	4.2
January, 1919	8.9 *
July, 1919	14.0
January, 1920	64.8
July, 1920	39.5
January, 1921	64.9
July, 1921	76.7
January, 1922	191.8
July, 1922	493.2
January, 1923	17,972.0
July, 1923	353,412.0
August, 1923	4,620,455.0
September, 1923	98,860,000.0
October, 1923	25,260,208,000.0
November 15, 1923	4,200,000,000,000.0

* Computed from Swiss quotations.

SOURCE: *Statistisches Jahrbuch für das Deutsche Reich,* 1921–22 to 1924–25.

The table shows the abrupt turn of events in July, 1921, following the London Ultimatum. The legendary inventor of the chess game, wishing to demonstrate to the Shah of Persia the meaning of a geometrical progression, is said to have asked as a favor to have his chessboard heaped with grains of corn in such a way that one was placed on the first field, two on the second, four on the third, and so on to the sixty-fourth field. The Shah soon realized that there were not enough grains in his realm to fill the last field alone. This legend became a bitter reality in the great German inflation.

SOARING PRICES

In the first inflationary period there was actually a considerable time lag between the movement of external exchange values and the domestic purchasing power of the mark. Commodity prices rose much more slowly than the dollar quotation. After the devaluation had gone wild, prices adapted themselves with increasing speed. Finally, after 1922, when the entire nation had come to understand the connection between *Devisen* quotations and commodity prices, the adjustment became almost immediate.

Accordingly, the dollar now became the yardstick of values and the determining factor for setting prices. The daily dollar quotation replaced the weather as a topic of conversation. Every guttersnipe was accurately in-

TABLE *II*

Indices of Depreciation of the Mark; January, 1920–November, 1923
(1913 = 1)

	MEASURED BY	
DATE	*Foreign exchange*	*Wholesale prices*
January, 1913	1.0	1.0
January, 1920	15.4	12.6
July, 1920	9.4	13.7
January, 1921	15.4	14.4
July, 1921	18.3	14.3
January, 1922	45.7	36.7
July, 1922	117.0	101.0
January, 1923	4,279.0	2,785.0
July, 1923	84,150.0	74,787.0
August, 1923	1,100,100.0	944,041.0
September, 1923	23,540,000.0	23,949,000.0
October, 1923	6,014,300,000.0	7,095,800,000.0
November 15, 1923	1,000,000,000,000.0	750,000,000,000.0

SOURCE: *Statistisches Jahrbuch für das Deutsche Reich*, 1921–22 to 1924–25.

TABLE 12

German Banknote Circulation, 1913 and 1920–23
(in gold marks)

Average, 1913	6,070,000,000
January, 1920	3,311,000,000
July, 1920	7,428,000,000
January, 1921	5,096,000,000
July, 1921	4,745,000,000
January, 1922	2,723,000,000
July, 1922	1,730,000,000
January, 1923	173,000,000
July, 1923	168,000,000
August, 1923	282,000,000
September, 1923	752,000,000
October, 1923	300,000,000

SOURCE: *Statistisches Jahrbuch für das Deutsche Reich,* 1921–22 to 1924–25.

formed about it, and of course every merchant had it at his fingertips, adjusting his prices automatically or even anticipating the forthcoming dollar rates. It became customary to close shop at lunch time and to reopen in the afternoon with new price tags after the dollar quotation of the day had been reported.

A comparison of the foreign-exchange index with the wholesale-price index reveals the growing speed of adjustment. The lag in adjusting retail prices was also diminishing.

In the headlong course of depreciation the volume of money in circulation began to lag behind the depreciation of the mark in terms of the dollar, particularly after the middle of 1921. Table 12 shows the banknote circulation computed in gold marks.

The paradoxical situation indicated by these figures can be clarified as follows: the increase in note circulation, especially in the last phase of the inflation, was so explosive that the printing presses were literally unable to keep up with demand. In the last months before the collapse more than 30 paper mills worked at top speed and capacity to deliver notepaper to the Reichsbank, and 150 printing firms had 2,000 presses running day and night to print the Reichsbank notes. Even with this mass production, disturbances in the money supply to the public could not be prevented. As prices followed the exchange quotations in ever closer succession, the commodity turnover had to be handled with a relatively shrinking money supply, and the velocity of circulation was accelerated even more. Since cash in hand was exposed to daily, later to hourly, devaluation, everyone took the utmost care to hold as little of it as possible. Money in the till burnt like fire and had to be gotten rid of at the first opportunity, preferably the minute it was received. While people became poorer and poorer there was a general scramble for goods.

As has been shown, the inflation resulted not only from the Reichsbank financing of government deficits but also from inflationary credits to business granted by the Reichsbank and commercial banks. In themselves these credits would have been normal features of an inflationary situation, but in the context of this particular German inflation they acquired a special economic and social connotation. With the growing speed of depreciation, credits made out in paper marks became an abundant and riskless source of profits and led to the accumulation of huge new fortunes.

The trick was simple. The businessman procured short-term bank credit not only to keep his shop going but also for investment in other "physical values." Such investment entailed long-term immobilization of the funds in expanding the debtor's own plant or in acquiring additional facilities. When the time came to repay the debt, payments were made with devalued money. Thus the new plants or the materials to run them were acquired virtually without cost. German industry experienced a time of frantic activity of the kind described, limited only by the availability of materials and manpower.

Naturally the demand for these magic credits rose by leaps and bounds, and private interest rates scaled astonishing heights, a progressively greater devaluation factor being calculated into the interest terms. Yet this devaluation premium usually lagged far behind the actual depreciation, mainly because the Reichsbank as the ultimate source of credit held interest rates down by granting voluminous business credits on short-term, low-interest bills.

This Reichsbank policy of pumping inflationary credits into business—aside from the inflationary credits to the government—began in 1922. At the end of 1921 commercial bills and acceptances in the Reichsbank portfolio amounted to only 1.1 billion marks. By the end of 1922 the portfolio had increased to 422 billion compared with a holding of Reich treasury bills of 1,185 billion. Thus, to the inflationary effects of Reich deficit financing, the Reichsbank added as much as another third in credits to business. Approximately the same ratio between public and private Reichsbank credits prevailed in 1923, the year of the Ruhr conflict and of the highest inflation fever.

The most objectionable feature of these inflationary business credits was the interest rate at which they were granted. Up to July, 1922, the Reichsbank kept its discount rate at 5 per cent. In August, 1923, it was still only 30 per cent; in September, 1923, it was raised to 90 per cent, where it was held to the end of the inflation. Thus the Reichsbank calculated a devaluation premium of from 25 to 85 per cent per annum while the actual devaluation rate was more than 3,000 per cent in 1922 and several million and billion per cent in 1923.

INFLATION PROFITEERS

Persons who were resourceful and had the necessary banking connections to procure a maximum of commercial credit had nothing to do but invest the money without delay in "physical values" in order to amass a gigantic fortune in no time at all. The most typical example of such practice and, in general, of the trend toward capital accumulation was the case of Hugo Stinnes.

Hugo Stinnes was not, as were so many other inflation figures, a newly rich man. He was heir to a large and reputable coal-mining and shipping firm and during the war had himself become a dominating force in the Rhenish-Westphalian heavy industry. When the first world war started he held the majority of shares of the *Deutsch-Luxemburgische Bergwerksgesellschaft,* one of the largest German steel and coal-mining companies, and of the Rhenish-Westphalian Electricity Company, the leading power producer in this foremost industrial area. Not until the postwar inflation did the Stinnes group become the voracious octopus of world fame.

The resources with which this group expanded came in one part from contributions paid by the Reich for properties ceded in Alsace-Lorraine, in another part from inflationary credits. Stinnes used these means to strengthen his position in heavy industry by forming a "joint venture" (*Interessengemeinschaft*) with another large group, the *Gelsenkirchener Bergwerksgesellschaft,* in 1920. In the same year he formed a further joint venture with the powerful electricity group of Siemens-Schuckert. In addition, he began to buy up at random and in large numbers the most varied businesses, including banks, hotels, paper mills, newspapers and other publishing concerns.

With Stinnes' economic power his political role grew apace. Stinnes was among the few German business men—Walter Rathenau occupying a comparable position at the opposite political pole—who had the courage to descend in person into the political arena in order to exercise in a straightforward manner the political influence inherent in his economic position. He did this both as one of the leaders in Gustav Stresemann's German People's Party (*Deutsche Volkspartei*) and through a daily newspaper which he had recently acquired, the *Deutsche Allgemeine Zeitung*.

Stinnes died in April, 1924, almost immediately after the mark was stabilized, just in time to save his reputation. For with the end of the inflation boom the inorganic giant business agglomerations were doomed. As soon as inflation was replaced by stabilization, prices inevitably began to decline and as the nominal value of the excessive debts that had been incurred remained unchanged, the burden became overwhelming. With uncanny speed the entire structure Stinnes had built foundered. His heirs retained a comparatively insignificant remainder of the industrial grouping, and the central concern disintegrated into its elements. Only the "community of interests" between the Deutsch-Luxemburgische Bergwerksgesellschaft and the Gelsenkirchener Bergwerksgesellschaft survived under different management, later to become the nucleus of the German steel trust, the *Vereinigte Stahlwerke*.

INFLATION VICTIMS

Thus, while immense fortunes were piled up, the broad strata of the middle classes sank into poverty. All property invested at fixed money values, such as government bonds, mortgages, mortgage bonds, savings bank deposits, and the like, became worthless. Hence the economic basis of a social class that had been so important in prewar German society and politics was destroyed.

After the end of inflation various efforts were made to repair, at least in part, the ravages to Germany's political and social life wrought by the pauperization of the rentier class. All long-term money debts were "revalued" by law at a certain percentage of their original gold value. Mortgages were revalued at 25 per cent, all other titles at lower rates. But these efforts did not suffice to reconcile the estranged rentiers to the young Republic, which they held responsible for the catastrophe. Naturally, the ones to fight with most energy for a policy of revaluation were the anti-Republican parties on the Right, while the Republican parties on the Left showed little understanding for the real social and political problems involved.

As the inflation progressed the number of victims kept growing while that of the profiteers dwindled. In the first phase of the inflation boom, industry and trade had profited much more by the opportunities opened to them in the consecutive waves of rising prices than they were harmed by the secondary effects of inflation. Since at that time the domestic price level lagged far behind prices on foreign markets the margin gave exporters a welcome incentive. This created the appearance of an industrial boom, at least as far as the volume of production and employment was concerned. Not even the world depression of 1921 interrupted this German boom.

Only slowly, frequently not before the end of inflation, did German businessmen realize that the prosperity of industry and trade during the inflation boom had been utterly imaginary. The great bargain turnover in the end stood revealed as a huge liquidation sale. No one experienced any difficulty in finding customers for his wares, which were on the contrary pulled out of the tradesmen's hands. But as costs of replacement continuously exceeded selling prices, stocks dwindled and plants were worn down. At the same time, in view of the prevailing "seller's market" at home and abroad, incentives for technical progress disappeared.

Gradually everyone came to realize that the industrial boom fed on a waste of substance. Now the workers and white-collar employees too began to notice that high employment was purchased at the price of decreasing real wages. Although the unions puzzled out ingenious devices to adapt wages to living costs, in this breathtaking chase prices outpaced wages by growing margins.

Finally the collapse of the monetary system was complete, and all and sundry were swept into the disaster. Money no longer fulfilled its essential functions for a modern economic system. Hence some people reverted to primitive methods such as barter. Domestic trade resorted to pricing in foreign money denominations. Business calculations and every sort of economic relationship became utterly confused. In the end, the disruption of every economic mechanism was so acute that unemployment increased despite a continued rise in prices.

3. *Stabilization*

BY THE AUTUMN of 1923 fundamental reform of the currency system had become a matter of life and death. How was the transition from an inflated to a stable currency to be brought about? Immense obstacles lay in the path, of which the following were the most thorny:

1. At no other time and in no other place had a currency and the faith in its functioning been undermined so thoroughly. Yet, without advance confi-

dence it would be impossible to build up a new currency. Lacking such initial confidence the new currency was bound to be rushed into rapid circulation again, which would spell a new depreciation.

2. There was no hope of a foreign loan, which in other cases of exhausted reserves had been the main step toward stabilization.

3. The central problem was how to procure resources for the time of transition. The Reich Treasury's principal source of revenue had been the printing press. How could normal revenues be found to replace banknote creation? From what source could the Reich draw a fund sufficient to carry the administration through the interval until taxes would once more begin to flow with regularity? During this time of suspense it would be just as impossible to float a domestic as a foreign loan.

4. Any plan of currency reform would be doomed unless there were at least an armistice in the reparations conflict and a breathing spell in reparations payments.

After the Ruhr struggle had been abandoned in September, 1923, and after negotiations between the occupying powers and the Ruhr industries had been initiated—which was tantamount to an armistice in the reparations struggle—with the aid of some imagination all other problems began to appear solvable. Even the particularly perplexing problem of how to stabilize the currency while continuing to resort to the printing press for the government's immediate financial needs was found to yield to simple theoretical reasoning.

As described above, the public's cash reserves in terms of gold had finally dwindled to almost nothing. Such cash reserves would presumably regain their normal proportions as soon as the public became convinced that no further devaluation was in the offing. A certain supply of newly printed currency would therefore not exert inflationary stimuli but only prevent deflationary pressures on prices from developing. Within these limits there would be little danger attached to the further temporary use of the printing press.

THE "MIRACLE OF THE RENTENMARK"

To implement this reasoning, all that seemed to be required was to convince the public of the soundness of the new currency and to keep the circulation within narrow bounds. This was achieved by a psychological device which has been written into history under the label of "the miracle of the *Rentenmark*."

Basically the idea of the Rentenmark had some resemblance to the assignats of the French revolution of 1789. In the case of the assignats the collateral for the money issued consisted of real estate. In the case of the Rentenmark collateral consisted of the "real-estate debts" of agriculture and of the analogous debts of industrial companies. In both cases the "backing" was fictitious since it could be used neither abroad to regulate foreign exchanges nor at home by being turned into cash. More significant than the similarities between the assignats and the Rentenmark, however, was one decisive difference: the fictitious backing of the assignats was devised to cover up inflationary designs, whereas for the Rentenmark it was a psychological device used in a determined effort at stabilization.

These scruples over how to "back" the Rentenmark were really beside the point and arose either from a misconception of the nature and function of a modern currency or from the notion that it was of the essence to "create confidence." All through the inflation period the Reichsbank had managed to preserve a certain gold holding which, to be sure, in the end amounted to only a few hundred million marks. As against the flood of paper issuing from the Reichsbank this gold fund was obviously without power to stem the inflationary tide; any amount used would have dissipated like a drop of water on a hot stone. When in 1924, by means of the Dawes Loan, a sizable gold fund was once more accumulated in the Reichsbank, the currency had already been stabilized. It remained stable not because of any "backing" but because the Reich budget had been balanced and the currency in circulation could be kept scarce.

As often happens when an idea is "in the air," the Rentenmark had many inventors. There was a Minoux Plan with the first germs of the mature idea. Then the former Secretary of the Treasury, Karl Helfferich, proposed a plan that closely resembled the ultimate policy; he suggested a "rye mark," a new currency unit to be defined in rye instead of gold, even though rye prices were especially unstable from year to year depending on the harvests. Rudolf Hilferding, Finance Minister in the first Stresemann cabinet, replaced rye with gold. Finally Hans Luther, at that time Food Minister, a few days later Finance Minister, afterwards—in the days of Locarno—Reich Chancellor, proposed the Rentenmark.

This stage was reached September 17, 1923. Nine days later the hopeless Ruhr struggle was abandoned. On October 15, the Rentenbank Decree was published, and on November 15 the mark could be stabilized at the rate of 1,000,000,000,000 paper marks for 1 gold mark, which at least gave Germany title to the uniqueness of her inflation.

The German currency was reconstructed in the following manner: the Reichsbank fully retained its function as a bank of issue, but it was prohibited from further discounting Reich or state Treasury bills. As in the prewar period, only genuine commercial paper was eligible for rediscount. Moreover, a second bank of issue was founded, under the name of Deutsche Rentenbank. It was nominally furnished with a capital of 3.2 billion Rentenmarks, not one cent of which, however, was actually paid in, the capital consisting exclusively of agricultural "soil debts" and analogous industrial debts. These obligations paid interest to the Rentenbank, constituting in essence a special tax on agriculture and industry; from this source the bank was in due time to accumulate a genuine capital. (It is a curious detail that this tax in the form of revenue from the Rentenbank real-estate obligations outlasted the Weimar Republic and Hitler's Third Reich, and continued to be levied on agriculture up to 1959.) The Rentenbank claims on agriculture and industry served as collateral for the Rentenbank notes which the bank was allowed to issue to a maximum of 2.4 billion Rentenmarks. These *Rentenbankscheine* were not legal tender but had to be accepted in payments to public agencies and thus circulated alongside the Reichsbank notes. Half of the maximum amount of Rentenbank notes, 1.2 billion Rentenmarks, was to be issued as credit to the Reich government, the balance in credits to business.

The basic question was not whether the collateral was fictitious or real; it was, rather, whether the public could be made to believe that the currency had a "stable value," an expression in fashion at that time. This was actually accomplished, primarily because it proved feasible to implement the plan from beginning to end exactly as scheduled. The Rentenmarks in strictly limited amounts flowed into the gap opened by the depleted cash holdings of the public. The Reich government received its credit of 1.2 billion Rentenmarks, and with this it managed to bridge over the time until tax revenues would once more begin to flow.

This favorable situation was temporarily interrupted when the government suggested to the board of directors of the Reichsbank that the credit to the Treasury be increased to 1.6 billion Rentenmarks. Immediately the foreign exchanges resumed their upward movement. The Reichsbank directors turned the proposal down and this negative decision, undoubtedly justified at this juncture, contributed a great deal to strengthening confidence in the soundness of the new currency. Before long taxes, having at last been restored to a stable currency basis and slightly increased at the end of 1923, began to yield returns sufficient to re-establish a balanced budget. The situation was of course materially improved by the temporary breathing spell in reparations. When in March and April of 1924 the foreign exchanges again threatened to slip, the Reichsbank imposed a radical credit freeze, thereby demonstrating its steadfast determination to fend off all dangers to the new currency. The definitive settlement of international currency relations was reserved for international agreements to be drawn up within the framework of the Dawes Plan.

4. *Plans for Reparations Payments*

THE DAWES PLAN

IN OCTOBER, 1923, the President of the United States, Calvin Coolidge, took up a suggestion made by Secretary of State Charles Evans Hughes that the reparations problem be submitted to an inquiry by nonpolitical experts. On November 30, 1923, after the Ruhr struggle had been called off, the Reparations Commission nominated two committees of experts to study various aspects of the problem and to propose—though this was not officially required—a new payments plan. The more important of these committees worked under the chairmanship of General Charles C. Dawes, later Vice-President of the United States. After careful studies the Dawes Committee presented the Reparations Commission with a new payments plan on April 9, 1924. A few days later it became evident that peace in the reparations controversies had thereby been assured for a considerable time to come. The plan was at once accepted by the Reparations Commission, and immediately afterward by the German government. After the French general elections in May, 1924, the Poincaré government that had waged the Ruhr conflict was replaced by Edouard Herriot's cabinet of the Left, which was favorably inclined toward peaceful arrangements. In July a Reparations Conference assembled in London, in August the Dawes Plan was adopted by all governments concerned, and on September 1, 1924, the Plan went into force. On August 30, 1924, Germany passed a monetary law giving the new currency the name of *Reichsmark* (RM).

Although the Dawes Plan was meant to offer only a temporary solution—a fact emphasized by the plan's failure to determine a definite total for reparations payments—it had two decisive merits as compared with all previous arrangements. First, the fantastic annuities of former plans were replaced, at least for the first few years, by more manageable amounts, which promised a fair period of quiet relations between Germany and the Allies. Second, the plan contained the acknowledgment that Germany was in need of a period of recovery. The experts realized that the German economy, buffetted by the most harrowing experiences for almost a decade, had to be granted a respite if it were to produce surpluses for delivery abroad. This time of grace was to be divided into two periods, one of nearly total indulgence and one of a partial resumption of payments.

The first period was to last one year, September 1, 1924, to August 31, 1925, in which time Germany was expected to mobilize only 200 million marks in cash from her own resources. An international loan, to be known as the Dawes Loan, of 800 million RM (approximately 200 million dollars) with Germany as debtor was to procure the means to continue the reconstruction of the devastated areas in France and Belgium and to carry the interest payments on the inter-Allied debts, the United States being the foremost creditor. The service of this loan was to be deductible from reparations annuities, not added to them. In the first year of the Dawes Plan the direct German payments plus the proceeds from the loan were to net 1 billion marks. In the second phase of the period of respite the German payments were to increase year by year from 1.22 billion RM in 1925–26 until the "normal" annuities of 2.5 billion RM would be reached in 1928–29, the fifth year. Even this normal annuity was not to be regarded as a maximum, however, since the plan provided an intricate "prosperity index" by which the Allies would participate in any German business recovery. A "depression index" was not contemplated. The bases for all business indices from which the prosperity index would be derived were of course extremely low immediately after the inflation disaster.

An ample system of safeguards was built into the plan. The sources from which reparations payments would be derived and the sum to be collected from each source were narrowly defined. A part of the payments was to come from budget sources for which specific customs and tax receipts were mortgaged. A special transportation tax was introduced and earmarked for reparations. Bonds were to be issued—5 billion marks' worth secured by a first mortgage on all large industrial enterprises and another 11 billion secured by a first mortgage on the property of the Reichsbahn. The mortgagors had to service these obligations at 5 per cent interest and 1 per cent amortization. To insure that the Reichsbahn would comply with its obligations, a Reich Railroad Company was organized and "internationalized." This implied that the railroads were to be independent of the Reich government and to include foreign experts in their managing bodies. Similar devices were used to safeguard the Reichsbank against any repetition of inflationist government policies. Finally, the post of General Agent for Reparations was created with headquarters in Berlin. His function was to supervise compliance with all reparations obligations and to report at regular intervals to the Reparations Commission on the state of the German economy and finance and specifically on the mortgaged assets. It was one of his foremost duties to take care of the transfer abroad of German payments and thereby to watch over the stability of the German currency. To this post the American expert Parker Gilbert was appointed.

For five years the Dawes Plan worked with admirable precision. All payments were made promptly and fully on schedule. The safeguards functioned, the sources of revenue delivered the expected amounts. That at the beginning of 1929 the Dawes Plan was supplanted by the Young Plan was by no means due to Germany's inability to continue fulfilling the Dawes obligations. The renegotiation merely expressed the general desire to proceed from the provisional Dawes Plan to a definitive solution.

When at last Germany and the Allies were agreed that a final settlement was desirable, the general situation in world politics had undergone a radical change from what it had been in 1924. The Allies were no longer animated by a spirit of victory and revenge, and Germany, though disarmed, had regained the status of a great power. Germany therefore rightly assumed that the time was ripe for a downward revision of reparations. But, as from the very beginning, an insurmountable obstacle barred the road to a milder definition of amounts and timing of payments. The situation was deadlocked because the Allies were determined to maintain a close connection between the reparations payments they were to receive and the inter-Allied debts they had to service, whereas the United States, the chief creditor, strictly refused to admit that such a connection existed. The Allies were unwilling to budge from the notion that, in reality though not formally, Germany would have to bear the burden of their payments to the United States; consequently, any remission of German obligations was made conditional on equivalent concessions on the part of America. In this way the Allies tried to shift the responsibility for a reasonable solution of the entire problem to the United States. This attempt was bound to fail.

THE YOUNG PLAN

In essence, the Young Plan was devised to carry out this Allied policy. After prolonged negotiations in Paris the Young Plan was signed on January 30, 1930, which was about the time of the first "normal" reparations year according to the Dawes Plan. The new plan was based on the recommendations of a committee of experts, again headed by an American, Owen D. Young, chairman of the General Electric Company. The experts had been asked to set up a definitive schedule of payments, and this they did, providing for the payments to end in 1988! To the German negotiators the most important feature seemed to be that a new two-year respite was to be granted. Payments for these next two years were reduced from 2.5 to 1.7 billion marks. After this, in slow progression the maximum annuities were to be reached in 1965–66 with a payment of 2,429 million marks. From this high point the annuities were gradually to decrease to 898 million marks in the last reparations year, 1987–88. The capitalized present value of all payments was computed at just below 37 billion marks, in itself a remarkable reduction from the fantastic sum of 132 billion fixed by the Reparations Commission in 1921. The connection with the inter-Allied debts was maintained in the Young Plan in that the German annuities would be reduced by two-thirds of any reduction the United States might grant the Allies before 1965, and after that date by the total reduction.

Not only did the Young Plan allow for a substantial immediate alleviation of the reparations burden, it also did away with the humiliating control of German affairs by foreign agents. The American General Agent for Reparations disappeared, the foreign directors on the boards of the Reichsbank and Reichsbahn were recalled, and these two institutions regained full sovereignty. The controlling agencies of the Dawes Plan were replaced by a Bank for International Settlements, B.I.S., founded in Basle, Switzerland, which was to function simultaneously as a reparations bank and as a sort of "central bank of central banks." Any development along this second line was prevented for the time being by the outbreak of the international banking crisis.

From the German point of view, the advantages of the Young Plan were offset by a plan to "commercialize" a part of the reparations payments. For the Allies, however, this was the feature of greatest interest in the Plan, since they hoped in this way to mobilize considerable sums on the international capital markets, primarily in the United States. Allied experts at that time favored the idea of a huge international loan to be serviced by Germany, the interest payments to be credited on reparations account. Such an arrangement would have been similar to the Dawes Loan, but there was a twofold illusion involved. First, it was believed that a very large sector of reparations could be removed from the sphere of politics and be converted into a strictly commercial obligation. It was also believed that commercial debts, no matter in what amounts and under whatever conditions, were safer than political debts. It is true that the National Socialist government did continue to service the Dawes and Young Loans long after it had repudiated the other small reparations obligations still outstanding after the Lausanne Conference of 1932. But this apparent effect of the Young Plan was attributable to the fact that after all only a small fraction of the reparations debt had been commercialized. The Young Loan issued in June, 1930, netted 1.2 billion marks. The placing of further portions was prevented by the outbreak of the Great Depression.

5. *Prosperity*

THE DAWES PLAN sounded the signal for a period of recovery the scope and intensity of which were unparalleled in previous German history. The promoters' era of the 1870's had indeed shown some similarities, but at that time Germany had been victorious in several consecutive wars, while now prosperity followed upon a crushing defeat. At the earlier time there had been the stimulus of a war indemnity of more than 4 billion marks; this time Germany had to pay a war indemnity of proportions unheard of in the history of any country. As will be shown later, the Marshall Plan years after the second world war exhibited notable similarities to the Dawes Plan recovery period.

The industrial recovery in this second period of the Weimar Republic was characterized by a process usually called "rationalization." At that time the country was consciously orienting its economic and technological efforts on the American pattern. America, so to speak, was discovered all over again. After having been cut off by war and inflation for over a decade from competition in the world markets and even from the knowledge of foreign developments—only a few individuals had the foreign exchange necessary to procure foreign scientific and technical magazines and books, even fewer to travel abroad—Germany had to learn that the world had not stood still and that America in particular had adopted new production methods far superior to anything known at home. Pilgrimages across the Atlantic were made, and Germans gaped at the American "economic miracle"—an adventure that was to be repeated twenty-five years later after an even longer period of isolation.

Indeed, Germany managed to learn a great deal during the six or seven quiet years that followed the terrors of war and inflation. Her industries once more attained a high standard of technical proficiency and regained leading positions in those areas in which she had led before the war, such as the chemical, electrical, and optical industries, and partly in engineering and textiles, although other industrial countries had taken advantage of the involuntary autarky of the war and inflation period to build up competitive industries of their own in several lines.

It is not a mere figure of speech to say that in these years a new Germany was built. This is true not only of the industrial sphere. Stimulated by public subsidies, urban housing experienced an impressive expansion. Facing the old, ugly "rent barracks," the German equivalent of the British and American slums, new settlements of a type hitherto unknown sprouted up—bright, tasteful, sometimes artistically noteworthy, large- and small-scale buildings that breathed the air of a new era of increasing social wisdom. Municipalities competed in providing playgrounds, swimming pools, schools, and hospitals. Power transmission lines were strung across the countryside; highways were modernized, though they still lagged far behind American standards. The merchant fleet that had been handed over to the Allies as stipulated in the peace treaty had almost been replaced; by the end of 1930 it had reached 4.36 million gross register tons, as compared to 5.13 million in 1914, and this new merchant fleet consisted mainly of new units that were more efficient than the outdated lost ones. In these years construction was begun on the foremost ocean liners of the day, the *Bremen* and *Europa*. By 1926 German exports had regained their prewar level of over 10 billion marks. In 1929, despite the loss of territory in Europe and of all the colonies, exports exceeded the 1913 figure by 34 per cent.

How could this recovery, foreseen by no one, have come to pass? How was it possible that a country which in the first postwar years had stumbled into an abyss under the load of reparations, now managed not only to keep up reparations payments but besides to build up a prosperity unprecedented in its economic life, a true reconstruction and modernization? Although it is a fact that in these years of prosperity reparations were paid fully and on schedule, no historian has been able to produce an unequivocal answer to the question whether Germany was really able to support the burden of reparations.

During the inflation period, Germany indeed discharged her reparations obligations out of her own resources, without the crutch of foreign capital, but this brought her currency and finances down in ruins. After the end of inflation, reparations payments left the German currency unscathed, but until the depression struck hardly a cent of these payments came from Germany's own resources. During this entire period a steady stream of foreign capital poured into Germany, far in excess of what went out of the country in reparations. Under the Dawes and Young Plans, that is, from September, 1924, up to the Hoover moratorium in July, 1931, German reparations payments amounted to a total of 10.8 billion marks. Against these payments, German foreign indebtedness, most of which originated in this period, rose to something over 20.5 billion marks. To this might be added approximately 5 billion marks in direct foreign investments in Germany, which were, however, more than offset by about 10 billion marks of German capital invested abroad.

The conclusion from these facts is that in the prosperity era from 1924 to 1930 Germany did succeed in financing not only her reparations payments but also her industrial and agricultural reconstruction and the general recovery of her economy. The greater part of the credits which made this possible came from the United States, and unexpectedly this vast inflow of funds was a direct effect of the reparations plans. The mere fact that a General Agent for Reparations residing in Berlin, together with the Transfer Committee (both instituted by the Dawes Plan), had to watch over German finances and especially over the stability of the mark created such unquestioned confidence in the capitalist world that Germany became this era's principal goal of capital movements, much as the United States had been in the decades before the first world war.

This peculiar relationship between reparations and capital influx was soon noticed in Germany and gave rise to political and economic discussions of the problem: what could be the fate of a country which had to get more and more deeply into debt in order to discharge current obligations? The opponents of a "fulfillment policy" regarded this entire structure of reparations and foreign debts as a house of cards. Foreign creditors, not Germans, were paying reparations; for this Germany was currently debited with interest at high rates, which she was not paying either since interest was simply added to the capital debt. Were the influx of foreign credits, for whatever reason, to stop, the house of cards must instantly collapse. It would then be most doubtful whether the interest on the debt could be paid, to say nothing of the principal.

Partisans of the fulfillment policy countered by contending that the expansion of the German economy achieved with foreign help would in the end enable the country to garner larger economic surpluses from which payments on reparations accounts, both for principal and interest, could be made. Before this controversy could be tested by actual developments, the house of cards did collapse.

6. *Government and Business in Weimar Germany*

THE HERITAGE OF THE REVOLUTION OF 1918

AS FAR AS the revolution of 1918 was actually in search of any fundamental change in the economic system, the ideas of 1918 came down to two demands: (1) "workers' councils" were to be formed and closely woven into the fabric of government and business management; (2) the key industries were to be nationalized.

1. The "council scheme" was an offspring of the recent Russian revolution. In Russia the "workers', peasants', and soldiers' councils," the soviets, had become an instrument of the Bolshevik revolution, and the new state now formed had retained the name and in part the ideology of these councils. Their practical function, however, soon dwindled as they became submerged in the dictatorial system of the Union of Soviet Socialist Republics.

In Germany the workers' and soldiers' councils, improvised in the first revolutionary days of 1918, never played an important role. Where they had been formed they soon abdicated voluntarily in favor of the constitutional democratic institutions. But one remnant of the revolution survived throughout the lifetime of the Weimar Republic: the institution of shop or workers' councils (*Betriebsräte*), which will be described below.

2. The revolution of 1918 was carried forward by that majority of the German workers who had been brought up on the Social Democratic ideology. In the general elections of 1912, the last before the war, one-third of the electorate voted for Social Democrats. For decades the ultimate goal of this party had been proclaimed to be the socialization of the capitalistic means of production. What was more natural than that the believers in this idea should press for its realization now that the Social Democratic Party had come to power? Once this was attained, immediate material improvements in their distressing living conditions could be expected.

NATIONALIZATION OF KEY INDUSTRIES

An installment payment, at least, was due on the promises made by the revolutionary government which had declared in a proclamation that "socialization was on the march." This was to consist in the nationalization of the "key industries," a term that was then taken to include mining, the iron and steel industries, and power production.

The implementation of this program was thought to be perfectly simple. With few exceptions, public utilities, such as railroads, gasworks, waterworks, telephone, telegraph, and municipal transport, had long been under public ownership and management with satisfactory results. Besides, most of these key industries were concentrated in cartels and trusts to such an extent that they were regarded as ripe for nationalization.

Yet, the revolutionary momentum did not prove strong enough to enforce this program. In March, 1919, yielding to the impetuous demands of the socialist workers, the revolutionary government proclaimed a "socialization law" as a first step. At the same time a law for the administration of coal mining was published, followed in April, 1919, by a law for the administration of potash mining. In both these industries, as a little later in the steel industry, "autonomous authorities" were organized to carry out nationalization.

The supreme authority over coal mining was vested in the Reich Coal Council (*Reichskohlenrat*) on which the mining companies, the coal miners, the coal dealers, and independent experts were represented. Furthermore, the coal-mining companies were organized in the Reich Coal Association (*Reichskohlenverband*), a statutory cartel of the entire mining industry in which the Ruhr Coal Syndicate had actual leadership. The Reich Coal Council was a planning body with the task of determining output and prices. Ultimate decisions were referred to the Reich government. The other autonomous bodies were organized along similar lines.

The record of these organizations was less than glorious. As it turned out, they represented only a weak compromise between capitalist and socialist conceptions. In the steel industry the organization quickly degenerated. In coal and potash mining it was kept alive during the entire Weimar period, with questionable effects. All too often, producers and workers who together commanded majorities on the boards agreed on prices and wages at the consumers' expense. In many cases, the Reich had to use its veto to enforce price arrangements better suited to the public interest. This made a sham of the boards' autonomy, and in the end nothing remained but a number of statutory cartels with government supervision of their price policies.

This was about all that was done in the way of nationalization. The vague promises of the Weimar Constitution of August, 1919, based as they were on a compromise between the Social Democratic Party and the so-called bourgeois democratic parties, were never implemented. And yet, the economic system of the Weimar Republic, as it actually materialized in its peculiar mixture of private and state management of industry and in the legal conditions of labor relations, undoubtedly contained much stronger socialist elements than had the prewar system.

As pointed out before, in prewar times the government already played a much larger role in business in Germany than in Western countries. Now there was a further considerable advance in the direction of central government influence. The railroads of the federal states were transferred to Reich ownership, resulting in the largest operating railroad unit then in existence anywhere. In developing the power system the states and municipalities were in the lead. The trolleys, subways, and bus lines still in private hands were now with few exceptions taken over by the municipalities, and so were most gas- and waterworks, although some gasworks continued to be run by heavy industry.

HOUSING

Of all public activities in business enterprise, housing produced the finest achievements. During the war residential building had virtually stopped, and it was not revived to any considerable extent during the period of inflation. Thus a huge demand for houses and apartments had accumulated. While the system of war economy was in operation the entire field of housing had been placed under a number of legal controls. All rents were officially regulated, private rent contracts were pratically eliminated, and the occupants were given a legal claim to their apartments as long as they paid their rent. The public authorities also functioned as renting agents.

Had rents been freed from regulation at the time of the most severe housing shortage, they would have risen steeply and this would have accentuated the serious social emergency. On the other hand, had rents in old buildings been kept low and construction of new houses been left to the open market, rents in the two groups would have moved far apart, and this also would have resulted in social tensions. No better expedient was found than to hold all rents down to the old levels and at the same time subsidize housing construction and even embark on public construction and management on a large scale. This remained the characteristic system throughout the Weimar period.

The results were remarkable. The Reich, states, and municipalities vied with one another in erecting modern residential buildings which changed the appearance of the German cities and towns. Building was usually financed in the following way: fairly inexpensive first mortgages were granted at normal interest rates by savings banks, insurance companies, and mortgage banks (in some places mortgage banks were founded for this purpose), but only up to 50 per cent of construction costs; then the Reich government granted substantial second mortgages at nominal interest rates, finding the funds for this not through borrowing but through the proceeds of the house-rent tax (*Hauszinssteuer*). This interesting tax was a child of inflation. For house owners who had been mortgage debtors, the stabilization had brought handsome profits since mortgages were revalued only to the extent of 25 per cent. This revaluation profit was now in part taxed away by the house-rent tax, the proceeds of which the Treasury could easily increase by allowing rents to rise slowly above prewar standards. Thus ample funds were found to finance more housing activities. States and municipalities also went into construction on their own account or by undertaking sizable participations in nonprofit building societies and cooperatives.

THE GOVERNMENT AS BANKER

Subsequent developments, both political and economic, were strongly influenced by the fact that in this period government activities were also intensified in the field of banking.

The Reich founded a bank of its own, the *Reichskreditgesellschaft,* which soon rose to rank with the four big "D-Banks." Although fully owned by the Reich it functioned like any private bank. It did not build up a branch system, but it played a prominent role on the money market through its close association with provincial institutions. Those among the federal states which so far had owned no banks of their own now made up for the lag. Furthermore, the Reich and some federal states founded banks for special purposes, primarily for housing, such as the *Deutsche Bau- und Bodenbank,* a Reich institution for intermediary building credits, and several mortgage banks. The Reichsbahn also formed its own bank, the *Deutsche Verkehrs-Kredit-Bank,* to administer its liquid assets and to grant freight credits to large shippers. For some time a subsidiary of the Deutsche Rentenbank was the leader in the field of long-term agricultural credits. The Rentenbank itself, after having discharged its currency stabilization function, was left with little scope of activity, and the Reichsbank regained its monopoly as bank of issue. Meanwhile, however, the Rentenbank had accumulated large funds from the tax on industry and agriculture, and the Reich decided to utilize these funds through a special new bank, the *Rentenbank-Kreditanstalt.* Its task was to let agriculture participate in the blessings of foreign credits. The bank contracted loans abroad, mainly in the United States, which were passed on to farmers by mortgage banks and state agricultural banks.

In 1924 the Reichsbank founded the *Golddiskontbank* to assist in the linking up of the mark with the gold standard. In the course of the following years the functions of this Reichsbank subsidiary changed repeatedly. At the start it acted for the bank of issue in dealings abroad, primarily in procuring credits in foreign currencies. Therefore the Golddiskontbank accounts were at first carried in pound sterling. Later the bank served in financing foreign trade. In the banking crisis of 1931 the bank was instrumental in reorganizing bankrupt banks by putting up new capital against their common stock and by extending credit. During the National Socialist era its functions were mainly in open market operations involving those government bills that for technical reasons were not eligible for rediscount with the Reichsbank.

Thus, long before the banking crisis of 1931, the government had acquired a dominant position in German banking. The main function of the German credit system, the financing of industry and trade, to a large extent still remained in private hands. This changed by one stroke after the banking crisis wiped out the capital assets of the leading banks. As will be described in detail, the Reich then took over controlling capital participations in almost every one of the large banks and held them far into the National Socialist era. The later "re-privatizing" of the large banks had little meaning because in the meantime the National Socialist state had seized full powers over the entire economy.

GOVERNMENT IN INDUSTRY AND CARTEL LEGISLATION

Government-owned industries were as a rule eliminated from the framework of public administration and organized as separate companies run along the lines of private business. Thus stock companies were formed to administer, among others, the arsenals, which had been Reich-owned long before the war, and also power plants and other industrial enterprises founded after the war. The stocks of these companies were concentrated in a Reich-owned holding company, the *Vereinigte Industrie-A.G.,* V. I. A. G., with the Reichskreditgesellschaft as an affiliated financing institution. As provided by the Dawes Plan, the Reichsbahn was reorganized in the form of an autonomous corporation with special legal status; it issued preferred shares, incurred debt, and, as noted above, founded a bank to manage its banking activities.

In November, 1923, after inflation had been stopped, the first German cartel law was enacted. The aim was not to place cartel policy on production and prices under state control but rather to forge an instrument to restrain the "misuse of positions of economic power" and as far as possible to offset the influence of industrial monopoly organizations, which during the inflation period had become overbearing. As the main feature of the cartel legislation, a special supervisory agency and a cartel court were set up. Cartel agreements as such were still not prohibited; the two new institutions were only given the duty to protect outsiders and competitive enterprises.

The most momentous clause of the cartel law provided that every party to a cartel agreement had the right to withdraw at any time without previous notice for valid reasons. Such reasons were defined as any unfair restriction on economic freedom of action, primarily in production, sales, and prices. In cases of conflict the court had to decide what constituted an unfair restriction. Without the consent of the president of the cartel court, no bonds given to ensure compliance with cartel agreements could be declared forfeited and no boycott or similar pressure could be applied.

Although it is generally assumed that cartels and concentrations of all kinds mostly originate in times of depression, in Germany the post-inflation prosperity was a period of strong and comprehensive concentration. In 1925 the German dye trust, the I. G. *Farbenindustrie,* and in 1926 the German steel trust, the *Vereinigte Stahlwerke,* were founded: two industrial giants that maintained their powerful position until they were ordered dissolved after the second world war. In the middle of the 1920's the number of cartels was officially estimated at 2,500.

When, after 1930, the Great Depression was exerting its full impact, the Brüning administration went one step further and provided the legal facilities for exercising full government supervision of the cartels in all their activities. The cartels were included in Brüning's deflationary measures and enjoined to lower the general level of fixed prices. This was hardly conducive to recapturing for the price mechanism the flexibility it had lost through cartelization.

LABOR POLICY

In the field of labor relations Imperial Germany had bequeathed to the Republic a well-developed system of social security, the foundation of which Bismarck had created, and the first wartime shop councils that were now to be expanded.

With respect to the protection of the workers' welfare little needed to be added. According to the notions prevailing at the time, the employed were fairly well protected against most contingencies. Working hours were limited, minimum wages defined, women and children especially safeguarded. What remained to be done was to improve the application of some of the rules. The very first decree of the revolutionary government in November, 1918, proclaimed the eight-hour day as the legal maximum.

Likewise, in the field of social insurance no fundamental improvements of the admirable achievement of the Bismarck era were required for the old-age, health, disability, and accident insurance systems. Only in one important respect did the German social insurance system prove to be deficient, primarily in view of the violent trade-cycle fluctuations in the postwar era. While Britain had begun in 1911 to build up a system of unemployment insurance, Germany tried to improvise such a scheme only during the war. These measures were not based on the insurance principle, however, but on proof of need. A regular unemployment insurance scheme was not introduced before 1926, and it proved workable only in times of fairly normal employment. The mass unemployment of the depression years destroyed this scheme even though government subsidies increased and the benefits for the insured decreased, because the income of the insurance fund dwindled as the need for payments rose. Thus the masses of workers unemployed for more than six months depended once more on relief distributed upon proof of need. This emergency relief was mostly administered by the local authorities supported by Reich subsidies, which always lagged far behind the most urgent requirements. At the end of the Weimar period nothing remained of unemployment insurance except a payroll tax shared by employers and employed.

MEDIATION AND ARBITRATION

The one original contribution of the Weimar Republic to social reform was in the field of relations between management and labor. The regulations introduced rested on two pillars: organized mediation and shop councils.

The practice of mediation was based on collective bargaining between trade unions and employers or the employers' organizations in the various industries. Before the war collective bargaining was regarded as a purely private matter between the parties concerned. In the Weimar system the collective labor contract was acknowledged by the government as the normal and desirable way to regulate labor relations in the public interest.

The commonly used expression that in the Weimar Republic the unions were "recognized" by the state signifies that none but free and independent unions were qualified to bargain for collective agreements and to make them binding on the employed. This excluded both the so-called yellow unions (roughly: company unions) and isolated shop crews. Thus at the time of the Weimar government the German unions had a much stronger position than the American unions enjoyed far into the 1930's under Franklin D. Roosevelt.

Official mediation agencies were set up to intervene in difficult cases of collective bargaining and to work out compromises between the contending parties. In all cases where, with the benevolent aid of the government authorities, such mediation resulted in a collective agreement, the character of private and free labor contracts was not impaired. However, the practice of mediation soon went far beyond these theoretical limits. In the first place, such collective agreements did not permit an individual laborer to contract to work under poorer conditions than the collective agreement would allow. Perhaps this also could still be reconciled with the notion of a free collective bargain.

But the government had further privileges. It could declare labor contracts as "generally binding," thereby extending the scope of the agreement to include all employers and employees of one industry in one district, even if they had not participated in the negotiations. One more momentous new feature was added: in cases where voluntary agreements were not achieved the mediator pronounced his own decision, which, if accepted by only one of the parties, became binding on both and was treated under the law as if it had been voluntarily agreed upon. What was originally meant to be an exception to be avoided wherever possible gradually became the rule. Thus the government increasingly assumed responsibility for all labor relations. Precisely in the most difficult, critical, and important cases the determination of wage rates was taken away from the bargaining parties and the free interplay of economic forces and became subject to government policy. The fictitious guideline was maintained that the official wage decision was to state only what the parties themselves would have agreed upon in reason and fairness. But, obviously, reason and fairness could not be otherwise defined than as conforming to the actual economic views and intentions of the government of the day.

It was a tragically ironical development that a measure instituted in the revolution of 1918 to enhance the unions' scope, strength, and authority should have ended by depriving them of their proper function—to confront the power of the entrepreneurs with the comparable power of labor organizations—and left them as little more than administrative organs of the government.

On the other hand, by accepting the responsibility of fixing "political wages" the inexperienced democratic state exposed itself to a severe strain. During the prosperity period the entrepreneurs and a large section of economic journalism took the government's wage policies to task for "overraising" wages. With logical consistency the same groups later made the government responsible for the slump that at least in part could be attributed to the rigidity of the wage level. But the unions, too, made the government a scapegoat when wage demands were denied. With the deepening depression the workers definitely turned against the public authorities, blaming them for permitting wages to slide. Naturally the opposition, already at that time led by the National Socialists and Communists in unsavory cooperation, did their reckless best to arouse the passions of a desperate people against the constituted political system. Thus German democracy undermined its popular support by shouldering tasks which the far stronger Western democracies were still to shun for some time to come.

INDUSTRIAL DEMOCRACY

The second and more solid pillar on which labor relations rested in the Weimar Republic was referred to as "shop democracy." As shown above, nothing tangible had remained of the soviet idea except—disregarding the short-lived Reich Economic Council (*Reichswirtschaftsrat*)—the institution of shop councils. The Shop Council Act (*Betriebsrätegesetz*) of February, 1920, provided for the election of a single representative in every plant employing at least five persons, and a representative council consisting of several members in plants employing more than 20 persons. The shop councils were elected by proportional representation and lists of candidates, as in the case of political elections. Since there were three groups of unions, the Free, the Christian, and the Hirsch-Duncker unions, which differed very little in their practice, proportional representation succeeded in some measure in alleviating the competition among the unions. Where the workers in a single plant belonged to different unions, each union was represented on the council.

Industrial relations thus developed along the two separate lines of collective bargaining and the shop councils in a sensible division of functions. The unions' allotted field was that of bargaining for all agreements with groups of employers on wages, hours, paid vacations, and apprenticeships. Within the framework of such collective agreements the shop councils worked out the details of labor conditions with individual employers and served as connecting links and buffers between management and the workers in all major and minor controversies, primarily as to hiring and firing. The members of the shop councils were themselves protected against being fired except for compelling reasons and therefore enjoyed a measure of independence from the employer which created a satisfactory climate. This system of shop councils became so popular and useful to all concerned that, after twelve years of interruption by the Hitler regime, it was to be revived and to continue functioning with only minor modifications.

Aside from these tasks, which were discharged to everyone's satisfaction, the shop councils were saddled with a heritage from the heyday of the "council ideology" that brought them less success. According to the Shop Council Act they were to "assist the shop management with their advice in order to cooperate in securing high efficiency and economical production performance." Furthermore, the books of the company had to be open for inspection by the shop council, and, if the company were a stock company, the council was entitled to be represented with voting power on its board of directors.

It soon appeared that these clauses of the law were not functioning as planned. On the one hand, employers generally were not interested in implementing them but, rather, evaded them by withdrawing various functions from the boards of directors and assigning them to special committees. On the other hand, most workers' representatives were not sufficiently trained and experienced to discharge the management functions with which the law presented them and therefore were mostly unable to stand up to the other directors.

7. *Collapse*

IN THE COURSE of fifteen years Germany was stricken by three disasters. The first, the military collapse of 1918, gave birth to the Republic. From the second, the currency cataclysm of 1923, the young Republic appeared to have recovered in an almost miraculous way, but deeper down the aftereffects and social repercussions of inflation had badly sapped the nation's vitality. The third catastrophe, the Great Depression of the early 1930's, precipitated the downfall of the Republic.

For the background and causes of the German crisis and especially for its peculiar political aspects, we shall first review the agricultural situation.

THE AGRARIAN CRISIS

The general pressure on agricultural prices during the world depression made it imperative for the German government to come to the aid of agriculture by erecting some protective dams. This was done over the years by constructing an intricate scheme of staggered import duties, import quotas, embargoes, government purchases and stockpiling, a state monopoly for maize, and many other expedients. These measures were supplemented by a special provision for agricultural credits that more or less amounted to a debt moratorium.

The agricultural crisis of these years was particularly felt in wide areas of northern and northeastern Germany, where the predominant grain product was rye. For a long time rye had posed a special problem in German agriculture. Annual fluctuations in rye prices far exceeded those in other products. In years of poor wheat harvests rye was in great demand as a bread cereal and fetched high prices. In years of ample wheat harvests the price of rye was determined by the demand for it as fodder or for export to the world market, which for this commodity was quite narrow.

Thus the rye belt was hit extremely hard by the world crisis from its beginning in 1929. With price collapses in almost all commodity markets, rye exports practically ceased. Consequently, a large section of German agriculture faced about the same difficulties as the American farmer. In both countries—in Germany mostly in the rye belt—farmers were overburdened with debt and many were insolvent. In both countries the governments searched for solutions to the debt problem and tried to halt the downward price movements by buying up surplus agricultural products. However, political implications were not comparable in the two countries. By a fateful coincidence, this particular rye crisis was to heap up dangerous political explosives against the German Republic, although as a purely economic factor it had limited importance compared with the far wider and deeper industrial and banking crisis.

The rye country was primarily in the hands of large landowners. Thus the rye crisis became the crisis of the Junker class. The Weimar system had indeed gone far in undermining the political and social ascendancy this class had enjoyed in Imperial Germany, but the Republic never fully succeeded in deposing the Junkers. They and groups politically and socially related to them had a considerable share in the patronage of the higher ranks of the Prussian civil service; they had close ties with the Prussian Protestant Church and, most importantly, with the army, which had entrenched itself in an independent and authoritative position in the Weimar system. Finally the fact stands out that after 1925 a prominent member of this social class, Paul von Hindenburg, held the Reich Presidency.

If there was such a thing as a natural enemy of the German Republic, this assuredly was the Prussian landed aristocracy. It might have been in the line of historical logic for the German revolution of 1918—as it had become a rule for European revolutions ever since the French revolution of 1789—to seize the large estates and break them up for distribution among the landless agricultural laborers. (This was only to happen in parts of Germany after the second world war, and then under Communist auspices.) There were several reasons for the German failure to follow this pattern. An important feature was that the German Social Democratic Party, largely responsible for the first phase of postwar German developments, was by tradition almost exclusively concerned with the urban proletariat and its problems and had little understanding of agrarian problems. Further, the orthodox majority of the Social Democrats adhered to the principle of large-scale management in industry and agriculture and therefore did not believe in breaking up the large estates. Finally, after the years of starvation, the masses of the population were interested in little beyond assured supplies of food, and any interference with the large landowners would at first have been bound to decrease harvests rather than improve them.

Once the opportunity of a revolutionary change in the property distribution in German agriculture had been missed, all that the later Republican governments could achieve were compromise schemes of agricultural resettlement through purchases of parts of the large properties for distribution under favorable conditions to farmer-settlers. The resettlement activity of the Republican regime was certainly not negligible. By 1931, of 5.58 million hectares (approximately 13.8 million acres) that in 1907 had been under large-scale management, 600,000 hectares (about 1.5 million acres) had been turned over to settlers. But, as the figures show, a thorough change in the agricultural system could not emerge from these policies.

Since the survival of the large estates was a reality to be dealt with, the Republican government soon felt compelled to devote large amounts of financial aid to these archenemies of the Republic. For this there was no gratitude from any quarter. How could the urban masses, on whose support the government relied, be made to understand why millions upon millions of marks had to be thrown into the laps of reactionaries while, allegedly, millions of unemployed persons were waiting to be settled on the lands of the bankrupt Junkers? For their part, the large landowners were by no means satisfied with the amount of government aid and were deeply embittered because the government used their plight to acquire large tracts of resettlement land. When finally Chancellor Heinrich Brüning had the courage to embark on a scheme for the prompt liquidation of those estates, which not even large subsidies could restore to economic soundness, the threatened class of landed aristocrats appealed to the kindred feelings of the Reich President. The charge of "agrarian bolshevism" thrown at Brüning by his political foes played a prominent role in his downfall on May 30, 1932.

THE BANKING CRISIS

The economic effects of the industrial and banking crisis were much more severe. One of the main reasons for the banking crisis was founded in the very structure of the banking organization.

As shown in Chapter II, Section 4, German banking had developed a mixed type of deposit and investment bank which was particularly vulnerable in periods of cyclical downturn, much more so than purely commercial banks would have been. Yet, the German credit organization had weathered the storms of prewar depressions. However, these depressions were very much milder than what befell the late 1920's, and in addition the German banks in the earlier period disposed of substantial reserves and were comparatively independent of foreign credits.

One of the many unfortunate consequences of inflation was that the banks were almost completely deprived of their capital; it proved fatal that in the short recovery and reconstruction period they had failed to use an adequate part of inflowing funds to strengthen their capital basis. Instead of risking only their own capital and reserves, they invested their depositors' money in venturesome industrial and commercial enterprises. While before the war the ratio between the banks' own funds and their deposits was about 1 to 3 or 4, this ratio had deteriorated to 1 to 15 or 1 to 20 at the outbreak of the crisis. In this situation a loss of only 5 to 10 per cent of total assets was enough to wipe out a bank's capital.

The second major cause of the banking catastrophe is to be found in the specific character of the post-inflation credit business. Exactly one-half of the credits that flowed into Germany from abroad up to 1931, that is, 10.3 billion RM of a total of 20.6 billion, were short-term credits which were never consolidated into longer-term investments. Of these a major part was concentrated with the large Berlin banks, whose deposits came to consist to 40 or even 50 per cent of foreign money.

On the eve of the international break in the business cycle the German credit structure displayed these features: the investments of the era of rationalization, consisting in construction and plant improvements, the opening of new mines, the development of department stores, power plants, and so forth, had been largely financed by short-term deposits, a considerable portion of which belonged to foreign creditors who at the first approach of a slump had a claim to immediate repatriation of their funds.

Insiders were well aware of these weaknesses, but some of the leading bankers were wanting in a sense of responsibility. Besides, no legal rules existed to restrain the bank managers, no regulations governed the amounts of capital paid in, the required ratio of cash reserves, or the kind of transactions suitable to such institutions. As a bank for banks the Reichsbank had some influence, but it lacked the legal means to bring its views to bear on the practice of banking. Hjalmar Schacht, while he was Reichsbank president from the currency stabilization to the ratification of the Young Plan (which precipitated his resignation), fought against the growing foreign indebtedness but with little success. Only for municipalities in search of credits abroad did the government finally set up an advisory board with the power of veto. This enabled Schacht in some cases to apply brakes to the municipalities' excessive investments in their ambitious enterprises.

Two events brought the banking difficulties to a climax. The tidal wave of National Socialist votes in the general elections to the Reichstag of September, 1930, by which the number of their members rose from 12 to 107, caused the first panic among foreign creditors and a massive recall of short-term credits. This abated when it seemed likely that the Reich government would withstand the National Socialist onslaught. The second blow came from the Austrian banking crisis, which in May, 1931, culminated in the crash of the Austrian Creditanstalt, one of the oldest and largest international banks in central Europe. After the alarm from Austria, the run on the German banks developed such momentum that no one could master it.

Foreign governments and central banks were not insensitive to the dangers that threatened the entire structure of the European credit system in consequence of these events. They tried to check the German banking disaster by two means: by a moratorium on reparations and by extending direct credit. The first, crucial move was once again hampered by the tie-up between reparations and inter-Allied debts. The reparations moratorium proclaimed by President Herbert Hoover on June 19, 1931, could not begin to work before July 7, after weeks of cumbersome negotiations between the United States, the Allies, and Germany. This moratorium postponed all reparations and inter-Allied debt payments for the year from July 1, 1931, to June 30, 1932, except that the service of the Dawes and Young Loans was to continue. This was virtually the end of the era of reparations and inter-Allied debts. In accepting the Hoover Moratorium, Germany incurred the conditional obligation to resume payments after the moratorium expired, but this was never fulfilled. After July 1, 1931, German payments remained confined to servicing the two international loans.

The second move to aid the German banks got under way somewhat more speedily. On June 25, 1931, the Reichsbank, whose funds had been quickly depleted by withdrawals of foreign deposits, received from the central banks of Britain, France, and the United States and from the Bank for International Settlements a credit of 420 million RM to tide the Reichsbank over the June 30, 1931, payments deadline. This credit was renewed from time to time until it was finally repaid in the first months of the Hitler regime.

THE GERMAN MORATORIUM

Both moves failed to arrest the impending catastrophe. On July 13, 1931, one of the four large D-Banks, the *Darmstädter und Nationalbank,* was forced to suspend payments. Along with the other large banks the Darmstädter Bank had become involved on the widest scale in short-term financing of risky and even unsound ventures. Its insolvency followed immediately on the bankruptcy of the *Norddeutsche Wollkämmerei,* a large textile firm in Bremen, through which the bank lost more than its entire capital. The other banks, also heavily involved, were unable to salvage the Darmstädter Bank; hence its insolvency threatened to drive all bank depositors, deeply alarmed as they were by the crash of the Austrian Creditanstalt, into headlong panic. In this emergency the government declared a bank holiday that was lifted in several stages over the following weeks.

Above all else, the open bankruptcy of all banks had to be prevented. Although everyone was agreed that the stockholders should be left to sustain the heaviest possible losses, it seemed out of the question to allow institutions on whose functioning the economic life of the entire country depended simply to break down. Nor could the small depositors be delivered into the hands of the liquidators. These were the actions that the government undertook: first, a Reich guarantee of all deposits in the Darmstädter Bank was proclaimed at the same time as the bank holiday; second, government money was put up for the reorganization of the Darmstäder Bank and the other large banks. The original share capital of the banks was written down to a fraction of nominal values, and the government or Reichsbank provided them with new share capital. A single one among the old banks came through the ordeal without Reich or Reichsbank aid, the *Berliner Handelsgesellschaft*. All the others, though they remained private banks in form, were now actually state owned. The previous concentration in German banking was now carried one step further by government intervention. The most important amalgamation was that of the Dresdner Bank with the Darmstädter Bank which, after having touched off the crisis, was the worst hit.

It is a historic fact that deserves close attention that the German banking system had thus been virtually nationalized by the Republican government on the very eve of the National Socialist revolution. Indirectly, the process implied that the government had also gained control over the major part of German industry.

To counter the withdrawal of foreign credits, at the end of July, 1931, the government proclaimed a moratorium on short-term indebtedness to foreigners. Formally this was arranged between the foreign creditors and the German debtors as a "standstill agreement," which subsequently was prolonged at regular intervals. This prevented the recall of a further 10 billion marks of foreign debt, which might have thrown the German currency and finance system into a deeper abyss.

Rigid controls and restrictions supplementing the moratorium on short-term debts were introduced for trading in foreign exchange. For more than twenty years to come Germany was never able to fight free of these exchange restrictions. After 1931 people slowly stopped realizing how oppressive these government interferences were, especially when, as the world depression dragged on, other nations were also forced to resort to such emergency measures. Less than two years after the foreign exchange restrictions had been introduced in Germany the National Socialists came to power, and their totalitarian regime used the exchange and banking controls as another welcome tool.

The banking crisis was aggravated by severe difficulties in the export trade. It has been estimated that toward the end of the prosperity period about one-third of German industrial production went into exports—in other words, that one of every three industrial workers lived on export proceeds. When the international depression strangled foreign trade one of the essential links in the German economic network was broken. From 1929 to 1933 German exports decreased from 13.6 to 4.9 billion RM, or almost two-thirds, while imports had to be squeezed down even more. The question now was: should exports be stimulated by letting the mark slowly depreciate with a concomitant controlled inflation, or should the attempt be made to defend the mark parity by means of a deflationary policy? To find an answer became the more pressing after the pound sterling was devalued on September 19, 1931, and several other nations immediately followed suit.

DEFLATION

The deflationary policies upon which the German authorities now decided to embark imposed heavy sacrifices and yet remained largely ineffective. With hindsight it is easy to say that the correct policy would have been to increase, or at least to maintain, the amounts of public expenditures instead of curtailing them, or that taxes should have been forgiven instead of being rigidly collected, and that the mark should not have been defended but rather devalued following the British example. Such measures, especially a devaluation and a sizable budget deficit, would at that time immediately have been interpreted by the population as another destruction of the currency. Germany had become a prisoner of her inflation experiences. The horrors suffered less than ten years before were still so vivid in people's minds that the government was hardly free to make a decision which the entire population would at once have taken as a portent of a new disastrous inflation. Furthermore, by reacting excessively the public probably would have nullified any good effects a moderate inflation might otherwise have produced. The domestic credit system had sustained such deep shocks that, beside the foreign payments moratorium, presumably a domestic suspension of payments would have become unavoidable.

Thus deflation seemed to offer the only potential escape from the export crisis with its sequel, the general economic crisis. By exerting strong pressure on the domestic price level one could hope to offset the price declines in important purchaser and competitor countries. A certain success was in fact achieved by these methods. In 1931 exports still held a level of 9.6 billion RM, compared with 13.5 billion in 1929, while imports were cut to 6.7 billion RM in 1931 from 13.4 billion in 1929. This netted the remarkable export surplus of almost 3 billion marks! Thus, in theory, the deflationary measures seemed indeed to open a path which in time might lead out of the quandary, once the hurricane that raged over the markets of the world showed signs of blowing itself out. However, in political reality, the deflation proved to be one of the strongest agents working toward the Republic's downfall.

To understand the scope of the deflationary policies inaugurated under Chancellor Heinrich Brüning it is well to recall that, already in Weimar Germany and not only later under Hitler, prices and wages were largely determined by the government or by agencies under direct or indirect state influence. Prices were largely political or cartelized prices, wages were political wages. Closely tied as the price system was to government decisions and to monopolistic organizations or companies, it had lost much of the flexibility that prices display in a free capitalist economy. This rigidity had much more detrimental effects on the narrow free sector of business than on the controlled sector, another factor that disturbed the overall balance.

The theoretical objective of the deflationary policy was to force the political prices down to the very level they would have reached automatically in an elastic system. But the difference between sagging prices on a free market and a politically enforced price decline is that no one can find whom to hold responsible for the former, whereas for the latter the blame is directed with full impact against the government.

Deflationary measures are by necessity unpopular. The consumer indeed reaps some benefits, but, everybody being a consumer, individuals tend to be more interested in their fate as producers. Furthermore, producer interests are better defended by business associations and pressure groups. The strong, excellently organized cooperative movement also had weighty producer interests. Even the typical consumer groups such as civil servants and pensioners derived no comfort from the deflation, for it was part of the deflationary policy to curtail civil service salaries.

BRÜNING'S EMERGENCY DECREES

So unpopular was the deflationary policy and so severe were the political and psychological obstacles in its path that the democratic system failed to overcome them, weakened as it was by growing mass unemployment and by the ascendancy of antidemocratic elements on the extreme Right and the extreme Left of the political spectrum. The resignation in March, 1930, of the Hermann Müller cabinet, the last strictly parliamentary government of the Republic, had been caused by one of these deflationary issues, the question whether the workers' contribution to unemployment insurance should be raised by a fraction or, alternatively, the benefits should be cut.

The Brüning cabinet which followed on March 30, 1930, backed away from the task of finding a parliamentary majority for its numerous deflationary measures and instead took recourse to the unparliamentary practice of issuing emergency decrees, which were technically based on Article 48 of the Reich constitution. This article, which had been meant for use only in extraordinary emergencies, was obviously misused to cope with a difficult parliamentary situation. Nothing then remained of the democratic rules of procedure except that, after issuing an emergency decree, Brüning, by means of small favors to one or the other of the various parties, induced a majority in parliament to vote down a repeal.

In this manner the Brüning cabinet maintained itself in power for over two years. Meanwhile civil service salaries, wages, house rents, interest rates, and controlled prices were scaled down by decree. Specifically, the deplorable emergency decree of December 8, 1931, contained the following measures: first, a decrease by at least 10 per cent in prices established by cartel agreements; second, reduction of all wages and salaries either to the levels of 1927 or by 10 per cent, whichever was the lesser cut; third, a sliding decrease of all interest rates on loans to a flat 6 per cent, which indeed was still a very high rate since in the disorganized capital markets voluntary conversions were impossible to arrange; fourth, a decrease in rents for old dwellings by 10 per cent.

This deflationary policy drained the democratic system of all vitality. Most depressingly, it failed to achieve its purpose to stop the rise in unemployment. The number of unemployed receiving benefits rose from 2.3 million on March 15, 1930, two weeks before Brüning took over, to 6 million at the end of March, 1932.

Now at last all doubts were dispelled that the direction of economic policy must be radically reversed. Salvation lay not in re-enforcing the deflationary measures but, on the contrary, in expanding credit facilities while fending off inflationary effects through government price regulations. It is an historic fact that the Brüning government was preparing such a reversal. It was to be initiated by floating a premium bond issue (*Prämienanleihe,* the purchasers having a chance for a discount in a lottery), the proceeds of which would go into a program of public works. While he was preparing the groundwork for such a loan, Brüning was dismissed with his entire cabinet on May 30, 1932. The German democracy remained burdened with the full responsibility for the six million unemployed. The escape from the crisis, which the government hoped it was about to discover and for which it could have dispensed with emergency decrees, was abruptly cut off.

"ONE HUNDRED STEPS BEFORE THE GOAL"

Meanwhile, what had been the course of the world depression? With the exception of the United States, Germany had been the hardest hit among all industrial nations. The unanticipated recall of American credits placed in Germany, begun as early as the autumn of 1928, had toppled the German credit structure, and in this emergency Germany had embarked in 1930 on a deflationary policy which had sapped the economy's last vital powers. Both production and incomes now took a downward course at a speed and to an extent unparalleled in previous records. Classical theory had never foreseen an economic crisis of such dimensions.

In 1932, German industrial production was only 53 per cent of what it had been in 1929; in the same three years national income decreased from 73.4 to 45.2 billion RM, the price index for raw materials from 131 to 86 (1913 = 100). During the winters of 1931–32 and 1932–33, the number of unemployed registered with the employment exchanges remained above six million, which indeed meant, for technical reasons, a total unemployment of perhaps seven million. Stock quotations, which in 1928 averaged 148 (1924–26 = 100), had moved downward consistently to arrive at an average of 54 in 1932. Under the impact of the banking crisis banks were no longer trusted with savings and business deposits. This in turn cut down the funds available for credits to tide over other enterprises. Innumerable bankruptcies, liquidations, and forced auction sales destroyed huge property values. At this stage almost no one had the courage and daring to undertake even the most urgent investments. The German economy was devouring its substance. For 1931, disinvestment—decreases in inventory and the wearing down of industrial plant—was estimated at five billion marks.

Looking back, it seems clear that the low point of the business cycle had been reached and overcome by the summer of 1932, immediately after Brüning's dismissal. Production and employment did not move further downward, and the crisis in credit and the dwindling of bank deposits had reached a standstill. Quotations of certain securities and prices of crucial raw materials had begun to rise. A breathing spell was felt. To be sure, no one dared to assert that everything would now get better, and soon. On the contrary, in the midst of the economic plight that engulfed the country a mood of dejection and despair became even more prevalent. Hundreds of plans were propounded by demagogues, swindlers, and cranks, as well as by experts, of how to prime the pump of the economy. However, a theory of full employment, as developed in the middle 1930's by John Maynard Keynes on the basis of experience with the Great Depression, was not yet available.

With more or less credence people listened to the thesis, spread in ever more radical terms by voices from the Right and from the Left, that the Weimar system with its political and economic ideology could not be trusted ever to lead the country back to bearable conditions. Ruthless as were the fights between the Republic's two fiercest enemies, the National Socialists and the Communists, the two groups were agreed on one purpose: to sweep the Weimar system away and then to rebuild Germany from its very foundations. Even apart from the extremist fringe, the Brüning government had lost much faith and support. All too many who lacked sound judgment in political matters and who were also blind to the signs of beginning recovery felt that it would be the right policy to let the National Socialists attain governmental responsibility, the more surely and permanently to prove their futility.

On April 24, 1932, just before Brüning's fall from power, elections to the Prussian Diet had resulted in a majority for the combined opposition parties of the Right and Left. National Socialists and Communists together now outnumbered the representatives of all other parties. Since their oppositional votes were invariably cast in concert, while on the other hand they were barred by their contrasting ideologies from forming a government coalition, there existed in the leading German state no majority able to form a constitutional parliamentary government. The Republican cabinet of Otto Braun, based on a coalition of the Social Democrats, the Center Party, and the Democrats, remained in office as an acting government, an untenable situation. As Prussia was responsible for three-fifths of the Reich area, chaotic conditions rapidly ensued which invited the radicals to resort to putsches. Force now had to be pitted against force. Regardless of who would gain the upper hand, the legal foundations of the Republican regime had become brittle indeed.

Still supported by a Reichstag majority, Chancellor Brüning struggled to survive this turbulent period. He pinned his hope on garnering a striking success in the fields of reparations and disarmament. Promising negotiations were carried forward to get the Western Powers' consent to a considerable German rearmament, in the framework of a general agreement, and to the virtual end of reparations. Such an achievement, it was presumed, would raise the Republican regime's prestige and give it strength for a successful fight against the rising tide of destructive forces. But before Brüning could carry these international negotiations to an end, he succumbed—"one-hundred steps before the goal," as he sorrowfully put it—to a palace intrigue of the clique surrounding the venerated but senile Reich President Hindenburg, who was no longer able to comprehend or master the situation.

BETWEEN WEIMAR AND HITLER

On May 30, 1932, Dr. Heinrich Brüning was dismissed and replaced as chancellor by Franz von Papen, who was charged with forming, at least for a period of transition, an "authoritarian" regime. In what direction such a transition was supposed to lead remained an open question. Papen did not presume for a moment to represent a majority of the Reichstag or of the nation. In fact, his nomination was passionately opposed not only by the National Socialists and the Communists but also by all Republican parties. The one exception was the support he received from the German Nationalist People's Party (*Deutschnationale Volkspartei*), led by Alfred Hugenberg, which spoke for less than one-tenth of the voters.

Franz von Papen was a conservative Roman Catholic, a member of the Prussian Diet, the owner of several newspapers, a man of considerable wealth who had never played any conspicuous role in politics and had never been taken quite seriously. With utter recklessness he plunged into the adventure like a buoyant officer riding in a cavalry attack or a steeplechase. During the first weeks of his term in office he reaped the fruit of Brüning's labors. He represented Germany at the Lausanne Conference which on June 16, 1932, suspended reparations payments indefinitely. The Lausanne agreement was never ratified by any of the governments concerned, but the reparations policy of the Allies had run its course.

About one month later, on July 20, 1932, Papen deposed the Prussian government by a coup d'état and established himself as *Reichskommissar* for Prussia, an office unknown to the constitution. The Prussian government yielded with a verbal protest against the infringement of its constitutional rights but without resorting to action, and Papen was unperturbed when later the Supreme Court of the Reich (*Reichsgericht*) in Leipzig pronounced part of the measures of July 20 unconstitutional.

Precisely during these months signs of recovery became more generally visible, the causes being both international and domestic. The Lausanne Conference had improved international confidence. Britain and the United States experienced some revival of business activity. At home, Papen reversed the deflationary policies of his predecessor. A substantial public works program was initiated and private investments were encouraged by public subsidies in the form of tax certificates usable within five years for paying certain taxes on industry.

Meanwhile, on June 3, 1932, the Reichstag had been dissolved and an impassioned election campaign was being waged. The elections of July 31 resulted in another overwhelming victory for the National Socialists, who raised the number of their parliamentary seats from 107 to 230. Of a total of 608 members, the Social Democrats returned with 133, the Communists with 89. Attention must be drawn to the fact that in these last comparatively free elections—though Nazi terror was rife—the National Socialists mustered little more than one-third of the votes (37.2 per cent); however, the parties that threatened the very existence of the Republic, the National Socialists and Communists, together now commanded a solid majority in the Reichstag as they had done before in the Prussian Diet. In parliamentary terms the government's situation was hopeless, but Papen remained calm. The following months were filled with inconclusive negotiations between the cliques surrounding Hindenburg and Hitler. The country was swept by a rising tide of chaos in the form of riots, political murder, resistance to legal authority, assaults on party leaders, and uninhibited public slander. These were the circumstances under which the new Reichstag convened on August 30 only to be dissolved once more on September 12. General elections were again ordered, for November 6.

This time, hoping to cash in on his successes, Papen led a valiant attack against the National Socialists; although the National Socialist Party did suffer severe losses in the November elections with concomitant disarray in its fighting spirit and its party finances, the opposition against Papen nowhere abated, and a parliamentary majority eluded him as much as before. The revolutionary atmosphere across the country became ever more threatening, with large-scale political strikes spreading, especially in Hamburg and

Berlin. In these strike movements the mutually hostile, embattled comrades, the National Socialists and Communists, again worked hand-in-glove.

During all this time the power behind the throne had been the army, represented by a political general, Kurt von Schleicher. He was the man who had made and destroyed Brüning, who then made and backed Papen. When conditions in the Reich had become unmanageable once more, the general himself had finally to stand up and be counted. On December 2, 1932, Schleicher formed a government, even before the newly elected Reichstag had assembled. He soon proved to be as much of a political outsider as his predecessor. His plan was to begin by conciliating the workers who were embittered by Papen's highhanded behavior. He tried very hard to gain the unions' confidence and at the same time to split the National Socialist Party by winning over their left wing. Its leader, the chairman of the National Socialist Reichstag bloc, Gregor Strasser, was second only to Hitler himself in popularity with the party's rank and file. But Schleicher was never allowed to prove whether or not his political scheme was workable. The man who had maneuvered the Republic's political intrigues for years now himself fell victim to an intrigue. Schleicher's erstwhile friend and protégé Franz von Papen was out for revenge. Although quite recently as Chancellor he had fought with determination and success against the National Socialists, after his forced retirement Papen allied himself with Hitler. On January 30, 1933, Schleicher found himself confronted with an accomplished fact: a Hitler-Papen cabinet had been formed behind his back by the same camarilla around Hindenburg which ever since 1930 had been directing German politics from backstage.

A new chapter of history had begun.

PREPARED FOR HITLER

At its demise, the Weimar Republic bequeathed to the National Socialist state an economic system which came close to being a thoroughly developed state socialism. In command of the banking mechanism, the government was actually in control of the blood circulation of the body economic. The state was also at the helm in other crucial aspects of the economy, such as transportation, power supply, and the management of cartel prices. Furthermore, the state had appropriated vital functions of the trade unions and the employers' associations. Through taxation, customs duties, and social insurance contributions a large slice of the national income was pre-empted and redistributed. The public enterprises—railroads, public utilities, building construction—should also be included in the picture. In 1932, after national income had decreased faster than had tax receipts and social insurance payments, the proportion of national income determined by the state may well have been as high as 50 per cent. Government was omnipresent, and the individual had become used to turning to it in every need.

At last it became common knowledge that all this state interference, in the shape it had reached at the height of the prosperity period, was of no avail in the most disastrous economic crisis that had befallen Germany in the course of her history. Paradoxically, the system of state interference as such, being far too deeply rooted in the German political and economic tradition, was not blamed by the opposition. On the contrary, the general mood of the public backed the demands that this imperfect and incomplete system of state intervention be superseded by one more perfect and complete. This was the content of the so-called anticapitalistic yearning which, according to a National Socialist slogan of the time, was said to pervade the German nation. To be sure, in the last parliamentary elections the parties which stood for the greatest possible measure of government regulation of business had received a huge majority of the votes. It is also true that each of these parties demanded an entirely different approach. But it is a fact that those who pinned their faith and hope on the return to a free capitalist economy had been reduced to a minority. This explains why the opposition against the National Socialist dictatorship was much weaker in the field of economics than in the political and cultural spheres. The road to the totalitarian state had been well paved; all that the National Socialist government needed to do was to use for its own purposes the instruments of power forged by its predecessors.

If from the very first stages of the National Socialist regime the German economy displayed the aspect of a huge army camp, it is well to reflect how easy it had been thus to reshape the existing economic organization as it had gradually been built up by preceding regimes. However, a basic difference between the economic system of the Weimar Republic and what was now to develop under National Socialist principles should also be recognized: the economic system of the Republic had at all times been imbued with a democratic spirit based on democratic institutions and directed toward international cooperation.

V

THE THIRD REICH AND THE SECOND WORLD WAR

1. The "Unalterable" Party Program

IN ITS BEGINNINGS, National Socialism was certainly not an economic movement. However, both its initial expansion and its coming to power occurred in a period in which economic crises, deprivations, and passions were casting deep shadows over the land and men were forced to watch for economic ideas that might rescue them.

The National Socialist Party was founded in 1919 at a time in which the Weimar regime was struggling in vain to fend off the rising tide of inflation. It took its first revolutionary action in 1923 when, in consequence of the Franco-Belgian occupation of the Ruhr, the German currency and with it the entire economic structure had crumbled. The amateurish putsch of 1923 staged by Hitler with Ludendorff's assistance in Munich, the "capital of the movement," had a swift, sanguinary ending. Hitler was sentenced to five years' military confinement (*Festungshaft*), although he was released at the end of 1924. For a number of years Hitler's movement seemed to have faded away. In the Reichstags of the 1920's it was represented by about a dozen members. But in the elections of September, 1930, the National Socialist parliamentary representation jumped to 107 members. From the time of these elections to the end of the Republic marked by Hitler's appointment as Reich Chancellor on January 30, 1933, the National Socialists and the Communists combined their assaults with the identical goal of everywhere throwing the constitutional life of the Republic—specifically in the Reichstag and in the state diets, first of all that of Prussia—out of gear.

When in 1930 the National Socialists won their first spectacular victory, which raised them to the rank of a great power in German politics, Germany had not more than three million unemployed. Per capita, this would not have amounted to much more than Britain's unemployment in its last prosperity period before the second world war. Moreover, unemployment on this scale had then existed for only a few months. After years of prosperity and fairly full employment one and one-half million unemployed had still been on record in October, 1929. Thus, unemployment and depression could hardly in themselves account for the swelling tide of National Socialism. True, unemployment now increased by leaps and bounds and, as shown in the preceding chapter, grew beyond all previous experience. However, even in the last general elections of March 5, 1933, which were held under Hitler's rule with only scanty remnants of a free and secret vote, a large part of the working class remained loyal to what were then termed the proletarian parties. Social Democrats and Communists lost hardly any votes. Thus it could not have been the unemployed who carried Hitler to power. Yet, in the end it was undoubtedly the economic crisis that bred the climate of despair in which revolutionary and visionary movements are apt to become rampant.

We should note that the super-nationalistic movement of national socialism experienced its great surge after the foreign troops had been evacuated from the Rhineland, after Germany had been received on equal terms with the other great powers in the League of Nations, and after the Young Plan had considerably, though as yet insufficiently, cut down reparations. By the time that extreme nationalism became victorious, the Lausanne Agreement of July, 1932, had practically done away with reparations.

Although a simple economic interpretation of the National Socialist ascendancy is therefore not acceptable, undoubtedly economic arguments played a great role in their propaganda. In the "unalterable" party program, the so-called Twenty-Five Points proclaimed in public convention in Munich on February 24, 1920, economic and social demands dominated. This program was to remain the intellectual basis of the movement; the party's training courses were based on it, and, combined with Hitler's book *Mein Kampf,* it provided the guidelines for the party's philosophy and actions. As it turned out, however, the political points of the program were followed much more conscientiously than the economic promises. What may be regarded as the quintessential point in National Socialist economics, that of state initiative and control in all fields, was not spelled out in the program, but its spirit was kept alive and formed one of the decisive elements in German developments.

Among the twenty-five points of the program, the following concerned economic issues:

> . . . 3. We demand land and soil (colonies) to feed our people and to settle our surplus population. . . . 7. We demand that the state be obligated first of all to ensure the gainful employment and the livelihood of the citizens. . . . 10. It must be every citizen's first duty to work, intellectually or physically. The individual's activity must never collide with the interests of the community, but must be carried on within the collective framework and for the good of all. We demand therefore: 11. Abolition of income not earned by work and toil, breaking the bonds of interest slavery (*Brechung der Zinsknechtschaft*). 12. In view of the enormous sacrifices in life and property exacted in every war, personal enrichment through war must be regarded as a crime against the nation. We therefore demand total confiscation of all war profits. 13. We demand nationalization of all heretofore incorporated businesses (trusts). 14. We demand profit sharing in large enterprises. 15. We demand wide expansion of the care for the aged. 16. We demand that a healthy middle class be set up and maintained, immediate takeover of department stores by the municipalities in order to procure space at low rates for small tradespeople, and the utmost consideration for small trade in placing orders for deliveries to the Reich, the states, and the municipalities. 17. We demand a land reform suited to our national needs, a law providing for confiscation without compensation of soil for community purposes, abolition of land rent and prevention of land speculation. 18. We demand a ruthless fight against those whose acts are injurious to the common interest. Common crimes against the nation, usury, profiteering, and the like must be punished by death, irrespective of creed or race. . . . 24. . . . Public interest comes before self-interest. . . ."

ANTICAPITALISM AND COLLECTIVISM

From the outset the National Socialist Party was an anticapitalist party. As such it was at the same time fighting Marxism and competing with it. Originating immediately after the first world war when many believed that the socialization of Germany and possibly of the entire world was inevitable, the National Socialist program attacked the problem of the day from three angles, none of them novel or alien to the Weimar Constitution. In wooing the masses the National Socialists did not deny the principles of the existing economic order; they rather adopted and exaggerated them. The first angle was the moral principle, the second concerned the financial system, the third dealt with the issue of ownership. The moral principle proclaimed: public interest before self-interest. The financial goal was: breaking the bonds of interest slavery. The new order of ownership provided: nationalization of all previously incorporated businesses (trusts), municipalization of department stores, land reform.

By proclaiming the principle of public interest before self-interest National Socialism emphasized its antagonism to the spirit of ruthless competition allegedly represented by democratic capitalism. The masses were told that the capitalist doctrine gives free play to egotistical instincts to the detriment of community interests. In truth the liberal theory of early capitalism had asserted that the community interests were best served by each individual pursuing his self-interest as rationally as possible. The development of the social conscience in the nineteenth century had brought about changes in this theory and its application. But to the National Socialists the primacy of public interest signified only that the individual was unconditionally subordinate to the commands and demands of the state, and in this sense National Socialism was, true to its name, a system of extreme national socialism.

The slogan proclaiming the primacy of public interest was however sufficiently vague to take in all sorts of economic currents and contradictory interests. It allowed the regime to follow a course of unbridled opportunism since it was easy to assert that community interests required such and such a measure. Thus it was possible simultaneously to appeal to the profit interests of the business community and to the utmost radicalism of the laboring masses and the uprooted intellectuals. Discussions within the party, as far as permitted, had little concern for the principle, but rather for its practical interpretation. Hitler's promise had been to do away with conflicts of interests, with the class struggle, and with the struggles of political parties to dominate the state. What really happened was merely that these struggles went on inside the single party, hidden from public view.

In the first years after Hitler's coming to power the radical wing of his party seemed to gain strength as the labor leaders, the intellectuals, and the para-military party formations adopted a common line of action. These groups discussed and promoted a "second revolution." However, the conservative forces of the old regime, which were represented in Hitler's government, were still powerful, and Hitler felt that his coalition was endangered by the pressures from the rank and file to have a social revolution follow the political. He therefore decided to crush the leaders of the radicals. This was done on June 30, 1934, in the so-called "cleansing action," a murderous bloodbath carried out with no semblance of legal proceedings. Among the victims were several of the mightiest "old fighters" of the movement such as Major Ernst Röhm and Gregor Strasser. Again the primary motive of this purge was by no means an economic one. It was a power struggle within the party that had threatened Hitler's own position, a budding party revolt which had to be squelched before it could spread as several others had done in the years before the party's advent to power. For the time being, the effect of the purge was to give a victory to the conservative elements in the struggle over economic policies.

Only a few years later the logic underlying this political system had prevailed, and full domination by the state was established also in economic matters. Private ownership of the means of production was not abolished, provided that the owner in question had not voiced opposition to Hitler or the party and that he was not a Jew. Businessmen were even permitted to reap ample and easy profits, especially after the autumn of 1936 when the wage and price freeze allowed generous profit margins. Moreover, the state itself was welcomed by business as a safe customer. But certainly by 1936 the regime had gathered sufficient strength to draw each and every economic act under its command. As in all other fields, the final decision in economic matters was in the hands of the Führer, Adolf Hitler. Thus, in five years of peace the economic system had already undergone a change that amounted to a genuine revolution.

"BREAKING THE BONDS OF INTEREST SLAVERY"

Among the many quaint slogans invented by National Socialism, "breaking the bonds of interest slavery" was the most peculiar. Before long it disappeared almost completely from public discussion, but in the years of the party's ascendancy it probably had a greater appeal to the masses than many a more rational promise. This can be explained. Hardly any experience in history, not even the defeat in the world war or the Versailles treaty, had ever impressed the thoughts and sentiments of the German rank and file as deeply as the currency collapse. In the postwar years of uncontrollable inflation people had been driven into a hopeless fight against an unassailable monster, a specter beyond anyone's grasp. The entire nation had felt engulfed in a mire from which there was no escape. What wonder that at such a time all notions about money, banking, interest, and credit were drowned in utter confusion.

Only against this background of the great inflation can the economic and social thinking of the National Socialists be understood. Their ideology started from the odd distinction between "rapacious" and "creative" capital, terms which in German furnished a rhyme: *raffendes und schaffendes Kapital.* Creative capital was essentially industrial capital, rapacious capital was capital in finance and commerce. Rapacious capital, so the National Socialist saga went, had appropriated all power in modern society and had thrown men into slavery to toil for capital interest. By a second short-circuit in reasoning rapacious capital was declared to be Jewish and creative capital "Aryan." This application of the National Socialist racial theory was of course as irreconcilable with fact as is the race theory itself with scientific truth.

However, the groups to which National Socialism catered had little concern for historical or scientific facts. They had simply stared transfixed into the witches' cauldron of inflation and seen people become immensely rich overnight by the simple device of borrowing money to buy commodities. They had discovered that only a tiny fraction of the people had access to the sources of credit and that an even smaller number commanded the power to distribute the blessings of borrowing and lending, while at the same time virtually the entire middle class was helplessly caught with its savings accumulated over a lifetime in the maelstrom of the disintegrated currency and doomed to perdition. On the other hand, as has been shown, the inflation had accelerated the concentration of capital and of economic power. The little fellow felt himself overwhelmed—the artisan by the factory, the shopkeeper by the department store, the farmer by the stock and grain dealer. Finally, after the inflation had been overcome and a stable currency reestablished, the true dimensions of the impoverishment of the nation stood revealed. The capital shortage necessarily manifested itself in high interest rates. All those who had been expropriated by the inflation, cut off from credit, or oppressed by debt at high interest were easy believers in the truth of what the National Socialists were saying.

However, long before the National Socialists had come to power, the entire issue had lost any practical significance it might once have had. The Republican governments, particularly the Brüning cabinet, had reduced the interest rates by emergency decree, and the power of the banks had been destroyed in the 1931 crisis. At the end of the Weimar period virtually the whole banking and credit system was owned or controlled by the state.

There is another curious contradiction in the fact that the same National Socialist movement that had derived such a potent propagandistic advantage from exposing the inflation to popular odium was itself pledged to a decidedly inflationary program. For example, "Feder money" did not figure in the Twenty-Five Point program, but it played a prominent role in the history of the movement. It was named for Gottfried Feder, originally Hitler's most influential adviser in economic matters who dropped from favor soon after Hitler's advent to power. Feder's idea was to finance housing construction and other public works by issuing *Baugeld, i.e.,* money earmarked for construction of dwellings and "secured" by the value of the construction so financed.

This was just one of innumerable fancy monetary proposals that pop up everywhere and are given credence in times of crisis by people ignorant in money and credit matters. After Hitler had become Reich Chancellor he named Hjalmar Schacht, not Gottfried Feder, to be his responsible adviser in monetary affairs. In Schacht, Hitler found an expert collaborator. As president of the Reichsbank during the first six years of the National Socialist regime and as Minister of Economics from 1934 to 1937, Schacht refrained from opposing the National Socialist propaganda in money matters, but, using an orthodox-looking technique, he pursued his own inflationary policy. In the first two or three years, as will be shown in greater detail, this technique aptly served the purposes of expanding employment and economic pump priming. But when it was pressed into the service of rearmament and war preparations it again led down the road to currency destruction. Thanks to the technique developed by Schacht the realities were long hidden from public sight. They came into the full light of day only ten years later.

THE STATE IN CONTROL OF PRODUCTION

The nationalization of big business and the expropriation and distribution of agricultural land was never attempted by Hitler. This was not a betrayal of his program; the absolute domination of the entire economy, industrial and agricultural, by the state was achieved not by expropriation but by other means. In the end every sort of economic activity, not simply the large trusts as promised by the program of 1920, was made to conform to government regulation, leaving little more than the title of private ownership. Beginning step by step but then increasing in rapidity, first under the necessity of creating jobs, later in the course of rearmament, an economic system was constructed which made the state as much an economic dictator as it had been from the beginning a political dictator.

2. *National Socialist Economic Policy*

JOB CREATION

THE GOVERNMENT'S FIRST economic efforts were devoted to cutting down unemployment, soon to abolishing it. "Work and bread" had been Hitler's promise, and this was indeed fulfilled within but a few years. This accomplishment provided National Socialist propaganda with its strongest asset, for it could point out that it had succeeded in doing what governments and politicians before Hitler had been incapable of achieving: to cure the disease of unemployment, to guide the people back to normal incomes. After years of deprivation and disappointments the population could not but hail this turn of events, and even abroad the rapid recovery of Germany was observed with surprise, frequently with admiration. Dazzled by the economic success, many realized only too late that it had been paid for by the loss of every civic liberty.

As noted above, Hitler and the National Socialists came to power at the low point of the depression, which in Germany and the United States was reached simultaneously around the end of 1932. At that time Germany had six million registered unemployed and possibly an additional million not registered. Table 13 shows how speedily unemployment receded and employment increased in the following years.

How was this achieved? When Hitler assumed power he had formed no actual plan for economic recovery. The party program offered only vague and unrealistic suggestions. But there was a ruthless determination to disregard all obstacles and scruples which had hampered the preceding governments, and the power to proceed was firmly in hand. As long as money creation by the government set unused resources and unemployed labor to work this process was in tune with economic reasoning. Similar methods were at this time explored in the United States and in other countries. Difficulties emerged only later, after the economic limits for this expansion had been reached and the authoritarian regime, lured further by boundless political aspirations, overlooked or repressed the real facts.

TABLE *13*

German Employment and Unemployment, 1933–38
(*in millions*)

September 30	*Employed*	*Unemployed*
1933	14.5	3.7
1934	16.1	2.3
1935	17.0	1.8
1936	18.3	1.1
1937	19.7	0.5
1938	20.8	0.2

SOURCE: *Statistisches Handbuch von Deutschland 1928–1944* (Munich, 1949), pp. 474, 484.

The fight against unemployment was begun by means of extensive public works and was carried forward in more and more ambitious projects which necessitated full state control of production, distribution, and consumption. In the end the workers were deprived of their free choice of jobs. Still, there was no preconceived plan, and under the pressure of circumstances economic policies had to be repeatedly revised.

In the spring of 1933 Hitler and his first Minister of Economics, Alfred Hugenberg, issued a proclamation promising a Four-Year Plan "to rescue the German people, to safeguard German food supplies, and to rescue the German worker through a powerful attack on unemployment." In the same year construction was begun on the Reich superhighways (*Autobahnen*), for a long time the vaunted symbol of Hitler's economic success. A further raid on unemployment was made by organizing the Labor Service (*Arbeitsdienst*), at first voluntary, after 1935 conscripted. Young male adults, later also young women, were assembled in work camps all over the country and used as cheap hands for the construction of roads and footpaths, for agricultural work and land improvement. The pay rate for a labor conscript was 25 pfennige a day. At the same time the Labor Service was used to give military training in advance of actual army service.

In March, 1935, general military conscription was proclaimed and rearmament, which had earlier been pursued more or less secretly, was pushed forward on a monumental scale. In March, 1936, Hitler ordered his troops to march into the Rhineland, although Germany had pledged in the Treaties of Versailles and again of Locarno (1925) to keep this area demilitarized.

Despite protests from France and Britain the fortification of the Franco-German border was begun at once.

In spite of all this activity, unemployment once more rose to two million in the winter of 1935–36. Not until the spring of 1938 did unemployment virtually disappear and the German economy reach full employment. Soon thereafter new labor reserves were opened up by the conquest of Austria in March, 1938, and of the Sudetenland in September, 1938, and finally by subjecting the Czech and Slovak remainders of what had been Czechoslovakia to the Protectorate, March, 1939. In these conquered territories also unemployment disappeared within a few weeks after the German armies moved in.

PLANNED ECONOMY AND AUTARKY

To begin with, the entire complex of agriculture, commerce, and the trades, including all earners of salaries and wages, were forced to enter a system of associations grouped according to professions. These associations functioned under the orders and supervision of government authorities. Their duty was to regulate the market for each branch or profession, and they were in charge of making business decisions that had been formerly up to the entrepreneurs. Even before the war began in 1939, for a large sector of the producing and distributing economy the kinds and amounts of production were prescribed, the supplies of raw materials were allocated by quotas, bookkeeping methods were regulated, profits and sales were determined beforehand. Applications to the authorities had to be filed not only to procure materials needed for new plant investments but even for used machinery to be taken over from another plant.

Serious damage to the economy resulted from the abrupt and heavyhanded methods by which the market economy, only recently under the supervision of a democratic state, was now being remodeled, but the effects of errors in judgment often received attention only belatedly. The regime was a captive of its own dilettantism and improvisations. In deciding on an economic measure no thought was given to the sequels of second and third measures that were necessary but by no means desired. For example, in precipitately turning to job creation and rearmament no consideration was given to the consequences for foreign trade that might ensue. Any scarcity of goods for export resulted in a slackening of imports. As early as 1936, shortages developed both for production and consumption. In several industries skilled workers became scarce. Because the leadership refused to contemplate any curtailing of rearmament or of make-work schemes, it was forced into inflationary financing; prices for scarce commodities such as nonferrous metals, rubber, oils, and so forth began to rise.

To prevent price rises from becoming general the government, in that same year of 1936, decreed a price and wage freeze applicable to the entire economy. This, of course, did not end the shortages themselves; on the contrary, redundant demand only became more pressing. Consequently scarce goods, at first only in the field of production, had to be placed under strict management. Soon purchasing permits and selling orders were required in many segments of the market. The demand that could not be satisfied escaped to other markets and there created new scarcities. This further restricted the range of commodities on which the "vagabond" excess of purchasing power could escape. Within a short time all essential commodities and raw materials, including those partly or totally imported, were placed under strictly centralized management, both as to prices and quantities.

This planless planning experienced its heaviest strain from the fact that the German economy depended on imports to a comparatively high degree. As demonstrated by the first world war, this dependence could become fatal in wartime. But even in peacetime industry could not do without imports of certain metals, fuels, textile fibers, etc. In foodstuffs, it was particularly the much-discussed gap in fats that needed to be filled from abroad.

In order to be armed economically as well as militarily against any future emergency, especially a blockade such as had been imposed on Germany in the years from 1914 to 1919, Hitler decided to embark on a program of self-sufficiency and independence from outside markets. After having been in power for almost four years he proclaimed in the autumn of 1936 at the Nürnberg party convention a new Four-Year Plan which was intended to make Germany self-sufficient in food and industrial raw materials.

> Within four years Germany must be entirely independent from outside countries in all those raw materials which, in whatever way, can be made available through German ingenuity, through our chemical and mechanical industries and our mining . . . . The new development of such a great German raw material industry will also usefully and economically employ the masses of workers that shall become available once rearmament has been accomplished.

To set this program of autarky in motion, giant industries were developed for the production of ersatz materials to replace those hitherto imported. In the period of the second Four-Year Plan it became apparent that the plan was not meant to supply the nation with better and cheaper goods but to make Germany invincible.

Basically this program and the National Socialist economic setup in general had its model in the German war economy organized in 1914–19 as a response to the war blockade. After this experience Germany had never ceased to worry about how to produce ersatz commodities. The scientific and technical preconditions had been prepared long before Hitler came to power. The difficulties lay only in applying the scientific procedures economically and on a large scale. First, huge amounts of capital had to be diverted from existing industries for investment in new plants. Second, the production costs of the new materials were many times the costs of those they replaced. For instance, the price of synthetic rubber (buna) was originally about seven times that of natural rubber. The price spread between synthetic oil and synthetic dye stuffs and the respective natural materials was somewhat less, but in a free economy in which prices had to adjust to those prevailing on the market none of these synthetic materials would have been competitive. Within the closed and centrally managed economy which now prevailed such considerations had no relevance. The economic point of view had to yield to the military.

As the record shows, remarkable successes were achieved as to quantity, quality, and production costs of the ersatz materials. And yet, the goal of self-sufficiency and independence from imports was not much nearer. For textiles approximately 40 per cent of peacetime raw material requirements were met from domestic production. Among the basic raw materials the greatest progress was made in flax growing with the help of high cultivation subsidies and fixed prices. Wool production gained less. The most important textile ersatz materials were pulp (*Zellwolle*) made from cellulose, and "artificial silk," rayon and acetate. Their production depended on adequate supplies of cellulose and therefore was limited by the output of timber, the production of which material, essential for the most varied uses, was now pushed forward to the detriment of forest conservation. Mass production of synthetic rubber, a derivative of lime and coal, began only in 1939. Increasing quantities of motor fuels were derived from coal by hydrogenation and synthesis, but in 1938 natural oil from German wells plus synthetic oil covered only about one-half of peacetime demand. Any war was bound to multiply the requirements.

Apart from developing substitute materials, utmost efforts were made to raise domestic raw material production irrespective of costs. Even more essential than flax and oil were iron ore, copper, lead, and zinc. Here also only partial success was achieved. For iron ore in particular Germany remained dependent for more than two-thirds of her total requirements on imports, mostly from Sweden, although the exploitation of low-grade ores in Salzgitter and later, after the annexation of Austria, of Styrian ores was pushed to the limit, and although in 1937 the giant *Reichswerke* were founded to implement autarky plans.

As noted above, the stage of full employment was reached in 1938. It was now clear for anyone to see that a nation that undertakes so many large-scale projects all at one time must draw on its last physical and human resources without ever having enough of either. In Germany the manpower shortage was aggravated by the fact that about one and one-half million young men were currently kept outside the regular labor force in military service or work camps, and another one to two million were unproductively occupied in the service of the party, the police, and the management of the state controlled economy.

AGRICULTURE

The thorough reorganization of the entire economic order, which implementation of the economic and noneconomic aims of National Socialism required, necessarily had to extend to agriculture.

As early as the summer of 1933 the whole agricultural sector was organized into the so-called Reich Nutrition Estate (*Reichsnährstand*). This was a sort of statutory cartel which included not only every producer, that is, all landowners and tenants of every size of holding, but also the processors and wholesale and retail distributors of agricultural products. In the following years, marketing boards (*Marktverbände*) were set up, each under a market commissioner. The boards were to fix prices, regulate supplies, and prescribe what charges were permissible for every phase of processing—for instance, how much the miller was to charge for milling the grain, the baker for baking the flour, the retailer for selling the bread. Gradually the regulations grew tighter, especially for bread, butter, eggs, potatoes, wool, cattle, and hogs. In the framework of the overall cultivation plans, individual farmers were assigned production quotas, processors were ordered to produce only certain qualities, sales in some products were restricted to officially designated sellers and buyers. Even in choosing seeds, fertilizer, and technical appliances the farmer was under official guardianship.

The peculiar National Socialist ideology did not stop at such economic tutelage. As early as the autumn of 1933 the government published the Hereditary Farm Law (*Erbhofgesetz*), which declared all farms amounting to a full-sized agricultural unit (up to a maximum of 125 hectares;

TABLE 14

German Agricultural Production, 1933 and 1936–38
(in thousands of tons)

	1933	*1936*	*1937*	*1938*
Wheat and Spelt	5,765	4,523	4,576	5,682
Rye	8,727	7,386	6,917	8,606
Oats	6,334	5,618	5,919	6,366
Barley	3,468	3,399	3,638	4,249
Potatoes	41,472	46,324	55,310	50,894
Sugar beets	8,579	12,096	13,701	15,546
Milk	24,829	25,400	25,445	25,185
Herd size (in thousand head at end of year)				
Hogs	24,014	25,892	23,847	23,567
Cattle	19,811	20,088	20,503	19,434

SOURCE: *Statistisches Handbuch von Deutschland 1928–1944* (Munich, 1949), pp. 124 f., 190, 215.

1 hectare equals 2.47 acres) to be "hereditary farms." Farms so designated could not be sold or mortgaged, and claims pending against them could not be enforced. The law prescribed a certain order of heredity; as long as a "peasant-worthy" (*bauernfähig*) male heir existed and did not relinquish his claim, female heirs could not take over. The idea was that agriculture was obligated not only to ensure the supply of the nation's agricultural needs, but also, according to racist notions, to serve as the "blood source of the nation."

Such protection and regulation was no unmixed blessing for agriculture. Contrary to the plans of its well-wishers, the flight from the land only became more marked. Those children who were deprived of their rights of inheritance and were not landbound by the Hereditary Farm Law were practically urged to look for other means of livelihood. Furthermore, increasing numbers of agricultural laborers chose the freer air and higher income of the cities.

All the same, the farmers were at first not badly off since they enjoyed satisfactory prices that were shielded against world competition and therefore fairly stable. Also there were several good harvests in succession. And yet, as in industry, German agriculture did not come much closer to the goal of autarky in foodstuffs. In fact, agricultural production hardly increased between 1933 and the second world war, although the use of fertilizer doubled.

Notable success was achieved only in potato and sugar beet production. Sugar beets received particular support as a substitute product for scarce fats. Imports in several grains rose and considerable amounts of imported foodstuffs were stocked up as a war reserve. In meat and dairy products the situation was no better. The hog population even decreased between 1933 and 1938 from 24 to 23.6 million head. Milk production rose from 24.8 to 25.2 million tons, butter from 450,000 to 508,000 tons, but these increases were achieved only with the help of imported fodder. The scarcity in fats remained the most serious problem of German nutrition. Although imports of all kinds of fodder were substantial, it hardly seemed possible to reduce the importation of fats in six years of planned agriculture. German fat consumption was always low by American standards, but still Germany remained dependent on outside supplies for two-thirds of her requirements.

It was all the more surprising that results were so far from satisfactory in view of the facts that investment in agriculture in the form of machinery and other technical supplies kept growing year by year and that fertilizer prices were held down by government regulations. Farmers also received benefits in lower tax and interest rates. Thus from 1934 to 1938 taxes for farmers were cut by 60 million marks, interest payments by 280 million marks. Finally, at harvest time the various youth groups of the party were a source of cheap labor on the farms.

INDUSTRY AND COMMERCE

The organization of industry and trade was no less comprehensive than that of the agricultural sector. After some revolutionary experimentation in 1933, the organizational framework was set forth in the Law to Prepare the Organic Reconstruction of the German Economy (*Gesetz zur Vorbereitung des organischen Aufbaus der deutschen Wirtschaft*) of February 27, 1934. This laid down the German variety of the corporate state introduced in Italy under Mussolini; however, here it was very different in organization and intention. The idea behind the new law was to return in some fashion to the old and rather vague idea of the guild state, with the difference that this modern corporate state had no place for self-government, nor were labor relations within its scope. The law empowered the minister of economics: to license specific business organizations as the sole representatives of their repective industries, to organize, dissolve, or amalgamate trade associations, to order their charters and bylaws to be altered or implemented, and to name or replace their managers. The former chambers of commerce, which in Germany had been publicly regulated but self-governing agencies with a large sphere of activity, were placed under the so-called leadership principle, the "leader" to be named by the government.

The economy was comprehensively organized by industries and by territory. Geographical districts, *Gaue,* were defined, as were the chief economic sectors such as industry, handicrafts, commerce, banking, insurance, and power. These great sectors, or Reich Groups, were subdivided into numerous smaller groups, each under the command of a leader named or approved by the government. As a rule the leader was an executive in the respective industry who within his jurisdiction had considerable powers and responsibilities. All in all, this apparatus was very cumbersome; everyone in economic life without exception was a member and was subjected by it to all the regulations, instructions, and orders which the government was pleased to decree. From this system there was no escape.

Even before the war, managers were often told what to produce and by what methods, how much coal and raw materials would be available to them, what materials to use and not to use, what prices to pay and to charge, from whom to accept orders for delivery, to and through whom to sell, and in which order to fill requests. Thus, at some times government orders had priority, at other times export orders, and among government orders sometimes those of the army, at other times those of government plants were first in line.

All sectors were similarly organized. Each order was first enforceable by the punitive powers of the organization itself, after this by the courts, and finally, should these fail, by the Secret State Police (*Gestapo*). Each of the leading groups in industry and commerce had its own supervisory agency.

The tight control of imports and exports essential to a planned economy was tied up with the control of foreign exchange and foreign credit. No carload, no postal parcel could cross the German border inward or outward bound; no one could buy or sell abroad, except by specific government permit. Whether and when such a permit was granted did not depend on market conditions alone. The German importer could not buy where he found the best quality at the most reasonable price, the exporter could not choose the markets in which he was best able to compete.

An elaborate system was built up to manage foreign exchange. By 1934 there were control boards authorized to fix quotas for the purchase of foreign raw materials and to restrict stock accumulation by producers and traders. Only a few months later the Reichsbank moved on to a system of foreign exchange allocations. By this method the importation of materials needed for armament was safeguarded at the expense of supplies required by the public. The Reichsbank disposed of foreign exchange according to its list of priorities. In order to procure essential imports it was necessary to maintain exports at all cost. This was achieved with the development of a system of export subsidies, barter agreements, and clearing arrangements.

In the second Four-Year Plan of 1936 export inducements played an even greater role than in the first plan. The tight foreign trade controls had disrupted the connections between internal and external price levels. Because no free competition existed on the home market or between Germany and her foreign trade partners, prices lost much of their economic function as guides to producers. The domestic price level was strictly controlled to prevent an inflationary rise. Where needed the government paid subsidies to the exporter for transactions which it deemed essential. These subsidies sometimes amounted to 50 per cent and more of market value.

Only an enormous expansion of industrial production could carry the German regime closer to its twin goals of military superiority and autarky. It was a question of producing more steel and more automobiles than Britain, more iron and more airplanes than France. This would be feasible only if within a period of but a few years the available raw materials and other elements of production could be doubled and trebled. Accordingly, the Hitler government undertook essentially the same experiment that was already being carried out in Soviet Russia. Industrial investment was forced, most of all in production of basic raw materials and in the mechanical industries in which investments had sunk during the depression to a particularly low level. Gross annual investment in industrial plants rose eightfold from 1933, when in fact it had not been much above zero, to 1938. In transportation and the consumer industries, investment was only trebled, but in producer goods industries it rose to twelve times its 1933 volume.

Such efforts could not but produce effects. Propaganda represented them as solely attributable to Hitler's statesmanship. But if one considers how manifold and large-scale were the tasks which the state assigned to industry and the benefits it received, it is rather surprising that it took all of four years to overcome the contractions of the depression years. The 1929 level of production was not reached and passed until 1936. In 1938, after six years of planned economy, the volume of production of the entire industrial establishment had reached a level 25 per cent higher than ten years before, an increase which for the most part did not enhance the people's welfare but only the arsenal of arms. Consumer industries produced only 16 per cent more in 1938 than in 1928. Considering that the population increased by about 7 per cent in this decade and that the quantity and quality of the goods available to the consumers was seriously restricted, it will be seen that civilian supplies per capita had hardly increased at all. German industry indeed produced more in 1938 than ever before, not for the purpose of making life more abundant for the German people but to serve the bold political aspirations of the National Socialist Party. Table 15 gives the pertinent figures.

TABLE *15*

Index of German Industrial Production, 1929 and 1933–38
(1928 = 100)

	1929	*1933*	*1934*	*1935*	*1936*	*1937*	*1938*
Total production	100	66	83	96	107	117	125
Production goods	102	56	81	99	114	130	144
Consumption goods	97	80	91	95	100	107	116

SOURCES: *Statistisches Jahrbuch für das Deutsche Reich 1941–42*, p. 55 *; *Die deutsche Industrie* ("Schriftenreihe des Reichsamts für wehrwirtschaftliche Planung") (Berlin, 1939), Heft 1, pp. 39 ff.; *Bevölkerung und Wirtschaft. Statistik der Bundesrepublik Deustchland* (Stuttgart, 1958), vol. 199, p. 46.

In view of these facts, the economic recovery in the National Socialist era is not worthy of praise. Certainly the upward trend from the depth of the depression was striking, yet it lagged behind what would have been economically sound and attainable. Against all common sense Hitler assigned to an economy overstrained by the two Four-Year Plans additional ambitious schemes. He personally drew up grandiose plans for rebuilding Germany and insisted on their execution. The largest cities, primarily Berlin and secondarily Munich, the official capital of the National Socialist movement, were to be adorned by magnificent public buildings. Nothing was spared in the preparation of the spectacular Berlin Olympiad of 1936, and the personal luxury of party leaders was more and more in keeping with their concepts of national grandeur.

METHODS OF FOREIGN TRADE

As noted before, the inflationary methods used in all these efforts were predicated on total state control of foreign trade and foreign exchange. Because of the continuous recall of foreign credit, foreign exchange reserves were depleted by 1934. After the leading industrial countries had devalued their currencies, the Reichsmark seemed greatly overvalued; exchange ratios favored German imports and exporters were more and more at a disadvantage in foreign markets.

In this quandary Reichsbank President Hjalmar Schacht devised his New Plan for the implementation of the monopolistic foreign trade scheme. From its effective date, September, 1934, every dollar and ounce of gold had to be deposited with the Reichsbank; transgressors were given heavy prison terms. Schacht's New Plan cut Hitler's economy loose from international customs and manners. For decades the expression "Schachtianism" was used in the English-speaking world to characterize a policy of tricks, discrimination, and the ruthless pursuit of egotistical aims in world trade. The traditional methods of world trade, multilaterally open and regulated by nondiscriminatory agreements, were now replaced in German trade policy by bilateral arrangements. The example thus set was soon imitated by other countries and the old multilateral regime degenerated into more and more chaotic bilateralism.

Four methods were used to execute the New Plan.

CLEARING AGREEMENTS Their aim and their result was to finance foreign trade without foreign exchange. This presupposed an agreement between two countries to buy and sell identical amounts over a period of time so as to avoid debit or credit balances. Each country established a clearing office to which national importers paid the amounts they owed their foreign suppliers. From these funds the clearing offices paid the national exporter what the foreign importer abroad owed him. Thus, a Swiss importer of German goods did not pay his debt to his German supplier directly but instead through the clearing office in Switzerland to a Swiss citizen who had sold goods for delivery in Germany. In various bilateral relationships, in which Germany had an export surplus but owed interest on capital investments or other debts to the country concerned, the clearing office was used not only to settle with exporters but also, to a certain degree, with bondholders and other creditors. Such clearing agreements were arranged with all important trading countries except Britain and the United States.

BARTER AGREEMENTS These agreements represented an even more primitive form of bilateral arrangement. Two countries agreed to exchange a certain quantity of one kind of goods for a certain quantity of another kind, for instance Brazilian coffee for German locomotives, Mexican oil for German pipes, Turkish tobacco for German automobiles.

IMPORT LICENSING Nothing could now be imported that was not deemed vital for production or nutrition. Among the foodstuffs thus designated, priority was given to edible fats, meat, and (in winter) citrus fruit. Each intended importation had to be checked against a list of approved imports and to be licensed by the government import office. Traders and processors were required currently to report their stocks.

EXPORT SUBSIDIES Apart from clearing agreements and import licensing the ability to procure essential imports depended on the willingness of foreign countries to buy sufficient amounts of German goods. The export situation having deteriorated in consequence of Hitler's economic policies, drastic expedients had to be discovered. Export industries were given priority in their raw material purchases. Furthermore, a method was used which proved successful but was regarded abroad as unfair competition: where important transactions and large-scale deliveries were involved, German exporters ruthlessly undercut prices prevailing in their home market and offered goods abroad at prices below production costs. They received refunds for the difference from an equalization fund to which the whole industry had to contribute; this amounted to a general tax called Export Subsidy Turnover Assessment (*Ausfuhrförderungsumlage*). This dumping practice gave German export trade a bad name for many years.

In consequence of these practices five typical trends could be discerned after 1933:

1. A small and decreasing part of German foreign trade was transacted outside state-controlled arrangements.

2. German trade relations with foreign countries were increasingly treated as political matters. Every trade agreement and every fairly important private transaction was consciously and openly backed by the power and influence of the Reich. The government used its monopoly power to render foreign countries which were interested in entering clearing agreements but whose foreign exchange position was weak fully dependent on the Reich. This particularly applied to the Balkan countries, among whose trading partners the Reich traditionally held a prominent position.

3. Despite all government inducements during the Third Reich's six years of peace, foreign trade hardly made any progress, a fact the champions of autarky could partly claim as a success of their efforts. Imports and exports remained at about one-third of their 1928–29 levels. In relation to national income the volume of foreign trade declined. In 1933 imports and exports

TABLE *16*

Germany's Foreign Trade, 1928–38
(in billions of RM)

Year	*Imports*	*Exports*	*Surplus* (+) *Deficit* (—)
1928	14.0	12.3	—1.7
1929	13.4	13.5	+0.1
1930	10.4	12.0	+1.6
1931	6.7	9.6	+2.9
1932	4.7	5.7	+1.0
1933	4.2	4.9	+0.7
1934	4.5	4.2	—0.3
1935	4.2	4.3	+0.1
1936	4.2	4.8	+0.6
1937	5.5	5.9	+0.4
1938 *	5.4	5.3	—0.1

* Excluding Austria and the Sudetenland.

SOURCES: *Bevölkerung und Wirtschaft. Statistik der Bundesrepublik Deutschland* (Stuttgart, 1958), vol. 199, p. 52; *Statistisches Handbuch von Deutschland 1928–1944* (Munich, 1949), p. 392.

had amounted to about 10 per cent of national income; in 1938 they were barely 7 per cent.

4. As Germany emerged from the world depression during the Hitler years she was still an impoverished country. There were no foreign exchange reserves, and Germany enjoyed no credit abroad. The gold and foreign exchange holdings of the Reichsbank, which in 1932, thanks to the credits granted by Britain, France, and the United States to tide it over the banking crisis, still amounted to well over one billion Reichsmarks, had decreased by the end of 1934 to only about 200 million RM, equivalent to the foreign exchange requirements of perhaps two weeks. From this low point the reserves never rose; even in years with a small export surplus there was no influx of gold or foreign exchange because any potential surplus had to be employed for servicing foreign loans, at least whenever the creditor country had the power to withhold any surplus in its trading with Germany. This applied to almost every European creditor country.

5. As a result of its bilateralism and political orientation, German trade shifted from the centers of world trade to the Southern European, Latin

American, and Middle Eastern countries with which agreements existed. In 1938 two-fifths of German foreign trade was transacted with these groups of countries, which in the six preceding years had only taken half that ratio.

FINANCIAL POLICIES

When the National Socialist regime undertook an armament program of growing dimensions observers thought the main problem would be how the resources for such limitless plans could be financed. Many, both inside and outside the country, were convinced that National Socialist ambitions were bound to lead before very long to another runaway inflation and to bankruptcy. However, year after year went by without any apparent sign of financial weakness or of inflation. Hitler seemed to furnish proof for the rule that within an economic system anything that can be produced can also be financed. Where government is in full command of the entire labor force and of all material resources of the country, and when it controls the balance of payments, the expansion of production meets no limitations other than those of labor and resources.

In a free market society the individual is at liberty to eat more if he has the means to pay for more and to choose his food according to his predilections, for the market will provide him with anything he may desire. Under a reasonably efficient dictatorship people can eat only what the government is willing to grant them. In a free market society effective demand, prices, and available resources will determine what can be produced. If more automobiles are demanded production will be adapted to the expanding market and more steel, rubber, glass, copper, and cotton will be processed into automobiles. If, on the contrary, people demand and are ready to pay for more housing, additional steel and glass will be put into building construction and, instead of rubber, copper, and cotton, more cement, bricks, and timber will be produced or imported for the market. Should people wish to devote a larger share of their incomes to their beauty or amusements, more capital will be invested in beauty parlors, cosmetics, night clubs, and movie houses. Labor and capital are directed into those channels where there is promise of better profits. Such are roughly the dynamics of freely functioning economic forces in a capitalist market.

In a totalitarian system the individual consumer's free choice cannot determine how capital and labor will be employed. The state decides for what purposes, in what amounts, and by what methods the physical and material resources of a nation are to be used, and in doing so it is not guided by the expectation of profits or by consumers' desires but mostly by political motives. In the 1930's the dominant motive in the field of economics was to make Germany militarily the most powerful nation and to reduce her dependence on foreign supplies to a minimum.

By what means can a government direct the economic resources of a nation into the desired channels? In theory, either by exerting immediate command over men and goods, or by the indirect methods of taxation, credit regulation, and price and wage determination. The National Socialist regime used a combination of these methods. First an attempt was made to use prices as the regulating instrument. Government itself appeared in the markets as a purchaser, exerting its demand in the same way a potent consumer would in a free economy. This procedure naturally presupposed the command of sufficient financial means. How to procure these means was the foremost problem the method presented. Financial policies would thus decide whether some free play of market prices could be preserved or whether resort to a command economy would become imperative.

The financial policies of the National Socialist regime did not develop according to a preconceived plan, either. They were improvised and revised as things went along and new needs demanded attention. No one was in a position to say exactly in what measure the various methods were being employed because the publicity of statistical reporting, so essential in the modern world, had been largely abolished.

Schacht, to be sure, tried hard to defend as long as possible the internal purchasing power of the mark. He intervened wherever price rises turned up, for the first time in 1934 when several raw materials purchased abroad became scarce because of foreign exchange restrictions. But after 1936, when the entire price structure threatened to topple, it was a futile effort to look for currency stability merely by means of ordering a price freeze. Had price stability actually been the government's foremost concern in this critical phase, either incomes would have had to be partly taxed away or armaments outlays would have had to be reduced. Neither action was taken; armaments expenditures were further increased, and higher income taxes were not levied because to do so would have deprived Hitler of a decisive feather in his propagandistic cap—having helped the people attain higher income levels. Only the corporation income tax was raised from its long preserved level of 20 per cent, first to 25 per cent in 1936, then to 30 per cent in 1937.

The defense of the purchasing power of the mark was thus subordinated to other political goals. Even after full employment had been reached, further budget deficits were incurred. Such deficits had to be financed by new money. To procure it, the regime, immediately after coming to power, resorted to a device that had previously been experimented with by the Papen government. It seemed inadvisable for the treasury to take up a direct credit from the Reichsbank since this might have reminded the public at once of the practice in the early 1920's. Instead, the government paid its contractors in the form of three-month commercial paper which the creditors drew against financing agencies especially set up to execute this maneuver. These three-month bills, which were renewable for up to five years, were admitted for rediscount by the Reichsbank. Consequently they became highly liquid paper acceptable in payment to every creditor and bank. One of these financing agencies was the Metallurgical Research Institute (*Metallurgische Forschungsgesellschaft*), founded in 1933, best known for the ominous "Mefo" bills named for it. Such were the methods by which Schacht achieved the phenomenon that amazed observers at home and abroad, financing both job creation and armament.

The Reich debt at first appeared lower than it was because the obligations of these special financing agencies were not added to the records of Reich indebtedness. After 1935 such deception of the public became unnecessary because budgets and records of the Reich debt were simply no longer published. If the Mefo bills are included in the Reich debt, which at the end of March, 1933, amounted to only 12 billion RM, the total in 1939 may be computed at 43 billion RM. On the other hand, the debt burden had been somewhat alleviated by the fact that in April, 1935, a general limit on interest rates came in force. The Law to Limit Interest Rates (*Anleihestockgesetz*) of December 4, 1934, had decreed that all borrowing had to stop and that all bond interest and dividends were not to exceed 6 per cent.

It appears, therefore, that the roots of the second German inflation should not be looked for only in the second world war. Even in the preceding years of "peace," conditions had moved decidedly toward a galloping inflation. The climb in the public debt began in the fiscal years 1933 and 1934 with increases of 1.6 and 2 billion RM respectively. In the three following years, 1935–37, the debt rose precipitately by 15 billion RM, and in the last single fiscal year before the war, 1938, the increase was 10.5 billion. Thus, the increase of the public debt in six prewar years was as high as 30 billion RM.

With the rapid growth of nominal national income, tax receipts necessarily increased. The revenue of the Reich was derived mainly from income taxes, turnover taxes, and consumption taxes, three sources particularly susceptible to fluctuations with the business cycle. Thus tax receipts increased at an even more rapid pace than national income. The tax receipts of the Reich trebled in the first six years of the National Socialist regime, from 5 to 15 billion marks, while the receipts of the federal states and the municipalities amounted to another 5, later 7 billion. By indirection, through credits granted by one public corporation to another, the Reich also profited from the mounting incomes of the social security funds and from the party's various welfare funds and subagencies, such as the Winter Help Fund (*Winterhilfswerk*) and the German Labor Front (*Deutsche Arbeitsfront*), a government trade-union organization. But all these sources combined fell far short of balancing expenditures, which increased from 8 to 32 billion Reichsmarks during this same period. Armament proper participated in this expansion, rising from 2 to 18 billion Reichsmarks.

Three further extraordinary and nonrecurring sources of revenue were tapped. The first was the actual, though not formal, expropriation of foreign creditors. The second was the appropriation in 1938 and 1939 of the Austrian and Czech gold and foreign exchange reserves under the title of war booty. The third was the plundering of the property of the Jews.

As previously explained, German prosperity in the years from 1924 to 1929 was largely based on the influx of long-term and short-term capital from abroad. In these six years the annual capital influx was on the average approximately 2.3 billion Reichsmarks. Although much of this had to be sent out of the country again in reparations and in interest plus amortization payments to service the reparations loans, considerable surpluses in foreign exchange accumulated. When the National Socialists assumed power they at first even stressed their compliance with foreign obligations. By making a voluntary transfer of 485 million Reichsmarks in April, 1933, the Reichsbank repaid the loan received in 1931 from the central banks of Britain, France, the United States, and the Bank for International Settlements to help overcome the acute banking crisis. The new regime wished to demonstrate to the world that it was able and willing to satisfy its creditors abroad. This reduced the gold and foreign exchange reserves of the Reichsbank to 511 million marks at the end of April, 1933. Only a few weeks later, in May, 1933, a transfer moratorium was proclaimed, to begin July 1, which at first still permitted certain transfers of interest and amortization payments. In June, 1934, all transfers were stopped except those stipulated in special agreements with individual countries.

German debtors now had to deposit in blocked accounts in Germany the interest and amortization payments that they were not permitted to transfer abroad. The refusal to transfer capital and interest simply meant that monies which could be rightfully claimed by businessmen abroad were forcibly retained in Germany for continued investment. The exact amount of these involuntary foreign investments in the German economy is not known, but it reached many million Reichsmarks annually, and these were in steady use until the blocked accounts were gradually liquidated during the 1950's. As against this perennial boon, the confiscation of the assets of the Austrian and Czech central banks and the seizure of Jewish property were only one-time gains.

It is difficult to estimate the value of the confiscated Jewish property. After the outrage of the "crystal night" of November, 1938, a Reich law obligated the Jewish population to pay a property levy of one billion Reichsmarks. In addition they had to deliver to the Reich authorities all stocks and bonds in their possession and to relinquish their insurance claims. Emigrants and refugees as a rule lost their property. The Reich's booty must be presumed to have amounted to several billion Reichsmarks.

TRENDS IN INCOME AND THE STANDARD OF LIVING

Men deprived of their personal liberties may feel less bitterly abused if at the same time their material welfare improves. What were the economic benefits to the population that derived from National Socialist policies?

At first glance it may seem that the improvement in personal incomes was spectacular in the first six years, 1933 to 1938, during which national income almost doubled. Successful job creation necessarily expressed itself in a corresponding increase in incomes. This was continuously stressed in the official propaganda. However, as noted before, the real improvement in living standards did not keep pace with the development in the national income. Correctly interpreted, the picture conveyed by the official statistics was considerably less spectacular. Hitler's ambitious projects could be realized only insofar as the population allowed the government to use much of the national income for its own purposes. In one of his highly rhetorical orations Hermann Göring, the "Führer's faithful paladin," President of the Reichstag, Prussian Prime Minister, Commander in Chief of the Air Force, and Commissioner of the Four-Year Plan, coined the often quoted slogan "guns instead of butter." Indeed, butter had to be rationed even before the second world war.

How much the increase in wages and salaries lagged behind the increase in national income is shown in Table 17. Much the same is true of the earnings of small tradespeople and the revenues from agriculture and from inter-

TABLE *17*

National Income and Wages; Germany, 1928 and 1932–38

YEAR	NATIONAL INCOME AT FACTOR COST	TOTAL WAGES AND SALARIES		INDEX OF GROSS WEEKLY WAGES * (*1936 = 100*)	
	In billions of RM	*In billions of RM*	*As per cent of national income*	*In money wages*	*In real wages* **
1928	72.4	44.9	62	124.5	102.2
1932	42.6	27.4	64	85.8	88.5
1933	44.0	27.7	63	87.7	92.5
1934	50.4	31.2	62	94.1	96.7
1935	56.8	34.5	61	96.4	97.6
1936	63.6	37.7	59	100.0	100.0
1937	71.5	41.5	58	103.5	103.0
1938	79.8	45.7	57	108.5	107.5

* (Bruttowochenverdienste der Arbeiter.)

** Index of money wage divided by the consumer price index.

SOURCE: Statistisches Bundesamt Wiesbaden, *Bevölkerung und Wirtschaft. Langfristige Reihen 1871 bis 1957 für das Deutsche Reich und die Bundesrepublik Deutschland*, pp. 86 f., 91; recomputed by the author to account for territorial changes.

est, rent, and tenants' payments, although these earnings and revenues were made to participate in the growth of national income to a somewhat higher degree than wages and salaries. Who then reaped the lion's share of the accruing benefits? The large profiteers were the government and the firms involved in the armaments boom, which however were themselves largely government owned. These two recipients retained mounting ratios of the national income for disposal in investment and construction plans at the expense of the broad strata of the population. In the normal year of 1928, wage and salary earners received 62 per cent of the national income; in the depression year of 1932, the percentage even rose to 64. From this point the ratio went down continuously until it reached 57 per cent in 1938, the last year for which trustworthy figures are available. It is true that after 1933 the aggregate income of wage and salary earners increased year by year by about three to four billion Reichsmarks, but the number of men employed was increasing at the same time. After six years of economic prosperity the average income of employed blue- and white-collar workers had increased by only 200 Reichsmarks a year. Taking the price fluctuations in living costs into account it can be said that gross per capita income—before the deduction of taxes, social insurance contributions, contributions to the Arbeitsfront and the Winterhilfswerk, and other more or less voluntary donations—did not recover before 1937 to the gross per capita income of the normal year, 1928.

While national income almost doubled between 1933 and 1938, Reich expenditures almost quadrupled in the same period. The budgets of the federal states, the municipalities, and the social insurance system did not grow quite so fast, and yet they too contributed to making the state the chief beneficiary of the increases in production and income.

Thus the individual worker, white-collar employee, craftsman, and entrepreneur were deprived of the fruit of the much-vaunted boom. This remained true even in the face of the many projects that were cleverly exploited by propaganda to give people the impression that living standards were higher, such as annual paid vacations, inexpensive theaters and concerts, and all the other activities of the party's leisure time organization "Strength through Joy" (*Kraft durch Freude*).

The boldest project simulating higher standards of living was the *Volkswagenwerk*. Construction of this huge enterprise was largely financed through the savings deposits of 320,000 Volkswagen-savers who wished to secure a claim to one of the first automobiles to be produced at some time in the future, and who saved 285 million Reichsmarks for this purpose. In reality the Volkswagenwerk served primarily to provide the *Wehrmacht* (defense forces) with standardized, lightweight, and economical cars. Since production only began to flow with the outbreak of the war, the hoax succeeded very well; the savers, instead of receiving delivery of their cars, were reminded of their readiness for patriotic sacrifice. Almost 20 years were to elapse before the savers, after endless court proceedings, received payment of 10 to 60 per cent of what they had paid in. This was not the only instance of private savings being used for public expenditure. These sums must also be deducted from the apparent betterment of living standards. The long-shrouded reality was to be fully revealed only through the currency reform of 1948.

3. *The "Social Achievements" and Their Price*

NATIONAL SOCIALISM CAME to power by promising a new social order. Several articles of the party program refer to this claim. However, what really came to pass in 1933 and 1934 was not even hinted at in the party program. Having grown strong fighting Marxism, which was identified with the idea of the class struggle, National Socialism made every effort to exorcise the spirit of the class struggle and to raise the flag of national and racial unity.

The first opportunity the National Socialists had to demonstrate their "folk community" (*Volksgemeinschaft*) was May Day of 1933. For many decades the first day in May had been appropriated by the socialist parties and the unions as their day of protest against the existing social order. Now, suddenly, it was remodeled as a festive demonstration of fealty to the new system. On April 24, 1933, only seven weeks after the elections of March 5, 1933, which had firmly established the National Socialist dictatorship, Dr. Josef Goebbels, the Minister of Propaganda, issued this proclamation:

> The government of national revolution has exalted May 1 as a holy day of national labor . . . We have become a poor people! But the joyous affirmation of life's values, the courage to work and create, the stiff-necked optimism that overcomes all obstacles, nobody will be allowed to take away from us. The entire nation honors itself by paying labor the honor that is its due. Germans of all estates, lineages, and professions, join hands! In serried ranks we march into the new age.

May 1 was celebrated everywhere in the Reich with all the pomp and impressive staging for which the National Socialists since have become notorious. Together with their workers the big industrialists, company presidents and vice-presidents had to turn out in marching order, often finding themselves placed not in the lead but in the rear. The impression was overwhelming.

The morning after the grandiose May Day celebration the National Socialists felt strong enough to strike the decisive blow. On May 2, 1933, the S.A. (*Sturmabteilungen,* National Socialist para-military troops) closed down all trade-union locals and offices, seizing the union leaders and functionaries, whom they manhandled or sent to concentration camps, and sequestrating union properties. The independent workers' organizations which, built up over decades, had gained in power particularly in the fifteen years of the Republican regime, were struck down in one day. Their heir was the Deutsche Arbeitsfront. This, however, was no longer an organization of the workers but of the National Socialist party. Besides the blue- and white-collar workers, it included managers and members of the intellectual professions.

The legal basis for this revolutionary measure was established only after the fact, in January, 1934, with the Law to Regulate National Labor (*Gesetz zur Ordnung der nationalen Arbeit*), which was pretentiously referred to as the Magna Carta of German labor. Up to Brüning's emergency decrees, free collective bargaining between trade unions and employers' associations had been regarded as the normal and desirable method for regulating wages. Mediation by government organs was only admissible after free negotiations had failed. Strikes and lockouts were legal where collective bargaining had proved futile. Wildcat strikes and lockouts were not regarded as punishable crimes but only gave rise to claims for damages. After Brüning's emergency decrees, for the first time wages could be determined by government fiat even when no bargaining between the parties had been attempted.

What under Brüning was intended as an emergency measure was now made the basic rule. The Arbeitsfront and the so-called Labor Trustees (*Treuhänder der Arbeit*) were assigned the task of regulating wages and working conditions and of deciding labor disputes on final appeal. For each of the geographical divisions of the party, the fourteen Gaue, there was a Labor Trustee. These officials were under the Reich Labor Department and received their orders from there. It was thanks to them that wages were kept virtually unchanged after 1933. The old shop councils were retained under the new name of trusteeship councils (*Vertrauensräte*), but the members were now selected from a list of candidates which the employer proposed in cooperation with the representative of the National Socialist party shop cell. Only two shop elections were held, the last in 1935. Later, in every shop the leader of the party cell was the only workers' representative, and it depended on the interplay of personalities or on chance whether he or the employer wielded more influence with the party in important decisions. Wages and hours were removed from the jurisdiction of the councils which now functioned only in minor shop problems.

Besides regulating working conditions, the Arbeitsfront assumed duties never before dealt with by the trade unions. The law of January, 1934, gave expression to a significant new ideology. It introduced "social honor courts" which had to rule on all "serious violations of the intrinsic social duties of the working community." Such violations were committed whenever "the employer, shop manager, or other supervisor exploits his position of power in bad faith to the detriment of the followers' physical well-being or their honor." (For the members of the work force the designation of "followers," *Gefolgschaft,* now became the accepted term, for the boss, the term "leader," *Betriebsführer.*) The employer or his representative could be heavily fined or even deprived of his position, sometimes removed from the management of his own property. On the other hand, management could go to court with complaints against anyone who "willfully provoked the Gefolgschaft so as to endanger labor peace or to disturb community spirit in the shop." In fact, virtually every expression of discontent was punishable by dismissal or persecution.

Above all, the Arbeitsfront was a powerful propaganda agency. Besides the "honor of work," the concept of the "beauty of work" was proclaimed and promoted. Under this heading, for instance, the Arbeitsfront concerned itself to see that the lighting and ventilation of shops was improved, that recreational space was procured, that the place of work was beautified, and that gardens were "voluntarily" laid out on factory grounds. Under pressure of the Arbeitsfront, industry spent hundreds of millions annually on such improvements.

The most important duty of the Arbeitsfront was delegated to its affiliate Strength through Joy. Kraft durch Freude represented the ambitious attempt to regulate the workers' leisure time on a collective basis. To leave the individual to his own devices was not permissible, since a totalitarian state cannot tolerate private life. Recreation also had to be directed into channels which led to communal activities under the care of functionaries in brown uniform. Not only class distinctions, but also individual differences were negated. Personal initiative in the utilization of leisure time was progressively eliminated, for Kraft durch Freude took care of everything—vacation trips, theater productions, gymnastics and every kind of sports, lectures, and courses. The Arbeitsfront built or chartered steamers, built or bought giant resort hotels in the mountains or on the seashore, rented special trains and buses; all these facilities were at the members' disposal at moderate prices the workers could afford. Some of the projects were subsidized, but most were self-supporting, costs being cut by mass participation. The Arbeitsfront had an annual income of several hundred million RM procured by a levy of 1.5 per cent on all wages and salaries; this was added to the 6 per cent tax for unemployment relief which was still levied after unemployment had disappeared, and to the contributions for the other social insurance schemes.

However great may have been the new social achievements which many observers credited to Hitler, the workers had to pay a price: they lost their liberties, among others their freedom of movement. In a growing number of industries the employed were prohibited from leaving their jobs without permission of the authorities. If they insisted they lost their claims to unemployment insurance. Each worker was given a work book which contained information on all his places of employment. This meant that the individual blue- or white-collar worker sank back to the status of state serfdom. Not everyone was aware of this fact. On the other hand no worker could be dismissed at will by his employer; his dismissal could only be ordered on true or alleged political grounds by the party representative on the spot. Labor was assigned to industries in the same way and according to the same criteria as raw materials, and naturally in all cases the state had first claim. Thus after 1938 every worker could be drafted for trench work or other assignments in any place at any time. His family stayed at home and was entitled to relief at fixed rates.

UNDER PARTY COMMAND

Without seeming to notice it, within the space of a few months labor had lost its once mighty bastions. The groupings described so far were only one sector in a comprehensive organizational system.

The one reliable pillar of the totalitarian system, the party, gradually laid its hand on all and sundry. Membership in the party itself had to be reserved to a limited number of persons. In order not to insulate these more or less trustworthy followers from the rest of the people, but on the contrary to draw the entire nation together under immediate party influence, an auxiliary structure typical of totalitarian regimes was used. The various professional and interest groups were amalgamated in associations with politically innocent-sounding names and defined civic purposes. Thus the teachers were collected in the NS (*Nationalsozialistischer*) *Lehrerbund,* the academic professors in the NS *Dozentenbund,* the lawyers in the NS *Rechtswahrerbund,* the physicians in the NS *Ärztebund,* the civil servants in the *Reichsbund deutscher Beamten,* and so forth. Even charities could not be left outside party control: the NS *Volkswohlfahrt* (for the welfare of all and sundry), the NS *Kriegsopferversorgung* (for war veterans), and the *Winterhilfswerk* (to help the poor in winter) were party projects. Sports clubs were combined in the NS *Reichsbund für Leibesübungen.* The most intensive, truly inescapable influence was exerted on the young, who in 1936 were turned over by law to the *Hitler-Jugend,* which was to educate them "in the spirit of National Socialism and for the service to the people and the people's community." This law condemned to dissolution the youth groups still freely operating. This was also the fate of countless other large and small associations, scientific societies, and similar private groups which, deprived of any possibility of free action, disbanded or perished by attrition.

Within only a few years of Hitler's advent to power hardly anyone was left outside the reach of the party or its auxiliary organizations. Whoever was not yet "organized" came under suspicion. Thus many yielded to pressure and joined one of the more harmless-looking party auxiliaries such as the NS Volkswohlfahrt or the *Reichsluftschutzbund* (for protection against air attacks) or the *NS Fliegerkorps* (pilots) in order to escape membership in the genuine party formations, especially the SA and the SS, the NS *Kraftfahrerkorps* (motorists), and the NS *Frauenschaft* (women's corps). But even the less militant groups were not allowed to elect their governing boards or to decide on their own affairs. This would have smacked of democracy and liberalism, and hardly anything existed for which Hitler had found words of deeper contempt in *Mein Kampf*.

4. *The Second World War*

ONLY TWENTY YEARS after the first world war Germany was again being driven toward a horrendous conflict. She had pursued the first war to the point of military, political, and economic collapse, and had paid for it with the lives of 1.8 million able-bodied citizens, the impairment of her people's health, and the loss of her overseas possessions, one-eighth of her home territory, and one-tenth of her inhabitants. Anyone in possession of his senses had to tell himself that another war might bring the political if not the physical end of the Reich, especially if Germany were the instigator of the war and placed herself before the world in the position of a felon.

HITLER'S WAR AIMS

What should never have happened did happen. Hitler's determination to risk a war dated back at least as far as 1937, as proved by the so-called Hossbach Protocol, a record of one of Hitler's addresses to the top officers of the Wehrmacht. His declared purpose was to conquer more Lebensraum. Since regaining the old colonies was out of the question, all he could mean was the conquest of the less densely populated territories across Germany's eastern borders. The claim to these lands was bolstered with the notion of the alleged racial superiority of the German nation and revived legends of German colonizing feats in the East. Neither the fact that both Belgium and Britain had a much greater population density than Germany and yet had a much higher standard of living, nor even the terrifying possibility that in a defeated and territorially crippled Germany more people might have to live than ever before, could be imagined, much less be discussed aloud.

Although Hitler's goals lay in Poland and Russia, his policy of bluster, his repudiation of treaties, and finally his attack on Poland drew him inescapably into conflict with Britain and France. In order to protect the rear and prevent a two-front war from erupting once more, a blunder for which he had berated the men of 1914 in *Mein Kampf* with words of strongest condemnation, he decided that Germany must enter an unnatural alliance. In August, 1939, he concluded a nonaggression pact (the Ribbentrop-Stalin Pact) with Stalin, a man whom he had previously singled out from among all his adversaries for the crudest vituperation and whom he had offended by forming the so-called Anti-Comintern Pact with Italy and Japan. The price Hitler had to pay was a share of his prospective Polish conquest and the delivery of the Baltic republics into Russian dominion. This cleared the way in September, 1939, toward the destruction of Poland and the campaigns against the countries to the north, west, and southeast.

In the spring of 1940 first Denmark and Norway were overpowered, then France, Belgium, and the Netherlands. When finally the last resisting Balkan countries, Yugoslavia, Albania, and Greece, were subdued and the German armies were in command of the central territories on the European continent, Hitler became audacious enough to break the Ribbentrop-Stalin Pact and to attack Soviet Russia itself. On June 22, 1941, the German armies were ordered to start the fateful campaign against Russia, "in order to secure for the German people the soil on this earth which is its due." This "soil," according to Hitler, "on which future generations of German peasant stock will be able to rear mighty sons will justify the sacrifice of some sons of today." With these words of *Mein Kampf* Hitler had already proclaimed his true aims in 1926.

ECONOMIC MOBILIZATION

In contrast to the first world war the second did not find Germany unprepared. Repeatedly the man responsible for German destinies had conjured up the threat of a war: in 1935 he proclaimed general conscription; in 1936 he militarized the Rhineland; in 1938 he ordered the annexation of the Sudetenland and the march into Austria; and finally in March, 1939, he directed the seizure of what was left of Czechoslovakia. Only when on September 1, 1939, Hitler, without having consulted the shocked German population, ordered the attack on Poland did Britain and France decide to resist. The second world war began.

There was no need to reorganize the German economy from a peacetime to a wartime status. Economic mobilization had begun three years earlier with the second Four-Year Plan, when the order of the day was that Germany had to be made as independent as humanly possible from the world outside. Placing the economy on a war footing had received further impetus with every consecutive foreign crisis, the repeated military mobilizations, and finally, in 1938–39, the construction in nervous haste of the *"Westwall,"* a system of fortifications along the Franco-German border. After 1936 rationing and state control of prices played a growing role, and the consumer had to get used to the rationing of scarce foods one year before the war. Thus in peacetime, if such it could be called, the economy had already attained a high degree of war preparedness. The transition to actual fighting could therefore be carried through without major changes.

As was shown above, the coveted economic independence of Germany from foreign countries had by no means been achieved. Not more than 80 per cent of the minimum needs in food supplies were assured from domestic sources, and the raw material requirements of industry could be met only with certain critical exceptions. Above all oil and other fuels were in short supply, as were iron ore and nonferrous metals such as copper, nickel, manganese, chrome, wolfram, and zinc, as well as fibers, leather, and so forth. When the war started Germany was still importing 70 per cent of the iron ore needed by her industry, 80 per cent of copper, 65 per cent of petroleum and rubber, 50 per cent of fibers, 45 per cent of hides and pelts, and nearly 100 per cent of manganese, nickel, wolfram, and chrome. The production in quantity of synthetic rubber began during the war, and after 1942 minimum rubber requirements could be met from domestic production. Otherwise, except for coal, nitrates, potash, cement, timber, and electric power, the Reich hardly disposed of sufficient supplies of raw materials and producer goods. That Britain would again, as in the first war, cripple Germany's overseas trade with a blockade could not be doubted. Germany's only important allies, Italy and Japan, were themselves short of raw materials and dependent on imports, Italy even being dependent on German aid.

Only two lines of recourse remained: first, in the southeast, Germany's supplies of grain for bread, several other foodstuffs, and oil had to be procured from the resources of the Balkan states, which immediately found themselves under massive political pressure. Rumania, with its grain surplus and its oil fields, ranked especially high in German calculations. Second, in the north, neutral Sweden could provide Germany with high-grade iron ore. To safeguard against surprises at least for a few months, stocks of grain and of some of the scarce metals had previously been accumulated. They were supposed to fill the gap until self-sufficiency could be attained by forcible expansion of the German Lebensraum. Hitler never contemplated a long-drawn-out war. This was proved not only by his military but also by his economic strategy.

INTOXICATED WITH SUCCESS

In the beginning the progress of the war seemed to justify Hitler's and his henchmen's claims of easy success. The rapid defeat of Poland did not yet bear the coveted economic fruit, for this country which had no considerable agricultural surpluses even in peacetime now lay in ruins. But soon Hitler's military triumphs over nearly all of Europe were to ease his worries. Hitler countered Britain's attempt to cut Germany off from Swedish ore when in April, 1940, he occupied Denmark and overpowered unprepared Norway's brief and hopeless resistance. Immediately thereafter Hitler commanded and carried out the conquest of France, Belgium, and the Netherlands. In the spring of 1941 he had consolidated his domination of continental Europe for three years to come. Now Germany had at her disposal the ore mines and agricultural surpluses of France; she had the use of Swedish ore and Rumanian oil; she exploited Polish coal mines and forests; she received Hungarian and Rumanian surpluses of grain and meat; the industrial complexes of Austria and Czechoslovakia were expanded in haste; armies of millions of foreign workers were conscripted and set to work. Britain's dreaded weapon, the blockade, had been blunted, the prophecies of a rapid economic collapse of the Reich had become untenable.

For a while it even seemed that Britain, not Germany, would have to worry about necessary supplies. After the collapse of France, Britain at first stood facing its enemies alone. It had to sustain the full force of German air attacks and was under the immediate threat of invasion by German troops. At the same time the ruthlessly pursued submarine war hit the British Isles where it hurt most. The tonnage of cargo ships lost rose from 2.1 million gross register tons in 1941 to 6.2 million in the following year when the Battle of the Atlantic reached its climax. Food for the British people became scarce indeed.

On the other hand, during the first years of the war German food supplies at worst held steady at their peacetime levels, and occasionally even became somewhat more ample and diversified. It now proved a psychological blessing that the nation had not been used to material plenty even before the war, for the war economy was not regarded as oppressive, and the popular mood which, contrary to the widespread legends of German war lust, had been badly depressed at the outbreak of the war, began to improve. Evidently the war was not as onerous and Germany's situation not as precarious as had been feared. Did not Hitler's successes have to be accepted as an uncontrovertible reality? Was not the Western world in its decadence ripe for its downfall just as the official propaganda maintained? Could Germany ever again suffer defeat? These were the questions in many people's minds.

An objective judgment would have had to recognize that in military and economic preparedness Germany enjoyed an advantage of about two years over her foremost adversaries. By 1938 one-quarter of total German production was already devoted to war preparation. France lost the opportunity of catching up, but Britain, after rescuing her troops from Dunkirk in May, 1940, rearmed with all possible speed and was able within a comparatively short time to reach and surpass the German production figures in airplanes, trucks, tanks, and other vehicles.

While Britain, after the hour of its greatest peril, was straining all its forces, Hitler, dazed by his triumphs, believed no further economic exertions were necessary. In a speech after France's downfall he declared that it would now be possible to reconvert a part of war production facilities to civilian uses as there were stocks of arms and ammunition in plenty. A time without worries followed in which it was assumed that guns *and* butter would be available. This illusory abundance induced Hitler, as late as autumn 1941 when the Russian war was already on, to cut down on armament production. Only a few months later, of course, this order had to be rescinded.

In fact German industrial production made no progress at all from 1939 to 1942. Nevertheless goods and services available are likely to have increased somewhat because the occupied territories delivered their contributions to supplying the Reich.

A report on *The Effects of Strategic Bombing on the German War Economy,* worked out after the war by a team of British and American economists, characterized the first three war years as follows:

> The outstanding feature of the German war effort is the surprisingly low output of armaments in the first three years of the war. . . . For these early years the conclusion is inescapable that Germany's war production was not limited by her war potential—by the resources at her disposal—but by demand; in other

words, by the notions of the German war leaders as to what was required for achieving their aim." (U.S. Strategic Bombing Survey, Overall Economic Effects Division, October 31, 1945, p. 6.)

Before 1942 hardly any war plants worked more than one shift, and the number of working hours per man and day was raised only inconsiderably above peacetime levels. The average weekly hours worked in industry, about 47.8 in 1939, rose to a maximum of 49.1 in March, 1943. In contrast to Britain, women were employed in war work only late and in insufficient numbers; girls in domestic service were even more plentiful toward the end of the war than at its beginning.

Table 18 shows in what comparative abundance civilian consumption was allowed to be maintained, how naively and with what levity the forces of the adversaries were underrated, and how large the untapped reserves of German industry remained up to the year 1943.

TABLE *18*

Index of German Industrial Production, 1939–44
(1938 = 100)

	1939	*1940*	*1941*	*1942*	*1943*	*1944*
Total industry	106	102	105	106	119	117
Consumption goods	100	95	96	87	91	87
Armaments	125	220	220	320	500	425

SOURCE: Deutsches Institut für Wirtschaftsforschung, *Die deutsche Industrie im Kriege 1939–1945* (Berlin, 1954), p. 173.

The strategy of the Blitzkrieg produced two further and fateful consequences. First, it created the initial temptation to attack Russia, whose military might, on the analogy to the French example, was to be annihilated within a few weeks or months. Once again the initial success, with several terrible defeats of the Red Army, seemed to prove Hitler's tactics to be correct. Even after the inroads of winter and the first Russian counterstrokes had halted the German armies at the outskirts of Moscow, the German leadership did not believe a Napoleonic ending was possible. On the contrary, in the early summer of 1942 the German armies once more made a deep penetration into the wide open spaces of Russia. Hitler's dream of Lebensraum almost came true with the Ukrainian grain fields and the rich coal mines of the Donets basin in his hands and the oil fields of Baku seemingly within reach.

The second consequence of the Blitzkrieg strategy and its rapid early successes was that the absence of purposeful central planning of the country's entire production, which had characterized the first six years of Hitler's regime, was allowed to continue into the war years. The report on strategic bombing cited above describes this as follows:

> It must be emphasized that throughout this period the German economy met the limited demands placed upon it, not only without evidence of strain, but also without controls. The Wehrmacht supply offices were, until well into 1942, Germany's only war mobilization agencies and exercised power only over munitions producing enterprises. They had no control over the bulk of the economy, which was permitted to operate in a leisurely, semipeacetime fashion under the loose supervision of Funk's Economic Ministry. (*The Effects of Strategic Bombing on the German War Economy,* U.S. Strategic Bombing Survey, Overall Economic Effects Division, October 31, 1945, p. 23.)

The longstanding system of government price regulation and rationing was extended to cover more goods, but for the rest the system of war economy still differed little from the totalitarian "peace economy." Planning as well as execution lagged far behind the requirements of a large-scale aggressive war such as this.

Hitler's war strategy really would have demanded rigid planning of production and procurement on the basis of priorities extending to the entire economy and under the direction of the much-vaunted German talent for organization. In fact, however, no list of priorities and no central planning agency with comprehensive powers of decision existed. Instead, a number of "demand bearers" (*Bedarfsträger*) competed with each other for the use of raw materials and production facilities. As it turned out, the Wehrmacht and its supplier industries were so convinced of their priority that supply problems seemed to solve themselves automatically. The Wehrmacht agents handed their orders to their contractors, who in turn demanded and promptly received steel, oil, coal, chemicals, and so forth, as a rule in quantities even in excess of their immediate needs. Thus many raw materials were wasted on the production of unnecessary goods and were then unavailable for more essential purposes. Scarcity and abundance existed side by side.

Yet it would be erroneous to infer from the mistakes and failures of planning that Germany's defeat in the second world war is explainable by a series of missed opportunities. Neither thorough planning of production nor the timely mobilization of every last potential reserve could have saved Germany from ultimate catastrophe. However much Germany could do, the war would be won by those who had the larger capacity to produce airplanes, tanks, warships, and munitions, and therefore from the outset Germany had no chance to succeed. It was no secret that Britain, Russia, and the United States could together produce three times the war materials of every description that could be produced by the Axis powers, Germany, Italy, and Japan. Only an almost incredible lack of economic common sense and criminal arrogance could have misguided the Reich leadership into believing that their aggressive war could be won.

FINANCING THE WAR

In its methods of financing the war the Reich leadership also followed the line of least resistance. The same methods employed before for job creation and rearmament now continued to be applied, only on a much larger scale. The lessons that the first world war should have taught them had not been understood by the Reich leaders in either their political and military or their economic and financial implications. Only the man who had brought about the "financial miracle" of the 1930's, Hjalmar Schacht, took alarm when he saw what spirits he had summoned from the deep. In 1937 he resigned as Economics Minister (with Walter Funk as successor) and in 1939 as president of the Reichsbank.

There are, as noted before, only three possible methods of procuring the means for government purchases of armament materiel: either through additional taxation, or through loans extended by the private sector, or through recourse to the central bank. The first two methods make the costs and the shortages of wartime immediately visible to the public and thereby tend to counteract inflation. The third method creates the semblance of abundance—a true abundance of money, but not of goods. If this method is not to lead rapidly to open inflation, a price freeze and strict rationing must be enforced.

The second world war was mainly financed in Germany by the latter two methods. The mirage of a swift victory, to be followed by the losers being burdened with the war costs, prompted the leadership to employ the same easy financial methods as in the first world war. Instead of adjusting public consumption at once to war conditions, as Britain did, the German government permitted matters to drift. At the beginning of the war the rates of income and corporation taxes as well as of several consumer taxes were indeed raised, but the top rates for higher incomes were kept far below those exacted by the democratic governments of the United Kingdom and the United States in their time of peril. During the war less than one-third of

Reich expenditures was covered by taxation. Approximately 10 per cent of total government revenue came from the occupied countries in the form of payments for occupation costs and war contributions.

More than one-half of the financial requirements was not covered and had to be borrowed. For this purpose the Reich offered to the banks, savings institutions, and insurance companies the same kind of highly liquid bills of indebtedness described on page 148, which were readily rediscounted by the Reichsbank. Since in wartime almost everybody has disposable money and therefore private credits are not much in demand, the financial institutions were most willing to invest their liquid funds in these interest-bearing bills. In the measure in which they made use of the Reichsbank rediscount facilities, they had additional funds at their disposal. Thus, behind this "noiseless" method of war financing, much praised at the time, again stood the Reichsbank and nothing else. An immense volume of money accumulated, which for a time was hidden behind the curtain of bank balances. After the war it made itself felt as an oppressive burden.

TABLE 19

Reich Revenues, Expenditures, and Debt, 1939–45
(in billions of RM, for two fiscal years)

	1939–41	*1941–43*	*1943–45*
Total expenditure	130.1	230.5	324.3
For armaments	90.4	172.5	246.3
Current income	72.0	121.7	136.5
From taxes	51.7	75.0	75.5
Reich debt at end of period	86.0	195.6	379.8

SOURCE: *Statistisches Handbuch von Deutschland 1928–1944* (Munich, 1949), p. 555.

In the six wartime budget years, April 1, 1939, to March 31, 1945, the Reich (without the federal states and municipalities) spent 685 billion Reichsmarks. Of these, approximately 510 billion, almost three-quarters, went for the war and armaments proper (excluding relief to Wehrmacht dependents) and in an economic sense were a sheer loss. However, these figures fail to characterize even vaguely the true war burdens which extend far into the future. The bankruptcy balance sheet of Hitler's Third Reich, represented by the Reich debt, stood at almost 400 billion Reichsmarks when the war ended. Since the Reich debt was reported at 48 billion marks on April 1, 1940, an inflation loss of almost 350 billion appears, a loss which had to be borne for the most part by the Reich citizens themselves insofar as they had owned cash, bank deposits, or liquid assets.

THE WAR OUTLOOK DARKENS

Two almost simultaneous events clearly disclosed even to the National Socialists that the war would not end soon and that the efforts exerted so far were insufficient: America's entry into the war in December, 1941, and the first military reverses in Russia during the winter campaign of 1941–42. The full seriousness of the situation even then eluded the perception of Hitler and his entourage, however.

At least the need for precise planning in order to supply military and civilian requirements was now recognized. The Minister of Armaments and Munitions, Fritz Todt, whose duty such planning would have been, died in an accident in February, 1942. He was replaced by Hitler's architect, Albert Speer, and with him a new era began. The loose negotiations between the Wehrmacht, the Reichsbank, the industries and other agencies, through which the various requirements for steel and other critical materials had somehow been adjusted, were replaced in the spring of 1942 by a new Central Planning Agency (*Amt für zentrale Planung*). The Wehrmacht's orders retained their priority. In place of the free choice as to suppliers previously exercised by the Wehrmacht's various procurement agencies, the Speer ministry took entire control of all Wehrmacht procurement and decided which plants were to receive what orders and finally also which production methods were to be used. Numerous uneconomic plants were closed down. Industry was charged with developing technically and economically rational production methods and with using capacities to better effect. Competing plants were combined to form organizations under expert management by industrialists and technicians, who were given full powers to regulate entire fields of industry. Many existing industrial groups were unwilling to give up their inefficient activities, however, and so instead of one strictly rational organization, another unwieldy confusion of controlling agencies developed which worked partly with and partly against each other. Statistics and reporting were in a grotesque maze; for instance, the watch industry, which now had to produce ammunition, fuses, machine parts, and measuring instruments, belonged to about a dozen different committees, task forces, industrial groups, and craft and subsidiary groups and had to obey as many different commanding and controlling agencies.

Despite such drawbacks due to its rapid improvisation, Speer's agency achieved astounding results of rationalization within a short time. Not only was production increased, but great savings were also made in raw materials and labor. The production of arms and ammunition, which had been stagnating in 1941, increased in the first months of the Speer era, March to July, 1942, by no less than 55 per cent. This would not have been possible had capacities been used fairly rationally before. Speer's successes clearly show in what an unprofessional and heedless way things had been managed.

In the first phase of increased production all kinds of armaments profited more or less equally. Later, as military techniques underwent rapid change, production concentrated on tanks and airplanes. Adjustment to this new program was completed by November, 1942. In the second phase, within half a year tank production rose two and one-half times, the production of aircraft and weapons of all sorts by well over 60 per cent.

Now the production of consumer goods had to be sacrificed to war needs in considerable measure. To set labor free for more essential purposes, consumer products were reduced to a small number of models and production was concentrated on the most efficient plants. Total production of consumer goods was cut by 10 per cent. The supply of foodstuffs still remained fairly high, partly due to forced importation from occupied countries, which fared less well. However, whereas statistics seem to show that, measured in calories, the nation was supplied in the fourth year of war, 1943–44, just as well as it had been in the first, the impression conveyed is too favorable. The people's diet was now dominated by vegetable products. Bread, cereals, and potatoes were in such ample supply that rationing was hardly necessary. In contrast, during the first four war years rations of eggs and meat had to be reduced by almost one-half, those of animal fats and edible oils by well over one-fourth.

The supply of clothing, household appliances, and other consumer goods was much poorer. After 1942 not even one-half the prewar supply was available. For instance, in 1943 of 1,000 men only 4 could be supplied with a suit, one with a winter coat, 16 with work pants, and 31 with a shirt. Quality was inferior. When in 1943 the air attacks multiplied and people began to suffer in earnest, they had already been drawing on their reserves for many years. Essential objects of daily use had now to be reserved for bombed out households. Thus, despite an output of consumer goods that was statistically rather high and which in 1943 rose somewhat over the preceding year, there were noticeable shortages. Yet, the full weight of the war had still not been felt.

TOTAL WAR

A last call to supreme effort was sounded at the beginning of 1943 by a turn in the war which struck a body blow to Germany's military might: the defeat at Stalingrad and the simultaneous expulsion of the German armies from North Africa. Stalingrad, where an entire army was lost and the eastern front crumbled—it could be painfully reconstituted only several hundred miles to the west—and El Alamein, where Marshall Rommel's Africa Corps was defeated, signaled Hitler's impending downfall. The legend of the unconquerable German armies had lost its glamor and every German citizen was confronted with the grim question of whether this war could still be won. At last it began to dawn even on Hitler and his crowd how serious their predicament was and what sacrifices they would have to exact. In a rousing speech in the Berlin Sportpalast on February 19, 1943, Josef Goebbels, the party's master propagandist, proclaimed "total war." The time of the peacelike war economy was past. All men between the ages of 16 and 65 and all women from 17 to 45 years of age were made subject to conscription, with exceptions for valid health or family reasons.

The Wehrmacht's losses in men and materials became more severe. The capitulation at Stalingrad had cost 91,000 prisoners. In the preceding battle the casualties were considerably higher still. Up to 1941 more than six million men had been mobilized into Wehrmacht service, and by the end of 1943 this had increased to 12 million. The consequent manpower shortage in industry could be compensated for only to a modest degree with female workers. In many cases workers from other countries were recruited to work side by side with prisoners of war in filling the jobs the conscripts had vacated. Instead of highly skilled workers the plants now had to use mostly unskilled laborers, and yet a further considerable increase in production was achieved. Again the Speer ministry excelled. As far as feasible production was broken up into simple technical processes which could be managed by unskilled workers under the supervision of a few professionals.

Between the end of 1941 and mid-1944 employment in armaments work rose by only 28 per cent, but war production rose by 230 per cent, for which only about 50 per cent more iron was required. Rationalization together with the simplification of weapon models were responsible for the improved efficiency. For instance, far more assault guns were now manufactured, since

TABLE 20

Composition of the German Labor Force, 1939–44
(in millions)

	CIVILIAN LABOR FORCE			ARMED FORCES †
	Germans	*Foreigners* *	*Total*	
End of May, 1939	39.1	0.3	39.4	1.4
End of May, 1940	34.8	1.2	36.0	5.7
End of May, 1941	33.1	3.0	36.1	7.4
End of May, 1942	31.3	4.2	35.5	9.4
End of May, 1943	30.4	6.3	36.6	11.2
End of September, 1944	28.4	7.5	35.9	13.0

* Including prisoners of war.

† Including fatalities.

SOURCE: Deutsches Institut für Wirtschaftsforschung, *Die deutsche Industrie im Kriege 1939–1945* (Berlin, 1954), p. 139.

these in many cases served the same purposes as the much more complicated and expensive tanks of the Tiger and Panther type.

In this phase of total war the armaments industry advanced to the very limits of available raw material resources, although no marked cuts in production were as yet made. The only really serious material deficiency, dating back to 1942, was in petroleum. Many persons converted their cars by replacing the gasoline motor with a wood-distilling apparatus.

The Reich still had access to the resources of the occupied countries. Even after the catastrophe of Stalingrad the Reich got from them about one-third of the aluminum it extracted and one-third of the iron ore it mined, about one-half its requirements in rayon, flax, hemp, and in pyrites and other basic chemicals, about three-fourths of its cellulose, and 30 per cent of its pulp and many other materials. After the war it was widely assumed that the production of basic materials (motor fuels and transportation excepted) had not in general been a limiting factor for the growing armaments requirements—this being the conclusion of the often cited Strategic Bombing Survey—yet one might doubt this judgment. But for the fact that material shortages did exist it would be incomprehensible that, despite desperate efforts to increase armament production, one-shift work still predominated in the factories. Without material shortages it would indeed be surprising that only about 10 per cent of the workers were employed in second or third shifts.

THE SECOND COLLAPSE

After the climactic reversal of the campaign in the Russian theater of war, Germany was on the defensive on all fronts. In the autumn of 1942 Marshall Rommel's Africa Corps lost ground to superior British forces. Soon the Americans appeared and compelled the German troops to leave North Africa. In July, 1943, the British-American attacks on Southern Europe began with the landings in Sicily and Southern Italy, and soon Mussolini's dictatorship fell to pieces. On the Channel coasts, it was no longer the British who lived in expectation of an invasion, but instead the German armies, decimated as they were by the losses on the Russian and Italian fronts. Now the drawbacks of Hitler's lightning victories and of extending German domination to so many countries became apparent. The more territory he dominated, the thinner his military defense had to be spread. It would no longer be impossible for the Allies to find in the thousands of miles of front the weak spots on which to exert their full force to achieve a breakthrough.

The Battle of the Atlantic and the battle in the air were both lost. The electronic spotting of ships and airplanes (radar), developed only during the war, had rapidly revolutionized air and ocean warfare and at last terminated the submarine threat. What finally decided the German collapse was the crushing superiority of the American and British air forces. To try to compete with American war production was an utter delusion. Before 1943 the productive power and the resistance of the German nation had not been seriously impaired by the war in the air; now the situation of the population deteriorated month by month. The attacks of the British and American bomber squadrons on the German cities grew in number and intensity.

In the first half of 1944 alone more bombs were dropped on Germany than in all four preceding years combined. One after the other the large cities were turned into rubble and ashes, while small towns, individual industrial plants, and transportation centers were also leveled through saturation bombing. Apart from destroying the towns the Allied air forces tried to cripple all of Germany's industry, or at least her war industry, by selecting key industries. Thus first the few ball-bearing factories were hit, among them those in Schweinfurt, Steyr (Austria), Bad Cannstadt, Erkner, Leipzig, and Elberfeld. After this the attacks singled out the submarine pens with their auxiliary industries and the docks; further targets were the airplane factories and the air fields, attacked in order to eliminate the *Luftwaffe*. Toward the end, oil refineries and storage facilities, plants to produce

TABLE 21

Bombs Dropped on Axis Europe by British and U.S. Strategic Air Forces, 1940–45
(in thousands of tons)

1940	12
1941	34
1942	46
1943	187
1944 January–June	406
July–December	684
1945 January–April	437

SOURCE: U.S. Strategic Bombing Survey, *The Effects of Strategic Bombing on the German War Economy,* Overall Economic Effects Division, Washington, D.C. (October 31, 1945), pp. 2–5.

synthetic rubber, and all transportation centers became strategic targets of the enemy air forces.

In the midst of the air offensive, the Allies mounted their decisive land offensive on the continent of Europe. In the early morning of June 6, 1944, they landed in Normandy, undeterred by the Atlantic Wall which had been erected with great effort to keep them off. Once more the will to resist was whipped up by the propaganda machine of the Third Reich. Hints were circulated about secret miracle weapons, which now indeed made their first appearance: the V-1, a small unmanned airplane or flying bomb, and the V-2, a rocket. They became operational only after the invasion began and were directed against the ports that supplied the Allied troops and against London in retaliation for the air raids on Germany. All efforts were concentrated on these new weapons, but they came too late, their accuracy was insufficient, and their numbers were too small to influence the course that events were now bound to take. As the invasion force advanced through France, London was soon out of range, and all other possibilities for obtaining military results from these miracle weapons became almost negligible.

Allied tank columns crossed the German frontiers simultaneously from the west and from the east. Once again the men in power tried to escape a quick collapse. In September, 1944, all men between the ages of 16 and 60 not yet conscripted were called up to serve in the National Assault (*Volkssturm*). These hastily assembled and mostly untrained units were thrown against the advancing armies. At the end of December the German leadership managed to inflict a last severe reverse on the Allies in the Battle of the Ardennes, but the attempted breakthrough to Liege came to a halt after three days. Meanwhile the Allies' superiority in the air had become so overwhelming that in daytime no planned movements were possible on the roads or by rail. As enemy mosquito bombers chased every single locomotive, disorganization became all-inclusive. With his still effectual and dreaded power to command Hitler forbade under penalty of death ordering any retreat. Germany was to be defended to the last square foot.

UNCONDITIONAL SURRENDER

From the very beginning Hitler and his team had been united in the determination that the war, once begun, must not end as in 1918 in surrender, should it be lost. In a speech at the outbreak of the war Hitler had exclaimed: "One word I have never learned to say: capitulation. . . . I wish to assure the world at large: a November, 1918, will never repeat itself in German history!" This made it certain beyond doubt that even a hopeless war would be continued as long as Hitler was alive. Faced with such an attitude and recalling the world's bitter experience with Hitler's Germany, the Allies had agreed among themselves that nothing but unconditional surrender could end the war with National Socialist Germany (agreements of Casablanca, 1943, and Quebec, 1944, between Churchill and Roosevelt; agreements of Teheran, 1944, and Yalta, 1945, between Churchill, Roosevelt, and Stalin).

The determination of patriotic officers and civilians to do away with Hitler and his clique in order to save the country from final destruction failed in the abortive attempt on Hitler's life of July 20, 1944; Hitler's revenge was taken at the cost of thousands of lives. Thus it was ordained that the militarily senseless war would continue into the cataclysm, which was finally reached with the armies in the east and west taken prisoner, with the towns and villages, roads and bridges, factories and public utilities under continuous bombardment, and with much of the population in chaotic mass flight to escape the onrushing Russian armies.

Only after Germany's occupation by the Allies did the extent of the crimes which had been committed under the symbol of the swastika come to light. Many Germans at first could not believe that the reports of the Allies were true and thought they were propaganda of the victors to justify harsh treatment of the defeated. Slowly the truth was revealed: in concentration camps and in infamous extermination establishments millions of men, women, and children had been murdered or had been left to perish from hunger, exhaustion, disease, or torture. The number of victims has never been even approximately ascertained, but it almost certainly adds up to six million. The large majority of the Jewish population of Germany and the countries she had occupied were among those killed. This frightful guilt of a criminal leadership will blacken the German name for generations.

When the end came, Hitler in his crazed condition proclaimed a scorched earth policy: the victors were to conquer nothing but a desert. This command was disobeyed wherever the disintegration of Nazi terror permitted evasion. Similarly, the call to wage a partisan war with packs of "werewolves" in the enemies' rear was no longer heeded. The German people, who to all appearances had stood so resolutely behind Hitler and who had showed hardly a sign of opposition to him, had now reached the end of the road. The subjects of the almighty state silently went their separate ways as soon as they ceased to feel its power.

Only against the Russians was the resistance carried on to the very last day in the vain hope that the Western Allies would march on as far as East Prussia. No one knew that the zones of occupation had been agreed upon long before and that the American and British forces would halt on the Elbe River while the Russians marched on into Berlin. Thus the capital city fell prey to the Red Army. When the Russian troops had advanced to the neighborhood of Hitler's bunker in the center of Berlin, he put an end to his life on April 30, 1945. Admiral Dönitz, whom Hitler had named in his testament as his successor, took over a government that existed only a few days. In the headquarters of General Dwight D. Eisenhower this government signed on May 7 the unconditional surrender of all German forces. Unconditional surrender also had to be offered to the Russians, and it was accepted by them on May 9. This is the day on which the Reich ceased to exist.

Hitler's Third Reich had lasted for twelve years, of which six were devoted to the war. Hitler's policies had led to the death of approximately 20 million people in Europe, of whom 6 million were citizens of the old Reich (4 million soldiers and almost 2 million civilians). To this number must be added about 1.5 million casualties among Germans abroad. But while biological losses, except those resulting from the years of hunger to follow, ended with the war, the political and economic catastrophe which Hitler had bequeathed to the German nation lingered on.

Politically, Germany had gambled away the elementary right of a nation to determine its own fate; in truth, there was no longer a German state. The territory was occupied by the four large victorious powers and by Poland,

and divided into five sovereignties. Economically, Germany's productive plant had been bombed into rubble, her storehouses were empty, her transportation facilities wrecked, her people wandering about in search of food, their families, and shelter.

What would now sustain the lives of these people? Would they ever recapture their inheritance from the past, their unity?

VI

THE PARTITION OF GERMANY

1. Under Allied Occupation

THE DOOM THAT now descended upon Germany can hardly be compared with what befell after the first world war. The collapse of 1918 had been bad enough. Then, too, the old Reich was totally defeated. But except for a brief incursion of the Russians into East Prussia at the beginning of the war, the fighting had not been carried on in Germany's own territory. In 1918 the government yielded to the armistice and peace conditions before one enemy soldier had crossed a German frontier. Despite the defeat and a considerable loss of territory the German Reich survived, and what was left of the German armies returned home without being molested by the erstwhile enemies. The soldiers could find their towns, their villages, their homes, their families. Except for the losses in dead and wounded and the biological damage incurred in the hungry years of the blockade, Germany had withstood the war unravaged. The productive plant and the transportation system were worn down, but they existed.

In the last phase of the second world war Germany herself had become the theater of war. Destruction did not cease before the last German soldier had laid down his arms and millions of his comrades were dead, wounded, or prisoners, nor before the last square foot of German soil had been conquered and Hitler's Reich wiped out. Germany was now an area without a state, a creature without a head or limbs, lacking its own law courts, administration, and constitution, utterly in the hands of the victors. No such catastrophe had faced the nation since the thirty years' war in the seventeenth century. The foreign powers had divided up their conquest into zones of occupation. The territory, already reduced in 1919, lost another quarter of its area; one-tenth of the people had been killed, the population was exposed to hunger, millions were without shelter or belongings, communications with the outside world were broken off. Railroads, mails, and telephones were out of commission, no newspaper could be printed; Germany had lost her voice. She had been carried back to the year zero of her political history. Did this Germany have any existence at all or was it but a geographical notion, politically a part of France, Britain, Poland, Russia, and the United States?

Everything now depended on what the Allies would do with the conquered land. However conflicting their interests may have been before the war, when confronted with Hitler's raids of conquest the Allies united, as a matter of self-preservation, for the one common objective of defeating Germany. Now this objective had been realized. Would the old conflicts spring up again in the face of the problem of how to deal with the defeated?

THE FOUR-POWER GOVERNMENT

Four weeks after the end of the war, on June 5, 1945, the four great powers who shared the occupation of Germany proclaimed that they had assumed supreme control over the country. They instituted the Allied Control Council as the central government. It consisted of the four supreme commanders of the Allied occupation forces and the administrative commands attached to them, with headquarters in Berlin. Members of the four powers took over all important administrative offices. Each of the four supreme commanders had complete executive power and sole responsibility for the territory under his command. The limits of the occupation zones had been drawn up in February, 1945, in the Yalta Agreement, and now the supreme commanders ordered their troops, as far as they were not already located in their respective zones at the end of the fighting, to take up their allotted positions. To the dismay of the people involved, the Americans vacated the federal states of Saxony (except for parts of Sachsen-Anhalt) and Thuringia which they had conquered, the British vacated parts of Mecklenburg, in order to turn these territories, as agreed, over to the Russians, who for their part allowed West Berlin to be occupied by the Western Allies.

For a time, the loose ties of the Allied Control Council precariously held together one central administration for all of Germany. However, this so-called Four-Power Government never achieved governmental authority. In fact the country was governed by each of the four military commanders who within their zones were responsible only to their own high commands. The Americans, British, and French acted along more or less parallel lines. Each power subdivided its zone into four parts under four military governments. Thus the three Western zones combined consisted of twelve (later eleven) state-like regions which did not in every instance correspond to the old federal *Länder* (states). The Americans organized military governments for Bavaria, Hesse, North Württemberg-North Baden, and Bremen; the British for Hamburg, Lower Saxony, North Rhine-Westphalia, and Schleswig-Holstein; the French for Lindau, Rhineland-Palatinate, South Baden, South Württemberg-Hohenzollern. In contrast with these arrangements, the Russians from the outset chose a centralized organization. Formally, they kept up the old Prussian division into provinces, but the territories in central Germany west of the Oder and Neisse Rivers were united under a single Soviet Military Administration, SMAD. What went on in eastern Germany, the provinces of Silesia, Pomerania, West Prussia, and East Prussia—the latter jointly occupied by Poland and Soviet Russia—at first remained uncertain and unknown.

THE POTSDAM CONFERENCE

Further decisions about the future fate of Germany were made at the Potsdam Conference of July 17–August 2, 1945. Still under the impact of the mortal danger to their countries and the victory won by their concerted effort, Harry S Truman for the United States, Winston Churchill (and, after his defeat in the general elections of July 26, Clement Attlee) for Britain, and Josef Stalin for the Soviet Union arrived at an understanding on the principles to be followed in the treatment of Germany. They imposed a sentence compared to which the fateful *Diktat* of Versailles of 1919 seemed almost benign. The German people were now to atone for "the terrible crimes committed under the leadership of those whom, in the hour of their success, they openly approved and blindly obeyed," as the Agreement expressed it.

The political part of the Potsdam Agreement signified that Germany remained decapitated and quartered. For the present, no central government was allowed to be formed and only the economic unity of the country was to be perpetuated. For this purpose a new central agency under Allied control was to be formed, "particularly in the fields of finance, transport, communications, foreign trade, and industry."

All matters affecting "Germany as a whole" were delegated to the Allied Control Council. But because this unnatural four-headed government had to be unanimous it soon turned out that decisions were arrived at only rarely, and then they were hardly in Germany's interest. The one thought the Allies had in common was to punish Germany, to uproot all traces of National Socialism, and to see to it that the German people would never again be in a position to bring down death and destruction upon the world. As soon as a positive action was on the agenda, however—for instance, the setting up of the projected central economic agency or indeed a decision about the shape of Germany's future—unanimity disappeared. The Allied Control Council having proved its inability to act, the zone commanders each took action on their own responsibility or under orders from their own governments.

Thus the idea of "Germany as a whole" more and more slipped into the realm of fiction, becoming a source not of consensus but of dissension among the Allies. Instead of the peace that the world craved after the fighting had ended, people found that the "German question" once again kept them in tension. According to the Potsdam Agreement, Germany's eastern frontiers remained undetermined until at some unspecified future time a peace treaty could be concluded. The former German territories east of the Oder and Neisse rivers were placed under Polish administration, a temporary solution which was in fact to last for decades. Northern East Prussia with the city of Königsberg was turned over to Soviet Russian sovereignty.

The economic clauses of the Potsdam Agreement were no less grievous than the political. In addition to the destruction and losses at home, Germany was now burdened with obligations toward the territories she had occupied and violated during the war. The damaged countries demanded reparations and effective guarantees against future threats. The Agreement provided that:

> Germany be compelled to compensate to the greatest possible extent for the loss and suffering that she has caused to the United Nations and for which the German people cannot escape responsibility . . . . [The] Allies will take in agreement together, now and in the future, the other measures necessary to assure that Germany never again will threaten her neighbors or the peace of the world.

Among other measures, the safeguards against future threats from Germany were to consist of making German industry incapable for all time of producing arms and war materials. The Potsdam Agreement did not determine precisely which industrial plants would and would not be allowed to function. But it contained a clause which declared that all "production of metals, chemicals, machinery, and other items that are directly necessary to a war economy shall be rigidly controlled and restricted . . . ." Directives for the execution of this clause, together with the list of the plants destined to be dismantled, were contained in the so-called Level of Industry Plan, issued by the Allied Control Council on March 28, 1946 after long discussions.

Three categories of reparations were demanded of Germany in execution of the Potsdam Agreement and the Level of Industry Plan: (1) all German property abroad, (2) the German navy and merchant fleet, and (3) the industrial installations designated for dismantling.

GERMAN PROPERTY ABROAD

While the war was still going on the nations at war with Germany that were not being occupied by her had seized all German assets in their own territories. Moreover, the powers which had reparations claims demanded the transfer of all German assets in neutral or nonbelligerent countries. This claim was not enforceable everywhere; later on in the war some countries refused to accede to this demand of the Allies. After the German Federal Government had been constituted, it entered into arrangements with Switzerland in 1950 and with Austria in 1957, which provided that German assets invested or deposited in these countries be restored to their owners. The United States, though a signatory to the Potsdam Agreement, was in due time willing to return German assets in part, and a settlement to this effect was signed on October 22, 1962.

A German estimate of the total foreign assets which Germany still owned at the end of the war puts them at 10 billion Reichsmarks. This does not include intangible assets such as patents, trademarks, and firm names which had also been taken over by the Allies and were lost to the German owners. These assets were estimated at another 10 billion. Patent protection against foreign countries was at first revoked inside Germany also, but the revocation was terminated for the Federal Republic in 1949, for the Russian zone in 1950.

The losses in German property rights abroad can only be assessed in rough approximation. Computing the physical assets seized by the Inter-Allied

Reparation Agency, IARA, a sum is found of about 1,000 million dollars at 1945 values. The amounts actually credited to reparations account came to only 293 million dollars at 1938 prices.

THE OCEANGOING FLEET AND AVIATION

By the Potsdam Agreement Germany was prohibited not only from building but also from owning ships. All seaworthy vessels had to be turned over to IARA. This ruling was not limited to warships, which in any case were regarded as booty and were not credited to the reparations account. At the outbreak of the war Germany had owned vessels totaling 4.5 million gross register tons, the fifth largest merchant fleet in the world. All oceangoing ships left at the end of the war had to be surrendered without compensation. This harsh measure was probably prompted by the recollection of the high-handed use Germany had made of the conquered units of the merchant fleets of the Netherlands, Norway, Greece, and others, which these countries now had laboriously to replace.

According to the IARA accounts, ships totaling 755,000 gross register tons were delivered, for which the reparations account was credited with 173 million Reichsmarks. According to unofficial German reports, almost 1.4 million gross register tons were actually transferred to Allied ownership. Years later many of these once German ships plowed the seven seas under different names and alien flags.

The prohibition against owning an ocean fleet condemned the main part of the German shipbuilding industry to idleness and potentially to dismantling. The floating docks which still existed and those parts of the shipbuilding plants which were usable for reparations, and which had not been designated for demolition, had to be surrendered to the reparations creditors and were hauled away. No ship under the German flag was in the future to ply the oceans; none was permitted to have more than 1,500 gross register tons, to have a speed exceeding 12 knots, or to be propelled by means other than steam. As a result of these measures, Germany was left with 140 steamships averaging over 45 years in age and usable only for coastal shipping.

These curbs remained in force only for a short time. Four years later, in April, 1949, a Washington agreement valid for the three Western zones permitted Germany to have ships up to 7,000 gross register tons, and after two further years the Federal Republic was freed from all restrictions on the construction of merchant ships or on civilian ocean traffic.

Restrictions parallel to those on shipping were imposed on aviation. Germany was neither to build nor to own airplanes or flying craft of any description. Even the practice of gliding and of balloon flying was prohibited, and to own a glider or a balloon was made illegal. These prohibitions continued in force in the three Western zones until 1955.

DISMANTLING AND REPARATIONS

The German population had been least prepared for the command to dismantle industrial installations. It expected harsh treatment after losing the war, but in view of the already incalculable destruction people could understand neither why the installations which had survived the bombing should not now be set to work, nor how anyone could profit by keeping Germany in perpetual destitution. Depression and despair spread; emigration and work as an agricultural laborer, household domestic, or chauffeur in any Western country seemed to many the only alternative to a life devoid of hope. When in May, 1947, two years after the end of the war, the majority of German prisoners of war in France were freed, 160,000 of them, a fifth of the total, decided to stay in France as free workers, preferring this lot for the present to returning to their families and homes.

THE LEVEL OF INDUSTRY PLAN

The devastation was far more severe and widespread after the second world war than it had been after the first. As a result, the victors were faced with an even greater temptation to heap economic burdens on Germany to such a degree as to preclude reasonable development. In fact, the Allies at first succumbed to this temptation, for the Level of Industry Plan of 1946 was simply a directive to hobble if not to destroy German industry.

In hindsight it is easy to state that the Allies' German policies of 1945 were misconceived. However, they followed almost necessarily from the horror and revulsion then felt in the entire world against Germany because of the immeasurable guilt she had heaped upon herself. At the Quebec Conference of September, 1944, Franklin D. Roosevelt and Winston S. Churchill had agreed upon the so-called Morgenthau Plan, named for Henry Morgenthau, then U.S. Secretary of the Treasury and Roosevelt's confidant. This plan contained the following sentences which are often quoted but were never implemented:

> . . . The industries in the Ruhr and the Saar would therefore [to destroy Germany's war potential] necessarily be put out of action, closed down. The districts

> should be put under some body of the World Organization which would supervise dismantling the industries, and make sure they are not started up again under some subterfuge. This program looks forward to converting Germany into a country principally agricultural and pastoral.

Had the Quebec Agreement and the Morgenthau Plan been implemented, the major part of German industry would have had to be dismantled.

At first this program was favorably regarded by all four Allied powers, even France and Russia who had not been signatories of the Quebec Agreement. Parts of these two countries had been severely devastated by the war and the German occupation; retribution and compensation were expected. Accordingly, the Allied Control Council set unhesitatingly to work at the job of destroying German war potential for what was then believed to be all time to come. The result was the "Plan of the Allied Control Council for Reparations and the Level of Post-War German Economy" of March, 1946, briefly referred to as the Level of Industry Plan, which had been worked out by a large team of Allied statisticians, economists, industrial experts, and military and government officials.

The original objective of the Morgenthau Plan, to reconstruct Germany as an agricultural economy and to deprive it of the character of an industrial country, was in fact already somewhat toned down in the Level of Industry Plan. But the restrictions that it placed on industrial production would undoubtedly have condemned the German people to extreme poverty and made them dependent on permanent economic aid from the occupying powers. To satisfy the countries whom Germany had attacked and ransacked, the Plan demanded that the average German standard of living was not to exceed "the average standard of living of European countries (excluding the United Kingdom and the Union of Soviet Socialist Republics)." To comply with this requirement, industrial production was to be scaled down to approximately 70 to 75 per cent of 1936 levels. This would have set Germany back to the levels of 1932, which were precisely the economic conditions that had propelled Hitler to power, an ironic consequence of the Level of Industry Plan that was at first appreciated by only a few clearsighted economists and statesmen.

Through the Level of Industry Plan the Allies hoped to achieve three policy aims: (1) Germany was never again to possess military equipment; (2) the character of the German economy was to be fundamentally altered and her industries restricted to a minimum; (3) the countries afflicted by the war were as far as possible to be indemnified out of German national property. These aims were implemented by categorically prohibiting some types of industrial production and by sharply cutting down others, thus rendering some industrial plants redundant and available for reparations purposes.

PROHIBITED INDUSTRIES

Among the industries to be prohibited and dismantled were those which produced not only weapons, ammunition, and other armament materials, but also the entire production of ball, roller, and cone bearings, the construction of heavy machine tools and tractors, and the synthetic production of gasoline, oil, rubber (buna), and ammonia. Likewise, all facilities for the construction of oceangoing ships and of airplanes of any description were to be dismantled. Even the production of aluminum and magnesium metal, radio appliances, and radioactive materials was forbidden. These prohibitions were aimed at least in part at the industrial plants built after 1936 and principally used for rearmament. To this extent their dismantling did not constitute an undue loss to German living standards.

RESTRICTED INDUSTRIES

The list of restrictions on industries entailed much greater hardships. It enumerated some branches of industrial production which formed the very core of the German industrial system and whose output was sorely needed for the country's reconstruction, as well as for the reconstruction of Europe —for instance, the steel, machinery and precision instrument, automobile, electrical, and chemical industries, and almost every other branch of capital equipment production. For every group a strict limit as to quantity and quality was laid down. Hardly any branch of industry was unaffected.

Under the restrictions, the motor vehicle industry was allowed an annual output of only 40,000 automobiles and as many trucks, which amounted to about one-fifth the 1938 production. For motorcycles only 10,000 units were permitted, their piston displacement not to exceed 250 cubic centimeters. Locomotive construction was to stop entirely for the present, not to be resumed until 1950 at the earliest. Equally drastic restrictions were imposed on the machine, optical, electrical, and chemical industries. The output of basic chemical materials was limited to 40 per cent of 1936 figures; for other chemical products the quota was as high as 70 per cent. The most severe and damaging restriction was imposed on steel output, which was not to exceed 5.8 million tons; the capacity of the blast furnaces that had survived the war was to be cut down to 7.5 million tons, less than one-third of 1938 capacity. This particular restriction would have set back one of the most important key industries to 30 per cent of 1936 production and alone would have limited the output in the other branches of industry to such an extent that not even the quotas permissible under the Level of Industry Plan could have been filled.

Even the production of electric power, cement, and shoes was rigidly limited. The volume of foreign trade was to be reduced to three-fifths of the already low level of 1936.

TABLE 22

1946 Level of Industry Plan: Permitted Production Capacities
(in per cent of 1938 production)

Basic materials and production goods		*Investment and consumption goods*	
Steel	25 *	Electricity	50 *
Basic chemicals	32	Shoes	50 *
Other chemicals	50 *	Precision tool and optical equipment	50 *
Aluminum	0	Automobiles	20
Cement	53	Textiles	55 *
		Machine tools	11 *
		Heavy machinery	31
		Other machinery	50 *

* Approximate.

SOURCES: Gustav Stolper, *German Realities,* New York, 1948, pp. 295 ff.; Deutsches Institut für Wirtschaftsforschung, *Die deutsche Wirtschaft zwei Jahre nach dem Zusammenbruch* (Berlin, 1947), pp. 115 ff.

UNRESTRICTED INDUSTRIES

Not even the few branches of industry for which the Plan provided no restrictions could have developed freely. It was estimated that the insufficient supply of steel and other basic materials would have held down the remaining industries to 35 to 40 per cent of their 1936 production levels. In fact, during 1946 and 1947 industrial production did remain at this miserable level; in the British and American zones combined 1946 output came to only 33 per cent of that of 1936, and 1947 output to 39 per cent.

The one industry which the Allies wished to support in their own interest was the production of Ruhr coal. France in particular, never having been happy about the concentrated industrial power of the Ruhr basin, was interested in this exception to the rule of restrictions, for its steel industry was dependent on Ruhr coal.

What could have been Germany's prospects under such conditions? Any future relaxation of these hardships was bound to have a liberating effect, and the shackled energies of the people might then be expected to revive with greater strength. Such development was in fact about to begin.

INTER-ALLIED CONTROVERSIES

The dismantling of complete factory installations of the type contemplated by the Morgenthau Plan and the Level of Industry Plan at first seemed to offer the Western Allies their one chance to proceed in agreement with Russian policies. Comparisons of the capacity that survived in the heavily damaged European countries recently under German occupation with German capacity pointed in the same direction. Russia had urgently demanded aid in rebuilding its ravaged economy. The Western Allies complied by offering to transfer to Russia a major part of Germany's industrial equipment.

It was agreed that Russia was to receive, in addition to a share in the German foreign assets and merchant fleet and the entire proceeds of dismantling in its own occupation zone, one-quarter of the industrial installations dismantled in the Western zones. Three-fifths of the deliveries from Western dismantling were to be in exchange for food and raw materials, which were less scarce in the Russian zone. These exchanges, it was thought, would keep alive a fair amount of the traditional trade relations among all the zones.

However, dismantling did not prove helpful in preserving the desired measure of German economic unity. When the question arose as to how the concerted program should be implemented, serious rifts appeared in the compact of the Allies. The dismantling program turned out to be a heavy political mortgage for the Western Allies. It was the one postwar measure to which the German population reacted with strikes and agitation, and soon the British and American occupation authorities themselves began to doubt its rationality. In consequence, each of the four powers followed divergent lines in carrying out the dismantling program.

One of the differences of opinion concerned the interpretation of reparations agreements. In Yalta the Allies had mutually assured one another and "recognized it as just that Germany be obliged to make compensation for this damage in kind to the greatest extent possible." In an effort to avoid the mistakes of the Versailles treaty and to circumvent the thorny transfer problem, which more than twenty years before had poisoned international economic relations, this time payments in kind were to be the only reparations made. However, the German assets that could be made available for reparations obviously would not satisfy more than a fraction of the claims. The Russians therefore interpreted "compensation in kind" to include parts of Germany's future production. In formulating the Level of Industry Plan, the Western Allies (without France) had not contemplated reparations as being taken from current production. If Soviet Russia were to insist on such claims the production quotas of the Level of Industry Plan would seem insufficient even to the Western powers. To increase the quotas would have meant that more industrial plants would have to be saved and fewer made available for dismantling and delivery. This consequence, however, was repugnant to the Russians.

REPARATIONS FROM THE SOVIET ZONE

The harshest fate was meted out to the inhabitants of the Soviet zone of occupation. In Potsdam the Russians had insisted on reparations to the value of 10 billion dollars. Although the damage suffered by Soviet Russia certainly was in excess of this sum, the Americans and British were not willing to approve such a high total for the Russian claims, to which those of the other Allies would have to be added.

However, the Russians stuck to their demand. They were determined to recoup their losses as far as could be done from their own zone. According to the Potsdam Agreement, "the U.S.S.R. undertakes to settle the reparation claims of Poland from its own share of reparations." How much Poland received from the Russian booty has never been revealed. In any event, the Soviets began at once to dismantle and remove reparations materials with such thoroughness that even railroad tracks, the insulation on high voltage and telegraph lines and the plumbing installations in dwellings and offices were not spared. On almost all double-track railroads the second track including ties was removed and sent east. Even several one-track lines lost their rails and were shut down. The same happened to other production facilities. By the end of 1947 the Soviet zone of occupation possessed only about one-fifth of its former production potential for the processing of iron ore, rolling of steel, and manufacturing of machines and electrical goods; about one-fourth of its former capacity for vehicles, precision instruments, and optics;

and practically nothing in the field of plywood. The Zeiss Works in Jena—famous around the world for its high-quality optical instruments and as an original and successful social experiment by which as early as 1891 this company was turned into a foundation using its profits for the benefit of its workers and staff—was not spared total dismantling.

Although the Russians' craving for industrial goods resulted in some of the industrial plants in their zone getting back into production even faster than in the Western zones, their dismantling practice was harmful to their own interests. It can be assumed with certainty that much of the hastily dismantled machinery and installations could not be made to function quickly at appropriate new locations but rather stood around somewhere until it rusted and became useless. Many lucky coincidences would have had to occur for success to be achieved in dismantling and removing a productive complex that had taken decades to build up—along with its supplies of materials and energy, its transport and marketing facilities, and the technical skills of its work force—and in setting it up again in an alien environment.

One thing is certain, the Russians ruined the productive power of their zone for several years to come. The affluence of this part of Germany had been founded on a highly developed export industry and on its agriculture. The export industries were practically destroyed, and agriculture was deprived by the occupation authorities of the larger part of its livestock and implements. The Russian zone, however, escaped famine conditions.

Two years after the occupation, "the Zone" (as the territory occupied by the Russians came to be popularly known) had been squeezed so dry that dismantling stopped automatically. By January, 1947, the Soviet Military Administration proclaimed that "the dismantling of plants" had ceased. As far as is known the last productive facility mentioned on the reparations list was dismantled in the spring of 1948. Yet, freight trains loaded with raw materials, machinery, and appliances of every sort did not stop rolling eastward. The Zone's deliveries to Russia merely took on different forms.

In addition to dismantling the Russians resorted to two further sources of reparations: human labor and goods from current production. These sources had the advantages of not running dry and that they could be set to work immediately for reconstruction without transit losses. The simplest transfer of reparations was achieved by mobilizing labor. Soviet Russia replaced a part of the millions of her war dead, now so sadly missed for reconstruction work, by using German prisoners of war and deported civilian workers. "Victory or Siberia," a National Socialist propaganda slogan used in the last phases of the war to arouse the ultimate will to resist and still legible where it had been painted on the walls of houses in eastern German towns, for many now seemed a tragically accurate forecast.

Only the disabled and sick among the prisoners of war were allowed to return home. The majority of the prisoners retained on Russian territory—insofar as they survived and did not succumb to sickness, undernourishment, and misery—saw their homes again only after many years. How many prisoners were retained in Russia is still undetermined. At the beginning of May, 1945, the Soviet Army High Command placed their number at over 3 million. But in May, 1947, the official press agency Tass mentioned roughly 890,000 prisoners. On the other hand, the Soviet Union declared in May, 1950, that nearly 2 million German prisoners of war had been repatriated and that the process had now come to an end. Another 5½ years later, in an agreement concluded in September, 1955, the Federal Republic was promised the repatriation of additional war prisoners and civilians, and by the end of 1961 another 11,000 persons had returned. The number of civilian workers deported to Russia for forced labor is also unknown. Among them were some highly qualified experts and scientists whose training benefited the Russian economy. As late as 1950 the Soviets launched a campaign in their zone to recruit aviation engineers. To be sure, in "dismantling" of technical know-how the Americans had quite frequently outraced the Russians by offering the sought-after physicists, chemists, and engineers favorable long-term contracts for work in the United States.

Not surprisingly, the Russians also made use of reparations as a lever to introduce Communism into their new dominion. The dismantlings were a nonrecurrent opportunity to seize private property and to remodel the social framework on Marxist patterns. This was the design behind the sequestration without compensation of the large landed estates and the destruction of numerous castles and mansions in line with the precedents of the Russian revolution. In industry also dismantling turned into expropriation. The largest and most important industrial complexes were seized and reorganized in the form of Soviet Corporations (*Sowjetische Aktiengesellschaften,* SAG).

The first SAG's were founded in June, 1946, at the command of the Soviet Military Administration. Altogether, 213 large industrial complexes and mining companies were transferred to Soviet ownership for an indefinite period of time. Thus, about 30 per cent of the industrial capacity in the Zone became a part of the Soviet Russian national economy. One of these complexes was the biggest chemical plant of Europe, the *Leunawerk,* originally owned by the I. G. Farbenindustrie; another one was the foremost producer of synthetic rubber in Germany, the *Bunawerk* in Schkopau near Merseburg. A number of less profitable companies were returned to German ownership, though not to the private owners, by 1947. As late as 1951 the Soviet Union still retained title to almost the entire large-scale chemical industry, four-fifths of potash mining, about one-half of electrotechnical manufacturing, steel processing, and vehicle production; about two-fifths of the production of heavy machines, the processing of nonferrous metals, and the production of electric power; and many plants in various other industries.

The number of workers employed by the SAG's in the autumn of 1951 was estimated at about 325,000, which would mean every seventh industrial worker. To this should be added 150,000 to 200,000 miners—no precise figure has ever been revealed—working in the strategically important uranium mines for the Soviet company Wismut A.G., in the region of the Erzgebirge in Czechoslovakia and in the neighboring Vogtland. This mammoth organization was an original Soviet project and did not figure among the SAG's expropriated in the Zone for Russian purposes.

In the three Western zones reparations were wound up by 1951, but the Russians continued to exact high contributions from their zone. In May, 1950, they officially renounced their claims to half the outstanding reparations obligations; yet, at that time still about every fifth worker in industry and mining was employed in a Russian enterprise. In April, 1952, it was decided to return an additional 66 plants in the Zone from Russian to German management, but these plants, which had originally been expropriated, had to be bought back for a sum of roughly two billion Deutsche Marks. On August 22, 1953, a protocol was signed in Moscow which stated that Russia and Poland were foregoing further reparations. By this action, the last 33 SAG's, this time without a purchase price, reverted to German ownership. The one exception was the Wismut A.G. Because of its military significance this company has been accorded the highest priority in everything it might require, and it is surrounded with such security measures that it almost constitutes a secret state within the state. The large uranium mining territories were secluded from contact with the outside world.

How much the reparations payments from the Zone amounted to may never be known. According to the official Soviet accounting, the value of dismantled installations and other reparations equaled 4,292 million dollars at 1938 world market prices. Computations made in West Germany have arrived at figures about three times this amount. If reparations payments are valued at current prices, their total may be reckoned to be at least 40 to 50 billion Deutsche Marks for the eight reparations years through 1953, not counting payments for occupation costs estimated at another 15 billion marks. Although it should be noted that industrial capacity in the Zone had also been much expanded in many respects during the war and that war destruction there was somewhat less than in the Western zones, no exertions could hope to offset a bloodletting of such dimensions. For an indefinite length of time this part of Germany was condemned to backwardness and poverty.

REPARATIONS FROM THE WESTERN ZONES

Second to the Russian zone, the one most burdened by the reparation regime was the French zone. Like the Soviet Union, France had suffered so severely from the war and occupation that it sought to recoup from Germany as much as possible. The territories of southwestern Germany placed under France's authority were mostly agricultural and forest lands where industrial dismantling could not result in any considerable benefits; thus, current agricultural and forestry production were now all the more thoroughly utilized as a source for reparations. Since, discourteously, the Allies had not invited France to the Potsdam Conference, it was not a signatory to the agreement and therefore did not feel bound by its terms. France refused to admit refugees from the east and other useless eaters into its zone and instead lodged there large segments of her armies with their dependents and camp followers. The French zone was compelled to carry the costs of this occupation, primarily for the required food supplies. The rich forest lands, already ruthlessly exploited by Hitler for his war needs, provided the occupying power with timber which was transported to France and Switzerland to serve France as a welcome source of foreign exchange.

The flood of goods, services, and booty of all kinds that during the war had streamed from France into Germany now reversed its direction. Besides the materials taken from the French zone and used at home or for export France received a considerable part of the reparations goods delivered to the British and American zones. Thus it happened that Germany, which in 1946 had nothing to export, nevertheless ranked fourth that year in French import statistics, supplying France with as many imports as in 1938, the last year of peace.

However, for France the most important reparation asset was the Saar region. After the second world war, as after the first, France demanded the annexation of this small but economically most desirable district. Influenced by Germany's hopeless situation and the occupying power's requests, promises, and threats, the Saar population decided in 1947 in favor of political autonomy and economic union with France. This seemed to make Germany's loss of the Saar permanent. But thanks to this plebiscite the Saar industries, first among them the Röchling iron and steel works, escaped the dismantling process, and France's urgent need for Saar coal helped to return the Saar industries to peacetime production levels very promptly. Eight years later, on October 23, 1955, while Germany's economic recovery was surprising the world, this same population deliberately cancelled its previous decision in another plebiscite and prepared the return of the Saar to Germany. The return itself became effective on January 1, 1957.

The progress of dismantling and reparations in the three Western zones depended less on France than on Britain and the United States. Their policies and those of Soviet Russia determined the pace and direction of the operations. This led to repeated revisions of the dismantling lists.

Had the Level of Industry Plan in its 1946 version been followed, 1,800 factories would have had to be destroyed in the three Western zones. In the autumn of 1947, however, just 18 months after the Level of Industry Plan was adopted, a new shortened list of only 858 plants was issued, which another 18 months later was cut by an additional 160 installations. Considerable further cutbacks were made in November, 1949, saving from destruction some of the largest and most essential complexes—among others the *August-Thyssen* steel works in Duisburg, the *Borsig-Werke* in Berlin, and the steel works in Salzgitter. The removal of machinery and installations definitely ended only in April, 1951.

The end of dismantling was due to a swing of public opinion in the United States. Comparatively soon after the war responsible people realized that this policy was detrimental to America's own interests. In fact, only a small fraction of productive capacity removed from Germany was ever set to work in any of the Western countries. The following figures will show how insignificant were the results: the Inter-Allied Reparations Commission in Brussels credited Germany's reparations account for dismantled plants taken from the Western zones with 700 million marks at 1938 prices, which corresponded to a current value of about 1,500 million. A German estimate placed the dismantling losses at roughly 5,000 million marks. Both computations are subject to question. The one thing that is certain is that the losses to one party were by no means offset by the gains to the other.

The spontaneous resentment which the dismantling caused in the German public may explain why its real importance was at first considerably exaggerated. On the whole, the losses suffered by the German economy were more than compensated before too long. By 1950, new investment in the three Western zones amounted to three to four times the assets lost through dismantling. However, it should not be overlooked that frequently the dismantled plants held a key position within their industry and were badly missed until they were replaced by new, more modern units.

DEMILITARIZATION AND DENAZIFICATION

In its first phase the policy of "Dis- and De-" (*Ent- und De-*), as the saying then was in Germany, was not confined to production. Like the Russians, the Western Allies were convinced at that time that the leadership of big business, the owners of large estates, and all economically influential persons had worked hand-in-glove with the militarists and National Socialists. Democratic development in Germany, it was thought, would be possible only after the power of the armament industry, allegedly firmly entrenched under National Socialism, had been shattered. Accordingly, the policy of dismantling was supplemented by a policy of demilitarization, denazification, decentralization, and decartelization. These measures had been decided upon in the Allied Control Council with perfect unity among the four occupying powers.

First the Allies saw to it that all military installations were destroyed and all militaristic ideologies proscribed. Installations, machinery, and appliances that served military purposes had to be wiped out, demolished, or delivered to the occupiers. Even civilian air raid shelters, certain installations for telecommunications purposes, aircraft hangars, and the like had to disappear. In order to uproot the spirit of National Socialism and militarism completely, every adult German had to account for his behavior during the Hitler years before special courts of law, the *Spruchkammern*. Only those exonerated by these courts or declared to have been mere camp followers of the Nazis were admitted to public office or to leading positions in industry. Those pronounced "culpable to a minor degree" (*Minderbelastete*) were, for a probationary period, not even allowed to take charge of their own plants or offices. The "culpable" (*Belastete*) had to deliver a large part of their property, and the "most culpable" (*Hauptschuldige*) had to deliver all their property to a fund for the relief of victims of Nazi persecution, or they were condemned to temporary or permanent forced labor in labor camps. For the American zone of occupation this "Law for Liberation from National Socialism and Militarism" of March 5, 1946, and its frequently sluggish and contradictory execution caused additional economic disruption in the disorganized economy, at least for a certain time.

AGRARIAN REFORMS

In Potsdam the Allies were also agreed as to the necessity of agrarian reforms. However, in each zone the legal measures took a different shape. In the Soviet zone the reforms began with the expropriations mentioned above. Four months after the end of the fighting a law was promulgated for the sequestration of all property of "war criminals and Nazi activists" and of all property of more than 100 hectares. After the owners had been expelled, frequently their houses were demolished as being "survivals from feudalism." The expropriated lands were immediately distributed in lots of 5 to 8.5 hectares to small tenants, farmers with too little or no land, and to expellees. At that period, before the compulsory collectivization drive was set in motion, lands owned by the Reich, the federal states, and the municipalities were also in part distributed to settlers. Through the end of 1948, roughly 7,000 estates of more than 100 hectares each, or a total of about 2.6 million hectares, were transferred from private owners to new ownership.

In the Western zones, land reform was carried out by much milder and less rigorous methods. Each of the three military governments laid down its separate law. In the American zone, where large estates had never played an important role, owners of more than 100 hectares had to hand over part of their land (*Landabgabe*), the part being larger the larger the estate involved. The French, and the British under the influence of their Labour government, decreed an absolute maximum estate size permissible for one owner of 150 hectares. In all the Western zones the owners received some compensation for land legally expropriated. The application of these laws, especially in the French zone, later turned out to have been much less radical than was at first supposed. In the entire Western region comparatively little acreage was redistributed.

The regulations of the Western Allies governing transfers of land were more stringent. Perhaps unwittingly, they at first continued the National Socialist policy of making every transfer of agricultural or forest land, even the smallest, contingent upon official authorization in order to make sure that farmer-owners (*Bauernfähige*) received first consideration as purchasers. Since the German farmers willingly accepted this policy, it was preserved. Later, in the Federal Republic, still in the spirit of this law, farmers' courts officially decided whether the purchase of a parcel of farm or forest land by a nonfarmer might lead to "unsound property distribution" or "the accumulation of land in one hand."

DECONCENTRATION

The policy of the Allies was directed against concentration of ownership not only in agriculture but in all other sectors of the German economy. The Potsdam Agreement contained the following clause on this subject: "12. At the earliest practicable date, the German economy shall be decentralized for the purpose of eliminating the present excessive concentration of economic power as exemplified in particular by cartels, syndicates, trusts and other monopolistic arrangements." The motives of the four powers in supporting this clause were again not identical. The Americans and British believed, by analogy to problems often discussed in their own countries, that a conspiracy had existed between the large industrialists and business managers on the one hand and the military strongmen under Hitler on the other. The French were less concerned with theories about the political background of the German disaster, but they lived in fear of any concentration of power in Germany and therefore wished to deconcentrate the German political and economic system wherever possible. To the Russians, economic power of any sort in private hands was always evil.

In the Soviet zone, along with the owners of large landed estates, the owners of large industrial companies were expropriated or jailed as "war criminals and Nazi activists." Their plants were transferred to publicly owned (*volkseigen*) or Soviet owned companies. These measures, which by 1947 had resulted in the expropriation of about two-fifths of the industrial capacity in the Zone, were based partly on an ordinance of the Soviet Military Administration, SMAD (Ordinance No. 124 of October 30, 1945), partly on laws which were promulgated in the summer of 1946 almost simultaneously by the German Communist governments already functioning in the various federal states of the Zone. In Saxony the government, predominantly in the hands of Communists, organized a plebiscite on expropriations which was ratified by 77.7 per cent of the voters. In the other federal states of the Zone the formality of a plebiscite was dispensed with.

Basically, in the Russian zone decentralization did not occur, for the decartelization of private industry was immediately followed by state action centralizing entire industries and fields of trade. Since a Communist planned economy requires central direction and clearly defined lines of command, in a very short time new economic units were organized which were more rigidly centralized than ever before. In July, 1945, in the entire Zone and in East Berlin all banks and savings institutions were closed and, as a first move, all deposits were blocked. Since, however, traffic in checks, bank transfers, and clearing accounts could not be allowed to come to a standstill, new state owned banks (*Landeskreditbanken*) and municipal banking institutes were at once formed to take possession of the premises, installations, organizations, and staffs of the closed banks. In this way the mixed system of private, semiprivate, and public institutions was replaced by a concentrated, centrally directed banking organization. In like manner, private capital was eliminated from the insurance field, and the 54 existing companies had to stop transacting business. They were replaced by five new *Land* (state) insurance companies which took over all their business and installations.

In similar fashion retail stores and a number of wholesale firms were eliminated by expanding the operations of consumers' cooperatives; from the middle of 1945 to the end of 1946 these cooperatives increased their retail outlets from about 2,000 to 6,000. In line with the tactics of the regime there was never a formal socialization law in the Zone; rather, all expropriations and shut-downs were decreed as denazification, demilitarization, and decartelization measures, and later carried the threat of penalties against "enemies of the state."

In strong contrast to the Soviet zone, the occupation forces of the three Western zones pursued the goal of true decentralization both in the fields of politics and economics. In the United States especially decentralization was a goal with an old tradition, and it was now pursued in Germany with missionary zeal. To begin with, the best known captains of industry were arrested, among them Gustav Krupp von Bohlen und Halbach, soon replaced by his son and successor Alfried; also Herman Röchling, Friedrich Flick, and the heads of the I. G. Farbenindustrie. They were tried before an Allied court and accused of having "conspired" with Hitler in support of his war aims. Their property as well as that of all other large concerns was sequestered and placed under the management of trustees; several years later these properties were returned to their owners. But the notion of a culpable understanding between the industrial barons and Hitler agitated not only the Socialists but also many other observers who knew the early history of National Socialism and remembered the cooperation between Hitler and Hugenberg and Hitler's relationship with Fritz Thyssen. In reality the guilt of most of the leading industrialists lay in their lack of courage, resistance, and sound political judgment in dealing with Hitler, and in this they were on a par with the bankers, the farmers, the workers, and every other group and profession.

In order to break the power of the large concerns, the financial and corporate combinations in the economy of the three Western zones were examined at length, and an administrative body, the Liquidation Commission, was established to devise controls over the various trusts, cartels, and cartel-like combinations. Following these thorough studies, deconcentration measures were promulgated for three large business complexes: the I. G. Farben concern; the coal and steel concerns, including Vereinigte Stahlwerke, and a few other companies; and also for the three large banks, Commerzbank, Deutsche Bank, and Dresdner Bank.

I. G. Farbenindustrie, a giant enterprise, had maintained a predominant position in Germany. However, in this largest German concern no one had ever owned a majority of the stock, and the same was true of the Vereinigte Stahlwerke, the large banks, and the electrical concerns, AEG and Siemens. The shares were scattered among tens of thousands of mostly small shareholders, and no more than a minority participation was held by owners of large blocs of shares who, to be sure, just because of this widespread ownership were in a position to exert their influence. The most serious allegations were directed against the I. G. Farbenindustrie, an organization almost too large to be controlled by anyone and which, it was believed, had been used by Hitler and his aides for criminal actions. For a long time its fate remained uncertain. Finally in 1953 the Liquidation Commission pronounced its judgment. I. G. Farbenindustrie was to be divided into four successor firms, the *Badische Anilin- und Sodafabrik, Cassella Farbwerke, Farbenfabrik Bayer,* and *Höchster Farbwerke.* These four firms took over most of the chemical plants left in the Western zones. The I. G. Farben properties abroad had already been sequestered for reparations, and the works situated in the Eastern Zone, among them the Leunawerk, had been declared publicly owned plants. Only a dubious residual property under the name of *I. G. Liquidationsmasse* recalled the name of the one-time giant.

The deconcentration of the coal and steel concerns also proved to be a thorny and time-consuming undertaking. Large parts were family owned and the liquidators had the doubly arduous task of dividing up the total property into viable parts on the one hand, and, as far as feasible, of safeguarding property rights on the other. As a result, the 12 largest coal and steel companies, which controlled about 90 per cent of steel production and about half the coal mines, were divided into 28 independent companies. In contrast to the quartering of the I. G. Farbenindustrie, which potentially was a blessing to the German economy, many observers feared that too radical a dispersal of coal mines and steel mills would have technical and organizational drawbacks. The Allies' policies partly severed the combination of coal and steel production which had been typical of the organization in the Ruhr region. At the same time, the Allies themselves concentrated the production and the marketing of coal under the North German Coal Control, an organization resembling a syndicate that worked under Allied supervision. This agency was primarily meant to insure the production and distribution of the coveted Ruhr coal, especially the supplies for France.

The third great economic power concentration, that of the large commercial banks, was also divided up into many parts. The strength of the three large banks was based on their vast potential for credit creation and on their influence over numerous industrial firms. Through a network of branches spread over the country the banks were in a position to create a considerable part of the money in circulation on the strength of their own credit. Wherever a customer filed a transfer order, the bank by a simple entry in its books created this money, provided that the man to whom the sum was owed had an account with the bank also on which he could be credited with the sum involved. This method of money creation, as mentioned before, had helped with the "silent financing" of the war.

Besides, the banks—particularly the large ones—traditionally possessed a direct influence on many large enterprises. This power rested on two pillars. First, they exercised their depositors' voting rights by way of proxies in the stockholders' meetings. Most of the small shareholders allowed themselves to be represented in such meetings by their banks, which in this way were in a position to exert strong voting power for their own interests even if they did not hold a single share on their own account. Second, they delegated their officers to sit on the boards of directors of the industries in which they were interested. In most instances both parties expected to profit from such interrelations.

Faced with this situation the Allies judged it to be imperative to divide the large banks into a number of smaller institutions. Following the pattern that prevailed in the United States, each bank's activity was first confined within geographical limits. It was permitted to run branch offices only inside its own federal state. Since the three Western zones comprised several Länder, the three large banks were now to be divided into thirty successor institutions, not counting the Berlin offices.

Four years later, within each of the three Western zones separately the dismembered parts of each bank, never having become genuinely independent, united again. After five more years, zone lines were disregarded and the three large banks were restored to their initial grandeur under the old firm names.

In general, nothing remained of the deconcentration effort except the division of the I. G. Farbenindustrie, of the Vereinigte Stahlwerke and several coal and steel concerns, and of the former *UFA-Film* concern.

2. *The Bizonal Area*

IT IS GRATIFYING to observe that the West had learned a lesson from history and that after the second world war the initial mistakes, which had been made out of an understandable desire to mete out punishment, to exact retribution, to build safeguards, and to take out reparations, were recognized as such and came to be revised within a few years' time. Soon after the Potsdam Agreement men of insight and a sense of responsibility began to sound warnings against a repetition of the errors committed after Versailles. In 1919 Germany had had imposed upon her excessively harsh conditions, political and economic, and the victors conceded a revision only after a lag of twelve years and under the impact of a worldwide economic crisis. This time the degree of devastation sustained by Germany and, indeed, the whole of Europe was even greater than in 1918. The widespread havoc wrought on the entire continent of Europe caused statesmen, especially those of Britain and the United States, to make a careful reassessment of their policies.

In the United States a serious view was taken of the humanitarian obligation to assist a swift recovery of Europe, and many observers recognized at an early stage that to reduce Germany to a permanent state of destitution would be both inconsistent with the moral tenets of the American people and a disservice to the cause of reconstruction and America's own interests. Unless the occupying powers were prepared to accept the responsibility for letting people die of starvation or disease in the very heart of Europe, it would be necessary to help the Germans to get on their feet and back to work. The United States Military Government drew this conclusion as early as 1945, organizing GARIOA (Government Appropriations for Relief in Occupied Areas) to supplement scarce foodstuffs and raw materials.

Because the American and British zones were the most densely populated and had the greatest food production bottleneck, the problem of feeding the population was of immediate urgency. The estimate of the occupying authorities was that approximately 600 million dollars per annum (see Table

25 on page 209) would be required to keep life going and to prevent the two zones from continuing in the state of economic paralysis to which they had been reduced.

REVISION OF THE WEST'S GERMAN POLICIES

On December 12, 1945, three months before publication of the Level of Industry Plan, the U. S. State Department had begun to "interpret" the Potsdam Declaration. In a statement which at the time was mostly overlooked by the public, the State Department declared that the Potsdam clauses concerning reparations were only meant as "guideposts" for the assessment of available industrial plant, and it denied that the objective was to hold down the German economy permanently.

The next significant step toward a revision of the United States' German policies was taken when President Truman authorized his Secretary of State, James F. Byrnes, to declare in an address before the assembled German minister presidents in Stuttgart, on September 6, 1946:

> The German people were not denied . . . the possibility of improving their lot by hard work over the years . . . . Being obliged to start again like the people of other devastated countries . . . the German people were not to be denied the right . . . to build up their industries for peaceful purposes.

When it appeared in late 1946 and early 1947 that the directives of the military governments, conceived as they were in the spirit of Potsdam, were still paralyzing the German economy, President Truman decided that a further step must be taken. In February, 1947, he sent former President Herbert Hoover at the head of a mission of experts (including Gustav Stolper as Hoover's economic adviser) to Germany and Austria. The mission's assignment was to study the economic conditions prevailing in the center of Europe and to make recommendations upon "the problem of reviving German industry and thus exports with which to relieve American and British taxpayers from their burden in preventing starvation in Germany. These problems also involve the economic stability and peace in Europe." The detailed recommendations quickly formulated by Hoover in three reports were accepted by President Truman as the basis of American policy. On June 5, 1947, the Marshall Plan was outlined at Harvard University. On July 15, the U. S. government issued a substantially milder general directive to Lucius D. Clay, commander of the American zone. The most perilous postwar period had ended for the two zones, although calamitous economic conditions continued to prevail for one more year.

Aside from humanitarian motives, two further important considerations helped to change American foreign policy with respect to Germany. The first one involved Europe's economic reconstruction, the other Europe's political situation. Economic common sense demanded that, if only in the interest of Germany's neighbors, German industries must not be left to go to ruin. Particularly the Ruhr basin had in peacetime supplied the rest of Europe with considerable amounts of iron and steel products, machinery, electrical appliances, chemicals, coal, and many other commodities. The European countries ravaged by the war now more than ever had an interest in the recovery of their biggest workshop, German industry, to a level above mere self-sufficiency.

Political considerations provided the second stimulus for an early revision of the West's German policies. The Americans and the British viewed with growing concern the repeated revelations of Russia's true designs. In the course of Hitler's war and during the first postwar years, the Russians had brought all of Eastern Europe under their sway. Many signs suggested that Stalin would not be content with what he had achieved. Economic decline and political despair seemed once again to be preparing the soil in the center of Europe for extremist agitation of the kind that had convulsed the 1930's. If the Western powers were to continue their original policies of retribution they would help Communism in its westward sweep—or so it seemed to many observers in the West, who perhaps did not realize how immune to the Soviet lure millions of Germans had become as a result of their distressing personal encounters with Russian methods.

CONSTITUTIONAL PROBLEMS AND UNIFICATION OF THE ZONES

Parallel with their policies in economic matters, the Allies had at first pursued policies of decentralization with respect to political organization as well. Along with the Reich the federal state of Prussia—which for all intents and purposes had already succumbed to Hitler's Gau organization—was now also formally abolished. On March 10, 1947, the foreign ministers of the four victorious powers, assembled in Moscow, declared their approval of a law of the Allied Control Council which had pronounced the Prussian State liquidated. With this act, almost unnoticed by the German public, the state which had played such a decisive role in the unification of Germany was carried to its grave. One more pin that potentially might have held together vestiges of German unity across the four zones was thereby eliminated.

After the war autonomous political authority was lodged only in the municipalities, counties, and the Länder which, however, had been partly redesigned within borders that seemed more practical for the purposes of the occupying powers. The Moscow Conference of March, 1947, made it abundantly clear that it would not be possible to save even the economic unity of Germany that had been stipulated in the Potsdam Agreement. Thus the Americans and the British decided to act on their own. Each of them in their respective zones had already approved the establishment of a central authority, the Americans the *Länderrat* in Stuttgart, the British the *Zonenbeirat* in Hamburg. In doing so they were drawing even with the Russians, who had organized their own central administration shortly after the capitulation. On the other hand, the French still objected to any attempt, however tentative, to tie together the broken pieces of what had been the Reich. Within their zone the several Länder, some of tiny dimensions, were forced to live on in oppressive isolation.

The two English-speaking military governments now took further steps toward uniting the territories they occupied. First they decided to unify the economic administration of their zones under the Economic Administrative Council in Minden, Westphalia, which began to function on January 1, 1947. It was hoped that the joint economic administration of both regions would result in better supplies for the starving population and a more rational exploitation of available productive facilities, for instance more Bavarian foodstuffs in the towns of the Rhineland in exchange for more Ruhr coal in Munich and Nürnberg. Soon it appeared, however, that the two zones would make no marked progress toward unity as long as they remained divided by political and administrative frontiers.

When the two powers finally decided to proceed with the political unification of their territories, the population for the first time saw hope that they might one day again live in a state of their own. The political unit founded in June, 1947, was deliberately given a provisional status and modestly named United Economic Region (*Vereinigtes Wirtschaftsgebiet*). It provided forty million Germans with common political institutions consisting of a council for economic affairs (*Wirtschaftsrat*), which was a quasi-parliament; a second chamber (*Länderrat*), formed by representatives of the federal states; and a quasi-government at the administrative summit. The sphere of action of the so-called Bizonia was at first limited to economic, social, and financial functions; the laws voted by the Bizonal Economic Council could be promulgated only after they had been approved by the American-British control board. This experiment proved successful and served as a pattern when the time was finally ripe for a larger project, unification of the three Western zones.

Thus, Bizonia was the immediate predecessor of the Federal Republic founded two years later. A beginning had been made toward overcoming the chaos that followed the war.

REFUGEES AND HOUSING

At the time when Bizonia was founded the primary problems yet unsolved were the lack of food and of shelter. Despite the bloodletting that had cost the lives of almost one-tenth of the inhabitants, the population density had increased to a frightening degree, most of all in the American and British zones. In many of the large cities two-thirds of the homes lay in rubble and ashes, and homeless families were moved out to hamlets and villages and to those provincial towns that had been spared by the war. In this exodus to the countryside the bombed-out townspeople were joined by the millions of Germans expelled from the East who mostly brought along only what they wore on their bodies and carried on their backs. Due to this mass influx of refugees and expellees it came about that in the predominantly agrarian Land of Schleswig-Holstein, for instance, the number of inhabitants increased by 70 per cent, and in the end every third man, woman, or child was an indigent, aimlessly wandering stranger. There was hardly a farmhouse that did not shelter at least one additional family. However, the fate of those who had found a refuge in the countryside was comparatively enviable, since in the neighborhood of their new homes there was something to eat and wood for a warming fire. In the cities and towns starvation was rampant.

Together with most other goods, housing space had to be rationed. No one remained master of his own apartment or house. In many large cities a person was normally given the right to occupy up to 12 square meters of living space, whether in a kitchen, room, bathroom, or hallway. Proliferating housing authorities hunted for spare rooms to be requisitioned and decided which families had to double up and which had to sublet. Many found shelter in air raid bunkers, barracks, and garden plot sheds. As late as 1949, only one refugee family in four had had the luck to rent a place all its own, and even ten years later the housing emergency among refugees had not been entirely overcome.

The number of dwellings destroyed or lost through the war will never be exactly ascertained, but the magnitude of the emergency may be gauged by the fact that in the Federal Republic and West Berlin 5.4 million people had been bombed out who with their homes had lost all their belongings. To them must be added approximately 6 million expellees and refugees from outside the West German territory, a number that during the following fifteen years was doubled by newcomers, especially fugitives from the Soviet zone. It has been estimated that in 1946, nine million dwellings still existed, but that this was about six million short of minimum requirements if people were to be accommodated according to prewar standards.

For a time it was feared that the refugees and expellees might form a separate group which could not be reabsorbed by the resident population. It almost seemed that a new class distinction cutting across all previous class lines might arise between the refugees and the old residents, as they differed in customs, dialects, and religion; and also a second class distinction seemed to emerge between those who had preserved their belongings and those who had been deprived through bombings and expulsion. The question was often heard: what justice was there in the distribution of property by the blind fortunes of war? Was there any connection with merit or performance? At once the attempt was made to organize a political party of the expellees and "Deprived of Rights" (*Partei der Heimatvertriebenen und Entrechteten*); however, the occupation authorities prohibited associations of this sort to prevent new radicalism from spreading. After lengthy deliberations in the Bizonal Economic Council, a Law for Immediate Relief (*Soforthilfegesetz*) was passed, which laid down provisional regulations to even out the incidence of war burdens, but not before 1949 did it finally receive the approval of the Allied authorities.

In the course of the growing prosperity of the 1950's, the refugee problem lost much of its bitterness. The older persons suffered sorely by being transplanted from their traditional homes, but the younger generation managed to integrate fully into its new community.

3. The Collapse of the Controlled Economy

WHEN NATIONAL SOCIALISM was defeated it left behind an economic system in which the government was omnipresent and paramount. Almost everything was rationed, subject to official price fixing, or allocated and distributed by public authorities. Yet nothing was in sufficient supply to fill the most immediate needs. No one even dared hope for better days.

In unprecedented circumstances, when all ties to traditional civic values have been lost, a nation frequently falls prey to radical upheavals, to a revolution. Not so Germany after the second world war. Finally blind faith in a beneficial state and wise authorities, long characteristic of German historical development, had been thoroughly shattered. People now had only one urgent desire: to be rid of every sort of tutelage, to see state regulation dismantled, to recover the freedom to exert individual energies. In short, the nation craved a more liberal economic order. And indeed, as soon as the system of command economy in force for about two decades had been swept away, expansionist forces were set free such as even the strongest believers in a free market economy had hardly anticipated.

AN ECONOMY OF SHORTAGES

In 1945 the Allies had no choice but to take over and administer Hitler's war economy. Had they tried to abolish the prevailing system at one stroke, the chaos would have been even worse. Since at that moment the Western Allies were seeking ways to save German economic unity, they postponed reforms until parallel actions could be taken in all four zones. Three years thus passed in which attempts to deal with the shortages in all vital goods by strict official regulation became increasingly hopeless.

As noted before, government regulation of the economy had been introduced by the National Socialists as early as 1935 when several raw materials were becoming scarce. A year later a general price and wage freeze was resorted to. Since that time, for more than ten years, prices and price relations between various goods had been held artificially stable. Under the military government this system was now to assume utmost rigidity. Every consumer —man, woman, or child—still received his food tickets valid for four weeks, which entitled him to purchase his rations always at the same prices. The rations per day for a "normal consumer" (the official term for an adult in office or household work) in one of the large cities, say Berlin, was, in September, 1946, 40 grams of meat, 13 grams of fat, 300 grams of bread, 43 grams of legumes, 24 grams of sugar, 400 grams of potatoes, 44 grams of skimmed milk, and 5 grams of coffee substitutes. Cheese, fish, eggs, fruit, and vegetables were almost never available. Clothing, fuel, and furniture were delivered only against a permit personally made out to the purchaser, which was almost impossible to obtain. Business firms too had to show permits entitling them to raw materials, spare parts, and other essentials. A huge organization was required to administer this system; even in the smallest municipality the mayor had to set up a ration office. The very paper for all these forms became scarce since the paper industry also was paralyzed. At best, rigid control could try to spread the scarcity fairly, but it would never get rid of it by stimulating production. By and by, this system of a command economy became absurd.

Various economic data illustrating prewar and postwar conditions are listed in Table 23.

TABLE 23

Population, Employment, and Production

	1936 *	*1939* *	*1946* †
Population (millions)	58	60	66
Gainfully employed (millions)	29	30	26.5
National income (billions of RM, prices of 1936)	58.7	76	32
Index of industrial production (1936 = 100)	100	116	27
Wheat and rye harvested (million tons)	9.2	10.3	5.5
Potatoes harvested (million tons)	36	40	22
Cattle, herd size (million head)	16	16	14
Hogs, herd size (million head)	18.3	19.4	7.5
Rail freight (million tons)	439	547	180
Food consumption per person (calories per day)	3,113	—	1,729 §

* Germany including the Saar territory.

† The territory of the four zones of occupation, including Berlin.

§ Residents of Berlin, September, 1946.

SOURCE: Deutsches Institut für Wirtschaftsforschung, *Die deutsche Wirtschaft zwei Jahre nach dem Zusammenbruch* (Berlin, 1947), pp. 266–77; partly expanded by the author's computations.

The centralized and planned economy had functioned not too badly during the war for which it had been created. Since wages, prices, and incomes were determined, people could manage as long as their rations of food, clothing, and fuel sufficed to sustain life. Economic crimes were harshly punished in the Third Reich, even by sentences of death, for such a transgression could easily be defined as implying a crime against the state. Under such severe sanctions, production and trade had in general moved along the lines prescribed by the authorities.

After the war, both conditions changed. Supplies had been more or less sufficient up to the end of fighting, but after 1945 they sank below the minimum needed to support life; also, the brutal, terrorist penalties for economic crimes gave way to more humane measures. Small transgressions were punished by money fines; in serious cases arrests were made. But even jail sentences failed to deter after so many decent citizens had experienced similar sentences for being considered Nazis, militarists, or black marketeers, or sometimes simply as a result of a misunderstanding with the occupiers. So great had want become that in an emergency the necessities of life simply had to be found, even if by illegal means.

That production still moved somewhat along prescribed lines was due to an effective device of planned economy: a ration permit, in German called the *durchlaufende Bezugsrecht,* which followed the consecutive phases of processing from raw material to finished goods. This device came into use in the Reich only during the war. The producer was issued a permit to buy raw materials according to the amounts of processed goods he was delivering in exchange for purchase permits to his customers. The consumer's permit ran backwards, so to speak, down the ladder to the first producer, who used it to substantiate the amounts of raw materials he could rightfully buy, based on the quantities of finished products he had contributed to the market at official prices. This device was hardly of use, however, in the field of agricultural production, where there is little processing of raw materials. And even in industry this sophisticated practice failed to give the producer the assurance that his supplier would have sufficient stocks of raw materials to honor the permit. Neither could he count on getting spare parts for his worn machinery, new tires for his automobile, or additional production facilities. As time went on even the most loyal and patient manager found that to keep up his production he could not simply rely on the ration office. As during the inflation in the early 1920's, numerous essential goods, obtainable by official permit at best only after lengthy delays, could be procured more quickly and reliably on the black market or through barter deals. Personal initiative, the black market, and bartering rapidly assumed greater importance. They withdrew from the officially managed economy increasing proportions of a diminishing production, and thus the ultimate bankruptcy of the command economy became only a matter of time.

REPRESSED INFLATION

In the first postwar years the German economy suffered from problems not only of scarcity but also of affluence. The hopeless shortage of goods was confronted with a no less dangerous plethora of money. Everyone had money, certainly more of it than he could use to buy his rations, pay his rent, and purchase his fuel supply. What then was the good of working if expending energy only made you hungrier and wore down your clothing and shoes, and when for the money you earned there was neither food to be bought nor household appliances nor anything useful or attractive? To pay black-market prices the wages would not be sufficient anyway. For one cigarette you paid in the large cities 3 to 5 marks, for one pound of butter 150 to 300 marks; at prevailing wages a worker would have had to put in three hours' work for one cigarette and two or three weeks for one pound of butter. The proceeds from one pack of cigarettes sold in the black market would easily buy one month's ration for one person at official prices. More and more people gave in to the temptation to make much more money with much less effort on the black market than through normal labor. Since the Reichsmark failed to fulfill its function as a trustworthy means of exchange, an ersatz currency was sought; it was found in the cigarette, usually American, which displaced the Reichsmark in the black market.

TABLE 24

Volume of Money and Net National Product; Selected Years, 1913–46*
(in billions of current marks)

	1913	*1932*	*1938*	*1945*	*1946*
Coins and banknotes †	6.6	5.6	10.4	73 §	—
Demand deposits †	12.3	12.7	18.7	100 §	—
Savings deposits †	24.5	15.3	27.3	125 §	—
Total money volume †	43.4	33.6	56.4	298 §	—
Net national product at factor cost	49.5	42.6	79.8	—	40 §

* Territory as applicable at given date.

† Status at end of year; for 1945, at end of war.

§ Approximate.

SOURCES: Deutsches Institut für Wirtschaftsforschung, *Die deutsche Wirtschaft zwei Jahre nach dem Zusammenbruch* (Berlin, 1947), pp. 206, 274; Statistisches Bundesamt Wiesbaden, *Bevölkerung und Wirtschaft. Langfristige Reihen 1871 bis 1957 für das Deutsche Reich und die Bundesrepublik Deutschland,* p. 87; W. G. Hoffmann and J. H. Müller, *Das deutsche Volkseinkommen 1851–1957* (Tübingen, 1959), p. 40.

Now at last the population came to see the results of the National Socialists' financial wizzardry. Job creation, armament, and war had been paid for by printing money for which there were no additional goods from current production for the civilian population. The ever-rising flood of money which, if savings accounts were added, amounted to about 300 billion Reichsmarks by the end of the war, could no longer be contained behind the governmental dams once the Hitler regime had disappeared.

To be sure, the loss of territory in the East and the Saar and the closing down of the banks in the Soviet zone had immobilized some of the active money supply, but the major part of the 300 billion Reichsmarks which Hitler had bequeathed to the economy still filled to overflowing the cash tills and savings accounts of the population. This inflationary power in search of goods now insinuated itself wraith-like throughout the German economy. Because the legal markets were depleted, prices on the illegal ones climbed to dizzy heights. These black-market prices, twenty to fifty times the legal ones, were more in tune with actual market conditions and more apt to give some direction to production than the utterly fictitious prices of the controlled economy.

While more and more of the essential goods escaped from state management, entrepreneurial activity turned to inessential products that were not subject to any regulations. On street corners barter exchanges opened up where people offered their wares. The department stores carried the most curious "free economy" items. Never before or after has anyone seen such an odd supply of lamp shades, painted wooden plates, ash trays, razor blades, doorstops, cigarette lighters, and what not. While the button industry flourished, sewing needles, ribbons, nails, and screws became unobtainable treasures. Before long, production statistics in the several zones showed increasing output. And yet, the population's supply of the most essential mass consumption goods, rather than improving, sank to new lows.

According to Allied plans, food supplies were to rise during the summer of 1947 from 1,550 calories per person per day to 1,800 (the normal food supply for a laborer being 3,000 calories). Actually, food allowances in the Ruhr cities decreased during this summer to less than 900 calories. Under such conditions, foraging expeditions growingly disrupted working schedules in the factories. In order to preserve any willingness to work, some production managers distributed to their workers a part of the goods they produced for use on the barter markets.

The economy drifted without rudder or pilot. Money had lost its function as a yardstick of value and as a compass for production. Any profit that a firm might figure on the basis of official prices and costs and accumulate in its cash registers or bank accounts was actually a loss in substance. Following the material destruction of the war, now for the second time in one generation the paralysis of inflation had descended upon Germany.

WESTERN GERMAN FOREIGN TRADE

Since in her dealings with the outside world Germany was represented by the occupying powers, all aspects of her foreign trade including her monetary foreign exchanges were under the control of the Allies. For the American and British zones, and later for the French zone also, this control was administered by the Joint Export-Import Agency, JEIA, which acted as intermediary agent for all German business transactions abroad, and in a number of major transactions even as a contracting partner in its own right. Only after the Federal Republic of Germany had taken over independent administration of foreign trade and exchanges in 1950 was the cumbersome, bureaucratic JEIA administration liquidated. Of course, in these years only an inconsiderable fraction of Germany's import needs could be filled by way of private commercial transactions, because as yet hardly any part of current production was available for export. Of the meager import volume only one-third could be paid for from domestic funds; two-thirds had the character of foreign aid. The most aid came from the United States Military Government which, at high cost to the American taxpayer, shipped foodstuffs and essential raw

TABLE 25

*Foreign Trade; West Germany * and West Berlin, 1945–48*
(in millions of U.S. dollars)

	EXPORTS	IMPORTS			
		Total	*Commercial*	*Foreign Aid Deliveries*	
				Total	GARIOA
1945 (August–December)	52	96	32	64	64
1946	201	689	221	468	468
1947	315	843	243	600	600
1948	642	1,588	562	1,026	884

* Territory of the Federal Republic without the Saar.

SOURCE: *Geschäftsbericht der Bank deutscher Länder,* 1948 and 1949, pp. 31, 33.

materials to Germany without asking questions about how or when a German government would pay for them. These GARIOA deliveries, together with countless private food parcels sent from Western countries, saved tens of thousands of families from inanition, sickness, and death. Roughly two-thirds of the GARIOA deliveries of this period were finally donated by the London debt settlement of 1953 (see page 252) to the German economy.

4. *Currency Reform and Division of Germany*

TWO YEARS AFTER the end of the war Germany was not only a territory without a visible political configuration but also a country without a currency. The Reichsmark had lost its essential functions. It was not usable for computing profits and losses nor was it a common medium of exchange. An instrument indispensable to a modern economy was destroyed.

Both the Allies and the Germans had long realized that only a thorough currency reform could set production facilities to work and restore an approximation of normal economic conditions. Such a reform would have to do more than dispose of the redundant masses of money. It would have to be based on a decision as to who would be responsible for the new currency and how it should be managed. Whichever solution were adopted, a previous determination was required of the measure of self-government which the occupying powers wished to allow a future Germany. The following fateful questions also demanded answers: would a currency reform be introduced simultaneously in all four occupation zones? If the Russians were willing to cooperate, where should the new central bank be located? Who would direct its policies? Would the principles of a free economy be applicable once more so that prices and market trends would determine and direct production? Or would the government still have to prescribe the kind, size, and distribution of production?

Thus, the problem of currency reform led straight to the most momentous political decisions. Two years after Potsdam the common currency was the last, though precarious and purely formal, tie between the economies of the four zones. Without doubt a currency valid only for parts of Germany would put a final seal on the political division along the currency frontier. This frontier would soon become the border between separate economic systems in both domestic and foreign trade. These were ample reasons for the Americans and British to hesitate in embarking on a reform as long as there was any hope that agreements with the French and Russians could still be reached on how to save Germany's economic unity.

This hope for an agreement was definitely ended by the attitude the Russians took at the four-power London Conference of Foreign Ministers in late 1947; but only after the Russians had also withdrawn their cooperation from the Allied Control Council in March, 1948, and begun to blockade Western traffic to Berlin in April, 1948, did the three Western Allies take the decision to proceed on their own. Their concerted actions toward currency reform became the basis for the economic unification of the three zones. Unavoidably, this would in due course be followed by political unification. The borders of the future Federal Republic of Germany were thus drawn.

CURRENCY REFORM IN THE WESTERN ZONES

By what steps was the currency reform to be accomplished? The first preparations involved the reconstruction of a central banking system. In 1947 and 1948 the Allies organized in each of the Länder central banks (*Landeszentralbanken*) to replace the former central offices and branches of the defunct Reichsbank. This trunk with unconnected limbs was given a head: in March, 1948, the *Bank deutscher Länder* came into existence in Frankfurt. It was at first placed under the surveillance of an Allied Banking Commission, but the direction of its activities was already in German hands. The new central banking system, built up from below very much on the American pattern, was characterized by decentralization in its decisions and functions. The basic problems of monetary policy were not decided by the bank directorate itself but by a central banking committee on which the presidents of the eleven Landeszentralbanken predominated.

Once a central banking system had been organized, the three occupying powers assumed responsibility for the currency reform proper. The German authorities were placed in charge only of the technical execution. After careful preparations it was decided that the Reichsmark would be abolished and a new payment unit, the Deutsche Mark (D-Mark or DM), introduced.

June 20, 1948, was the day when the event, long awaited by the German population but kept secret until the preceding day, finally came to pass. On this memorable Sunday every inhabitant of the three Western zones was handed—together with his ration cards—40 Deutsche Marks in exchange for 40 Reichsmarks. On the day the new currency was born every person owned the same amount of money. But the very next day efforts began to increase the sum through gainful work. What seemed almost incredible happened. Literally from one day to the next fresh vegetables appeared in the windows of the food stores empty for years; shoes, clothing, and underwear, unobtainable for money the Saturday before, could once more be bought. It now made sense to supply the markets with hidden goods and subsequently to produce goods for these markets. To achieve output and to offer it in exchange for money promised a reward.

Handing out the per capita quota—which two months later was increased by another 20 D-Marks—was only the beginning of the transition from the R-Mark (Reichsmark) to D-Mark. All other private claims were cut down to 10 per cent of their nominal value. Cash and especially bank deposits were put through a complicated exchange process. To prevent a shortage of small coins, for the present the coins from one Reichspfennig to one Reichsmark were kept in circulation at 10 per cent of their former value. All other old money for which an exchange was claimed had to be paid into bank accounts on which the owners were credited with D-Marks at the ratio of 1 to 10. But only half the new account, that is, 5 per cent of the original amount, was unblocked immediately after the tax authorities had checked the legality of the assets' origin. Even in this late phase an effort was made to spot the black market profiteers, but this proved futile. Of the 5 per cent still blocked, one-fifth was unblocked in October, 1948, and later another one-tenth. The remaining seven-tenths were finally cancelled. Thus, aside from the per capita quota of 60 marks, in the end 100 R-Marks in cash were turned into 6.5 D-Marks, which means that the Reichsmark had been devalued for internal circulation to approximately one-fifteenth of its nominal value.

The worst complications were encountered in figuring out the devaluation for the banks and insurance companies. Along with their cash balances, their claims on the Reich, which they had acquired in huge amounts during the war and even before, were now wiped out. To balance their accounts they received what were called equalization claims, for which at first the Länder served as debtors. These rather illiquid, low-interest debentures were issued in a total amount of 21 billion D-Marks and may be regarded as the share in bankruptcy of the old Reich debt. The currency reform thus finally liquidated the huge debt left behind by the Third Reich through the device of a state bankruptcy. Except for the equalization claims which would have to be acknowledged as indebtedness, a future government would be able to begin its new financial existence almost unencumbered. For the time being, then, a new central banking system and a new currency existed but not yet a new nation.

The most difficult part of the reform was yet to come. On the one hand, the reestablishment of a sound currency was a precondition for reestablishing a working market. On the other hand, the new money would perform its function only on the condition that authoritarian management of the economy could be terminated and production once more be placed under the rules of the market. The Allies had assumed the responsibility of introducing the currency reform; now it was left to the Germans to shoulder the risk of radically changing their economic structure together with their currency. The more remote consequences of the reform were viewed therefore with apprehension as well as hope. Could an economy so severely disorganized that it failed to provide the people with the necessities of life conjure up a sufficient supply of goods simply through a currency reform and a reorganization of its economic system? Would a free development of prices direct production toward the desired goals? Was there any assurance that a transition from the established directed economy to a self-regulating system could be made in a very short time? Would producers, from now on necessarily faced with risks, discover the right methods, prices, and quantities and make fairly accurate forecasts of purchasing power and purchasing needs?

The major credit for the success of this experiment belongs to one man who summoned the courage and assumed the responsibility for breaking the vicious circle of poverty–rationing–controlled economy–low production–poverty. This man was Ludwig Erhard, at that time administrative director of the United Economic Region. He proposed that only the most essential foodstuffs and raw materials, such as bread, milk, fats, cereals, coal, electric power, iron, and steel, for the time being continue to be rationed at fixed prices, but that less essential goods should at once be exposed to the fresh currents of the free market. One year before, another liberal, the economist and later President of Italy Luigi Einaudi, had courageously led his country in the same experiment. Experience in Italy had shown that with the end of rationing, strong energies were at once released which benefited production and stimulated workers and entrepreneurs to provide the markets with greatly increased supplies. Wider production and increasing incomes would then cooperate to overcome poverty and make the rationing system obsolete.

This reckoning proved correct. Production increased in amounts and at a speed which even optimists had not dared predict. In the second half of 1948 industrial production rose by no less than 50 per cent and once more during the following year by well over 25 per cent. Everyone felt the relief of no longer having to stand in queues for ration cards, of not being obliged to have daily dealings with bureaucrats, and of being able to rely on his own abilities. The success in removing authoritarian shackles raised German self-confidence from the depths to which it had declined. The conviction that this liberal economic order was right took such firm roots that it became the political creed of most citizens in the Western zones.

CURRENCY REFORM IN THE SOVIET ZONE

At first sight a currency reform seemed to be less imperative in the Soviet zone than it had been in the West. The closing of the banks in 1945 and the blocking of large parts of the bank deposits had already markedly decreased the amount of money in circulation. A planned economy, Soviet style, would in any event be less dependent on the services of a sound currency than a free market economy.

Nevertheless, the Western currency reform forced the Soviet zone also to act with speed because the cash already devalued in the West continued to circulate freely at its face value in the East and could be used for payments. In order to prevent the Zone from being flooded with currency from the West, the Soviets followed the Western example after only four days. A new currency was also introduced here, the D-Mark East.

How little the Zone authorities were prepared for this departure is shown by the absence of new notes. The old Reichsmark notes retained their validity and an official stamp was simply affixed to them. After June 23, 1948, only notes with such stamps were legal tender.

Through the measures of 1945 an estimated 70 billion Reichsmarks had been taken out of circulation; therefore, the currency reform of the Zone did not need to be as drastic as in the West. Every person was allowed to exchange 70 Reichsmarks for 70 new D-Marks East, and the same ratio was applied to savings accounts up to 100 Reichsmarks. Bank deposits up to 1,000 Reichsmarks were exchanged at the rate of 5 old for 1 new unit, and larger deposits at 10 for 1. The ratio 10 to 1 was also applicable to all other bank assets and debtor-creditor relations. Assets in excess of 5,000 Reichsmarks were subjected to special examination which they only rarely survived.

As in the West, the new currency of the Soviet zone required the setting up of a new central banking institution. Almost simultaneously with the Bank deutscher Länder, in the spring of 1948 the *Emissions- und Giro-Bank* was founded in East Berlin, which in the course of the currency reform was renamed *Deutsche Notenbank* and three years later once more renamed *Staatsbank*. The principal function of this institution was to replace the provisional notes by new notes which bore the name of the Deutsche Notenbank.

While a new economic system was inaugurated with the Western currency reform, no one in the East could expect the currency reform to result in a comparable economic change. Rationing, planning, and price controls were carried over and adapted to the new system. The amount of money in circulation was only a minor problem.

DIVIDING GERMANY AND SPLITTING BERLIN

The political conclusions which the Soviet occupying power drew from the currency reform and political decisions of the Western powers were of incomparably greater significance than the Eastern currency measures. In the three Western zones the currency reform had logically led to constitutional reforms. The three years that followed the end of the war had proved that it was futile to wait and hope for a common German policy of the four Allies. The currency reform was indeed a symbol of the determination of three of the four to hasten German reconstruction within their immediate spheres of responsibility. Certainly this could never entail a renunciation by the Germans of all zones of their right to self-determination.

Efforts to create a new democratic constitution began in September, 1948, ten weeks after the currency reform. Over the following months they resulted in the foundation of the Federal Republic of Germany which, in accordance with accepted international law, raised the claim to the right of self-determination for all of postwar Germany. This new German state was constituted by several steps. In September, 1948, delegates of the Länder parliaments of the three Western zones assembled in Bonn and organized a Parliamentary Council (*Parlamentarischer Rat*) with the assignment of drafting a constitution. This Council drafted the Bonn Basic Law (*Bonner Grundgesetz*), which was approved by majorities in ten of the eleven Länder parliaments, Bavaria alone disapproving. On the force of this majority, the Parliamentary Council was empowered to proclaim the acceptance of the Constitution on May 23, 1949.

The first general elections were held three months later, in August, 1949. The Christian Democratic Union, CDU (in Bavaria CSU), received a narrow majority over the Social Democrats, and the Free Democrats followed at some distance. After another month, on September 21, 1949, for the first time in seventeen years a government based on free elections could take office under a constitutional president. Theodor Heuss was elected the first Federal President. The federal government was formed by a coalition of the Christian Democrats, Free Democrats, and several smaller parties. The first

Federal Chancellor was Konrad Adenauer, the first Minister of Economics Ludwig Erhard. This settled the political leadership for the next decade and a half.

These developments in the Western zones forced a decision on the Soviets. Would they allow their zone to exercise the same process of self-determination as the Western zones? This was made impossible by the evident discrepancy between the basic views of a majority of the population and those of the occupying power. The alternative was determinedly to carry through political separation. Although no doubts existed as to the will of the people, the will of the occupiers prevailed. The Bonn Constitution and the Federal Republic of Germany were confronted by the Moscow authorities with another concept of state established in the Soviet zone of occupation under the name of the German Democratic Republic (*Deutsche Demokratische Republik,* DDR), for which, however, they found no recognition in international law within the Western world. The Soviets went so far as to declare their sector of Berlin a part of this quasi-state.

Although the Soviet zone of occupation had been organized from the start on centralist principles and thus could easily have been given a government by fiat from above, those in authority sought to endow the territory under their power with the prestige of a democratically constituted state. To give their creation a semblance of legality they used a People's Congress, a People's Chamber, and popular elections based on a single list of candidates under the dominating influence of the Socialist Unity Party of Germany (*Sozialistische Einheitspartei Deutschlands,* SED). On October 7, 1949, this quasi-constitution went into effect, and therewith the Soviet zone laid claim to being a second German state.

The first victim of the division that was imposed on the country following currency reform was the city of Berlin. In the beginning, the two new currencies, DM-West and DM-East, circulated side by side with equal value and had the character of legal tender throughout the four-sector city. All official agencies maintained this fictitious equality, but the public soon did not, and a growing discrepancy in the two currencies' market values developed. By the end of July, 1948, one month after the reform, free market quotations for the DM-East had fallen to half the rate of the DM-West, and after another three months the public exchanged the two currencies at a rate of one to four.

This parallelism of two currencies of different value and of two antagonistic economic systems in one city could not last. The cleavage between the Soviet sector and the other three areas of occupation kept growing. At the end of November, 1948, the Communist representatives in the Berlin city parliament—which until then had precariously held together—declared themselves independent. Although they numbered only one-fifth of all Berlin representatives, they set up a government and an administration of their own for the Soviet sector. Within a few weeks this resulted in a political frontier arising between the Eastern and the Western sectors. For several more years a comparatively free exchange of persons and goods on both sides of the dividing line was maintained, but gradually the Eastern sector restricted this freedom of movement by various means until on August 13, 1961, the construction of the Berlin Wall began, which made the severance of the two parts of the city and the two regions complete. West Berlin became more and more isolated from its geographic surroundings, an island separated by about 100 miles from the mainland of the free world.

Not much more than three years after the end of the war the territory left to Germany was divided into two parts, separated by their currencies, their mutually antagonistic economic systems and their hostile political systems. For the third time in the course of only thirty years, within one generation, the foundations of German statehood were basically altered. And again many citizens found themselves unable to identify with the new state. Would time and wise leadership give the new political structure firm roots in the minds of the people? Would the citizens manage to become reconciled to the existence of two states? Or was it imperative to regard Germany as it emerged into the postwar world as still being in transition to something unknown?

[illegible]

[illegible] 1990, [illegible] communiqué expressing [illegible] [illegible] until [illegible] and [illegible] been [illegible] independent. Although they practiced only one [illegible] [illegible] [illegible] of the Soviet sector. Within a few weeks this resulted in a political [illegible] between the Eastern and the Western sectors. [illegible] [illegible] consumer goods [illegible] [illegible] [illegible] repeated the [illegible] by various means until on August 13, 1961, the [illegible] of the Berlin Wall [illegible] the two parts of the city and the two regions completely. West Berlin became [illegible] surrounded [illegible] about 100 miles from the mainland of the free world.

But much more than [illegible] of the [illegible] the territory left [illegible] divided the two parts, separated by their currencies, their [illegible] antagonistic economic systems and their hostile [illegible] to [illegible] in the course of only thirty years, within one generation, the foundations of [illegible] were basically altered. [illegible] with the [illegible] [illegible] support the new political structure [illegible] in the [illegible] Would the citizens [illegible] to become [illegible] [illegible] regard Germany [illegible] and the [illegible] still being in transition to something [illegible]?

VII

THE FEDERAL REPUBLIC OF GERMANY

1. The "Economic Miracle"

WITH THE CURRENCY reform of 1948 the first epoch of German economic history after the second world war had come to an end. As in the case of every rigid line drawn across historical developments, this one is somewhat arbitrary. Furthermore, it may be slightly misleading. Stressing the importance of the currency reform too much could easily create the impression that the years before were dark as night—thus overlooking the early beginnings of sound economic growth—and that the years after it were brilliant simply on account of the reform. The currency reform alone, however, could not have brought about the massive recuperation that now ensued. But because the currency reform, the Marshall Plan, and the enthusiastically awaited liberation of the German economy from oppressive administrative shackles all became operative at about the same time, there was some justification in the feeling people had that they were witnessing a historic turning point. Compared with these economic events, the political efforts to develop the constitution of the Federal Republic and gradually to recapture independence from the Allies did not attract as much public attention. The first steps toward organizing a new state in their divided country were generally re-

TABLE 26

Economic Development of the Federal Republic of Germany, 1948–65*

	GROSS NATIONAL PRODUCT			
Year	*In current prices (billions of DM)*	*In 1954 prices (billions of DM)*	*Per capita, in 1954 prices (in DM)*	*Index of industrial production (1958 = 100)*
1	*2*	*3*	*4*	*5*
Second half 1948	36.4	—	—	27 ||
1949	81.8	—	—	39 ||
1950	97.9	112.9	2,368	49
1951	119.5	125.5	2,608	58
1952	136.6	136.5	2,815	61
1953	147.1	147.3	3,038	67
1954	157.9	157.9	3,189	74
1955	180.4	176.9	3,537	86
1956	198.8	189.3	3,741	92
1957	216.3	200.2	3,926	97
1958	231.5	206.8	4,051	100
1959	250.9	221.0	4,281	107
1960	296.8	254.9	4,598	119
1961	326.2	268.6	4,781	127
1962	354.5	279.6	4,911	132
1963	376.5	288.6	5,012	138
1964	412.5	307.3	5,274	149
1965	448.8	322.3	5,470	156

* Unless otherwise stated, the territory referred to is that of the Federal Republic without the Saar and West Berlin for the period 1948 to 1959; from 1960, including the Saar and West Berlin.

† As of December 31.

§ Cols. 8 and 9: the territory referred to, 1950 to 1959, includes the Saar but excludes West Berlin.

|| Per working day.

GOLD AND OTHER FOREIGN EXCHANGE RESERVES † (*in millions of DM*)			
Total	*Gold*	*Gainfully employed, yearly average (in thousands)* §	*Registered unemployed, yearly average (in per cent of employed)* §
6	*7*	*8*	*9*
+168	—	13,544	4.6
—1,375	—	13,524	8.4
—1,129	—	13,963	9.5
+1,737	116	14,580	9.0
+4,635	587	15,055	8.4
8,158	1,367	15,645	7.5
10,930	2,628	16,280	7.0
12,781	3,862	17,160	5.2
17,795	6,275	17,805	4.1
22,917	10,674	18,317	3.5
26,105	11,085	18,519	3.6
23,621	11,077	18,865	2.5
31,628	12,479	20,331	1.2
28,281	14,654	20,730	0.9
27,729	14,716	21,053	0.7
30,301	15,374	21,303	0.9
30,313	16,992	21,547	0.8
29,719	17,371	21,840	0.4

SOURCES: Cols. 2 and 3: *Vierteljahreshefte zur Wirtschaftsforschung* (1951), p. 17; *Statistisches Jahrbuch für die Bundesrepublik Deutschland 1965,* p. 552. Col. 4: computed from *Statistisches Jahrbuch für die Bundesrepublik Deutschland 1965,* pp. 31, 552. Col. 5: *Statistisches Jahrbuch für die Bundesrepublik Deutschland 1965,* p. 246; for 1948 and 1949, estimated on the basis of *Monatsberichte der Bank deutscher Länder* (August, 1952), p. 110. Cols. 6 and 7: *Monatsberichte der Bank deutscher Länder* and *Monatsberichte der Deutschen Bundesbank,* 1951–65, statistical annexes. Cols. 8 and 9: *Statistisches Jahrbuch für die Bundesrepublik Deutschland 1965,* p. 151; *Monatsberichte der Bank deutscher Länder* (October, 1950), p. 81.

garded by the Germans as a transitory phase. Although they consented, they didn't feel enthusiastic about it. Sentiments were entirely different toward the economic recovery. Not only did the standard of living rise steeply, the recovery also laid a balm on the deep wounds that the nation's self-respect had suffered with the collapse of the Weimar Republic and throughout the Hitler epoch.

Economic recovery was responsible to a large extent for the enduring stability of political conditions in the Federal Republic. Contentment with developments was so widespread that the phrase "no experimentation" became the most usual and successful slogan of candidates in the following general elections. What a contrast to the instability of the first German Republic! At that time the helplessness of wavering governments in the face of economic catastrophes had made the nation feel deserted by its leaders, and this had prepared the soil for the foolhardy political aberrations that ensued. Compared with these recollections the scope and steadiness of the recovery after 1948 seemed indeed like a miracle, even more so because the abyss into which the nation had fallen in 1945 was still deeper than the one of 1918.

What actually happened after the currency reform to create the impression of a miracle? Table 26 gives a rough survey of a period of recovery unparalleled in German history.

Between 1948 and 1964, industrial production increased almost six times, in the first years by leaps and bounds, but also in the following years at a consistently high average rate of growth. Real gross national product rose almost threefold in the 14 years after 1950; per capita it increased more rapidly in the Federal Republic (BRD) than in other Western European or the North American countries.

Table 27 shows that Austria and Italy had almost as high a growth rate as Germany, and Japan an even higher one. In these countries, too, people spoke of an economic miracle.

Compared with prewar developments, the growth in the national product was surprisingly steady. Not one year showed complete stagnation; however, years of very fast growth alternated with years of more modest growth. In this Germany did not differ from her neighbors. Thanks to the general progress achieved in business cycle policy after the second world war, few countries showed the traditional pattern of business cycles that included years of economic contraction and lower incomes.

Among the figures in Table 26, those on employment and unemployment stand out as most indicative of the expansion. In the first years after currency reform the number of unemployed was still high although employment rose

TABLE 27

Indices of Per Capita Gross National Product; Selected Countries, 1950–64
(at constant market prices; 1958 = 100)

Year	Federal Republic	France	Britain	Italy	Austria	U.S.A.	Japan
1950	59	76	88	—	64	91	—
1953	75	84	92	80	71	104	77
1955	89	90	99	87	86	103	86
1957	98	98	101	95	96	103	98
1959	106	102	104	106	102	105	116
1961	118	112	110	121	114	106	150
1963	124	121	113	134	120	113	173
1964	131	126	119	136	126	117	191

SOURCE: *Statistical Yearbook of the United Nations, 1965* (New York, 1966), pp. 539–41.

at the same time. In the first six years after the reform three million new jobs were created and filled, twice as many as the average number of unemployed registered during the year 1950. When this development began, the unemployment rate in Germany was about as high as in Belgium, Denmark, and Italy. Before long, unemployment in Germany sank to the level of countries with virtually full employment such as Britain, the Netherlands, Norway, and Sweden. In the autumn of 1965 the registered unemployed were confronted with job openings almost seven times their number, although by that time more than one million foreign workers had found employment in the Federal Republic.

Foreign trade, which in 1948 had still been practically dormant, rose more rapidly than the national product and industrial output. In one year, 1949–50, exports doubled, and in the following year they increased another 74 per cent. In later years also the rate of growth, viewed in the international context, remained very high (see Table 28 on page 247). Eliminating the uncharacteristic year 1949 and disregarding the price changes for imports and exports, the fourteen years to 1964 show a six-fold increase in the volume of imports and exports. In 1960, the Federal Republic's share in total world exports had risen to more than 10 per cent, and the country had overtaken Britain to rank next to the United States. Germany's balance of trade, which in the period from 1948 to 1950 had been badly unfavorable, turned in the following year to a steadily favorable one, and with the help of these export surpluses it became possible to increase monetary reserves almost every year from 1951 to 1960. After 1960 there were also some years in which foreign exchange reserves decreased; yet the gold reserve rose from year to year to almost 17 billion DM in 1964, an amount never equalled even in the gold standard epoch of the old Reich. With surprising speed the Deutsche Mark became a hard currency trusted by foreign investors.

Did all this constitute a miracle? With the advantage of hindsight the brilliant record of reconstruction and growth, as exemplified by the few selected facts of Table 26, can be logically explained; there is no mystery. The following features are the most important: as early as 1948 the international political climate had improved in favor of the Western zones of Germany. The occupying powers had begun to treat Germany not as a defeated enemy but as a partner and finally as an ally. In marked contrast to what had happened after the first world war, they gave the German economy massive aid and prepared it for a return to the free world economy. This world economy itself developed more favorably than after the first world war. While the volume of world trade regained the pre-1914 level only in 1924, by 1950 it had risen far above the levels of the 1930's, and it continued to grow with only mild fluctuations of the business cycle. This naturally helped the German exporters to regain footholds in the world markets.

Furthermore, the German economists proved to be much more expert in dealing with the problems of reconstruction and the following expansion than they had been after the first world war. Varying combinations of government interference and aid within the basic framework of the free market economy, preferred in principle, exerted their influence on the volume and structure of investment, secured the favorable balance of international payments, and for some time maintained a stable price level. Such general conditions favored the full utilization of the intelligence and willingness of the individuals who were prepared to work hard to regain their former standard of living. When, in about 1953, people in West Germany were on the average as well supplied as before the war, their standard of living still remained considerably below the standards reached in the meantime in comparable Western countries. This left German development with sufficient further incentives. Just as a baby after overcoming a severe illness often increases rapidly in weight for a period until he recaptures the weight normally corresponding to his age, such high national product growth rates are not infrequent in economies which temporarily have strayed off the normal path.

In 1948, Germany's industrial production was no higher than it had been at the turn of the century or immediately after the first world war. This could not last if general world conditions continued to be fairly satisfactory. Rapid growth could therefore have been predicted, especially for the initial phase of reconstruction in which comparatively little capital was required. Despite all the devastation, the basic structure of production and distribution had survived. What was most needed to set the entire mechanism going once more was to repair and to replace missing parts. Overall, the capacity of the remaining industrial plant was not substantially less in 1948 than before the war, since the destruction was approximately balanced by what had been added to capacity in the years from 1939 to 1944. To be sure, such a global view hides the realities of the chaotic destruction which were described above in some detail. Certain specialized plant had been totally eliminated, which resulted in bottlenecks and therefore underutilization of the capacity that did exist. Furthermore, the structure of the existing plant was obsolete in view of the fundamentally changed new needs. And yet, a considerable basic reservoir of productive installations had survived. Also, manpower in plenty was available in 1948. If industrial production still was only half of what it had been before 1939 this could be assumed to be due to faulty—but promptly reparable—organization and to lack of raw materials. Was it a miracle that the economy, after these faults had been eliminated and more imports were available, became healthy and strong?

Does this mean that there actually was no German economic miracle? Did everything develop as a matter of course? Surely not in the view of contemporary observers of the currency reform and its outcome. Not one expert at the time accurately predicted what the economic future of the Federal Republic would be. Even optimistic forecasts lagged far behind the reality that emerged in the following years. The explanation is that no one could know beforehand how the various favorable elements, characterized above, would coincide to make such growth possible. To the Germans it seemed miraculous how everything operated in their favor and how even what were initially severe handicaps turned into blessings.

Thus few observers would have guessed in 1948 that the influx of refugees would one day be counted as one of the contributing factors of economic growth. At first they multiplied the misery; more food and shelter had to be supplied, more public funds had to be devoted to social aid, relatively high unemployment had to be carried. But after the loss of life the nation had suffered, this population influx offered the Federal Republic valuable workers, many of them skilled, all intent on finding gainful employment. The stock of human capital, of such crucial importance to economic growth, was augmented. And when in due time it became possible to secure the necessary physical capital, the movement of refugees, which continued up to the construction of the Berlin Wall in 1961, turned out to be a boon. It was one of the most potent stimuli for economic development.

The period from 1948 to 1965 may be divided, according to its economic aspects, into three phases:

The first phase, 1948 to 1951, was the time of reconstruction proper. These were critical years in the effort to return to a free market economy. It was the phase when the Marshall Plan and the balance of payments recovery made their most significant contributions. The Federal Republic was received as a member by the Organization of European Economic Cooperation, OEEC, although she still lacked sovereign status. In 1951 the dismantling program was officially declared to be terminated.

In the second phase, 1952 to 1956, the Federal Republic was accepted as a sovereign nation among equals, but at the same time it transferred some of these sovereign rights to a number of supra-national institutions, such as the European Coal and Steel Community (in German usually referred to as *Montan-Union*); the North Atlantic Treaty Organization, NATO; and finally the European Economic Community, EEC (*Europäische Wirtschaftsgemeinschaft,* EWG), the so-called Common Market. The international efforts to liberate world trade from administrative controls culminated in 1958 when the Deutsche Mark became fully convertible, in law as well as in fact. After lengthy deliberations a law against restraint of competition was enacted in 1957 and came into force in 1958. The year 1957 marks the achievement of full employment, which persisted even when in 1958 German economic growth was somewhat retarded by the repercussions of the American recession.

The third phase began in 1959 with a new ascent into boom conditions which in 1960 resulted in another spectacular growth of the national product, by 9 per cent. However, since there were no longer any manpower reserves available—on the contrary, a state of "over-full employment" could be said to exist—prices rose more rapidly than before. The Deutsche Mark was revalued in March, 1961 (see p. 273) to reduce the balance of trade surpluses which seemed to pose the greatest threat to the domestic price level. The revaluation had the desired effect of slowing down the growth in exports and foreign investment in the following few years, and for the first time there were even adverse payments balances. By 1963 the overall economic growth rate decreased to 3 per cent. However, in 1964 a strong new expansion set in. The Federal Republic was now definitely one of the wealthy countries and in this third phase began to participate in international efforts to aid developing countries. There is no visible sign that this third phase of economic expansion is approaching its end. Possibly a future observer may judge the year 1965 to have been an important turning point, the year when Western European attempts at integration came to a crisis. Perhaps the year 1963, when Konrad Adenauer was replaced by Ludwig Erhard as Federal Chancellor, may be seen as another sort of dividing line. The general elections of September 19, 1965, did not change the alignment of the political parties, however; the "economic miracle" still dominated the voters' preferences.

2. *Reconstruction 1948 to 1951*

THE FIRST YEARS after the currency reform were devoted to reconstruction. Ruined productive facilities and houses and a huge amount of household goods, furniture, and clothing lost as a result of bombing and expulsion had to be replaced. The renewal of worn-out goods had been neglected even before the war and all the more during and after it. What personal property was left was overage. Everywhere there was an enormous hunger for commodities of every description, besides the physical hunger and undernourishment which persisted in many places. The industrial plant which still existed worked only poorly, if at all. The demand that now pressed upon the market was the accumulation of many lean years. It was both for consumption and for investment, both for domestic production and for imports.

The task of reconstruction posed the challenge of how to reconcile all these demands, which in sum total certainly far exceeded productive capacity. Above all, large investment was essential to make general economic productivity grow. The one overriding problem of postwar economic development was how to bring about the necessary investment. As will be shown, through these years more than 22 per cent of the gross national product was continuously made available for investment purposes. A second pressing problem was the seemingly hopeless condition of the balance of foreign trade. In these early years it was only through foreign aid that the minimum of essential imports could be procured. Up to 1951, exports were not nearly sufficient to pay for essential imports. Reconstruction could be said to have been accomplished when capacity surpassed prewar levels and when the

Federal Republic managed to pay for its imports out of its own resources. Both happened in 1951.

Reconstruction, however, did not simply mean the rebuilding of what had been destroyed. The process of reconstruction already heralded the economic growth to follow. Wherever ruined plants had to be rebuilt, this would obviously not be done merely by duplicating former patterns. The new installations were mostly much better than the old ones, with the result that as capacity expanded production costs declined. The firms evacuated from the eastern parts of Germany and from Berlin to new locations in the Federal Republic reopened with modern plants. Even during the reconstruction phase German industry largely made the transition to up-to-date methods.

The greatly changed conditions under which the people of the Federal Republic would have to live in the future demanded much more than mere reconstruction. In 1948, approximately six million more people than before the war lived in this area. The economic unity of the Reich being lost, the multiple relations that had connected both parts of Germany with one another and with the countries that were now about to disappear behind the "iron curtain" had been disrupted. The structure of production and foreign trade had to adapt to all these changes. Fortunately, these changes not only posed difficulties but also offered new opportunities. Many a product could be bought or sold to better advantage in the world market than it had previously been in the now severed parts of the Reich.

FROM THE CURRENCY REFORM TO THE KOREAN WAR

The currency reform had been a project of the Allies. It would hardly have been possible for a German agency to impose such a hard cut; only the military government could take in its stride a responsibility of such magnitude. On the other hand, the simultaneous transition from a controlled to a market economy was the work of German agencies, carried out with the tacit approval of the occupying authorities. On the day that the new currency was introduced, 400 items were taken off the list of controlled commodities. A Law setting forth Guidelines for Controls and Price Policy After Currency Reform (*Leitsätze für die Bewirtschaftung und Preispolitik nach der Geldreform*) proclaimed the intention of the Economic Council of Bizonia to decontrol as soon as possible those sectors of the economy that seemed ready for free competition. In July, 1948, 90 per cent of the then existing price controls were abolished, and the general price freeze, in force ever since 1936, was terminated. As stated before, this did not mean that the end of government regulation of prices and distribution had come, for certain relevant parts of the economy still remained under the old controls. However, the lifting of controls was sufficiently general to change the entire economic climate at one stroke. Within three months the production of bicycles doubled and that of shoes more than doubled. The index of industrial production climbed as much per month between June and December, 1948, as it would later do only in whole years.

Prices also rose, however. It had been expected that not all prices would remain at their old levels. After all, production costs had changed since 1936 and at different rates for various items. But soon the market went beyond adjusting the price structure to the new conditions. The entire price level climbed, and so did living costs. The higher prices could not be fully accounted for by rising costs of production, although wages did rise after the wage freeze was lifted and more had to be paid for raw materials. But in general, costs still lagged behind commodity prices. Demand simply exceeded supply. Either the devaluation had not sufficed to eliminate redundant purchasing power, or monetary liquidity was now increasing too rapidly. It may be assumed that both alternatives were true to some degree. The scarcity of goods resulted in handsome profits.

These were critical weeks for the market economy. Advantages and disadvantages appeared at the same time, and it was hard to judge which outweighed the other. The advantages consisted in the stimuli to entrepreneurs to expand production, the disadvantages in the obviously unjust distribution of incomes. On November 12, 1948, a general strike broke out in Bizonia, the unions demanding that an economic emergency be declared and a price commissioner installed. This was not granted by the Bizonal administration, but it was evident that a further rise in prices, despite its usefulness in some respects, had to be prevented. By now, high profits had enabled business to accumulate the means needed for economic expansion.

Financing investment out of profits played a very important role in the process of reconstruction. The currency reform had made this possible on a large scale for the first time. In view of their urgent replacement needs, consumers were not yet able to accumulate any considerable savings. What other means were available for financing investment? As things stood, only the state and the business firms were potential savers. The state accumulated funds by way of taxation, businesses by way of the gap between their costs and high selling prices. In both cases, the consumers' spending was cut, not by their free choice, but by compulsion. The government had even planned its methods of taxation so as to enhance the accumulation of business profits and had promised greater tax privileges to those businesses which would embark on large investments. These inducements worked well in view of the assured demand for goods and the very tight credit conditions.

The occupying powers had introduced exorbitant rates of income taxation, one of the purposes being to reduce redundant purchasing power. At the time of the currency reform these rates had already been lowered, but not far enough. An unmarried man who earned 2,000 marks a month had to pay almost 1,000 marks in taxes. And if he earned 830 DM a month, any wage rise would benefit him only to the extent of 50 per cent. Who could be expected to take risks or to exert himself under such circumstances? But this was exactly what everything depended on now. The plan was to decrease the confiscatory tax rates, but the Allies objected, fearful that new budget deficits might once more endanger the price level. In this situation the German authorities resorted to several devices. They permitted business managers to manipulate book values of assets and depreciation allowances by various accounting maneuvers in order to reduce taxable income. If the companies plowed back the profits thus retained into their enterprises, they received further tax benefits. In this way, self-financing was promoted on a large scale. In fact, until the end of the reconstruction period in 1951, promoting investment was one of the foremost aims of tax policy.

These tax policies purposely ignored the criticism about the lack of social justice in exempting those most able to bear taxes. Entrepreneurs and private companies were by that time in a position to accumulate large properties while their workers were still living on a meager standard. Yet, this was believed to be the only available way to assure equitable supplies for all in the future. That in these years social peace was preserved may be attributed to the indisputable improvement in general living conditions, the moderation of trade union policies, and the various social measures adopted by the government, to be described below.

By the beginning of 1949, the first peril for the free economy, the threat of inflation, appeared to have been overcome. Supply had by then succeeded in catching up with demand. The Bank deutscher Länder had been busy stopping various potential sources of inflation. Among other devices, it used a sort of credit ceiling in an attempt to hold credit creation down to a certain level; in this it was not entirely successful. Also, the commercial banks were urged to raise their minimum reserves in order to decrease the volume of bank credit. Following the British example, Bizonia had proclaimed a "utility program" (*Jedermann-Programm*) with the object of providing the market with consumer goods at subsidized prices. But before this program had begun to yield results the business cycle had once more changed its direction and prices developed a downward trend. At this point, a new threat appeared: unemployment began to rise. Before the currency reform there had been practically no unemployment, or at least no visible unemployment, since it was veiled by the flood of money. During that time businessmen did not have to keep accurate accounts, and everyone could work at something or other irrespective of economic results. It had been a foregone conclusion that unemployment would have to rise after currency reform. However, the magnitude of the increase was a surprise. The number of unemployed rose month by month and at the beginning of 1950 it was four times what it had been on the day of currency reform. Not only were workers idle, but many factories as well were not running at full capacity.

Thus the market economy had reached a second critical point. Many observers accused the system of having permitted unemployment to occur and demanded a return to a controlled economy. However, the more farsighted were convinced that this would not be the right remedy. Some occupation agencies and German critics of the policy of waiting exhorted the administrators to find ways to stimulate demand. They suggested that the Central Bank should finance public and private spending programs even at the risk of causing a slight new rise in prices. In an emergency, it was thought, full employment should have preference over price stability. To be sure, no real danger of a steep rise in prices was thought to exist, since the incidence of unemployment seemed to show the possibility of a further expansion of production without reaching the limits of capacity.

The Central Bank and the federal government took a different view. They maintained that the emerging unemployment was not, as it had been in the world depression after 1929, a problem of the business cycle but rather of the structure of the economy. According to their view, the continuing influx of refugees and expellees and their unfortunate concentration in regions with few employment opportunities were primarily responsible. Actually, unemployment was much lower in the industrial centers than in Schleswig-Holstein, Lower Saxony, and Bavaria. Industry as a whole had not been discharging workers; on the contrary, it was able and anxious to expand its labor force. Under such circumstances, a large program of financing additional demand would very probably have induced another general price rise, and this would have seriously worsened the second persistent difficulty of the time, the balance of payments.

Meanwhile, in 1949 West Germany had been accepted as a member in the Organization of European Economic Cooperation, OEEC, whose mission was to promote the reconstruction of Europe and, for this purpose, to liberate trade among its member nations. Along with other European countries, the three Western zones had already abolished a number of quotas that had restricted imports. No sooner had the gates been raised than a broad stream of goods began to flow. Had domestic prices moved upward just at this time, the rush of imports would have been even greater while exports—now more expensive—would have had to be cut back. As long as exports were not yet sufficient to pay for essential imports and American aid was required to finance the balance, the country's economy was particularly vulnerable to rising prices.

In the autumn of 1949 the Deutsche Mark was devalued. The rate of 3.3 marks to one dollar, which had been set by the Allies, proved to be very damaging to exports. The new rate of 4.20 marks to one dollar lowered the price of German goods on foreign markets and raised the price of imports. At the same time many competitor countries had also devalued their currencies, some more than West Germany, so that in some respects the German situation was even worse than before. At the end of 1949, the deficit of the balance of payments rose, a warning to the German authorities that this was not the time for large-scale make-work programs.

However, at the beginning of 1950 the period of watchful waiting appeared to have reached its end. It may have been a favorable development that the cost of living index had returned to the level that had existed at the time of the currency reform, but the young Republic could not simply accept without a fight the perils of renewed mass unemployment. Therefore, housing construction and other schemes meant to generate employment were planned, to be financed by the Central Bank. But before these programs could begin the business cycle took another turn, this time for the better: production rose faster than was usual in spring. By itself this turn might not have gained sufficient momentum to bring about a quick and strong change in general conditions. Such a change was brought about, however, by an unforeseen event in a different quarter of the globe: the outbreak of hostilities in Korea in June, 1950. At one stroke, the situation in the world markets and consequently for the German economy was changed.

A violent upsurge of activity began, at first stimulated by a speculative demand for raw materials which soon spread to capital goods, foodstuffs, textiles, and a wide range of goods. Stocks of whatever commodity could be found were accumulated at home and abroad. The faster a trader could buy the better, for prices were rising steeply. This posed the third critical point for the German market economy, for again the market was accused by many of being helpless as a regulator in a difficult emergency. Again, central management of commodity markets and a general price freeze were urgently demanded. The Central Bank immediately tried to dampen the boom by tightening credit with but mediocre success. The most critical element was the condition of international exchanges. Panic buying had at once swelled imports; but also the interests of export business demanded that means be available to pay for extensive raw material purchases. Thus, foreign exchange reserves dwindled rapidly. Only thanks to credits granted Germany by her European neighbors was she able to procure the needed imports. However, these credits were not inexhaustible and finally it became necessary in the spring of 1951 to revert temporarily to import restrictions.

Only when the principle of free trade had thus been breached did it appear through the rising value of exports what a brilliant opportunity had opened up for German business. Rearmament and a domestic boom in all Western countries stimulated their import requirements. West Germany was in the fortunate position that her industries were able to fill foreign orders not only comparatively cheaply but above all quickly. In hindsight the cautious policy in the period preceding the Korea boom of deferring a rapid expansion of the domestic economy proved to have been correct. This policy had directed German producers to foreign markets where now, thanks to the sudden boom, they found ready customers. Within one year the influx of foreign exchange in payment for exports doubled and new monetary reserves accumulated. After 1951, when world markets had successfully been entered, Germany's worries over monetary reserves were mostly a thing of the past. It is true that in the early years, among the foreign currencies received in payment there were too many that were not freely convertible, and the dollar shortage still persisted. Therefore imports from dollar markets remained restricted longer than from other areas.

THE MARKET ECONOMY

The market economy had overcome its third crisis. This gave it sufficient prestige to escape fundamental controversy in succeeding years, which were indeed easier ones. The advocates of the free market increased. It characterizes the German situation that discussions over the basic tenets of the economic order were of much wider public concern than in other countries. After the first world war all countries, excepting only the Soviet Union, had rapidly returned to market economies as the natural way an economy should work. After the second world war the United States, for one, did not hesitate to do so again. Of course, as a wealthy country, it had not been forced even during the war to introduce controls on a scale at all comparable to what was done in Germany. Furthermore, Italy, Belgium, and Austria had already begun to relax controls before Germany decided on a similar course. On the other hand, there were also countries that held fast to controlled economies, among them some that were far in advance of Germany in their economic performance.

In this situation a technical discussion among experts of the various practical methods of procedure would have been appropriate, especially because no one contemplated turning over the direction of economic processes to the market forces entirely and at once, nor did more than a few experts favor a permanently government-planned economy. In Germany, however, this most important problem of economic policy, of how functions should be distributed between the government and the market, became not a technical but a philosophical controversy with all the characteristics of dogmatic cleavages between extreme positions. This was regrettable and seemed to denote a deficient sense of realism. But the controversy resulted partly from the German trend of decades toward growing government influence on the economy, and it may be attributed partly to the German tendency to convert all political and economic problems into ideologies inviting fundamental discussion.

In these controversies the partisans of a market economy referred to two sets of ideas that had been formulated and developed during the 1920's and later in the 1930's as local points of oppositional forces against the Hitler regime. One doctrine was propounded by a group of economists around Professor Walter Eucken of Freiburg University. They outlined a program for a return to free competition and free trade—for which in Europe the accepted term is "liberalism"—with the intent of avoiding liberalism's traditional flaws. The terms "neo-liberalism" or "ordo-liberalism" were coined by this Freiburg school ("ordo" meaning that the free economy was to perform within an orderly structure). Independently but simultaneously, Professor Alfred Müller-Armack of the University of Münster, later state secretary of the Federal Economics Ministry, sought an organic compromise between the spheres of the government, the markets, and the interest groups. For this intermediary position Müller-Armack used the designation of "social market economy" (*soziale Marktwirtschaft*) which had so much popular appeal that it came to characterize the overall economic policies of the Federal Republic, a remarkable testimonial to the power of a well-chosen phrase.

The propounders of neo-liberalism based their opinions on the conviction that political liberty could not prevail without economic freedom. Whoever opposed dictatorships had to oppose systems of "planned economy." To them, the market place and the democratic forum were correlative. However, liberty was not to be understood as an attitude that merely negated government interference. Such an attitude, they claimed, had led old-fashioned liberalism to its downfall. As newly formulated, economic freedom on the contrary presupposed a very active government, although the government's functions should be confined to combatting crises, to safeguarding the currency, and, above all, to guarding against private positions of monopoly power. Monopolies were to be prohibited or placed under public control, and free competition was to be guaranteed by the public authorities. Thus, it was hoped, would economic efficiency be enhanced and a just distribution of incomes be most closely approximated.

What for Germany was new in these ideas was the fundamental connection they established between the problems of the economic and the political order, although in other countries this connection may long have been a matter of discussion and experimentation. Neo-liberalism as a doctrine had its uses in overcoming the anticapitalist sentiments of the public which, as has been seen, had helped to seal the fate of the Weimar Republic. After the currency reform, the doctrine of the market economy gained wide acclaim.

Yet it was by no means unopposed. Critics pointed out that very old democracies existed where, without endangering their systems of political liberty, central controls and economic planning were being used and developed. In Germany primarily the Social Democratic Party (*Sozialdemokratische Partei,* SPD) and the trade unions opposed Economics Minister Erhard's experiment. These groups, with their traditional faith in strong government guidance, were concerned that without it reconstruction might be imperiled. Developments soon dispelled such concern. However, the opposition was also politically motivated by a dread of the possible revival of the elements against which they had fought for generations and which now, in the eyes of many Germans, had emerged from the Hitler era burdened with guilt.

The argument for and against the market economy was in Germany much more than a mere controversy among experts as to the best way to carry out reconstruction. It was also a struggle to build a new society. In the opinion of the public the argument was soon settled. On the one hand, there was discernible a wide-spread disgust with state regulations in whatever shape; people had simply had more than enough of them. On the other hand, for many the argument was clinched by the progress of reconstruction itself, which was attributed by propagandists to the market economy, to a greater extent, probably, than was justified by the facts. Finally, a large variety of social and economic welfare measures saw to it that the masses accepted the existing system and even its designation as a market economy. The Government continued to intervene wherever the market process seemed to show flaws or failed to deal with present needs.

The SPD continued its opposition for several years, but in the end it adopted the concepts of the market economy under the formula: "Competition as far as feasible, planning as far as necessary." This slogan was sufficiently general and flexible to enlist the support of the partisans of the "social market economy" in the Bonn ministries, and it gave a rather accurate description of what actually happened at the time the market economy was reintroduced. Rationing of consumption ended at the beginning of 1950, and the relations between the producers were largely left to be determined by market forces. However, in 1951 price controls had not as yet been abolished for coal, steel, flour and bread, dwellings, or electric power. Nor was German foreign trade decontrolled, and foreign exchange transactions were kept under many restraints. The domestic capital market was a sickly problem child which, with rigid interest rates, required a variety of government support. In this respect the second phase of reconstruction was to show some progress. However, as of 1966 the free market had not yet been restored either in agriculture or in some aspects of housing.

THE MARSHALL PLAN

Currency reform and the decision in favor of the market economy were two pillars on which reconstruction was based. The third was the inclusion of the Western zones of Germany in the Marshall Plan in April, 1948.

Unlike the period after the first world war, the United States had not withdrawn from the European continent after the second. As an occupying power it shared the responsibility for Germany. Although factories were still being dismantled and certain kinds of production remained forbidden, aid to the defeated country in its struggle against hunger and disease was organized at a very early stage. As noted before, ever since 1945 the GARIOA funds of the American army had been flowing in, along with the contributions of numerous private agencies such as CARE and of innumerable individual package senders. The official aid was aimed at immediate emergency needs; foodstuffs were therefore far in the foreground.

Of course, West Germany was not alone in needing help. All of Europe was struggling against heavy odds to restore some order to the chaotic economy and hasten reconstruction. Raw materials, machinery, and foodstuffs, which the United States was in a position to deliver but which Europe was unable to pay for, were lacking. When, very shortly after the war, the dream of perpetual peace had given way in the face of the cruel reality of East-West tensions, the political perils of abandoning Europe to its weakened condition became vividly apparent. Already Soviet power had entrenched itself in the territories under its immediate sway. Turkey and Greece were threatened. In France the Communists had become the strongest party, and in other countries also, especially Italy, revolutionary upheavals were feared. These massive dangers could not be dealt with by occasional aid schemes, be they ever so costly. If substantial progress was to be achieved, a constructive master plan would have to be devised.

This master plan was formulated by Secretary of State George C. Marshall on June 5, 1947, at Harvard University. The United States offered the European countries substantial aid on the condition that they propose a concerted plan of reconstruction. Europe received this offer with enthusiasm. Even several Eastern states, primarily Czechoslovakia, voted to adopt the plan, before being forced to withdraw by Soviet pressure. In the end, 16 European countries were represented at the preparatory conference. Here for the first time in its history Western Europe made its appearance as an economic unit. The Marshall Plan (the European Recovery Program, ERP) began to spin the threads which later were woven into more far-reaching integration efforts. The Western zones of Germany, not yet members in their own right, were represented by the respective occupying powers. The decision had already been made to utilize Germany's resources for the reconstruction of Europe, which without them was difficult to imagine. The revision of the Level of Industry plan, described above, was the logical consequence of this decision.

On the basis of the proposals made by the European experts, the United States Congress passed the Foreign Aid Bill in April, 1948. A total of approximately 17 billion dollars was provided, of which 7 billion were allocated at once. The European member countries founded the Organization for European Economic Cooperation, OEEC (in German, the *Organisation für europäische wirtschaftliche Zusammenarbeit,* sometimes referred to as *Europäischer Wirtschaftsrat*), for the concerted execution of the Marshall Plan. The Western zones of Germany were represented by their military governors, but as soon as the Federal Republic was established, it assumed membership in its own right.

What benefits did the Marshall Plan bestow upon Germany? The first effect was that the Plan was of the greatest help in providing foreign foodstuffs, raw materials, and machinery, the payment for which was deferred to some later date. In the first year alone, to the middle of 1949, West Germany received deliveries valued at over 600 million dollars. In total, she received one and a half billion dollars, or $29 per capita. This aid given by an erstwhile enemy marks an extraordinary political departure. It created a precedent in the history of peace settlements, which up to that time had known only war contributions paid by the defeated to the victors. Materially, the effect was great and immediate. In 1948, two-thirds of German imports were paid not from earnings but through foreign aid. Without it, shortages would have been felt everywhere, notably in foodstuffs, raw materials, and badly needed special machinery; reconstruction would have been long delayed. At that period every dollar had a far greater effect than indicated by its nominal value or even more through its official exchange value in Deutsche Marks. In exhausted postwar Europe, American commodities were precious treasures; they helped to break many a bottleneck.

A second effect was connected with the Marshall Plan. The American imports did not have to be paid for immediately to the United States; but to the German individual they were not free gifts, he had to buy them for Deutsche Marks. As had been the practice with the GARIOA deliveries, these payments were booked on a special account, the so-called counterpart funds. German agencies, at first in cooperation with the United States Marshall Plan administration, disposed of these funds, mostly by granting low-interest investment credits. In this way, power stations, plants for the iron and steel industry, shipbuilding, and housing were financed. Coal mining and agriculture were also among the favored recipients. The counterpart funds were at the disposal of the government, an operation reserve which could be set to work wherever the other available means—retained earnings, the capital market, or the public budget—proved insufficient. The beneficial effects of this reserve continued long beyond the Marshall Plan period. After 1952, only Berlin was still a recipient of direct Marshall aid, but credits from the counterpart funds continued to be available. After only a few years credits began to be repaid and could be expended a second time. Total expenditures from ERP counterpart funds reached 18.6 billion D-Marks by 1964.

THE ORGANIZATION OF EUROPEAN ECONOMIC COOPERATION AND THE EUROPEAN PAYMENTS UNION

A third initiative of the Marshall Plan may have been of even greater importance than direct aid and counterpart funds credits: the effort to establish a community of the Western European countries with the primary aim of liberalizing their mutual trade. Again in contrast to what had happened after the first world war, after the second national frontiers remained closed to free trading relationships for a long time. So strong had the distortions become as a result that many believed none of the national economies could suddenly be exposed to the harsh winds of free trade. However, the persistence of measures intended to protect countries from one another was especially harmful in Europe to the recovery of any of them. It was therefore only logical that the United States should wish, by way of the Marshall Plan, to exert a certain pressure on the European countries to "liberalize" their trade relations. The OEEC regarded just this as its main assignment; in the middle of 1949 its Council of Ministers decided to abolish all administrative trade restrictions for about 50 per cent of mutual imports and, step by step, to proceed with further foreign trade liberalization. It was a special misadventure that Germany's efforts in this direction had to suffer a setback during the Korean crisis. Led by Minister Ludwig Erhard, the German government had originally embraced the program for reestablishing freer world trade with greater enthusiasm than many other governments and had included it in their general concept of a market economy. The Federal Republic was able to resume the program only in 1952, but then pursued it with determination. Among the OEEC countries, commerce was almost entirely freed of all quota restrictions, and as a result it was possible for OEEC to wind up its activities in 1961. This was all the more appropriate since by that time the newly organized economic groupings, the EEC (European Economic Community, consisting of France, Italy, the Federal Republic of Germany, and the Low Countries) and EFTA (European Free Trade Association, consisting of Britain, three Scandinavian countries, Switzerland, Portugal, and Austria) had assumed some of OEEC's previous functions. The organization which succeeded OEEC, the Organization for Economic Cooperation and Development, OECD, located in Brussels, has as its foremost tasks the coordination of its member nations' economic policies and the promotion of developmental aid.

While trade among the European nations was thus rapidly freed from administrative shackles, the liberalization of trade with third countries proceeded at a slow pace. As late as 1965 German imports of 105 commodities (mostly textiles) from non-European "capitalist" countries required special licenses, and imports from countries belonging to the Soviet bloc were persistently tied to bilateral trade treaties and individual licenses.

All efforts to liberalize Western Europe's commerce in commodities might have come to little, had not international payments been liberated at the same time. To achieve this purpose, on July 1, 1950, the European Payments Union, EPU, was founded. Until that date every country was intent on balancing its accounts individually with every other country with which it traded, and so could buy from any partner only as much as the latter was buying from it. In the absence of a bilateral balance a country would have to pay the deficiency in gold or dollars, which the country either did not have or could not spare except for essential purchases from the United States. Gold and dollars were the only means of payment that were entirely free and usable anywhere. A few other currencies, such as the Swiss franc and the convertible pound sterling, approached the dollar as foreign payments media. It was obvious that as long as there was no other way of balancing payments, international trade must be restricted to an unsatisfactory volume. If a country did not need the tomatoes that a trading partner had to offer, this partner could not buy the machinery that he needed. Another partner who might have liked the tomatoes possibly had nothing to offer in return that the tomato grower wanted. In such a system all nations were cut off from the advantages of an international division of labor and multilateral trade.

This is where EPU came in; it organized a European clearing system by establishing current accounts through which Britain, France, Italy, West Germany, and the other member nations balanced off their mutual claims. The Bank for International Settlements, BIS, in Basle, the institution which had been founded in 1930 as a reparations bank in connection with the Young Plan, carried the current accounts of each member country. The activities of EPU were not restricted to accounting operations. As soon as BIS reported that one country had bought more from all other countries combined than it had sold them, clauses on multilateral credits began to function. A country with an adverse trade balance previously would have had to pay the deficiency in cash, which at that time meant gold or dollars. This was now avoided by opening a line of credit. Only a part of the deficit had to be paid in gold or dollars; for the rest EPU extended credit within a framework of agreed quotas, in the hope that the country concerned would in time have more to sell and thus be able to wipe out its debt. This system soon proved its merits in further diminishing the need for gold or dollar transfers among the European trading nations.

In addition to clearing facilities and multilateral credits, a third facility of the EPU was made available to Germany as the first recipient among member nations when, in the winter of 1950–51, the Korea panic caused her to take in imports in excess of the quotas for which the automatic credit clauses would have come into play. She also lacked any other means to pay for the excess imports. Here EPU came to the rescue by allowing a special credit. It had the financial power to do so because the United States had granted EPU 350 million dollars from Marshall Plan funds. Germany quickly overcame the crisis with a temporary suspension of trade liberalization, as described before. Rapidly rising exports made it possible to repay the special credit within a few months. With this repayment, the Federal Republic joined the countries which normally export more than they import. It became a permanent creditor of EPU, but withdrew only part of the balance in gold or dollars, leaving the rest on account. Since other countries, on the contrary, were structurally debtors, hopes that over the years a balance would result between temporary credits and debits did not materialize. However, EPU was gradually able to increase the quotas of cash payments, so that in the end credits were only required for one-quarter of the clearing balances. This process led to the so-called hardening of the European currencies and in 1958 to the resumption of their general convertibility and the consequent demise of EPU. Since then there has been a loose coordination of monetary policies among the former member countries of EPU, in the framework of the European Payments Agreements, EPA. The second phase of the German recovery ended along with EPU.

THE SYSTEM OF PUBLIC FINANCE IN THE FEDERAL REPUBLIC

In the preparatory deliberations on a constitution for the new West German state which began in 1948, an important issue was the allocation of fiscal powers among the various levels of government. In every community the division of fiscal prerogatives is decisive for the overall internal balance of governmental authorities. The Federal Republic was to be, as the name indicates, a Federation. But what should be the functions as well as the revenues of the federal, the Land, and the local authorities? Above all, should the Federation (*Bund*) be largely dependent on the Länder, as it had been before the first world war, or were the Länder on the contrary to be dependent on the central authority, as they had been under the Weimar constitution? The Western Allies favored as weak a central authority as possible. The representative of France especially tried to stunt every effort to build up strong centralized government functions. The draft constitution that was at first submitted to the Western military commanders and foreign ministers was judged by them to be too centralistic. The German parties themselves did not agree in that matter. The Social Democratic Party pressed for a strong power at the center; the Bavarian Christian Social Union believed in reserving important governmental functions to the Länder. Because of the refusal of the Social Democrats to submit, the military commanders did not succeed in having the draft constitution revised in the direction of more extensive decentralization. At last a compromise was reached in April and May, 1949, with the result that Article 109 of the Basic Law (*Grundgesetz*) of May 23, 1949, stated: "The Bund and the Länder are fiscal authorities in their own right and independent from one another."

The Basic Law declared that it was the function of the Länder to discharge all duties of government not specifically delegated to the Bund. The competencies of the Bund were specified as follows: all foreign affairs, provisions for occupation costs and other obligations derived from the war, restitution, national insurance subsidies, matters relating to currency, money, and coinage (*Währungs-, Geld- und Münzwesen*), foreign trade, and others. Several important matters were left to "concurrent legislation" by the Bund and the Länder, which meant that the Länder had the power to legislate on their own unless the Bund had acted. A number of functions of primary importance were unequivocally assigned to the Länder and the local authorities, such as the administration of justice, police, public health, education and cultural affairs. Soon the Bund became the stronger competitor in the field of "concurrent legislation," with the result that after all a wide measure of legal and administrative uniformity was established in Western Germany. Actually, over the years political, economic, and social considerations worked toward transferring to the Bund functions in many fields which originally had been intended for the Länder. Thus the central power came more and more to the fore in promoting industry and trade, in transportation, and even in the area of government aid for science and research.

The various governmental units were assigned several specific forms of taxation and to the extent of these revenues, they were indeed independent. Luckily, the legislative powers reserved to the Bund were sufficiently comprehensive to prevent serious local inequalities in taxation from developing. However, the local authorities could freely define the rates of the business tax (*Gewerbesteuer*) and the land tax (*Grundsteuer*) assigned to them. Among the taxes reserved to the Bund were the general turnover tax, customs duties, and other indirect taxes (except for the tax on beer). The Basic Law assigned to the Länder the following taxes, among others: personal income and corporation income taxes, property taxes, and inheritance taxes;

the Länder were also in charge of collecting the real estate taxes assigned to the local governments.

It could be foreseen that the Bund tax revenues would not suffice to cover the very extensive centralized functions of government. It was therefore provided that the Länder could be called upon to participate in financing some areas of Bund expenditures. This power was used once in 1950; after 1951, recourse was had to Article 106 of the Basic Law which allows the Bund to claim a certain quota of the income and corporation taxes levied by the Länder. The size of this quota annually became a source of irritation and controversy. In 1955, an amendment to the Basic Law allotted to the Bund 33.3 per cent of these state taxes, but this very soon again proved insufficient. A further revision followed in 1958 giving the Bund 35 per cent of income and corporation taxes up to 1962, and even more thereafter. In 1955 the Bund was given the privilege of levying surtaxes on income and corporation taxes, but so far no use has been made of this title. A comparison between the fiscal systems of the Bonn Republic with those of the old Reich and the Weimar Republic reveals that the Bonn system is based on a series of compromises best characterized as negations: neither is the Bund as dependent on the Länder as in the old Reich, nor are the Länder dependent on fiscal revenues doled out to them by the central authority as in the Weimar Republic.

Furthermore, the Federal Republic does not follow the Weimar precedents in the field of fiscal administration. Unified administration was replaced by a peculiar dualism. Only customs revenues and indirect taxes were to be administered by Bund agencies, all other taxes by the Länder fiscal authorities which, as far as revenues for the Bund are concerned, act as its agents. Consequently it happened that, despite the unified tax laws, tax collection followed differing practices in the different Länder, with the taxpayers placed under territorially unequal conditions.

After all these measures, the distribution of tax revenues among the Bund, Länder and local authorities still failed to correspond to their respective functions. Therefore many adjustments had to be made through horizontal and vertical intergovernmental transfers of funds between the various fiscal authorities (*Finanzausgleich*). Thus, the local authorities received considerable funds from the Länder in addition to the revenues from their own taxes; funds were also transferred between one Land and the other and between local governments. For instance, the financially weak Land of Schleswig-Holstein, burdened more than others by the influx of refugees and expellees, received financial aid from the "wealthy" Länder Rhineland-

Westphalia and Baden-Württemberg. Moreover, West Berlin was regularly subsidized from the Federal budget.

The specific fiscal policies, expenditures, and individual tax arrangements for various purposes are treated in the pertinent chapters.

3. *Consolidation*

THE END OF THE OCCUPATION REGIME

WITH THE SIGNING of a treaty on the relations between the Federal Republic and the three occupying powers (*Deutschlandvertrag*) in Bonn in 1952, the status of an occupied power practically ended for the Federal Republic. However the treaty itself had to be revised in London and Paris agreements of 1954 because originally the Bonn treaty had been projected in conjunction with a treaty to establish a European Defense Community, EDC, which in 1954 the French parliament refused to ratify. Thus the Bonn Treaty of 1952 became fully effective only on May 5, 1955. But even before, there had been constant progress toward the status of equality for the Federal Republic and toward a normalization of political conditions within West Germany as well as in all of Western Europe.

Up to 1955 the Federal Republic had indeed possessed a parliament (the Bundestag), a federal government, and a federal president, but it was still somewhat comparable to a minor in whose name a guardian acts and in whose education and vital decisions the guardian takes a prominent part. When in November, 1949, the Federal Republic was permitted to join OEEC and EPU, and several further important industries were struck off the list for dismantling, the Bonn government agreed to become a signatory to the Ruhr Statute, which had been devised by the Western Allies in 1948 and signed by seven Western nations on April 18, 1949. This statute provided that an international agency would be in charge of the Ruhr basin to regulate production and distribution of coal, coke, and steel. Now German representatives would at least participate in the Ruhr agency's decisions. In the years 1950 to 1952 more of the production controls of the Allies were lifted, for instance on shipbuilding and the production of synthetic rubber and synthetic petroleum. Actually, the synthesis of rubber and gasoline never regained the role in German industry which it had had during the war and prewar periods. Freer world trade and increased German production of natural oil made it less urgent to expand capacities for synthetics production. On the other hand, the lifting of restrictions on shipbuilding opened the way for an amazing expansion of the German merchant fleet, which by 1960 was greater than before the war.

The dismantling ended in 1951 with the cancellation of the dismantling order for the steel mill in Salzgitter, part of the former *Hermann Göring Werke*. It was Germany's good fortune that by this time she had found sympathetic assistance abroad in combatting the irrational dismantling policy. On the initiative of Walter Reuther, president of the American Automobile Workers' Union, the leadership of the American trade unions sought to influence public opinion to pressure the Administration and Congress to stop dismantling. A private estimate is that in 1954 more than half the German heavy industry, machine, and chemical exports came from plants which only five years before had been on the dismantling list.

In 1950, after the outbreak of the Korean war, American, British, and French statesmen for the first time expressed their inclination to see Germany rearm, and Chancellor Konrad Adenauer on his part formulated a proposal in this direction. In view of recent history any scheme for German rearmament seemed fantastic. But the Korean conflict as well as the emergence of the paramilitary "people's police" (*Volkspolizei*) in the Soviet zone made rearmament seem urgent. Only five years after the defeat of the adversary whose disarmament for all time to come had been solemnly vowed, a divided Germany was once more drawn into the vortex of an armaments race. The East-West conflict did not admit of neutrality in the heart of Europe.

Following Winston Churchill's proposal of August, 1950, French Premier René Pleven suggested in October of the same year that a European army be formed with German participation. He made France's consent to German rearmament conditional on Germany's agreement to join a European Coal and Steel Community. France had a vital interest in having a pledge in hand to assure Germany's peaceful intentions before allowing her to rearm. A community for coal and steel had been proposed earlier, in May, 1950, by the French Foreign Minister Robert Schuman as a first step toward European unification. For Germany, the concept of a common market for coal and steel was a decisive improvement over the Ruhr Statute, which had retained discriminatory controls against her. Now Belgium, Luxembourg, the Netherlands, France, and Italy were to submit their industries to the same controls as Germany, thereby renouncing their separate national coal and steel policies. The Treaty of Paris of April 18, 1951, establishing the European

Coal and Steel Community (in Germany usually referred to as *Montan-Union*) became effective in 1952.

Despite the failure of the European Defense Community Treaty, on May 5, 1955, Germany was at last admitted in her own right to the North Atlantic Treaty Organization, NATO, and the Western European Union, which in addition to the Montan-Union countries included Britain. At the same date, the occupation regime for the Federal Republic was terminated. The Allied High Commissioners now became their countries' ambassadors. The occupation forces, which between 1950 and 1955 had cost the Federal Republic 34 billion Deutsche Marks, were transformed into allied protective forces. Immediately the build-up of the German army within the NATO framework began.

Because of the division of Germany, a formal peace treaty to end the second world war could not be negotiated and concluded. Consequently Germany had no hope for the foreseeable future of joining the United Nations, and so her international status remained below that of more than one hundred other nations. At the United Nations in New York, the Federal Republic is represented by an observer with the rank of ambassador but without voting power, while it has a full membership in some of the UN's specialized agencies.

GROWTH AND EXPORT

In 1952 the federal government resumed its policy of liberalizing its trade relations with the OEEC countries that it had been forced to interrupt in connection with the Korean crisis. Developments in the following seven years were less hectic than in the preceding period. The demand of consumers, domestic investors, and importing countries for German goods was strong enough to raise the gross national product by almost two-thirds. Yet, up to 1955 the volume of demand posed no serious threat to the price level. Nor did prices in general recede noticeably after the end of the Korean crisis, in contrast to the period after the first buying rush following the currency reform (see Table 30 on page 249). A decrease in the price level could probably have been achieved only by the Central Bank pursuing a deflationary policy, which no one favored. Unemployment, averaging more than 8 per cent annually in 1952, was still considerable. The Central Bank and the government were satisfied so long as prices did not continue their upward trend, and thereafter they concentrated their efforts on keeping prices stable at the level they had reached.

TABLE 28

Foreign Trade of the Federal Republic; Selected Years, 1950–65

YEAR	IMPORTS				EXPORTS			
	Total (billions of DM)	*Foodstuffs*	*Raw materials*	*Semifinished and finished goods*	*Total (billions of DM)*	*Foodstuffs*	*Raw materials*	*Semifinished and finished goods*
		(as per cent of total)				*(as per cent of total)*		
1950	11,374	44.1	29.6	26.3	8,362	2.3	14.0	83.7
1952	16,203	37.4	34.8	27.8	16,909	2.2	7.6	90.2
1954	19,337	37.0	28.5	34.5	22,035	2.3	7.7	90.0
1956	27,964	32.8	29.4	37.8	30,861	2.7	5.6	91.7
1958	31,133	30.2	24.7	44.1	36,998	2.4	4.6	93.0
1960	42,723	26.3	21.7	51.0	47,946	2.3	4.6	93.1
1962	49,498	27.6	17.8	54.6	52,975	2.2	4.5	93.3
1964	58,839	23.9	18.6	56.6	64,920	2.5	3.9	93.6
1965	70,448	23.9	16.2	58.8	71,651	2.8	3.6	93.2

SOURCE: *Statistisches Jahrbuch für die Bundesrepublik Deutschland 1966*, p. 320.

Economic expansion after 1951 essentially was carried along by the continuous expansion of exports, as shown by Table 28 on page 247. The success in exports had several reasons, among which the most decisive were the strength of the world markets, the structure of German industry, the country's comparatively prudent monetary and fiscal policies, the support export industries were given by the government, and a general undervaluation of the Deutsche Mark.

That a large slice of the remarkable expansion in world trade was filled from German sources can again be traced to several causes. Germany was favored by the nature of her industrial structure. She possessed and was able to expand precisely those industries—such as machinery, vehicles, electrical products, and chemical products—which were among the front runners in international trade and enjoyed constantly growing markets. During the first years following Germany's reentry in the world markets exports of raw materials and semifinished goods had made up abnormally large shares of total exports, but thereafter German exports consisted principally of the goods with the best demand expectations. (See Tables 28 and 29.)

The strength of the export industries was enhanced by the fact that, at prevailing exchange rates, prices were relatively low. Because unemployment still persisted, rapidly growing productivity was not outstripped by rising

TABLE 29

Exports by Commodity Groups; Federal Republic, 1950–65
(as per cent of total exports)

Group	*1950*	*1965*
Machinery	14.1	20.9
Iron and iron goods	21.4	12.3
Vehicles	5.7	15.1
Chemical products	11.2	12.4
Electrical products	3.7	9.0
Textiles and clothing	6.5	5.7
Coal and coke	15.8	2.9
Nonferrous and precious metals and products	5.4	3.7
Precision tools, optical goods, watches	2.1	2.5
Others	14.1	15.5
Total:	100.0	100.0

SOURCE: *Statistisches Jahrbuch für die Bundesrepublik Deutschland 1952*, pp. 243–45; *ibid., 1966*, p. 327.

TABLE 30

Volume of Money and Cost of Living Index; Federal Republic, 1948–65

Year	Money in Circulation,* December 31 (in millions of DM)	Cost of Living Index † (1962 = 100)
	I	II
1948, Second half	14,263	85.1
1949	17,599	84.0
1950	19,152	78.8
1951	23,341	84.9
1952	26,011	86.7
1953	29,441	85.1
1954	34,155	85.3
1955	37,969	86.7
1956	41,083	88.9
1957	42,397	90.7
1958	46,849	92.7
1959	48,855	93.6
1960	54,456	94.9
1961	63,381	97.1
1962	67,534	100.0
1963	71,779	103.0
1964	76,147	105.4
1965	80,553	109.0

* Cash and domestic demand deposits.

† Cost of living for a four-person wage-earner family with medium income of head of household as the only wage earned.

SOURCES: Col. I: computed from *Monatsberichte der Bank deutscher Länder* and *Monatsberichte der Deutschen Bundesbank*, 1950–66, statistical annexes. Col. II. *Statistisches Jahrbuch für die Bundesrepublik Deutschland 1965*, p. 497; *ibid., 1966*, p. 495.

wages; while at the same time after 1951 import prices took a favorable turn. These two conditions held down German production costs in comparison with those of other countries, and Germany's monetary and fiscal policies tended in the same direction. As has been pointed out, the Central Bank did not resort to extensive spending programs whenever a lag in demand appeared on the horizon, but neither did it withhold the money and credit required by a growing economy.

However, after 1955 the Central Bank again had cause to counteract a threat that the business boom might become overheated. In itself, the growth of demand was no larger than in previous years but it was confronted with a less elastic supply as the Federal Republic approached full employment. This set a limit on the real possibilities for continued expansion of the economy as a whole, and the danger of a rise in prices increased. And price stability remained the overriding concern of economic policy.

Therefore, the rediscount rate was raised from 3 to 3.5 per cent at the end of 1955, and once more to 4.5 per cent in March, 1956. When in May the Bank deutscher Länder went one step further by raising the rediscount rate to 5.5 per cent and at the same time cancelling the rediscount privileges of exporters, the industries involved raised a storm of protest and within the cabinet itself violent differences of opinion were voiced. At an annual meeting of the association of manufacturers, Chancellor Konrad Adenauer publicly rebuked Economics Minister Ludwig Erhard and Finance Minister Fritz Schäffer for having approved the measures of the Central Bank; the Chancellor denounced them as having dealt body blows to the economy.

This conflict of the Chancellor with the Bank deutscher Länder taught the public a lesson on the importance of the Central Bank's statutory independence from government interference. This was especially essential in 1956, when the Bank deutscher Länder, organized in 1948 by the Allies, was finally about to be replaced by the federal bank (*Bundesbank*) called for by Article 88 of the Basic Law. In July, 1957, the Bundestag voted the Law on the German Federal Bank, which in Article 12 obligated the new bank to work in harmony with the government's general economic policies, but then limited this obligation by establishing the bank's responsibility for safeguarding the currency. It was expressly stated that within the bounds of its authority the bank was to act independently of government directives. All the same, the government continued to wield considerable political influence over the bank since it designated the members of the board of directors and thereby almost half the members of the Central Bank Council (*Zentralbankrat*), the bank's governing body.

Even before the Deutsche Bundesbank was formed, the Bank deutscher Länder had been aided in its endeavors to check inflationary pressures by certain developments in the federal budget, which however had not been planned for the purpose. In the years from 1952 to 1956, the budgets showed considerable surpluses because the occupation forces did not make full use of the funds that had been allotted to them. Finance Minister Schäffer transferred these surpluses to the Bank deutscher Länder, thus practically steriliz-

TABLE *31*

Cost of Living Indices in Selected Countries; Selected Years, 1948–65
(1958 = 100)

Year	*Federal Republic*	*France*	*Italy*	*Netherlands*	*Sweden*	*Britain*	*U.S.A.*
1948	92	57	78	—	65	—	83
1950	85	64	72	75	67	68	83
1954	92	82	91	86	85	85	93
1955	94	83	93	87	88	89	93
1956	96	85	96	89	92	94	94
1957	98	87	97	98	96	97	97
1958	100	100	100	100	100	100	100
1959	101	106	100	101	101	101	101
1960	102	110 *	102 *	103 *	105	102 *	102
1961	105	113	104	105	107	105	103
1962	108	119	109	106	112	109	105
1963	111	127 *	117	109	116	112	106
1964	114	131	124	115	119	115	107
1965	118	132	130	122	125	120	109

* Change in basis of index; figures in columns not entirely comparable.

SOURCES: *Statistical Yearbook of the United Nations, 1964* (New York, 1965), pp. 520 ff.; *Statistisches Jahrbuch für die Bundesrepublik Deutschland 1966,* p. 131.*

ing them in taking them out of circulation. The sterile fund thus accumulating was nicknamed "Julius Tower" with reference to the Spandau fortress tower near Berlin in which Frederick the Great kept his war treasure and in which part of the five billion gold franc French war contribution of 1871 was held by the Reich, again as a war treasure. Salting away Schäffer's Julius Tower may have had some beneficial effects on the business cycle up to 1956. However, the termination of this reserve fund, finally amounting to over seven billion marks, was managed with just as little planning as had gone into accumulating it. The cash reserves raised the parliament's appetite, and several additional expenditures were voted. Only the fact that the government had at that time to make payments abroad for various purposes prevented a major inflationary effect from developing in the course of the Julius Tower liquidation. On the whole, the cost of living rose less than in some of the other Western countries.

The anti-inflationary policy which the Bank deutscher Länder followed up to 1957 and the accumulation of the Julius Tower treasure contributed to a further expansion of German exports and to renewed foreign exchange surpluses, as had been the case in 1949–50 when the Central Bank refused to stimulate economic activity at home, thereby favoring exports. Business experienced certain difficulties in selling its products in the home market and therefore looked abroad, where the markets offered better prices.

The government's fiscal and general economic policies were also favorable to the export business. The exporters were given government guarantees against various risks in international trade. After 1951 they enjoyed a number of tax privileges, some of which however had to be rescinded on protests from OEEC. Exporters had access to cheap credit, and when now and then the Central Bank caused the commercial banks to tighten credit, exceptions were made in favor of exporters. Finally, it was helpful to exporters that the Central Bank stood ready at all times to buy foreign exchange and export drafts. All in all, direct government aid was probably not decisive for the development of exports, but neither was it negligible. No doubt, the presence of the Allied military forces also contributed a great deal to strengthening Germany's foreign exchange position. Whenever the foreign soldiers used German services other than those financed by the German defense contributions they had to procure D-Marks in exchange for French francs, pounds sterling, or the dollars which had been in such desperate demand in the days of the dollar shortage. Every serviceman who bought a German car or spent his furlough in Berchtesgaden strengthened the German monetary reserves.

THE LONDON DEBTS AGREEMENT OF 1953

The need to accumulate monetary reserves was not the only reason for regarding export surpluses as absolutely essential. The government had to face a number of obligations which could only be discharged under conditions of a favorable balance of trade and services. How the Hitler regime deviously expropriated Germany's foreign creditors has been described above. After the war, there were many claims from abroad which the federal government acknowledged, at least in part. Among other liabilities, the Dawes and the Young Loans were mostly still outstanding. Their service had to be resumed, back interest had to be paid. The occupation powers even made the recognition of German sovereignty conditional on a settlement of prewar debts, and they desired to make arrangements for that part of the immediate postwar aid which had been given on credit.

In the London negotiations, conducted for Germany by the banker Hermann J. Abs, the federal government acknowledged the principal of all the old debts and offered to pay back interest also, although at reduced rates. Payments were spread over longer terms and interest charges were redefined. The creditors were prepared to concede that, although the Federal Republic was indeed regarded as the legal successor of the German Reich, economically she could not, being a divided country, possibly assume all the Reich liabilities.

The settlement of prewar debts became possible only through the waiver by the United States of two-thirds of its claims for repayment of postwar economic aid in order not to damage Germany's future international exchange position. According to the London Agreement of February, 1953, the total debt outstanding amounted to roughly 14 billion marks against which annual installments of at first 600 million, later of 750 million marks were to be paid. By the end of 1964 approximately three-quarters of the debt had been repaid.

It was not easy to arrive at this settlement because there was no way to determine in advance whether future economic developments would justify incurring obligations of this size. All partners to the Agreement were anxious not to repeat the mistakes made in the unfortunate debt arrangements after 1918. While negotiations were carried on in London, Germany already was in possession of a rather well-stuffed foreign exchange cushion. Doubts persisted, however, whether future payment balances would suffice, all the more so because other foreign obligations existed in addition to those dealt with in London, such as the payments to the State of Israel agreed to in 1952 as a partial material compensation for the irreparable wrongs inflicted on the Jews by the National Socialist regime. At the time of the London conference it was especially doubtful whether the required free dollars would be obtainable, though it might not prove too difficult to arrange transfers in European currencies. It was for these reasons that the United States decided on its generous self-denial.

THE CONVERTIBILITY OF THE MARK

In this second phase of development, 1952–58, foreign exchange holdings grew rapidly, as shown in Table 26 (see page 220–21). The Bundesbank was accordingly prepared in 1958 to declare, along with some other OEEC countries, the return of its currency to full convertibility against the dollar. Ever since 1931, when in the midst of the banking crisis exchange controls had been introduced to combat capital flight, such controls had assumed more and more rigorous forms until finally the management of foreign exchange became one of the main instruments of economic *dirigisme*. The reverse process of liberating the markets began in 1950 within the framework of the EPU, first for exchange transactions among European nations, soon to extend also to overseas countries. The formal declaration of general convertibility, on December 27, 1958, wrote finis to a sad chapter of German economic history. The D-Mark had in fact already been freely convertible for some years. By 1958, it had become a hard currency trusted by foreign investors, even though other European currencies were still plagued by frequent rumors of impending devaluation.

The liberalization of foreign exchange markets had several notable consequences for the countries involved. The most important may have been that countries with convertible currencies and stable exchange rates were left with only limited autonomy in influencing the business cycle. In illustration of this, German monetary policy furnished an impressive example. As has been mentioned before, the Central Bank had frequently suggested after 1948 that, in its estimation, the goals of keeping the currency stable and foreign payments balanced were paramount. In the course of the years this opinion led into a serious quandary. In the boom of 1955–56, the Central Bank tried to master the upward trends and to protect a steady price level by making money scarce. What followed was an increased influx of gold and foreign exchange because the high interest rates attracted capital to Germany. And since prices were kept low, exports were maintained or even increased. The commercial banks, because of their great liquidity, were able to expand credit without recourse to the rediscount facilities of the Central Bank, which was thus left with a narrow supply of commercial paper. There was a slight rise in prices besides. Now the Central Bank changed its course and cheapened credit. This relaxation seemed to be justified by the fact that the production boom abated somewhat in 1958–59; in previous years the reaction would probably have been different, and the Central Bank would simply have waited for the price increase to slow down. However, under conditions of free convertibility, the laws of a world-wide credit market are in effect. It was not possible any longer for a single country to keep credit tight and to stave off influences from outside. The German Central Bank went so far in relaxing credit as to set a rediscount rate of 2.75 per cent at the beginning of 1959, a low rate without precedent in the history of German central banking. This in turn helped to ignite another boom which introduced the third phase of the Federal Republic's economic development.

CAPITAL MARKET POLICY

After the Korean boom, the Bund thought the time had come to change its capital market policies. Almost three-fifths of all investment in new construction and producers equipment had before 1950 been financed out of the retained earnings of business; another quarter of the total was financed directly by public agencies; and only one-seventh was contributed by the capital market. In effect, practically no capital market as yet existed in Germany, not a satisfactory condition in the long run for a market economy. Although no one could expect that the self-financing of investments from undistributed profits would disappear entirely, efforts had to be exerted to change the proportional roles of the various methods used for investment and to promote financing from outside sources. Therefore, tax policy was tailored from 1951–54 to promote the capital market. However, tax policies were not all consistently in this direction. For instance, the so-called declining balance method of depreciation introduced in 1952 again favored self-financing, which nevertheless had been discouraged in 1951 by the repeal of several tax privileges. (Estimating depreciation by the declining balance method involves periodically writing off a constant percentage of the remaining book value of a property—rather than, by the straight-line method, a constant sum—and diminishes taxable profits, especially in the first years after construction, but also in total.) On the whole, the government's objective seems to have been to promote the development of a capital market while continuing to aid and guide investment. Economic expansion depended on a high rate of investment, and consumption was to be kept from expanding too much at the expense of investment growth. At the same time, the new tax policy was also directed after 1951 to inducing individual saving activity.

It may be that private saving could have been stimulated simply by lifting the interest ceiling and allowing interest rates to rise to a level that corresponded to actual market conditions. However, the responsible authorities were afraid to rely on a neutral interest policy because rising interest rates would have endangered housing construction, among other investment activities. As long as rents were controlled—and ending rent controls seemed impossible for the duration of the extreme shortage in dwellings—the cost of housing construction could not be allowed to rise above certain levels. The controlled rents would not yet have supported payments of interest rates as determined solely by supply and demand.

It therefore remained one of the tasks of tax policy to stimulate private saving. Savers who purchased bonds of public authorities or the mortgage bonds of the social housing program (*Sozialpfandbriefe*) were allowed to a limited extent to deduct the amounts invested from taxable income. Direct loans and subsidies for shipbuilding and housing were also encouraged (by the famous Article 7, Sections a–e, of the income tax law). These tax methods perhaps did not greatly increase the total capital available for investment, but they directed whatever capital there was toward the desired uses. Of the amounts invested in shipbuilding through 1958, more than one-quarter came from nontaxable loans and subsidies. The Law for the Encouragement of the Capital Market (*Kapitalmarktförderungsgesetz*) of 1952 favored bond issues of public authorities and of industry by exempting interest income totally or partly from income taxation while still keeping interest rates under controls. This law was successful in promoting the financing of investment of corporations from outside sources. But here, too, the government, wavering between two different purposes, decided in favor of capital investment and against an old social tenet of fiscal policy, less applicable under present conditions: that unearned income should bear a heavier tax burden than earned income.

It may be taken as a sign of economic consolidation that after 1953 measures were devised to encourage recipients of lower incomes to accumulate property commensurate with their growing saving power. To this end the prevailing tax incentives were of little use since they became interesting only for larger incomes with higher tax obligations. The attempt was therefore made to stimulate the propensity to save by granting direct subsidies rather than mere tax concessions. Savers who were willing to put their money in various kinds of long term investments were, within certain limits, extended opportunities to earn a bonus of 20 per cent of the amount saved. The programs of saving for housing and the savings accounts of banks benefited most from these provisions.

At the height of these efforts to encourage private saving the fiscal authorities forgave taxes to the extent of two billion marks annually. It is hard to be certain whether this tax policy should be credited with a major role in bringing about the very high postwar rates of investment. One might assume that the government would have made larger direct investments itself, had it not given such costly favors to private investors; or possibly companies and private investors would in any case have contributed to capital formation. What is certain, however, is that the flow of capital formation took a different direction from the one it would have taken in a free capital market without government subsidies.

One example of a conscious effort to influence the direction of investment was hotly contested at the time: the 1952 Investment Aid Law (*Investitionshilfegesetz*). In the course of the Korean crisis, serious bottlenecks appeared in coal, steel, electric power and gas, and transportation. These bottlenecks slowed down any additional general expansion, and because sufficient investment capital was not available they could not be quickly broken. In these fields prices were still held under public control; therefore no substantial profits could be expected and high interest could not be paid. To remedy this situation a law was passed which provided that the enterprises which were thought to be profiting from the low prices charged by the industries mentioned above—in reality, such profits were most unequally distributed—were to pay a total of one billion marks in the form of an extraordinary contribution to the tax collector. These funds were to be redistributed to the industries to be aided through a special bank, the *Industriekreditbank*. The contributors were to receive bonds of the debtor industries.

This law was at first regarded as successful. Together with other supporting measures it caused investment in the so-called bottleneck industries to double in the course of two years. However, five years later dark clouds gathered above some of these industries, primarily coal mining. Coal dumps grew and the industry, so highly favored until lately, became distressed. What had happened? For many years the coal industry had been unable to keep up with demand. Therefore, public funds were expended in many ways to build up capacity, and long-term contracts were signed to insure deliveries from the United States. But when the American deliveries began to flow, coal had ceased to be in short supply, petroleum having become a lively competitor. The growth rate of demand from the foremost customers had only to show a slight decrease for the alleged coal shortage to turn out to be illusory. Observers began to question whether, with more careful studies of the international markets, it would not have been possible to avoid paying high subsidies, first for the expansion of mines, and soon thereafter for closing them down. In the United States in the 1920's coal had already begun to lose its importance compared with oil, although the mining conditions for coal were much easier there than in the Ruhr and Saar basins. In Germany, on the other hand, hardly any petroleum was available in the first postwar years because there was no way to pay for it and because consumers were not yet technically prepared to use oil instead of coal—for instance, to heat their houses. Coal mining therefore is one of the outstanding examples of an expensive detour on the road toward the reconstruction of the German economy.

IN DEFENSE OF FREE COMPETITION

Only very late, nine years after the currency reform, did the German market economy receive what should have been its basic law, the Law Against Restraints on Competition (*Gesetz gegen Wettbewerbsbeschränkungen*). The very starting point for discussions about such a law had been unfortunate. The preamble of the Allies' decartellization decrees of 1947 had cited as their main purpose in breaking up cartels the wish to reduce Germany's industrial power. The traditional American antitrust principle of strengthening the market by safeguarding free competition was at first hardly discernible in these decrees.

These early decrees made it all the more difficult for Ludwig Erhard and his staff to take over the American heritage and to develop what in his judgment was appropriate in it for German requirements. The Law on Guidelines for Controls and Price Policy After Currency Reform (*Leitsätzegesetz*) of 1948 (see page 228) contained the following declaration: "Wherever economic monopolies develop they are to be abolished and until then placed under state control. The draft of a German bill on the matter is to be presented to the [Bizonal] Economic Council forthwith." A draft was prepared which was radical in its prohibitions and in the powers it assigned to a monopoly control agency. However, in long drawn out and tortured deliberations many teeth were pulled from this first draft and several succeeding ones. More and more consideration was given to what the various interest groups desired, and when the law finally was promulgated on July 27, 1957, the original spirit was hardly recognizable. Actually, the result pleased no one; some thought the law too weak, and others judged it to be a brutal interference with economic liberty.

The law indeed went considerably beyond the old Cartel Decree of 1923. It dealt not only with abuses of cartel power but introduced a prohibition in that it denied cartel agreements the aid of the courts. However, numerous exceptions were admitted, for example, agreements on terms of delivery and payment, on rebates, and on rationalization. Under certain conditions cartels to deal with structural difficulties in an industry and cartels for export could be permitted. The Economics Minister had the right to license any other cartel if the interests of the economy and the community at large required it. Furthermore, the law empowered industrial producers of articles with registered trademarks (*Markenartikel*) to prescribe sales prices to retailers.

Producers and traders who held dominant market power were to be placed under supervision to avoid the misuse of power, but the relevant clauses of the law were so loosely drafted that, at least in the first years following enactment, not one important case occurred in which they were applied. The difficulties that confront any legal treatment of this entire matter are indubitably great. The record of American antitrust practice also displays uncertainties and vacillations in interpreting the law. Whether an abuse of monopolistic power will be prosecuted or not depends less on legal formulae than on the work of the authorities and the courts. The Federal Cartel Authority (*Bundeskartellamt*), established by the law of 1957 and located in Berlin, as a rule tried to uphold the interests of free competition. The attitude of the courts that had to supervise the execution of the Authority's rulings was sometimes more attuned to old German cartel traditions. So far, the Authority has avoided taking radical decisions in order not to risk being restricted to a narrow field of activity right from the start by adverse rulings of the courts.

No one could entertain any illusions that after enactment of the law none but the duly registered and approved cartels would survive. By the end of 1964 roughly 260 cartel applications had been filed, of which 136 were approved. The number of cartels was estimated at 3,000 for 1930, and it must be assumed that after 1958 still more of them were in existence than were legally registered. Because the survival of secret cartels could not be ruled out, the rapid opening of the German borders to imports undoubtedly had a stronger effect on competitive behavior in the markets than the cartel law, although the law was of importance in those domestic markets that were not exposed to foreign competition. The German cartels had first become strong at the end of the nineteenth century under customs protection; later they increased their power when foreign exchange and import restrictions were instituted. Their power was bound to dwindle as soon as foreign competitors were free to enter the German market. Where secret cartels survived they now became less of a danger.

The anticartel regulations of the Allies were in force until 1957. Shorter lived was the effort of the U.S. Military Government in the autumn of 1948 to enforce in its zone the absolute freedom to establish new business firms. The so-called proof of the applicant's competence (*Befähigungsnachweis*) and of reasonable public demand for a new establishment (*Bedürfnisprüfung*) had played a varied role in the history of German handicraft and retail trade. Under National Socialism the conditions for licensing a business firm were tightened. When all these regulations were abolished in the American zone of occupation, the step could be justified not only on the basis of liberal principles but also of the necessity to integrate the expellees, many of whom at once began to improve their lot by opening shops. Formal proceedings in accordance with the old trade regulations would have been too slow, their outcome often uncertain. At a later stage, however, the federal government was not willing to implement the American practice, the less so since the British and French occupation authorities had not followed the American example in their zones. Conditions in Germany were very different from those in the United States where nothing at all comparable to the German artisan franchise existed. The Artisan Charter (*Handwerksordnung*) of September 17, 1953, reintroduced the requirement for proof of competence for craft licenses, and in 1957 the proof of expertness (*Sachkunde*) and reliability (*Zuverlässigkeit*) was also made a condition for admittance to retail trade. The reintroduction of the craft and trade regulations was motivated, as it had been for the past century, by the asserted need to help preserve the middle class. Some liberalization had been achieved, however; the worst obstacle for entry into the market, the requirement for proof of demand for an additional business, remained abolished except in a few trades.

It was fortunate for the market economy that even in cases dealing with the few excepted trades the courts repeatedly ruled in favor of market freedom. Thus the Federal Constitutional Court (*Bundesverfassungsgericht*) held that the requirement for proof of demand was generally unconstitutional. This 1958 decision ended the traditional monopoly of privileged pharmacies. Their number now increased dramatically as more traders wished to participate in the high profits derived under the protection of privilege. Among the few industries in which existing firms retained statutory protection against new competitors was long-distance transportation.

Nothing, however, could prevent the reemergence of great power concentration in industry, trade, banking, and insurance. The speed at which the giants expanded created the impression of a strongly growing concentration. Uneasiness and the demand for redress spread among the population, and the state could not deny sharing in the responsibility for the trend toward concentration, after having supported self-financing and having given other tax privileges to big business. To be sure, compared with the mammoth organizations of the world the size of the West German large enterprises was still modest. Of the hundred largest industrial enterprises in the world (measured by their turnover after a somewhat questionable currency adjustment), in 1964 only thirteen were West German companies, of which two were automobile producers, two electrical concerns, six enterprises in heavy industry and three successor organizations of the former I. G. Farben chemical group. The largest German enterprise ranked only twenty-seventh on the world scale, although altogether Germany took third position in industrial production behind the United States and Soviet Russia. Nevertheless, the problems of the concentration of economic power continued to worry many even after the Law Against Limitations on Competition had been enacted. Public hearings on the problem of concentration ordered by the Bundestag did little to clarify causes and effects. The general expectation was that the obvious trend toward concentration would in some measure be counteracted by the simultaneous expansion of the market, primarily within the framework of the European Economic Community, and that consequently the monopolistic power of the giants would not be substantially increased. The question remains, however, whether it makes sense to retain government measures, such as some contained in the tax laws, that directly or indirectly favor the growth of big business.

STRUCTURAL CHANGES IN INDUSTRY

Experience has shown that economic growth does not occur simultaneously and along parallel lines in all sectors of an economy. Thus, after 1948 consumption expanded in waves favoring now one, now the other industry. The first wave was nicknamed the "eating wave" (*Fresswelle*) during which people seemed involved in a race to use their rising incomes to gratify a long-repressed craving for food. This was followed by a "clothing wave" which benefited the textile and garment industries. The demand for house furnishings and appliances was less marked as a wave, but it increased as the construction of new homes and repair of old ones went forward. The vehicles industry first experienced a rise and subsequent fall in the demand for bicycles, then for motorcycles and "mopeds." In 1964 no limit on the expansion of the automobile industry was yet in sight, since the Federal Republic still ranked behind France and Britain and far behind the United States, having only 143 automobiles per 1,000 inhabitants as compared to 356 in America.

Only after the second world war did the automobile become an article of mass consumption in West Germany. Private cars were a rarity in 1948. Sixteen years later there were eight million cars on the highways, one for each seven inhabitants. As had happened decades earlier in the United States, the automobile industry had advanced to the rank of a key industry. Everything and everyone connected with the automobile prospered, the auxiliary industries, repair shops, service stations, the petroleum industry, tourist trade, and, not least, road construction. The Autobahn network as well as other highways and roads were expanded and improved at great cost to serve the suddenly multiplied needs. Road construction cost the public authorities more than what they spent on the institutions of public law and order and roughly one-half of their expenditures for schools, research, art, and culture combined.

Beside the industries most involved in catching up with the backlog of pent-up demand, some new industries were also in rapid expansion. Progress in production techniques and inventions of novel products were two factors that resulted in the sprouting up of new industries such as television, automatic washing machines, electronics, fully synthetic fibers, and numerous plastics. Finally there was a third factor that created marked shifts in the traditional industrial structure: the division of Germany. For instance, prior to the war, the electrical industry had been largely concentrated in Berlin. It was now reconstructed in the West and by 1960 had grown to eight times its size in 1936. The garment industry also had been centered in Berlin and in the Soviet zone, and therefore in the first phase of the reconstruction it was among the fastest growing industries in West Germany. On the other hand, the leather industry stagnated because it had always been concentrated in the

TABLE 32

Index of Industrial Production; Federal Republic, 1965
(1950 = 100)

All industries	319
Industries with above average growth	
Plastics	2,616
Petroleum products	918
Vehicles	663
Electrical products	601
Chemicals	471
Machinery	355
Industries with below average growth	
Coal mining	120
Textiles	238
Pulp, cellulose, cardboard, and paper	238

SOURCE: Computed from *Statistisches Jahrbuch für die Bundesrepublik Deutschland 1966,* pp. 240–44.

West and now felt the competition from synthetic materials. The plastics industry multiplied its products and, as in other countries, took the lead among growth industries, followed by the production of the new synthetic fibers, and petroleum and natural gas refining.

In the course of general reconstruction the Ruhr region lost some of its preponderance over the other industrial centers of Germany. The Rhine-Main-Neckar region attracted many additional industries, and new centers arose—such as the Munich area, which before the second world war had comparatively few industries but which now became an industrial focal point. In general, industries were spread more evenly throughout West Germany in 1965 than in the preceding decades. Railways and coal were no longer such decisive factors for the location of industries since automobiles, electricity, and new pipelines militated against centralization. The many settlements of refugees also resulted in a dispersal of industries over the agricultural countryside, where after 1956 the search for the last reserves in manpower was intense.

The older industrial areas kept growing also, the large cities expanded beyond their previous confines, and the character of the landscape changed. The need to plan the growth of the cities was urgent, but as yet only small beginnings were made. Cooperation between municipalities, counties, and the federal states left much to be desired, and many opportunities open during the reconstruction period were unfortunately missed. It remains a task for the future to clarify the aims and potentialities for a reasonable management of the available national space. The same applies to the all-too-slow beginnings of efforts to shield the population against water and air pollution by industry. The conviction is spreading that these blemishes are not unavoidable concomitants of rapid industrialization.

West Germany had been an industrial country for generations. Now the stormy postwar developments expanded industry even more. In 1964 almost half the labor force was active in industry and the crafts, compared with only two-fifths before the second world war. That such an increase was possible is due to a circumstance outside the realm of industry: the long overdue adjustment of agriculture to the changed technological and economic conditions of the modern world.

THE AGRARIAN REVOLUTION

After the currency reform the domestic supply of foodstuffs was much too small to satisfy the home market. Not enough foreign exchange was available to procure the immediately required imports. Accordingly, the chief goal of agricultural policy was to keep the population sufficiently supplied at moderate prices—agricultural policy was food policy. Prices remained under public control, subsidies stimulated cheap supplies. The import and warehousing agencies (*Einfuhr- und Vorratsstellen*) organized in 1950–51 had a public monopoly on the importation of cereals, fodder, livestock, meat, milk, and sugar. Because in these years prices in the world market were generally above those at home, these agencies had to pay more for the imported commodities than they received in selling them to the public. As late as 1952 the deficit amounted to approximately 350 million D-Marks, which had to be paid from tax revenues.

When the Korean boom was over and agricultural prices sagged everywhere, the structural weakness of German agriculture became manifest. It was unable to face foreign competition. Far too many people used technically deficient tools on irrationally shaped farms and often widely scattered parcels of land to produce commodities which could be bought much cheaper abroad.

What was to be done? First it was necessary to formulate fairly clear ideas as to the objectives to be pursued, but for several more years such clarity of purpose was lacking, and improvisations and haphazard protection against foreign competition continued. Where imports now were absolutely essential, the import and warehousing agencies raised the prices of the goods bought in the world market to the higher domestic levels. Grain and sugar remained under direct price control and the prices of other essentials were manipulated by opening and closing the import gates. Fuel for agricultural machinery was sold at subsidized prices; the government made funds available for refugee settlements; and there were other projects, all without following any clear line. The government also attempted to raise farmers' incomes by granting tax privileges and yet could never satisfy them. It became ever more apparent that the Hitler and postwar years had given German agriculture only the fictitious prosperity of a temporary monopoly situation which, especially after 1948, isolated it from the sound growth of the rest of the economy. In other sectors incomes rose much more rapidly. The slogan of the farmers' associations now was to demand "parity," which seemed to signify many things but above all that agriculture wanted a guarantee of its share in the national income.

The Agricultural Law of 1955 put an end to this floundering about of agrarian policy. The proclaimed aim of the new law was to render German agriculture competitive in world markets within a reasonable time and for the proper kinds of produce. This path had been followed by the Netherlands and Denmark in the nineteenth century without their ever having protected the farmers behind high customs barriers, as had Germany. Of course it was not possible at this late juncture to follow their example directly by permitting unrestricted importation. This would have spelled the ruin of millions of families. It was now up to the government, which was not without fault for the misdirected development of the past, to soften carefully the rigors of transition.

This goal was pursued in the "Green Plans" which after 1955 the government presented annually to the Bundestag. Within a year government subsidies were increased by almost a billion marks. Through their distribution to the individual farmers an attempt was made to influence private decisions in the desired direction. Hundreds of million marks were devoted to subsidizing the use of fertilizer. There were subsidies for milk and egg production and strong support for the consolidation of dispersed acreage and for resettlement. Substantial low-interest loans were made available from the Marshall Plan counterpart funds. Tax reductions were continued for agriculture, in 1959 to the tune of 400 million marks in taxes not collected. Actually, agricultural enterprises were practically free of income taxation.

What were the results? Agriculture experienced a veritable revolution comparable to that in most of the developed countries of western Europe and North America. Never in modern German history had conditions changed with such rapidity. Some of the credit belongs to the new government approach.

Alone among the major economic sectors, agriculture absorbed no part of the large growth in population. On the contrary, it more than ever served as a rich reservoir of manpower available for employment elsewhere. The total number of persons employed in agriculture decreased by more than one-third from 1950 to 1964, the number of landless agricultural laborers by two-thirds. Without this manpower reserve German industry could not have expanded so rapidly. In 1964, 3.1 million persons produced three-quarters of the foodstuffs required by 58 million inhabitants. This ratio was still less favorable than that prevailing in other countries, notably in the United States where only 7 million persons were needed to feed a population of 195 million, besides producing large surpluses for export. However, the American efforts to raise productivity by the application of investment capital had begun under exceptionally favorable geographic conditions and at a much earlier period than in Germany.

Motorization and mechanization produced a thorough revolution in technical methods; thereby the face of the countryside, of villages and farms was transformed. In the mechanization of agriculture Germany had been in the rearguard; all the faster, therefore, could the lag be made up, taking advantage of the latest technical advances. At last, small tractors, combines, and other kinds of farm machinery adapted to the normal size of West German holdings were available. Within thirteen years the number of tractors increased eightfold; in the foreseeable future horses will remain only as a luxury. While in 1952 combines were very rare, in 1960 one-third of the arable land was harvested with their help. In one-third of all dairy farms milking machines were used; milkmaids and farmers' wives were relieved of their chore, since the machines were serviced by men.

Due to changed techniques and the migration of agricultural workers from the countryside to other sectors of the economy, productivity per worker increased even more steeply in agriculture than in industry, a feature that could be noted also in other Western countries. Productivity increased not only per worker but also per acre: each cow gave more milk, each hog or steer more meat. Overall, in 1964 a much smaller number of workers produced 50 per cent more than before the war. The question may arise whether it would not have been advisable to allow domestic agricultural production to dwindle in Germany as in Britain. However, experts in the Ministry of Agriculture expressed the opinion that by 1960 one-third of the agricultural units were already able to withstand all competition from the world market and there was a fair chance that more would be added before too long. According to this opinion it would be a mistake to sacrifice German agriculture to open international competition at this time.

The unavoidable revolutionary change in the agricultural structure thus was well under way. For the first time in decades the number of small holdings decreased because there was no economic justification for their survival. Another traditional problem of German agriculture, particularly in southern Germany, was the fragmentation of viable farm units by inheritance. This posed an obstacle to technical progress and often turned the farmer into a commuter who had to spend many hours of his working year on the road between his scattered plots of land. After 1948 motorization brought some relief, but in the interest of rational management it became imperative to consolidate small parcels into larger units. This was promoted by the government in consolidation projects (*Flurbereinigung*) which before the war had been pursued with but little determination. Even now the resistance of individual farmers against exchanging some of their old acres for ones

TABLE 33

Agriculture in the Federal Republic, 1950–65*

Year	PERSONS EMPLOYED IN AGRICULTURE (*in thousands*)	(*as per cent of total employed*)	*Hired farm laborers* (*in thousands*)	*Tractors* (*in thousands*)	*Index of productivity* † (*1950 = 100*)
1950	5,020	22.0	999	138	100
1952	4,695	20.7	885	245	118
1954	4,400	18.6	785	371	136
1956	4,175	17.0	705	543	149
1958	3,972	15.8	611	696	170
1960	3,623	13.7	533	857	203
1962	3,383	12.6	460	999	212
1964	3,084	11.4	391	1,107	253
1965	2,966	10.9	370	1,164	—

* 1960–65, including West Berlin.
† Vegetable and animal production (in cereal units) per capita employed in agriculture.

SOURCES: *Statistisches Jahrbuch für die Bundesrepublik Deutschland,* 1952–66; *Bericht der Bundesregierung über die Lage der Landwirtschaft 1965.*

more adjacent was stiff and at times bitter. By 1963 about one-fourth of all agricultural land had been consolidated.

The Agricultural Law of 1955, which had codified the views and measures of reform prevailing at that time, soon had to face another difficult argument. More rapidly and decisively than had been anticipated, the emergence of the European Economic Community in 1957 altered the competitive status of German agriculture in the EEC market. At the beginning of the 1960's individual farmers and farmers' associations again pressed for protection against the new dangers, and controversies on these matters once more caused unrest and vacillation in agricultural policy.

THE EUROPEAN COAL AND STEEL COMMUNITY AND THE EUROPEAN ECONOMIC COMMUNITY

As described above (see p. 245) the end of the occupation and of the international control of the Ruhr coincided with the founding of the European Coal and Steel Community, the Montan-Union. Possibly this institution was not in itself of very great importance—some observers regard it as only a sort of international super-cartel with some consumer protection. However in the conception of Robert Schuman of France, the Montan-Union was to be the first step toward a more comprehensive unification of Western Europe. Beside the Marshall Plan, the Schuman Plan was probably the most fruitful idea on how to cope with the devastating consequences of the second world war. A successful step toward a more hopeful future seemed to have been made. The same goal of European unification inspired the formation of the European Economic Community, EEC, colloquially referred to as the Common Market. The members of both the Montan-Union and EEC were Belgium, the Federal Republic of Germany, France, Italy, Luxembourg, and the Netherlands. The Montan-Union administrative body (the High Authority) is located in Luxembourg, the Common Market Commission in Brussels. The two communities promoted mutual trade, but they also impinged on the members' sovereign prerogatives and, in some measure, on their very national existence. Unlike several other postwar organizations, the communities were not concerned simply with removing obstacles to traffic, trade, and payments across national frontiers. The aim of the communities was larger: to let these national frontiers themselves disappear as important economic facts in order to gain all benefits, including political advantages, of a wide unified space.

In the twentieth century, efforts to establish larger economic units have a far greater bearing than in the nineteenth. In the earlier period it was much easier to promote economic unification by removing customs barriers and to proceed from there, as for instance in the step-by-step unification of Germany described above in the first chapter. By the middle of the twentieth century to create any new free trade area had become very difficult, but even had this been achieved it would not have resulted automatically in the establishment of a unified economic region. As long as the fiscal systems, monopoly legislation, social security laws and practices, monetary, trade cycle, and agricultural policies were not fully aligned among the member countries, the national frontiers would continue to be effective barriers to full exploitation of the opportunities for supra-national division of labor. Not before a common European system of taxation and commercial law, of monetary and trade-cycle policies were developed would the free movement of goods, capital, and labor be a reality. A development along these lines would, however, require that the individual nations be prepared to transfer some of their administrative sovereignty to supra-national authorities. The High Authority of the Montan-Union was the first institution of this kind in

Europe; in certain respects it had immediate authority over the citizens of the several member states and even the power to order member governments to take specific actions.

The foremost aim of the Economic Community was to establish a common market for coal, iron ore, scrap, and steel. This was achieved in 1953. The next year quality steels were included. All customs duties and quotas for coal, iron, and steel were abolished, actually not a difficult thing to do in these years since most countries were in urgent need of the commodities and were not intent on warding off imports.

However, the privileges of the High Authority were much more far-reaching. According to the Montan-Union agreement, not only duties and quotas but all discrimination in trade between citizens of the member countries, all export subsidies and export assistance measures are to be abolished, insofar as they interfere with free competition in the common market. Also freight rates across the frontiers are to be unified to prevent hidden aid or hindrance. The High Authority has the power to regulate imports and exports of coal and steel products that cross the Community's external borders, and it may formulate programs to stimulate or restrict investment. The Authority itself raises capital on the international capital market and disposes of the funds. It has the right to fix maximum prices in times of scarcity and minimum prices in times of glut. The Montan-Union agreement, as a matter of principle, prohibits cartels, and any association of firms requires special permission of the High Authority. Here is a large list of powers and duties which constitute an entirely novel type of supra-national economic union. The member governments indeed divested themselves of various privileges which up to that time had been regarded as inalienable attributes of sovereignty.

In its first years, the Authority had a scarce commodity to manage and this kept many of the potential problems out of sight. This happy situation ended rather abruptly in 1957–58. The developing coal glut and, soon thereafter, the steel slump in 1958, and again in 1961—not foreseen in time by the Authority, which stood by helplessly—aroused the opposition of regional interests, and it became imperative to put up a genuine fight for the Authority's principles, primarily for free competition and the prohibition against subsidies. Success was difficult and limited, and the problems to be faced by any such supra-national authority came into vivid focus. The Montan-Union was in control of only a narrow market and had no power over important determining factors of supply and demand. The devaluation of the French franc at the end of 1958 suddenly improved sales opportunities for the

French steel industry in the neighboring markets and caused competitors to take counter-measures. Also the divergent national regulatory methods for electric energy production and distribution reacted on the common coal market without the Authority being able to intervene directly. Harmonizing the tax systems proved more difficult than had been expected, and tax support for exports kept distorting the competitive situation. Observers soon realized that the Montan-Union was unlikely to furnish the model for wider integration, which was to have included one economic sector after another. Occasional plans for a "Green Union" for agriculture or a union of several electric power organizations were not realistic. Only one of the organizations founded in 1958 in conjunction with the EEC, the European Atomic Community, EURATOM, resembled the Montan-Union type. For the rest, the path of development led straight from the Montan-Union to the comprehensive European Economic Community.

The Treaty of Rome of March 25, 1957, continued the project of unification. This was the decisive step to create a market with 170 million people, comparable in economic capacity to the market of the United States and to that of the Soviet Union. It was planned that by 1969 a common market for all goods, services, and capital movements would have been established in successive steps and all restrictions on the free movement of persons removed.

The EEC was to have a common tariff against outside countries and a closer economic and political relationship among the members. A different system was established January 4, 1960, between seven other European countries, often referred to as the "outer seven," in the European Free Trade Association, EFTA. The seven EFTA countries which had not joined the EEC were Britain, Denmark, Sweden, Norway, Austria, Switzerland, and Portugal. These countries agreed among themselves that they would gradually eliminate all tariffs against one another but would retain their individual trade and tariff policies toward the outside world. Their decisions not to join the Common Market had various reasons. The main reason may have been an unwillingness to relinquish so much of their sovereignty as was contemplated in the Treaty of Rome; however, their refusals were also based on their differing political concepts. Austria was bound by her treaty with Soviet Russia to retain a neutral status, Switzerland and Sweden based their foreign relations on an old tradition of neutrality, Britain had its Commonwealth ties and Portugal an authoritarian regime. The Scandinavian countries maintained a close economic relationship with Britain. Differences over the Common Market ideas on future agricultural policies also played an important role.

German economic interests were bound to suffer from the persistent economic division of Europe. In 1960, 28 per cent of German exports still went to EFTA countries, only 1.5 per cent less than the share going to the Common Market countries. It was therefore clearly in Germany's interest to champion the entry of Britain into the Common Market, or alternatively to explore how the political nucleus of the EEC could be retained while offering nonmember countries association under looser terms.

Once the Common Market had begun to function, British statesmen and economists, who at first had opposed entering it, developed a lively interest in a common economic system for Europe. It was helpful that meanwhile the impulse toward a close political integration of Europe had somewhat abated. In August, 1961, the Conservative government of Harold Macmillan formally applied for British membership in the European Community. Negotiations dragged on, especially over problems of agricultural integration. They were abruptly terminated in January, 1963, when President de Gaulle made known France's disapproval of the planned combination. This turned out to be only the beginning of a separatist French policy which in 1965 resulted in an open crisis of the EEC when President de Gaulle declared that he would never consent to be bound by majority decisions of the Community members. France then substantially curtailed its collaboration in the EEC, and the French president worked toward a revision of the Treaty of Rome.

The now openly controversial political substance of the Treaty of Rome lay in the fixed procedure it provided for achieving a closer integration of the members' trade and economic policies. Integration was to begin with the common external tariff and to be carried on into the realm of the essential monetary and economic structure. Among other clauses, the Treaty of Rome provided for protection of free competition through the prohibition of cartels and measures against exploitation of dominant market positions. Other clauses prohibited discrimination for reasons of nationality and forbade export subsidies by individual member countries. An adjustment was outlined for the systems of taxation, social security, and labor and trade legislation. One of the main duties assigned the Common Market was to carry out a concerted balance of payments and trade-cycle policy. Once individual national policies to assure full employment and economic growth were well adjusted to a common pattern, the Common Market would indeed have become an economic unity. This, however, is a task for the future to achieve.

Optimism in the initial phase was followed by more skeptical judgments as to the possibility of ever fully reaching the ideal of supra-national integration. And in 1965 doubts were spreading that the Common Market would ever be more than a simple customs union.

In contrast to the Montan-Union, the Common Market agencies had from the very beginning less power to issue orders directly to the citizens of the member states. Their sovereign authority was more restricted, and their activities generally depended on convincing the member governments that certain concerted steps should be taken. The "perpetual" Treaty of Rome, not subject to cancellation by any member, in reality represented a collection of rules which the Council of Ministers of the Community was to follow in creating supra-national legal systems in the future. For some of these measures the Treaty laid down a fixed timetable. For instance, within a maximum of 15 years tariffs inside the Community were to be abolished in three stages. Such stages were also to be applied in establishing the common external tariff.

The scaling down of tariffs within the Community was carried out more rapidly than anticipated. The Federal Republic in particular had, by 1965, reduced import duties for industrial goods from member states by 80 per cent and for agricultural products by about 60 per cent. The first moves toward establishing a common external tariff were made for industrial goods in 1961 and for agricultural goods in 1962. The common marketing system for agricultural products called for by the Treaty of Rome was decided upon in 1962, but the question of the levels of agricultural prices toward which the Community was to strive was left open. Similarly, opinions still differed widely among the members about what practical measures the policies in defense of free competition ought to lead to. Despite such uncertainties, the volume of trade among the member countries experienced a far larger growth than the trade between the Community and third countries.

In the efforts toward integration Europe has seen the promise of a further heightening of its prosperity. The great influx into the European continent of the investment funds of American firms, meant to insure a favorable initial position in a growing market, may be taken as proof that these are not futile hopes. The boom which began in 1959 can with some justification also be attributed to the Community. Within the member countries entrepreneurs invested at a lively rate to prepare for new opportunities and keener competition.

4. *Continued Prosperity*

IMPORTED INFLATION AND REVALUATION

THE RISING DEMAND for investment in the Common Market increased the demand for investment in Germany and for German exports. It would not be correct, however, to regard rising investment demand of the Common Market partners as the sole cause of the 1959–62 expansion. Demand was increasing in the whole world, and inside the Federal Republic a multiple combination of influences was at work. The demand for consumer goods, which had been lagging in 1957–58, revived and the construction industry showed veritable boom conditions. What two years before hardly anyone would have thought possible came to pass: industrial production leapt forward by another 11 per cent from 1959 to 1960, and gross national product by 9 per cent. At the same time the German economy entered the phase of "over-full employment." In the autumns of 1961 and 1962, only 0.5 per cent of the labor force was unemployed, and for each unemployed person there were five unfilled jobs.

The reservoir of domestic manpower having been drained, by 1961 more than a half million foreign workers had entered the country, primarily Italians, Spaniards, and Greeks. The price level, which had remained stationary in 1958–59, began to rise once more. Reference was made to "imported inflation," meaning that the rise in prices was primarily attributable to the export boom and the continued influx of foreign money. In this situation the credit needs of business could be largely met without recourse to the Bundesbank, which thereby lost much of its influence. As long as business enjoyed a lively boom the demands of the trade unions could be easily granted. By repeatedly cutting the rediscount rate in 1958–59 the Bundesbank had tried to check the excessive inflow of foreign funds. In the beginning of 1959 the lowest discount rate in the history of German monetary policy was reached at 2.75 per cent (see p. 254). And yet the desired effect was not achieved; possibly the low interest rate did keep out some foreign money, but at the same time it added even more stimulus to the domestic boom. In view of this frustrating experience, the Bundesbank again tried the policy of tight money in 1959–60, with as little effect. After 1960, the influx of gold and foreign exchange rose once again, and the export surplus persisted.

It appeared that a structural imbalance had developed. The trade partner countries voiced harsh criticism of Germany because they saw their currency reserves being drained away, while within the Federal Republic itself many were hurt by the "imported" inflation. There were only two possible correctives: either to allow domestic prices to rise to levels at which the pressure for exports would diminish, or to alter the exchange rate of the mark. In essence, the problem now was to terminate the policy which in the postwar period had favored the producer at the expense of the consumer. For several years past, experts had been suggesting that the D-Mark be revalued. Instead, the authorities at first planned to give tax benefits to importers and to discontinue the various benefits to exporters, but they were unable to convince the Bundestag of the merits of such measures. Industry tried to defend itself against the threat to its export enterprises which a revaluation of the mark would pose by suggesting that the German economy raise a loan for investment in developing countries. Such a loan would only have transformed the current surpluses of the balance of payments into long-term assets abroad, however.

On March 6, 1961, the decision was taken to revalue the mark by 5 per cent, from DM 4.20 to DM 4.00 to the dollar. Many judged this revaluation to have been too timid, and a raise by 10 or even 15 per cent had been widely expected. This would surely have been exaggerated, but developments over the following years showed that further adjustments in the domestic price level were still required. The dire consequences predicted by some exporters did not materialize, nor was the home market flooded with imported goods, which could have been anticipated, since in the preceding years the average prices for imports had indeed fallen by more than the 5 per cent of revaluation with no notable turn in the foreign trade picture in favor of imports.

The renewed boom that followed carried West Germany to the ranks of the "have" nations, and this necessitated a good deal of rethinking. The export ideology of the postwar period which, as in the days of mercantilism, had raised exporting to the glory of a national achievement, had now to be reconsidered. Likewise, the hopes that an all-wise central bank could always successfully control the ups and downs of the business cycle had to be given up, and the question whether the government was well advised to remain as passive toward booms and depressions as in the past aroused discussion. However, the revaluation combined with some price rises was indeed successful for a time in cutting down entrepreneurial profits and the surpluses of the balance of payments. At the same time investment demand decreased.

The rate of growth of the economy decreased somewhat in 1962–63 but increased again in 1964.

Thus, in the third phase of development after currency reform, beginning in 1959, it was already possible to review more than one complete business cycle. A characteristic feature, without parallel in previous experience, is the high ratio of investment to gross national product in the years after 1959. In 1964, almost 30 per cent of GNP was devoted to gross investment (new and replacement), exceeding by far the investment ratios in the reconstruction phase, ratios which at that time had themselves been regarded as miraculously high. Abnormally high prevailing interest rates did not perceptibly decrease the demand of private and government enterprises for investment funds. In the face of this home demand, the opportunities for German investment abroad and other forms of development aid were unable to attract a larger portion of national income despite the growing wealth of the country.

DEVELOPMENT AID

It may be regarded as fortunate in many ways that Germany was now a country without colonies. She was spared the worries and disappointments of the great colonial powers which had emerged victorious from the wars and yet had to divest themselves of one colonial possession after another. Where they had not withdrawn in good time, bitter colonial wars were a heavy drain on the human and material substance of the mother country. Where no wars ensued the economic development of these vast, recently colonial territories required substantial help. Year in and year out France and Britain devoted huge sums to these tasks. Their contributions were even exceeded by those of the United States in pursuance of aims in which, as in the Marshall Plan, humanitarian, political, and economic motives merged. As the leading power of the Western world, the United States sought to win the cooperation of the neutral nations in the West-East conflict, but it was also motivated by repugnance against starvation in the world at large and stimulated by the challenge of opportunities in the expanding world market.

West Germany was so long exclusively absorbed in the task of her own reconstruction that only in 1956 were her first timid steps taken to aid developing countries. Lacking previous experience Germany naïvely improvised technical development programs. What should be done? Who should do it? How should the financing be handled? Elsewhere the problems of the developing countries were being explored in a well-publicized literature, but German aid remained hesitant and inexpert.

The easiest opportunities were found in multilateral aid programs. The Federal Republic participated with contributions or credits in the work of international organizations such as the International Bank for Reconstruction and Development, IBRD, the International Monetary Fund, IMF, and special funds of the United Nations. Also the private export credits listed in German statistics as development aid as a rule posed no considerable problems. Export credits to support German trade had always been available. They actually could hardly be regarded as development aid except in cases where the needs of the recipients had taken precedence over the profits of the providers. But the statistics offer no basis for distinguishing the two kinds of credits.

Portfolio and direct investment in the developing countries involved much more difficult problems since they were often politically and economically risky. Who would guarantee the security of property abroad in case of political unrest? And if factories were set up in these countries, how was a market to be found, how were costs to be assessed beforehand in dealing with foreign labor in unfamiliar surroundings? Also, the questions of how profits were to be remitted and how the foreign exchange problems of the country concerned were to be solved deterred many potential investors. Moreover, the interest level in Germany was so high that investment at home brought very satisfactory returns without the risks of development investments. Of the almost 8 billion marks, which by 1965 had been directly invested abroad by Germans in factories, trading organizations, and suchlike, only 9 per cent went to the high risk countries of Asia and Africa. German investors preferred Europe (53 per cent) and the Americas (36 per cent).

To be sure, development aid did not consist of money alone. Knowledge and experience were exported in many cases when foreigners received their education and training in Germany and when skilled Germans worked abroad. But technical assistance without capital aid has only limited effects. As in the case of other countries, genuine capital aid had to be given primarily from public sources. The government could charge interest rates for credits that were below market rates and could be lenient as to security and terms of payment in a way not possible for private investors. The government could grant capital aid for the so-called infrastructure investments in developing countries, consisting of roads, railroads, and power lines, none of which could well be financed by private means. Unlike the United States and other countries, Germany insisted on granting credits in preference to donating capital. The questions involved in these matters are still so much debated and experience is as yet so limited that knowledgeable judgments on the respective value of this or that method of giving aid are hardly possible. On the international level the decision of the federal government to give development aid only in the form of credits met with some regret as being narrow in scope and of little political effect. Also the amounts of German development aid were criticized on the grounds that the productivity of the German economy would warrant larger contributions. More than anything, the balance of payments surplus gave force to this criticism and, in fact, these surpluses would have supported greater efforts. On the other hand, responsible persons in Germany pointed to her extraordinary position with regard to the East-West conflict which immobilized considerable public and private funds, not to mention the duty to continue internal reconstruction and to defray social obligations stemming from the war.

5. *Social Policy in the Social Market Economy*

WHEN IN 1948 the decision was taken in favor of a market economy, the government by no means retreated completely from economic life. As was shown above, various opportunities were made use of by public agencies to engage in economic policy. The fiscal authorities paid special attention to economic growth. One-third of the accretion to saving and investment was due to public activity. The public authorities also played a prominent role in directing saving and investment by firms and private capitalists. The statement may be justified that altogether about half the capital formation in the Federal Republic was directly or indirectly financed by public means.

It is not surprising that after 1948 government (federal, state, and local) still remained the largest entrepreneur, as it had been in the preceding decades. This was obviously true in the traditional fields of activity of the German states and municipalities—railroads, electric power, water and gas works—but in productive industry also the participation of public agencies remained considerable. The federal government was in control of about one-third of the output of iron ore, one-fourth of coal, more than two-thirds of aluminum production, one-fifth of shipbuilding and, until 1960, about half of automobile production. The public hand was engaged in approximately 60 per cent of the credit volume of banking—the Bundesbank excluded.

Even had one wished to do so, the heritage of earlier decades could not be rapidly disposed of. Three industrial enterprises of the Federal Republic were at least in part "reprivatized": in 1959 PREUSSAG (*Preussische Bergwerks- und Hütten A. G.*), whose shares had a nominal value (*Nominalwert*) of 82 million DM and a real value (*Kurswert*) of about 100 million DM; in 1961 the Volkswagenwerk, at 360 million DM nominal and 668 million DM real value; and in 1965 VEBA (*Vereinigte Elektrizitäts- und Bergwerks A. G.*), at 528 million DM nominal and 1,256 million DM real value. In these reprivatizing projects the objective was not primarily to lighten the burden of the government's entrepreneurial functions, for it continued to participate in ownership and therefore to influence management. Rather, the idea was to stimulate private saving among the masses of the population by means of a wide dispersal of share holdings. Due to attractive issue prices and substantial "social rebates" for persons with low incomes, 1.5 million citizens acquired Volkswagen shares and 2.8 million savers subscribed to VEBA shares. The Volkswagen shareholders at first enjoyed a rapid but short-lived appreciation of their holdings to almost three times the issue price. But just as rapidly this bounty melted away, leaving the owners with the experience that shares were risky investments. For a time this experience dampened further efforts at reprivatization, all the more so in that the government could not well be expected to make free gifts of all or most of its profitable enterprises. However, the Bundestag elections of September, 1965, brought to fruition the plans to reprivatize VEBA, just as the Volkswagen plan had been carried out in an election year.

The reprivatization of public property through the wide dispersal of shares among the less propertied classes belongs to the third or post-1959 phase of West Germany's economic development (see page 226). Only ten years before no one would have thought such schemes had any urgency. At that time social policy had posed entirely different problems. The refugees and expellees had to be integrated, housing to be procured, war losses to be equalized, the rates for social insurance contributions and benefits to be redefined, the issue of workers' co-determination in the industrial establishments to be taken up once more. In these matters the social market economy was required to prove that the word "social" referred to more than a decorative sideshow to old-style private capitalism and that the community intended to be serious about redistributing property and incomes and caring for the needy. It might have appeared at first that the government was prepared in its economic policy to sacrifice more equitable distribution to more rapid growth. And yet much more progress toward social justice was actually achieved by government action than the easy slogan "the market economy without government intervention" indicated. Even in the market economy the government took an active part in the distribution of the national product. This explains why, even though the contributions to Allied occupation costs and autonomous German defense expenditures remained below the average defense expenditures of other countries, taxation was higher in the Federal Republic than in most other Western countries. The tax load kept growing over the years, and in 1963 the revenues from taxes and contributions of all public authorities including the social insurance system amounted to 36 per cent of gross national product, almost 5,000 DM annually for each gainfully employed person.

INTEGRATING THE EXPELLEES AND REFUGEES

By 1950, about eight million German expellees from the regions east of the Oder-Neisse line, Czechoslovakia, and the other eastern and southeastern territories had been taken in by the Federal Republic. In the following ten years another 1.7 million were added, partly making their way through the Soviet zone. In 1962, almost every fifth citizen of the Federal Republic was an expellee. In addition, Western Germany was the goal of a massive flight from the central German regions under Soviet occupation. Between 1950 and 1962, about 3.6 million people came through the Iron Curtain, mostly in Berlin, to settle in the free West.

As noted above, in the first years after the war the mass influx of expellees and refugees was a catastrophe, not only in terms of human distress but also for the economy. In the midst of the general destruction and economic disarray, additional millions of men, women, and children had to be fed, clothed, housed, and directed to places of work. At first the success was only partial. The postwar suffering had fallen hardest upon those who had lost their homelands, and the various improvised methods of public help could bring them only scanty aid. The newcomers were not equally distributed over the country, and unemployment was particularly high in those regions in which the newcomers were most concentrated. In 1950 every fourth person in the labor force in Schleswig-Holstein was unemployed, two years later still every fifth person. Two-thirds of the expellees were located in the Länder with only one-fourth of West Germany's industry. Over the years a certain redistribution of persons and of industries was achieved, followed by decreasing unemployment and soon full employment. Housing conditions improved at a much slower pace. Yet before long the expellees ceased to constitute a separate political group, as can be seen from the dwindling membership and votes of the once numerous expellee party, the *Bund der Heimatvertriebenen und Entrechteten.*

Integration was not achieved without painful dislocations, however. Many expellees were forced to engage in new professions, many formerly self employed became laborers. Only a minority managed to continue in their former careers. Integration was particularly difficult in the field of agriculture, since there was hardly any space for establishing new independent units. In these years an exciting social experiment remodeled the ancient shape of many hamlets, villages, and towns; a seemingly permanent social stratification was subjected to a process of change. In their drive to recapture status and incomes the expellees worked hard and thereby gave a strong impetus to reconstruction. They represented a manpower reserve of rare mobility which eased the necessary adaptation of the economic structure to the new conditions. It has been estimated that the expellees, by bringing with them the value of their training, made a present of human capital to the Federal Republic on the order of 30 billion marks. Without doubt, the labor supply they offered was one of the reasons why wages in West Germany at first increased more slowly than productivity, a phenomenon which enabled the country to reenter the world market as a strong competitor.

HOUSING CONSTRUCTION

Even before the second world war Germany had been short of housing. During the war, one-fourth of the roughly 10 million existing dwelling units were destroyed, creating a desperate problem for both the old residents and the newcomers. Because of the terrifying scarcity it was clearly out of the question to establish a free housing market. Rents would have risen to levels totally unacceptable to the masses of the population. In the interest of social peace it was unavoidable to continue rent control and the public allocation of dwellings, practices well known in Germany since the days of the Weimar Republic and in many countries after the war.

How was the housing supply to be increased as long as there was no profit to private industry in providing it? It could only be done by public construction and by subsidies to private builders. The first Housing Act of 1950 provided for three kinds of construction: (1) publicly promoted social housing projects leading to dwellings with subsidized rents (*sozialer Wohnungsbau*); (2) housing projects aided by tax preference; and (3) free, privately financed building projects.

To provide dwellings in the first category the government contributed a large part of the capital in the form of interest-free or low-interest loans with various advantages in their servicing. In return, the government determined what rents were to be paid and admitted only low-income occupants. In the second category, the government gave aid by reducing taxes somewhat and in return retained some influence on rents. In the third category there was no control of rents and no government allocation of the new apartments. The private capitalists who financed the construction benefited only from the tax reductions generally granted to savers and investors. More than half the housing constructed up to 1961 belonged to the first category, which included a special building program for miners and resettlers (*Umsiedler*). Altogether, one-third of the capital invested in housing construction came from public funds. In addition, the Federal Republic, the states, and the municipalities forgave part of the taxes owed by those who invested their savings in housing projects. Capital thus was channelled into this bottleneck situation while at the same time interest rates still were kept low. The tax benefits considerably improved the effective interest rate for private capital devoted to housing. If the total amount of taxes not collected is added to the public funds actually spent on housing, the public sector is seen to have provided more than half of the capital used for housing construction.

In this cooperation of public agencies with private enterprise astonishing results were achieved. Between 1949 and 1964 approximately eight million dwelling units were constructed, at first 215,000 units annually, after 1953 more than 500,000 units annually. Per capita, more dwellings were built in West Germany than in any other Western country.

However, admiration for this performance must be tempered with criticism. Building activity indeed produced quick results, but soon it appeared that important opportunities had been missed. The social housing projects, first inhabited by families selected from among the neediest, often turned out to be below the standards of quality that came to be expected in the following years. Many of the rebuilt cities were unsightly and poorly planned. The experiences accumulated in the splendid construction periods of the 1920's were hardly put to use. In many places the task of finding thoroughgoing solutions to old problems of town planning was not tackled. Long-term planning was only stressed at a later stage. Often the haphazard plugging of holes cost many times what would have had to be invested in well planned, farsighted projects. It is, however, not fair to level serious reproaches against the responsible agencies. In 1948, everyone was under the impression that for generations to come Germany would be the scene of destitution and suffering. Hardly anyone could imagine the rapid recovery and rise in quality standards.

In the public control and management of housing serious shortcomings also emerged over the following years. Those who by chance were able to remain in an old dwelling enjoyed very low rents, and so did the lucky residents of the social housing projects. It happened, however, that the persons who got priority for these new projects were not always the most needy. The opposite injustice also emerged; those who had to pay double and triple rents in the housing market as compared to their privileged neighbors were not always the well-to-do. Among them were young married couples who were not willing to wait for several years until the authorities would assign them a low-rent apartment. Thus chance and injustice were common. In general, the habit had grown of paying a much smaller part of one's income in rent than before the war. Therefore, even after the worst scarcity was overcome, there was popular reluctance to part with rent control, for this would necessarily have brought some rent increases. Nevertheless, rent decontrol was begun in 1960, and proceeded in stages. By the end of 1963, for the first time in forty years, rents were actually free in large parts of the country, including the rents of dwellings constructed before 1948. Even after decontrol, tenants enjoyed more legal protection against the rigors of a free market (profiteering, eviction) than before government controls were first introduced.

EQUALIZATION OF WAR BURDENS

Presumably the effects of the fateful war will reach far into the future and public funds will long be needed to deal with its manifold ills. The "financial liquidation of the war" has not yet been carried to its end. It is impossible to assess accurately the social costs caused by the war; they are hopelessly intermingled with normal costs in the accounts of every one of the social security operations. In the twenty years after 1945, for the support of war victims alone roughly 60 billion marks from public funds had to be spent, and in the framework of local welfare administration, for relief to those who suffered other war distress (*Kriegsfolgenhilfe der Fürsorge*), an additional 14 billion marks. But these sums fall far short of indicating the full social costs of the war. The ravages of the second world war were incomparably worse and were much more widely, yet unequally, dispersed among the citizens and regions than those of the war of 1914–18. When the war ended, those who had by chance been spared from bombing and expulsion lived side by side with those who had literally lost everything. The currency reform added more injustice by wiping out with a stroke of a pen the money claims of creditors while favoring debtors. The incidence of the burdens of war was so plainly unjust that the demands for redress could not be disregarded. In connection with the currency reform an equalization of burdens had already been promised. A beginning was made in the Immediate Aid Law of 1949 (*Soforthilfegesetz*); in 1952 the definitive Equalization of Burdens Law (*Lastenausgleichsgesetz*) followed. This legislation, together with the sections of the Basic Law concerning intergovernmental financial relations, represented the most important departure in public finance from the practice of the Weimar Republic. These laws established a special Equalization Fund (first called *Soforthilfefonds,* later *Lastenausgleichsfonds*) outside the federal budget, which was to receive the contributions of those taxed and redistribute them to those entitled to relief. The contributions consisted of a tax on the devaluation profits from mortgages and credits realized in connection with the currency reform, of subsidies from the federal and state treasuries, and above all of a levy on property which was to be determined uniformly at 50 per cent of the assets owned on June 21, 1948.

Naturally, a sudden redistribution of all property was not possible; this would have been technically unfeasible and economically undesirable. Business firms could not allow just any person to participate in their property and its management; neither could they place on the market part of their property in order to satisfy with cash the persons entitled to a share. There were no persons able to buy facing those forced to sell. Therefore, the property levy was converted from a lump sum to be paid at once into a series of yearly installments to be paid into the Equalization Fund until 1979. All the installments are to add up to approximately 84 billion marks.

To assist the needy at a faster pace than would be possible on the basis alone of the installments coming in, the Equalization Fund also borrowed in the capital market. Nevertheless, Fund relief disbursements remained dilatory. Many who were entitled to relief died before help reached them, and as time passed the idea of redistributing property seemed more dubious. Those obligated were as a rule able to defray their payments without touching their assets. Over the years their payments became minimal as measured by their property. The annual receipts from the levy were less than the revenue from the automobile tax and not much above the receipts from the ordinary property tax. It appeared that the values assessed in 1948 for shares, land, buildings, or machinery were far below actual values. Instead of taking 50 per cent of assets, the levy in fact netted only 10 to 20 per cent; and the longer payments were delayed the more their real value was cut by the prevailing slight inflation. The Equalization of Burdens Law did not fulfill the promises made in good faith in 1948–49 and did not live up to its name.

By 1964, more than 55 billion marks had been distributed through the Equalization Fund. Of this sum only about one-third went to individuals who had sustained actual losses of property. The Fund was used to a large extent to pay relief in urgent cases, to secure the livelihood of war victims, to build apartment houses for the expellees and those who had been bombed out, to finance small refugee enterprises, and so forth. Among the equalization payments proper the "household goods compensation" (*Hausratsentschädigung*) took first place and was granted according to the greatest need. The doctrine that the "equalization of burdens" constituted a legal claim irrespective of immediate need began to dominate Fund practice only in 1961, when payments for the so-called main compensation (*Hauptentschädigung*) began to require larger payments. Only then did public discussion begin about how damages should be treated that were sustained through the expropriation of German assets abroad, dismantling, or reparations; and in general about the problem of damage to juridical persons, which so far had not been considered. Expropriation and dismantling had caused a total of 17 to 18 billion marks in property losses. These problems remain for future legislation.

There was another matter that was far more urgent and required immediate action: the restitutions (*Wiedergutmachung*) for National Socialist crimes, which took a variety of shapes. Persons persecuted by the National Socialist regime on political, religious, or racial grounds, who had lost their relatives, their health, their liberty, who had been damaged in their incomes, deprived of their careers, or who had sustained enormous property losses were to be given payments in redress. True reparation for all these outrages to life and soul was obviously impossible. As for property losses, the Jewish citizens of Germany alone had been deprived of property estimated at seven billion marks.

Personal self-esteem at home and the Federal Republic's prestige abroad depended on positive proof that Germany was willing to repair as much as could be repaired of the damage done in the name of the nation during the Hitler years. This was the objective of the restitution laws which among other things gave the victims a legal claim to restitution of what was left of their lost property, or to damages. Thus there were filed more than three million individual claims, in settlement of which 18 billion marks were disbursed between 1945 and the spring of 1964. Restitution was made of physically existent property items valued at approximately two billion marks, and in addition one billion was paid to settle outstanding money claims. In order to help those who for some reason had no legal claims, various hardship funds were created—for instance, for the hapless victims of medical experimentation in eastern European concentration camps.

Comprehensive restitution agreements were arranged with several countries to afford some redress to residents of those countries who had been persecuted by National Socialism. By far the most important was the agreement of 1952 with the State of Israel; in it the Federal Republic undertook to pay three billion marks to the Israeli government, in acknowledgment of the fact that Israel had opened its doors to the Jews persecuted in Europe. Moreover, a Jewish Claims Conference received from the Federal Republic an additional 450 million marks for restitution to Jews living outside of Israel. Up to the end of 1964 a total of 26 billion marks had been raised and for the most part transferred abroad for restitution. Germany's favorable balance of payments was helpful in carrying through this project.

THE SOCIAL SECURITY SYSTEM

After the second world war Germany no longer ranked as the prototype welfare state. Although in 1963 West Germans paid almost 14 per cent of their national income in contributions to the social insurance system, Germany had been overtaken by other countries which originally had been slower in recognizing the obligation of a national community to care for its sick, elderly, disabled, and unemployed. The German system (see pages 45, 106) was old, people had become used to it, there was nothing in it to arouse enthusiasm or particular gratitude. Aside from occasional election giveaways, official propaganda laid much greater stress on the freedom of Germany's market economy than on the government's achievements in the area of social insurance benefits. The impression spread that other countries were more progressive in social policy than Germany.

It is true that at first the Federal Republic merely rebuilt the traditional institutions of social insurance which the Hitler regime had wrecked. The government was so preoccupied with reshaping the legal order for dealing with the social consequences of the war that the field of social insurance was somewhat neglected. Yet, contributions and benefits were increased. In 1963, employers and employees paid contributions equal to roughly 30 per cent of the total wage bill to the social insurance system. Repeatedly the circle of obligatory membership was enlarged. By 1965 all workers and persons earning salaries up to 1,800 marks per month were included in the old age pension plan. Coverage was extended to various groups of the self-employed: in 1961 the artisans and in 1963 the farmers were drawn into the insurance scheme. Finally, a majority of the population had in one way or another acquired membership in the social insurance system; for instance, almost nine-tenths of the people were covered by the system's health insurance. The simple expansion of the system's coverage to more people was only one of the ways it developed after the war.

In 1955 the Federal Republic began an imaginative reform that would eventually lead to the reconstruction of the entire social insurance system. In the field of retirement benefits, the reorganization of the three separate pension systems for workers, salaried white-collar employees, and mining personnel was completed by 1957. The first feature of this reorganization was a new formula to determine the amount of individual benefits. It had been observed that upon his retirement from the working process a person often experienced a sharp cut in his living standard because the retirement benefits he received, which were based on his total lifetime contributions, were in marked contrast to his last earnings. This happened whenever wages and salaries in general, for whatever reasons, had an upward trend. The newly introduced formula for pension payments did not, like the old formula, take into account only the total of an individual's contributions; it also examined whether a person's working income at the time it was earned was relatively high or low. The new formula compared the individual's contributions with the average contributions over the same period and applied the ratio found to the benefits to be allowed. The reform's second feature was the provision for the current reviewing of benefits paid. In order to let those already receiving pensions participate in any general improvement in productivity and incomes, a yearly adjustment of benefits must be made in accordance with the rise in the general level of income. Thus, between 1958 and 1965 pensions were raised seven different times, by an average of 6.7 per cent. In 1959, workmen's compensation insurance payments were similarly adjusted. This reform was described as "dynamizing" the benefits or as instituting "productivity benefits."

Along with the methods of calculating pension payments the method of financing them was changed. The former principle of accumulating the contributions of the insured and paying out in benefits only the accruing interest on the accumulated capital was discontinued. The fact that twice within one generation the fund had been wiped out by inflation without this necessitating the interruption of benefit payments made the responsible managers aware of how superfluous the accumulation of a fund really was. An individual can accumulate wealth through saving, from which he can in due time sustain his existence. But this is possible only because there are others who are willing to buy what he wants to sell (for example bonds), thus enabling him to buy currently produced consumer goods for the proceeds of his savings. The moment a large part of the population has become involved in the social insurance system, no separate stock or flow of goods exists on which the insured could draw in case of an emergency. The fixed assets of the nation cannot be consumed. Therefore, those gainfully employed today producing national income have to give up some consumption in favor of those currently retired from work. Contributors expect that the coming generation will treat them in the same way. Accordingly, it is in principle correct to burden those gainfully employed today with the costs of the social insurance system, and in fact nothing else is workable.

A remarkable new objective was added to the traditional insurance system in 1954, with the introduction of "children's allowances" (*Kindergeld*). All parents of three or more children received 25 marks a month for their third and each succeeding child. In 1965 the rates were increased to 60 marks for the third child and 70 marks for each additional child. Parents with low incomes might be allowed 25 marks for the second child. The costs were carried in a special family equalization account by the employers and the treasury. This experiment in the "equalization of family burdens" represents a feature somewhat alien to the idea of a market economy since the family wage has no connection with the worker's performance but is predicated solely on his need. On the other hand, society as a whole is interested in raising a sound posterity. Family allowances, which have an old tradition in New Zealand for instance, are not completely new in Germany. Before the first world war the government paid its civil servants and other employees wages and salaries graduated according to the number of their children. The income tax legislation also recognized a kind of family allowance in that it granted tax deductions for each child, but those most in need of consideration profited least from this because the low-income brackets were exempted from tax anyway. Direct relief had to be provided for the recipients of low incomes, once the principle that family assistance was up to the state had been accepted. In the overall framework of the German social insurance system, however, family benefits continued to play a minor role. While in 1964 family allowances in the other member nations of the Common Market involved one-fifth to one-third of all social security expenditures, in Germany

Kindergeld payments amounted to only 3 per cent of all social security disbursements. This comparison does not, however, give a complete picture of family assistance since families are aided in various other ways in Germany. Tax benefits, preferential transportation fares, and aid for education are available to increase the effective income of large families.

Taken together, the various changes in the social security system in a way amount to a break with the old principle of social insurance, especially since almost every citizen is now covered. Originally it had made sense to think that, by insuring certain low-income groups and making them contribute only modestly to the general fund—the difference paid by employers and taxpayers—income would be channelled from the better-off to those in greater need. This concept now became less and less applicable. The larger the number of persons covered by the insurance system, the greater the case load became and the more government drew on tax receipts and business raised prices to finance the growing burden. Finally, the benefits were being paid from the very pockets of those to be benefited. Actually, distributions and redistributions of income have become so confused that even experts lose their way. No one can say with any accuracy who in the end carries the burden of the system.

THE LABOR MARKET

When in November, 1948, the wage freeze was terminated and wages once again became subject to free bargaining, people tried to take up the threads that had been broken in 1933, in labor relations as in every other field. Unions and employers again faced one another to arrive at collective agreements. The old party-line unions were now replaced by unified trade unions representative of all those employed within one industry or trade. Representing the several industrial unions (*Industriegewerkschaften*) was a summit organization founded in 1949, the German Trade Union Federation (*Deutscher Gewerkschaftsbund,* DGB). The Allies had hoped that this umbrella organization would not become too powerful. Therefore, the industrial unions retained their autonomy and only they acted as the participants of collective bargaining with management. The DGB in turn spoke for labor in basic matters of economic and social principle, and it tried to coordinate the policies of the various member unions.

The idea of single unified trade unions was the outgrowth of bitter experience in the Hitler years during which all unions, whatever their political line, had faced the same oppression and persecution. This prompted union leaders not to revive old animosities but to stress common interests. There were various motives for combining all available forces. Some hoped that the absence of competition among the unions would strengthen the workers. Others expected that out of consideration for the non-Marxist members the identification of the major part of the unions with the Social Democratic Party would be weakened. Finally, it was hoped that a powerful centralized umbrella organization would strengthen labor's and its leaders' sense of responsibility for the general well-being. This hope, particularly under the leadership of the first chairman of the DGB, Hans Böckler, was largely justified by results.

Labor conflicts in the Federal Republic were infrequent. Although almost half the labor force was unionized, and the unions therefore commanded a position of strength, this was not fully exploited in open pressure for higher wages. To a large extent such restraint was due to the unemployment that persisted until 1955 and to the low ebb in union funds. However, in Belgium, France, and Italy unemployment was also high and yet there were continuous severe labor conflicts. In Germany, this was the period in which the unions pressed their demands for and won the right of codetermination (*Mitbestimmung*) (see pages 292 ff.), which disproves the argument that their weakness alone compelled them to forego wage demands.

What other reasons were there for the unions' reluctance to strike? They will be found in the workers' and their unions' attitude toward reconstruction. After the currency reform, everybody was ready to work hard. Naturally the general aim was to achieve a higher standard of living, but this was not all. To rebuild the factories was in itself a goal worth striving for. Moreover, the workers placed their confidence in the new system of society, the market economy, and also in the government. Germany remained free of extreme political tensions which might have found expression in strikes. It is true that in the first years after currency reform the unions made the market economy a target of their criticism, but just in this the membership often refused to follow its leaders. Why strike if year by year real income improved (see Table 34), or, more precisely, money wages rose and prices lagged behind? After the wave of readjustments at the end of 1948, consumer goods prices even decreased for a time, and the Korean boom raised them not much above their initial level. Altogether, the uncontrolled prices rose comparatively little prior to 1955, while rents were kept low. Thus, except for the first few months in the first years after the currency reform, the impulse to adapt wages to rising prices, so strong in other countries, was lacking in Germany.

TABLE 34

Indices of Money Wages, Real Wages, Working Hours; Federal Republic, 1950–65*
(industrial workers; 1950 = 100)

YEAR	GROSS WEEKLY WAGES		HOURS WORKED YEARLY
	Money wages I	*Real wages *** II	III
1950	100	100	100
1951	114	108	99.5
1952	123	112	98.8
1953	129	119	98.3
1954	134	124	98.6
1955	143	130	98.6
1956	155	137	96.2
1957	163	142	90.8
1958	171	145	88.5
1959	180	152	87.1
1960	197	164	86.1
1961	217	176	83.7
1962	239	188	81.0
1963	255	195	79.0
1964	275	202	78.9
1965	304	219	78.0

* 1950–60, without the Saar and West Berlin; 1961–64, without West Berlin.
** Index of money wages divided by cost-of-living index.
SOURCES: Col. I and II: Computed from *Statistisches Jahrbuch für die Bundesrepublik Deutschland, 1952–66.* Col. III: Computed from *ibid., 1966,* p. 227.

With growing prosperity and the achievement of full and even over-full employment the scene on the labor market became livelier. At the same time, it became plain that the umbrella association of the unions, the DGB, in reality was weaker than it appeared. After the death of Hans Böckler in 1951, the DGB's policies seemed to be nothing more than compromises of the differing ideas of the leaders of the largest industrial unions. The incomplete centralization of the unions began to be felt as a distinct problem. Because of rivalries among the various unions, the wage increases gained by one union were often costly to the membership of other unions. A wage increase—and possibly a resulting price increase—in one industry stimulated the leaders of other industrial unions to demand equal benefits for their members.

After 1959 wage policies approached a danger zone. As long as the industrial boom lasted, employers felt able to grant almost any wage increase and to recoup the outlay by raising their prices. Accordingly, the public began to hold rising wages responsible for rising prices. It was noted that the unions now hardly ever needed to strike to achieve higher wages, and this led to doubts whether the unions really should remain autonomous in collective bargaining. Remembering the sad results of compulsory arbitration through government intervention in the last years of the Weimar Republic, the authors of the Wage Agreements Act of 1949 (*Tarifvertragsgesetz*) had declined to provide for such a procedure. Now some people wished to revive compulsory arbitration or to let experts determine "objectively correct" wages.

Moreover, the postwar years presented a new circumstance which made all comparisons with former conditions inapplicable: the commitment to full employment. In the Federal Republic both the government and the Central Bank were pledged to guarantee full employment, a fact that was decisive for wage policies. If costs were to rise and profits decrease because of higher wages, and consequently the employers dismissed an unusually high percentage of the labor force, the government would have the obligation to stimulate demand and induce prices to rise in order to prevent unemployment from developing. If, on the other hand, the government wanted to avoid rising prices, it would be forced either to give up the guarantee of full employment, or it would need sufficient power to put pressure on the unions and employers or to take over direct control of wage movements. In the Federal Republic influential voices were heard in favor of the last two alternatives. As of 1966, however, no actual measures had been taken.

For several years the DGB had not been alone in representing the interests of the employed. In addition to the DGB unions there were the German Office Workers' Union (*Deutsche Angestellten-Gewerkschaft*), the Clerks' Association (*Handels- und Industriegehilfen-Verband,* revived in 1950), and several associations of civil servants. In 1955 the Christian Workers' Union reappeared, which had serious implications for the unity of the labor movement. It had been founded because many union members believed that the DGB was not politically neutral. In fact, in a number of important matters the DGB and the Social Democratic Party held the same views, while there was some serious opposition on the part of the DGB to policies of the majority party, the CDU-CSU. These conflicts became manifest when the unions actively participated in the political discussions on German rearmament. The agitation after 1952 against the reintroduction of conscription, and after 1958 against providing the Bundeswehr with atomic war heads strongly implicated the union leadership in political action. The new Christian unions tried to intervene, without gaining much influence.

CODETERMINATION

When after the first world war the attempt was made to introduce a new social order, the unions made an effort to "democratize" the management of industry and business. Democratization was to be achieved by the formation of shop councils (*Betriebsräte*), whose functions, however, had been narrowly defined. After the second world war a new effort was made to give the employed coresponsibility with management in the shops and offices. The opportunity seemed favorable since management wished the cooperation of the trade unions in the fight against dismantling and decartelization. It was therefore understandable that in 1950 the unions insisted that at last the time had come to devise a system of codetermination (*Mitbestimmung*), to begin with the mining and steel industries. Labor threatened to strike unless the Bundestag passed an appropriate law without delay. This threat came in a critical phase of reconstruction when immobilizing the coal and steel industries would have paralyzed the entire economy. At the last moment an understanding was reached and, still under the strike threat, on May 21, 1951, the Bundestag passed the Law on Codetermination of the Employees on the Supervisory Boards and the Management Boards of the Companies in the Mining and the Iron and Steel Industries (*Gesetz über die Mitbestimmung der Arbeitnehmer in den Aufsichtsräten und Vorständen der Unternehmen des Bergbaus und der eisen- und stahlerzeugenden Industrie*).

[At this point an explanation may be useful of the typical governing bodies of German corporations. A German enterprise as a rule has two boards, each of which performs some of the functions performed by the board of directors in American enterprises. The *Aufsichtsrat* (supervisory board or board of overseers) is normally composed of shareholders, elected by the general meeting of shareholders and determining only matters of general policy. The *Vorstand* (management board or executive board), on the other hand, is normally composed exclusively of executives active in the enterprise and is collectively responsible to the shareholders for its actual management. The membership of the two boards usually does not overlap. An analogous form of organization is offered by Harvard University with its Board of Overseers and its President and Fellows.]

According to this law, the supervisory board of every enterprise was divided evenly between representatives of the shareholders and of labor, with one neutral member appointed by both sides. A labor member was added to the management board as representative of the trade union and the shop council. The position of the neutral member between the bargaining parties was difficult, but in general few cases of serious disagreement became public. On the management boards there was not much dispute since the interests of the enterprise as a whole mostly enjoyed the allegiance of the labor representatives who often gave management valuable support in their discussions with the Bonn authorities and with the High Authority in Luxembourg. Codetermination basically resulted in a sort of cartel of all those involved in the production process directed against the consumers. Many observers believe that this institution can be credited with the comparative absence of social tensions during the painful contraction of the mining industry. It might be remarked that it was precisely in the mining industry where the decisions of the individual firm in which labor participated where comparatively insignificant, since the European Coal and Steel Community had absorbed important managerial responsibilities. Thus, codetermination did not initiate any revolutionary change in the German economic system.

It is too early for a conclusive evaluation of the prospects for lasting peace between management and labor. No law on codetermination can alter the fact that, whoever manages the firm, one authority must issue the orders and everyone else must follow. The relationship between an upper and a lower echelon necessarily gives rise to conflict situations. It is questionable whether labor will find in codetermination a method of deciding conflicts more satisfactory than the traditional ones, or whether on the contrary labor might become a captive of codetermination, which in the end might serve management better than labor.

After codetermination had been introduced in the mining and iron industry in 1951, the unions continued to press for its introduction in other industries. Meanwhile, however, conditions had undergone further changes. Economic expansion was all-pervasive, the market economy was solidly established, the revolutionary impulse had subsided, and therefore attempts to apply the new model introduced in the mining and iron industry to all other fields of business had no success. The threat of a general strike was indeed repeated about this time, to prevent the passage of the Act Concerning Industrial Constitution (*Betriebsverfassungsgesetz*), which labor regarded as too mild, but the strike did not come off. A newspaper strike which did begin was unpopular and was even pronounced illegal by a court decision against the union involved. On October 11, 1952, the Act Concerning Industrial Constitution passed the Bundestag without difficulty. In the future one-third of the members of the supervisory boards of all stock companies would have to be labor representatives, who could of course always be outvoted. The shop councils as a rule were only to participate in decisions concerning social security and personnel matters and in rare cases were accorded codetermination with a power of veto. This law did not constitute an important step toward fulfilling union aspirations. Unions continued their struggle for codetermination and in the election campaign of 1953, in cooperation with the Social Democratic Party, they made it one of the main planks in their program. However, a decisive victory went to the CDU-CSU, which was able to raise its percentage of votes from 31 to 45. Evidently the voters were satisfied with the economic success that had been achieved and were not particularly interested in changing the status quo. Twelve years later, in the general elections of 1965, the unions put new steam behind the old ideas by again demanding codetermination in those industries in which it was not yet applied.

Waning fervor for codetermination was characteristic of the climate of political reform during the second and third legislative periods of the Bundestag (1953–57 and 1957–61). As the preceding pages show, there was no lack of new ideas in the realm of social policy to supplement the ideology of the "social market economy." But over the years it appeared more and more that a fundamental examination of the existing social structure and the equitableness of the distribution of wealth was overdue. Everyone, indeed, had profited from the economic expansion, but the results of increases in productivity were by no means equally apportioned. The market and government policy both favored the accumulation of wealth by businesses, and the haves gained more than the have-nots. Possibly no alternative policy would have been viable at first, and in the last resort the little man also improved his income and even his property. But what could be accepted in an exceptional situation became more of a problem once the sense of emergency had faded from men's minds.

Accordingly, at the end of the 1950's, the aims and methods of income and wealth distribution were more widely discussed. In contrast to the arguments in the days of the old Reich and of the Weimar Republic, the discussion now centered less on the distribution of incomes than on the distribution of property, for which a much wider dispersion was declared by many critics to be highly desirable. However, opinions differed as to the methods by which labor should receive its due share of new productive capital. Various experimental measures followed. Business firms made it easier for their employees to acquire shares of their stock; the federal government reprivatized three of its largest concerns; tax policy was shaped in favor of savings by low-income groups. Yet, the main problem, the concentration of economic power in a comparatively narrow stratum of the propertied few, was hardly to be solved by such methods. It may be that the coming period of economic development in the Federal Republic will witness more discussion of the problems of equitable distribution of wealth and power than those of growth. If this should come to pass, the debate on codetermination, interrupted in 1953 but resumed in 1965, may take on greater significance.

6. *Economic Problems at the Iron Curtain*

WEST BERLIN

MUCH OF WHAT has been reported in the preceding pages concerning the West German economy also applies to West Berlin. De facto, West Berlin is one of the Länder and played its part in founding the Federal Republic. It developed the same institutions and professes the same ideas. And yet, the city, separated politically and physically from the West since 1945, and divided moreover since 1948, has had to find its own, much more thorny, path.

Immediately following the war, the Reich's capital city lost its functions as the center of administration, trade, and banking, and with these functions several hundred thousand inhabitants lost their livelihood. More than two-thirds of West Berlin's industries had been dismantled by the Russians and to a lesser extent by the French occupation authorities. The blockade imposed by the Soviets in 1948 and 1949 crippled the beginnings of reconstruction and threw the economy even further back than it had been at the end of the war. The air lift organized by the Allies was successful, but it could secure only the absolute minimum of supplies for the population. While by 1950 Western Germany had returned to prewar production figures, the level of production in West Berlin amounted to no more than one-third of 1936 volume, and the prewar level was surpassed only seven years later.

Unemployment took a long time to overcome. Following currency reform, in West Berlin, a city of two million, as many as one-third of the labor force remained without regular employment, and in 1952 unemployment was still at the rate of 25 per cent. Not before 1959 did the unemployment rate fall below 5 per cent. After that the West Berlin economy proved strong enough to offer employment to the many thousands of refugees who, year by year, entered the city from the east. Ever since 1949, West Berlin had made every effort to expand its industrial base. In 1950, less than one-fourth of those employed were working in industry; ten years later it was one-half. The electrical, ladies' garment, and engineering industries became again, as in the years before 1945, the main industries of Berlin and resumed their important role in the context of Western German production. Lured by tax benefits, the cigarette industry relocated in West Berlin, with the result that in 1962 every third cigarette smoked in Western Germany was produced in West Berlin.

The revival of West Berlin cannot be understood without considering the many subsidies its industries received. The island city needed them to compensate the disadvantages of location and the catastrophic conditions from which development had to begin. Contributions from Marshall Plan funds made possible the reconstruction of industrial plant, transportation, and housing. Massive tax benefits persuaded business to invest in Berlin or to buy its products. However, the city remained under constant threat of political intervention and these risks could not be fully shouldered by private business. In the years after 1958 Khrushchev repeated his Berlin ultimatum from time to time, demanding the removal of the Western occupation forces and the political divorcement of West Berlin from West Germany, and at the same time proclaiming the right of the so-called German Democratic Republic to control the means of communication with Berlin. The Federal Republic then gave certain guarantees to compensate importers and exporters for the higher transit costs caused by the risk of Soviet interference. The Federal Republic and Marshall Plan funds also dealt with the considerable budget deficits of the city administration in view of the heavier burden of war damages that Berlin had to carry as compared with the other Länder. Freight subsidies were given in order to even out the additional production costs in Berlin caused by its remoteness from sources of supply and centers of demand. As the years went by the city became more and more able to manage on its own.

On August 13, 1961, the DDR began to construct the Berlin Wall and the Death Border (*Todesstreifen*); these measures put the seal on the division of Berlin and completed the insulation of West Berlin. The 60,000 workers who until that time had daily come in from the East to work in the West were now shut off from their customary jobs. West Berlin's businesses succeeded in surviving this further shock, but the question of the economic future of this insulated community was now posed with greater insistence. Never in the past had a metropolis kept alive through time on the basis of its residents only, but had always depended on migrants attracted to it. Berlin had been a city of people from Brandenburg, Silesia, Mecklenburg, Pomerania. In order not to die out, Berlin was now forced to attract families from West Germany and to stop the trend toward emigration to the West. To achieve this, the wage level had to be kept higher in West Berlin than in the rest of the country, although on the other hand labor costs could not be allowed to rise so far as to wipe out business profits. Therefore, subsidizing in many forms was necessary. This was a political not an economic task. Even before August 13, 1961, Federal and West Berlin authorities had cooperated in this respect, but now they had to multiply their efforts. In 1962, the Bundestag, in which representatives of West Berlin had seats but not the right to vote, passed laws which accorded more privileges to Berlin taxpayers and more inducements to private investors and which promoted the sale of Berlin products in West German markets.

INTERZONAL TRADE

The favorable developments in the Federal Republic's foreign trade and the progress of its integration with its European neighbors present a striking contrast with the developments of interzonal trade, the last vestige of the lively trade relations that had once prevailed between the western, central, and eastern parts of Germany. This residual trade was called "interzonal trade" in order to indicate that no genuine "foreign" trade could exist between the various parts of Germany; and indeed, there were no customs duties. However, neither could these trade exchanges be called domestic trade, as they were carried on between regions with differing currency systems and had to be arranged by means of agreements between separate governmental authorities and by a sort of foreign exchange clearing system. The interzonal trade involved two economic systems of extreme divergence; it was under stricter control than most of the real foreign trade of the Federal Republic; and it was not included in the Common Market arrangements. The amounts and composition of the goods that crossed the borders in either direction were decided mainly on the basis of political considerations on both sides.

The Federal Republic exchanged only about 2 to 3 per cent of its foreign trade by way of the interzonal arrangements, but in West Berlin the ratio was much higher for both imports and exports. Berlin's main imports from the DDR were coal, meat, and sugar. For the DDR, interzonal trade was of greater importance, accounting for about 12 per cent of its total foreign trade. The DDR could in this way procure essential goods, which were not to be found in the eastern territories, for building up its heavy industries. It exported to the Federal Republic primarily lignite, petroleum, and textiles. In return it bought in the Federal Republic chemicals, machinery, steel, iron, and Ruhr coal. For reasons of quality and price there was little demand in West Germany for the many consumer goods the DDR tried to sell. West German merchants also dreaded the cumbersome licensing and trading methods and of course the political risk. No one could hope to build up steady business connections, since the decisions of the all-powerful planning authorities in the East and political considerations in the West determined what could be bought and sold. On one occasion in 1960 the Federal Republic cancelled the interzonal agreement in protest against infringements by the Zone authorities on communication procedures with West Berlin; however, later the agreement was extended. The modest interzonal trade could hardly constitute an instrument of economic pressures in the East-West conflict. For this reason it was allowed to survive after August 13, 1961, under the regime of the Wall.

VIII

GERMANY'S OTHER PART

1. An Eastern Economic Miracle?

WHEN IN 1949 the Federal Republic of Germany and the so-called German Democratic Republic prepared to organize their separate statehood, the disjointed parts of Germany were progressively drawn into the fields of force of two divergent economic as well as political systems. Just as the two large powers, the United States and the Soviet Union, confronted one another in their rivalry of military organization, propaganda, economics, science, and technology in many other places, this contest of fundamentally opposed orders of society had to be played out here also, in the very heart of Europe. As material evidence of the superiority of their respective political and economic systems, both parties pointed to criteria of reconstruction and standards of living.

Over the first decade, the race went in favor of West Germany. It must be conceded that no such indubitably accurate statistical material concerning the Soviet zone and the Soviet sector of Berlin is available as there is for West Germany and West Berlin, and it is often necessary to depend on rougher estimates. It may be stated, however, that the Socialist Unity Party (*Sozialistische Einheitspartei,* SED, the single powerful political organization of the DDR) has so far not succeeded in attaining its goal of surpassing the standard of living of "capitalist" West Germany or even of coming close to this standard. The gross national product of the DDR, that is, the sum of consumption, investment, and excess of exports over imports, showed a somewhat more favorable development than private consumption alone; however, in 1950 it still remained about one-fifth less than the level of 1936, at a time when West Germany had already surpassed the prewar standard. After 1950, the per capita gross national product increased in the East at about the same rate as in the West, at which rate the East could not catch up with the West, much less overtake it.

Can the economic system of the DDR be judged unsuccessful merely on the grounds that it failed to attain one of the goals stressed in its propaganda? Were the West to arrive at such a conclusion, it would be deluding itself. True, even had the DDR achieved a better growth rate and its standard of living improved more rapidly, this would still be questionable proof of the system's success. The growth of Germany's national income after Hitler's accession to power could hardly have recommended this system because the methods by which this expansion was achieved were also relevant. In the same manner, economic growth in the East and the West can only be compared if account is taken of the sacrifices at the expense of which the development occurred. These sacrifices weighed incomparably more heavily on the people of the Soviet zone.

Moreover, growth was in fact not faster in the DDR than in West Germany. Is not this sufficient ground on which to pronounce judgment about the Eastern system's inefficiency? The answer still is no. To begin with, as has been seen, conditions at the outset were much more unfavorable for the parts of Germany occupied by the Soviets than for the West. Dismantling had hit the eastern industries more brutally and the expropriations of industrial property in favor of the Soviet Union had deprived the reconstruction effort of essential facilities. While West Germany began to enjoy international economic aid, East Germany received no help; on the contrary, it had to contribute heavily to the reconstruction of eastern Europe, at least until 1953. In the period from 1945 to 1953 the Soviets took from current production massive reparations whose worth was set by experts at a minimum of 40 billion DM-East. Consequently, a smaller part of domestic production as compared with West Germany was available for investment and consumption. For political reasons the Soviet zone was forced to concentrate its foreign trade progressively on the Eastern countries; it was therefore able to import only little of the cheaper and better Western products offered in the free world markets and had to be content with the goods that the badly damaged and less efficient Eastern economies had to offer. Finally, the Soviet zone was constantly drained by emigration. Among the emigrants were many highly skilled experts through whom the West enjoyed a corresponding addition to its productive potential. However, this last unfortunate feature of the Eastern economy cannot be regarded as a factor independent from the system itself. The mass migration which lasted until forcibly stopped in August, 1961, was on the contrary a significant proof that the people concerned regarded the sacrifices demanded of them in the process of reconstruction as excessive. People escaped from the totalitarian compulsions which they had no democratic means to alleviate, and they were drawn toward the lure of the obviously more successful system.

If it is thus true that reconstruction as it evolved under particularly difficult conditions in the DDR did not satisfy the population, can it then be justly said that the system had suffered a shipwreck? This must depend on the yardsticks an observer applies. Whether a planned economy is successful or not does not depend on any comparison with different systems but only on the criterion of whether or not it achieved its own goals. In this connection it should be admitted that the aim of raising the standards of living, dominant in the West, is actually of secondary importance to the responsible planners in the Soviet zone. Other planning goals rank higher, and in achieving these the system was successful. The reconstruction of the Soviet Union was appreciably advanced, and in the Soviet zone a new social and economic system was introduced, the structure of domestic production was basically changed, and a disengagement from the capitalist West was carried through. These were political goals derived from the power structure and the dominant ideologies, and therefore no comparison with western economic successes can tell the whole story.

In consecutive phases of development the aims of the planners underwent some modifications, mostly in step with political events in the Soviet Union. After 1948, the DDR took part in the harsh Stalinist course; after Stalin's death, on March 5, 1953, and the revolt of the Zone on June 17, 1953, policies were temporarily made somewhat milder. At the end of 1956, influences were felt across the borders from the Polish "thaw" and the Hungarian uprising, which jolted all the countries of the Eastern bloc. Yet, policy may be said to have followed a generally consistent direction in compliance with the Soviet pattern. While in 1945 functionaries of the Communist party in the Zone might still have dreamed of an independent German way to Communism, it soon appeared that the Russian occupation forces and the central body of functionaries surrounding the leader, Walter Ulbricht, were not in sympathy with such a course.

After 1960, practically no private property was left in agriculture and forest lands (see Table 36 on page 308). With insignificant exceptions, the state was sole owner of the means of production in industry (see Table 37 on page 310). There was no private wholesale and very little private retail trade. The small enclaves of private business remaining in industry, trade, and the handicrafts were caught up in the net of rigid central controls, unable to take independent action of any consequence. The labor organizations had lost their power; codetermination, shop councils, and the like were alien to the system. The unions had become an auxiliary organ of the state in administering controls. Strikes were unthinkable since according to the dominant ideology no conflict of interests could arise between the workers and the state-run industries. The Party and the government apparatus it controls maintain that in all their decisions they know better than the workers themselves how to serve the workers' welfare, and so any democratic control would be beside the point. Some observers think that the elections of 1946 still retained vestiges of free choice; however this may be, since then no more free and secret elections have been held in the DDR to give the voters any alternative whatsoever.

These policies, accompanied by terror as they undeniably were, were based on the evolving Marxist-Leninist-Stalinist doctrine. This doctrine was inspired by the expectation that a future stage of society would be paradise and by the conviction that a specific minority group, the capitalists, are the preordained obstacles to the realization of this paradise. According to Communist ideology, the dictatorship of the party elite is justified because the workers could attain the right state of mind only after the end phase of social development had been reached. Before this consummation there would always be vestiges of the so-called capitalist economic behavior that was so hard to eradicate and that obstructed the workers' better appreciation of their own good. It therefore remained the duty of the leadership to enforce the desired social conditions, if necessary against the opposition of a majority, to prevent "the majority defeating the truth" (Khrushchev).

Such a doctrine does not lend itself to discussion with its followers since criticism, coming from nonbelievers in the underlying ideology, is at once branded as biased by self-interest. But criticism of individual measures leveled from the point of view of this ideology itself is equally futile because, allegedly, the leadership alone is in command of the truth and of its correct interpretation. No judgment is made here whether in fact all the leaders believe in this doctrine or whether some of them, perhaps the most important ones, are only technicians of power. One thing is certain, that without this ideology the Soviet system, as it prevails in Russia and in the Soviet zone of Germany, would be unthinkable. The ideology creates the minimum of consensus among the members of the governing group without which no totalitarian government can survive.

In the first years after 1945 the dogma was instrumental in carrying out the expropriations which marked a definite end to the capitalist relationships and conditions of production and which were supposed to secure the new order. Since then, Yugoslavia and also Poland have each, in its own way, expressed some doubts as to whether the Marxist system must necessarily enforce rigid nationalization of all means of production. In the Soviet zone also the argument that society must be entirely reconstructed temporarily dropped somewhat into the background. Thus, in the spring of 1961 the official reason given for carrying the collectivization of agriculture through to its very end was the urgency of raising productivity. When this renewed campaign of expropriation led to a crisis in supply, and it became evident that collectivization had failed to improve productivity, the campaign was nevertheless not called off. Obviously the leadership had not really expected a rapid improvement in harvests but had simply assumed that the power structure was sufficiently consolidated to dare to rescind the 1945 distribution of lands among the farmers.

Thus the fact that living standards were not increasing more rapidly could partly be attributed to the extraordinarily difficult conditions of reconstruction, combined with some planning errors. But partly also the failure followed from the political aim of economic independence from the non-Communist world. It is a fundamental Communist postulate that in order to attain the ultimate goal you must first strengthen the heavy industries and the production of investment goods. Accordingly, the iron and steel industry, sheet rolling plants, capital equipment manufacturing, and shipbuilding were energetically promoted. Giant socialist plants were founded such as the iron and steel complex in Stalinstadt (in 1961 renamed *Eisenhüttenstadt*) on the Oder, the lignite complex Black Pump near Hoyerswerda, and the large coke works for the processing of lignite at Lauchhammer. In comparison, the consumer goods industries, in the DDR as in the Soviet Union, lagged behind. It would have been entirely feasible to increase the supply of consumer goods, and it seemed even ideologically possible after 1953 when criticism was voiced in the Soviet Union of the prejudice in favor of heavy industry. However, except for some insignificant waverings, the party line remained chained to the goals of the fastest possible growth of the economy as a whole and its independence from the West; and these goals were believed attainable only by forced investment at the expense of consumption.

Nevertheless, toward the end of the 1950's the most onerous and unpopular method of restricting consumption, the ration card system, was at last terminated even in the DDR, though with exceptions. On principle, the government had the power to adjust demand to supply without rationing. To restrict excess demand all that was necessary was to raise prices energetically. In practice there was reluctance to rely exclusively on this method which most hurt the neediest, and this is why the hated card system was retained for so many years. Ever since 1952 the full abolition of rationing had been repeatedly promised, but the promise was finally kept only in 1958. Two years later, catastrophic developments in agriculture forced a new reversal. Winter potatoes were now issued only against ration cards, meat and butter only to registered customers according to certain norms. For the rest, the consumer could spend his money freely on supplies as they became available. This did not mean that production would mainly be determined by private demand or that the desired goods would be forthcoming. Even fifteen years after the currency reform there were queues in front of the shops whenever scarce commodities were being offered. Occasionally customers had to wait for many years for delivery of a refrigerator, a television set, a radio, or a motorcycle.

After the currency reform an effort had been made to siphon off excess money through a governmental trading organization (*Handelsorganisation*, HO). In the stores, restaurants, and hotels of this organization, rationed goods could be bought freely, though at a multiple of their controlled prices. The margin between free and controlled prices was in effect a kind of consumption tax. Nevertheless, considerable amounts of cash accumulated in the hands of the consumers after 1948. Without rationing, this cash would have spilled into the market with the force of an avalanche. This problem brought about a second currency reform in 1957 that went by the name of "currency exchange." Savings accounts were not involved but large sums of cash were destroyed after the possession of cash was limited by law.

In comparing the Western "economic miracle" with the Eastern reconstruction, the large discrepancy in housing construction is striking. While in the years 1950 to 1964, 8.0 million dwelling units were built in the Federal Republic, the number in the DDR was only 0.9 million. Had building proceeded at the same per capita rate as in the West, the number would have been 2.6 million. The apartments offered in the East were on the average smaller and of poorer quality. In the Federal Republic one-third of all units available in 1958 had been built after 1945, in the DDR not quite one-tenth.

TABLE 35

Migration from Soviet Zone to Federal Republic, 1950–62*

Year	*Persons*	*Year*	*Persons*
1950	337,300	1957	384,700
1951	287,800	1958	226,300
1952	232,100	1959	173,800
1953	408,100	1960	225,400
1954	295,400	1961 †	214,100
1955	381,800	1962 §	21,356
1956	396,300		

* Including West Berlin.
† To September 30, 1961.
§ Accounted for later in the course of the Federal Emergency Procedures.

SOURCES: Reports of the *Bundesminister für Vertriebene, Flüchtlinge und Kriegsbeschädigte an die Landesflüchtlingsverwaltungen* (June 19, 1961), p. 4, and (January 28, 1963), pp. 4 ff.

In many instances towns in the DDR damaged in the war had not yet been rebuilt in the early 1960's. Clearly, housing did not enjoy high priority with the planners but ranked as low as other consumer needs. It may be granted that housing construction was not as urgent in the DDR, where population decreased, as in West Germany, where the population increased.

In 1960 there were 6.5 per cent fewer residents in the Soviet zone and East Berlin than ten years before. The number was roughly the same as in this territory in 1938, while in the West the population had increased by one-third between 1938 and 1960. The decrease in population in the DDR, particularly in the early years, happened as many who had first settled in the Soviet zone joined the enormous wave of expellees from the East who continued their trek until they reached West Germany. After 1948 the political motive for leaving the DDR became predominant. This flight assumed such proportions that the natural excess of births over deaths could not compensate for it, particularly since, as of 1960, this natural excess was only 3.4 per thousand inhabitants compared with 6.4 per thousand in the Federal Republic. The exodus (see Table 35) was at first not unwelcome to the DDR authorities since, it was hoped, it would help cut down unemployment and rid the economy of many old-age pensioners at the expense of West Germany. In the first Five Year Plan, prepared in 1950, the emigration had actually been included in the plans. However, when it appeared after 1953 that too many young people, skilled workers, physicians, technicians, and scientists were joining the flight and that the potential labor force had begun to deteriorate, the battle against the "Flight from the Republic" was proclaimed. After 1957 flight was made a crime, but prevention proved impossible until on August 13, 1961, the Wall was erected. Therewith the citizens lost their last way of expressing opposition to the system.

2. *Nationalization and Collectivization*

THE ECONOMY OF the DDR was planned and controlled by a bureaucracy. Under Hitler a bureaucracy had also been in command, but the economy still existed as a partner to the state authorities. Through National Socialism the entrepreneur had lost his liberty; in the DDR, but for inconsequential exceptions, he was eradicated. The state was the only producing agent. To adherents of economic planning this was logical. As long as free entrepreneurs survived the plan could not but be incomplete. The expropriations therefore seemed to follow from the logic of planning. In reality, the sequence was exactly the reverse: because society was to be revolutionized and, by definition of the dogma, the privately owned "means of production" were to be confiscated and turned over to the state, the individual economic decisions of the entrepreneurs had to be replaced by a total state plan. Nationalization and collectivization were, in the DDR just as in the USSR, the factors that dominated society and economy, and the Plan was the result. This is clearly revealed in the history of Marxism and the Soviet Union. In Germany, this sequence was easily overlooked because a system of detailed economic controls had already been developed in wartime. For Germany, planning had preceded expropriation.

In the DDR the fundamental decision had been taken before 1948, that is, before the currency reform had made a wider public aware of what was happening in divided Germany. As early as 1945 the private banks and insurance companies had been closed down and replaced by government institutions. This fulfilled the first point on the program; the allegedly dominant role of "finance capitalism" in the late phase of the capitalist era was eliminated. The expropriation of the large estates finally disposed of the dreaded power of the Junkers. The nationalization of industry and the takeover of the large industrial plants under Soviet management had broken the influence of the entrepreneurial class as a whole, not only that of the "monopolists and war criminals."

In the course of the land reform the large agricultural estates were initially not turned into collective farms to conform with Soviet Russia; they were cut up and distributed in small parcels of land, which mostly were not viable. There is little doubt that the authorities never meant to deviate from the Soviet pattern but merely found it politically inexpedient to nationalize the large estates immediately. Also, hundreds of thousands of expellees had to be integrated in the economy and no thought could be given to organizing mechanized agricultural units on which few hands would be needed. Thus, up to 1955 more people were occupied in producing less food than before.

But after 1952 the government openly proclaimed its goal of collectivization and had by then prepared the instrument to be used in organizing so-called Production Cooperatives (*Produktionsgenossenschaften*). This instrument was the Machine Lending Stations, MAS, after 1952 called Machine Tractor Stations, MTS. Originally planned as collection and distribution agencies for the material expropriated from the large estates, they had been reorganized as nationalized workshops (*volkseigene Betriebe*); they held a dominant position in the countryside because every farmer depended on the use of their pool of machines. Further collectivization was once more slowed down for a time when after Stalin's death the "quickening of the class war," proclaimed in 1952, was postponed. The prestige of the SED regime, which had suffered a bad reverse in the revolt of June 17, 1953, needed a respite. On that day, only the intervention of the Soviet troops had prevented the population from driving out its masters. Consequently, the pace of land collectivization and of expropriation in other sectors of the economy was for a few years somewhat lessened. However, the process of nationalization never came to a halt; bedeviling of the remaining private enterprises with taxes, insufficient raw material deliveries, and many other chicaneries caused numerous farmers, tradesmen, artisans, and industrialists to divest themselves of their businesses.

After 1956 the tempo of socialization quickened again. In this year a Chinese method was introduced, the so-called state participation. By taking a certain interest in the capital of a business firm the state acquired a partnership and, as by private contract, the right to participate in the firm's management. In this case, too, the private owners were usually placed under heavy political and economic pressure. Thus, the state banks refused to give them credits and, on the other hand, they were promised tax benefits as well as favorable production quotas and advantageous raw material deliveries if they accepted the state as partner. In such a semi-state enterprise the former owners were kept on as managers and received a salary in addition to a share in the profit. However, no attempt was made to hide the expectation that such partnership was only the preparation for full nationalization; the erstwhile "capitalist" was transformed into a "workingman" (*Werktätiger*) whose property rights were protected just as long as he and his experience were in demand.

In the spring of 1960 the efforts to complete the nationalization of all enterprises reached their climax up to the present when, with the application of unrestricted terror, the farmers who had still preserved a degree of independence were forced to enter the Production Cooperatives. In 1959 about one-half of all arable land was still managed by farmer-owners; now within only a few months this ratio declined to 7.6 per cent (see Table 36).

There are three types of Production Cooperatives differing according to whether the arable land only, all the farm land, or the land and also the live stock are collectivized. These three types were to be regarded as preparatory

TABLE 36

Agricultural Acreage by Type of Ownership; Soviet Zone, 1950–64
(in per cent)

	SOCIALIZED FARMS				OTHER FARMS *
Year	*Total*	*State farms*	*Other socialized units*	*Agricultural production cooperatives*	
1950	5.7	2.7	3.0	—	94.3
1955	27.3	4.4	4.4	18.6	72.7
1956	30.4	4.4	3.4	22.6	69.6
1957	32.7	4.6	4.0	24.2	67.3
1958	37.8	5.8	2.6	29.4	62.2
1959	48.2	6.0	1.9	40.2	51.8
1960	92.4	6.3	1.8	84.2	7.6
1961	92.7	6.3	1.7	84.7	7.3
1962	93.3	6.4	1.5	85.4	6.7
1963	93.6	6.4	—	85.4	6.4
1964	93.7	6.4	—	85.6	6.3

* Private farms and, after 1956, also church-owned farms.

SOURCE: *Statistisches Jahrbuch der Deutschen Demokratischen Republik* (1965), p. 259.

stages toward full collectivization, Soviet style. Already at the end of 1962 type III, with full collectivization of farm property, predominated. But at that time, in contrast to the Soviet pattern, in the DDR the returns of harvests were distributed in some measure according to how much property a member had contributed.

In 1963 only 8 per cent of production in the DDR came from private producers, mainly from artisans and retailers who until then had escaped collectivization (see Table 37). In industry nationalization had been practically completed in the 1950's; only 2 per cent of production originated with private firms, generally small producers of consumer goods. In 1959 only six private firms had more than 500 employees, none had more than 1,000. Commerce remained a special problem child to the authorities. The independent merchant can hardly be replaced in his functions of finding the proper channels for the distribution of goods and services and of acting as the middleman between producer and consumer. The plan set forth the major guidelines for production and distribution, but to have the goods available at the right time in the right place, to grade their quality and to stock them properly often requires risky decisions which private enterprise is better prepared to take. The handling of the wholesale trade and of the likewise thoroughly nationalized retail trade by state functionaries proved less than a success. To be sure, commerce was held responsible for many troubles that actually originated with all sorts of planning errors. When too little had been produced the government frequently blamed the trade agencies for not having distributed the goods correctly. Some of the numerous changes in the organization of commerce were made for reasons of propaganda.

To sum up, the goal of decisively altering property relationships was attained. According to Party doctrine, socialist property does away with the former relationships between masters and subjects. Because by definition only the "capitalists" had been the masters and in the DDR no private capitalists were to be found, there was no more domination and no more exploitation. What did persist, however, was that orders were issued and obeyed, and indeed the relationships of subordination to command under sanction of force were immeasurably widened in scope. The "capitalist" was replaced by the all-powerful state which undertook to achieve the ultimate well-being of the masses—some day.

TABLE 37

Gross National Product by Type of Ownership and Economic Sector; Soviet Zone, 1950, 1958, 1963
(in per cent)

	1950			*1958*	
	Nationalized	*Cooperative*	*Private*	*Nationalized*	*Cooperative*
Industry	75.5	2.0	22.4	84.9	3.6
Construction	31.6	—	68.4	60.1	4.0
Artisans, excluding construction	—	—	100.0	—	5.6
Agriculture and forestry	12.1	—	87.9	14.4	25.3
Transport, post, telecommunications	86.0	—	14.0	91.8	—
Commerce	21.5	36.5	41.9	35.1	44.6
Other sectors	92.5	—	7.5	97.1	—
TOTAL	53.6	5.8	40.6	67.6	9.2

SOURCE: *Statistisches Jahrbuch der Deutschen Demokratischen Republik* (1964), p. 27.

3. *The Planning System*

THE DDR WISHED to emulate the Soviet model and technique of centralized planning. Numerous Soviet experts in the various government agencies collaborated in adapting the system to the new locale, and they saw to it that in the form and content of planning the DDR was integrated with the rest of the Soviet Bloc. The parallel with the planning methods of the Soviet Union was so close that every change in the planning system of the USSR was immediately duplicated in the DDR.

At the latest by 1950, when the State Planning Commission was organized, the basic features of the planning system were firmly established. Until then the economic controls taken over from National Socialism were only adjusted piecemeal in order to serve the most urgent requirements, above all that of expediting reparations transfers to Soviet Russia. As soon as the new central agency for economic management began to function it carried out a number of short-term planning experiments. The first Five Year Plan started in 1951.

1958		*1963*			
Semi–state owned	*Private*	*Nationalized*	*Cooperative*	*Semi–state owned*	*Private*
3.4	8.1	85.3	3.4	8.8	2.4
3.5	32.3	63.9	15.3	9.1	9.1
—	94.4	—	29.8	—	70.2
—	60.3	16.7	72.6	—	10.7
—	8.2	94.7	—	2.3	3.0
2.1	18.2	38.6	42.6	7.7	11.1
—	2.8	97.0	—	1.0	1.9
2.5	20.7	70.4	14.6	7.1	8.0

In theory, planning was comprehensive. It reached to all parts of the economy and beyond this included other essential spheres of society. Naturally, it did not prove practicable for one central agency to decree every detail, and therefore a hierarchy of authorities was made responsible for the many large and small decisions. The bureaucratic planning system underwent continuous changes, and the privileges and duties of the various ministries, Länder, and district offices were frequently revised. One principle remained unchanged, that the SED leadership together with the Soviet authorities laid down the basic directives. The domination of the state by the Party was no longer concealed; it was on the contrary legally formalized. Planning objectives were usually made public at Party gatherings and from there were handed down to the government and the competent planning agencies. In 1960 a ministry was set up to ensure that the decisions of the Party and of the planning authorities were in accord. Since the incumbents of the superior administrative offices were at the same time high Party functionaries who were beholden for their state offices only to the Party the coordination was safely secured.

After the Politbureau and the Central Committee of the SED had issued the binding directives, the State Planning Commission as a rule worked out the fundamentals of the multi-year plan, the so-called Perspective Plan, and also the annual economic plans. The ministries, state factory managers, and district economic offices took over the further shaping and specification of details for their areas and then turned over the plan directives to the individual production plants. These on their part made suggestions as to the execution of the directives; they stated what they could produce and what materials they would need. Thereafter the plan proposals went in reverse, from below to the top, to be shaped into a consistent pattern by the State Planning Commission. During this ascent, at each level there were usually wide discrepancies from the original directives which had to be ironed out in negotiations; or quite frequently they were decided by fiat in higher or the highest Party echelons.

Understandably, the planning proposals in general differed from the directives. Every agency, whether a ministry or an association of nationalized factories or a district economic council, was afraid later not to be able to fulfill the plan, and each of them was therefore interested in keeping its plan figures (*Plansoll*) at as low a level as possible. In consequence, the proposals coming from the lower ranks contained a good deal of "air," which means that they did not show what the economy could actually produce. Sophisticated methods of control had to be devised, much experience and, in the last resort, strict enforcement measures had to be applied to detect and correct fictitious figures. For their part, the central planning agencies tended to put their figures unrealistically high for reasons of political propaganda. Frequently in the midst of the production process and of the planning period it became necessary, in spite of strict controls of the workshops, to adjust aims to realities. After such readjustments, the reports of quota fulfillment by factories, districts, and central ministries referred to the new specifications. Thus it happened that, precisely because of the frequent plan revisions, many details of the yearly economic plans and of the first Five Year Plan were reported as fulfilled. A second Five Year Plan, which was to begin in 1955, could only be formulated two years later, and after one further year it had to be abandoned because in 1958 the Soviet Union changed from the Five to a Seven Year Plan and the DDR wished to draw even. But this Seven Year Plan also failed despite frequent readjustments.

The plans were primarily expressed in quantities for production and distribution, with the stress on material balances. Because the DDR is not a barter but a money economy, the flows of money also needed planning so that the spheres of commodities and of money could be attuned to one another.

The ordinary state budget was only one item in the financial master plan of the economy as a whole. The state budget not only listed the normal government receipts and expenditures but on principle also all receipts and expenditures of the nationalized enterprises. According to the agreed plans, the individual state plants had to be furnished at the right moment with the funds for materials, wages, and capital equipment, and they had to make their payments according to the plans. Understandably again, every plant was interested in holding back reserves for emergencies; however, it was one of the principles of planning to keep money as scarce as possible and to prescribe its use in detail so that the material plan could be kept under control by the financial plan.

In order to hold the money and commodity flows in close accord, wages and prices were fixed by law. Consumption goods which were in strong demand but were not planned for mass production were highly priced; however, the factories and agencies that produced and sold them were charged high turnover taxes. The prices of other goods were subsidized. Thus, there was also some central direction of the economy by the price system. The fundamental difference between a market economy and an economy planned by the state is that in the first a multitude of individuals, in expressing their needs and desires as consumers on the market, has a direct influence on production and distribution; in the centrally planned state economy, production and distribution are directed according to the people's needs and desires as formulated by the state authorities.

In 1958, a reform of the planning system was begun which reached a climax in the 1963 decision on "The New Economic System of Planning and Direction of the National Economy." Experiences over the preceding years had taught that a central plan worked out in too great detail does not function properly and that in the long run the administrative departments as well as the factories have a better chance to be efficient if they are allowed some personal responsibility and material incentives. Accordingly, decision making was decentralized in some measure and the top planning and directing agencies were freed from the responsibility for much small detail. The state enterprises were empowered to arrange deliveries among themselves in elaborating and making specific the over-all plans. In the DDR it even became possible for state enterprises to sue one another like private business firms whenever one partner was remiss in his delivery obligations or did not make payments at the appointed time. The reform of 1963 went even further. Administrative direction of production was confined within limits; a large part of the detailed planning expressed in physical quantities was discontinued and "economic levers" were inserted in the process which were supposed to furnish some autonomous self-direction to the economy in pursuing the centrally determined goals. It is easy to see that some of these economic levers—which were expected to stimulate the factories themselves to look for the best means to achieve their goals—have a strong similarity with the forces of a market economy. It now became possible to achieve profits in the factories, and correct accounting of profits and costs was expressly required. The managers were allowed to participate in the profits they helped to achieve, and the leaders of the Association of People-owned Works (*Vereinigung Volkseigener Betriebe*), who before had only an intermediary function between the ministries and the factories, were given powers of free decision, which made them look like "socialist captains of industry." To assure that profits really reflected productive efficiency, it became necessary for the price system to function more or less reliably. It is therefore only logical that since 1964 a reform of the price system has been under way which in part will drastically alter price ratios among various goods. Thus in 1964 prices of basic materials and of electric power were raised by 75 per cent. However, these rising production costs are not allowed to be reflected in the prices for the end products. There is also reluctance for the present to tackle agricultural prices, the raising of which would without doubt produce a marked rise in living costs.

For a long time efforts have been devoted to avoiding some of the drawbacks of centralized and bureaucratic economic management by organizing a movement of "socialist competition." In the DDR as in the USSR competitions are constantly held between factories, workers' brigades, and individual workmen. As Russia had its Stakhanov, so the Zone had its Adolf Henneke, a miner who in 1948, after careful preparation of his coal-drift, exceeded his quota by 287 per cent. He became the symbol for the "Activist Movement," an allegedly voluntary effort of workmen in competition with each other to improve productivity, lower production costs, and introduce better working methods. Planning benefited somewhat from such movements, not only in directly increasing production and thus helping to fulfill the plans, but above all in enabling the authorities to keep better informed of the actual or alleged working capability of the labor rank and file than they could have been by using time-consuming investigations. Thus, the authorities were able to point to pioneering performances in laying down production plans and working norms.

4. *Integration Into the Soviet Bloc*

WHEN THE MARSHALL PLAN began to function in 1948, the American offer of aid also extended to some of the Eastern European countries. As noted above, Poland, Czechoslovakia, and Yugoslavia seemed inclined to accept the offer, but under Soviet pressure they had to refuse collaboration with the OEEC. To compensate them for this forced self-denial and as a propagandistic countermove, Soviet Russia organized a Council of Mutual Economic Cooperation, COMECON, which in 1950 admitted the DDR to its membership. At that time the USSR had not yet recovered sufficiently to give the COMECON countries much aid; neither were the individual members able to develop independent economic action as equal partners within the framework of Soviet domination. Thus until 1953 the COMECON had but a shadowy existence and began to show more vitality only after Stalin's death.

More than the foreign trade of any other region, that of the DDR was completely dominated by the USSR, which not only dictated the amounts of reparations but also to a large extent the exports to be directed toward the other Eastern Bloc countries. Before the war, central Germany, now the Soviet zone, had been closely integrated with eastern Germany, Berlin, and the West. More than half its products had been sold and about the same proportion of its imports had been bought from across the present borders in other parts of Germany and abroad. The separation from the traditional trading partners was felt more keenly in the DDR than in West Germany. Moreover, having previously been an export region for agricultural products, the DDR was now forced to import considerable amounts of foodstuffs. These had to be found in the East and to be paid for by exports to the East. This was a bitter departure from old relationships in international trade. After 1950, roughly 80 per cent of the DDR's foreign trade (exclusive of interzonal trade) was transacted with Soviet Bloc countries, approximately 50 per cent with the USSR alone.

Up to 1954, the individual COMECON countries had sought separate economic autarky. They based their plans on broad industrial development and stressed investment in the production of basic materials and capital goods industries. Their foreign trade was geared to procuring the goods needed to implement these plans. The Moscow Conference of the COMECON in 1954 inaugurated a change in these practices. The economic value of international division of labor had been rediscovered and the goal now was to organize a "socialist system of world economy." Since all the countries concerned had planned economies and their foreign trade was handled by state monopolies, the idea of division of labor logically presupposed that the national plans be coordinated and, in the long run, that a unified plan be established.

In subsequent COMECON conferences the main topic of discussion was how to achieve this aim. In 1956, concrete procedures were formulated, to be implemented over many future years. None of the countries were ready to give up industries which they had by then developed; every decision was heavily contested: who, from now on, was to produce trucks, automobiles, textiles, shoes, machine tools, etc.? Though a division of labor might have evident economic virtues, the various countries were critical in their attitudes and apprehensive lest their relative strength be made to suffer. Because 1956 was the time when serious rifts appeared within the Soviet Bloc, and Poland especially seemed to be striking out on its own path, the leading functionaries showed but moderate enthusiasm for economic integration. Only after the domestic political consequences of the Hungarian revolt and the new Polish policies had been brought under control was the program of integration resumed. In 1962, it was resolved that production plants should be located in close proximity to their raw material bases. For example, the DDR was to expand its heavy chemical industries based on its lignite deposits and to cut down its production of iron and steel. Also, it was ordered to stop producing airplanes and automobiles and instead to specialize in certain types of machinery, the electrical industries, precision mechanics, optics and plastics.

In some countries, primarily Rumania, the heavy stress laid in 1962 on the division of labor within the Soviet Bloc seems to have been replaced by a renewed strong desire to develop national industries on a broad and independent basis. Also the growing conflict between Soviet Russia and Communist China reacted unfavorably on the COMECON system.

For trade relations among the Soviet Bloc countries the problem of pricing the goods to be exchanged posed a special difficulty. Since in each of the countries prices were necessarily determined by domestic considerations and plan requirements, they were not immediately applicable to foreign trade. If a commodity was cheaper in a neighboring country than at home this was not the reason for deciding to purchase that commodity abroad. The decision rested on whether the commodity was essential for plan fulfillment and whether goods were available which the partner country was willing to accept. Because there was no unified price system on which an exchange of goods could be figured, as an expedient the prices prevalent in the Western world markets were frequently used. In order to get rid of bilateral trade negotiations, plans were prepared looking toward the establishment of a price system and a multilateral clearing system within the Soviet Bloc. This turned out to be very difficult to achieve, and the matter is still pending.

5. *"Social Achievements"*

THE TERM "SOCIAL achievements" in the DDR denotes a much wider field of endeavors than in Western social policy. All the radical changes in the social and economic system described above fall under this heading. The top-priority efforts were to ensure the workers' and peasants' power in the state, to establish firmly the dominance of the SED, and to socialize and centrally plan the economy. Because, according to Soviet doctrine, these changes were putting an end to the exploitation of the workers, the continued fight for social legislation and for protection of the workers' legal status was less of a duty in the DDR than in the Western democracies. In countries with market economies, searching for a just balance between management and workers and, in numerous relationships, adjusting the distribution of income in favor of the needy were historical social aims. In the DDR, and for that matter in all countries which deny that they harbor any fundamental conflict between the interests of the workers and the allmighty State, the declared object of social policy is to raise production and productivity. For many years past all laws and ordinances in the field of social and workers' legislation were based on this supposition. Thus, Article 1 of the Labor Code of 1961 declares:

> The Work Code serves to establish the economic charter of Socialism. It promotes increasing productivity of labor on the basis of advanced science and technology and it contributes as fully as possible to supplying the steadily growing needs of all members of society and to their general development. The Work Code serves to implement the economic plans according to the principle of unity of central planning and direction and of the conscious creative efforts of every working man in production and in his participation in the leadership of the State and the Economy.

The association of unions in the DDR was no longer the representative of the interests of the workers since the state pretended that this was its function. Nor was it any longer organized along democratic principles since in the Association of Free German Unions (*Freier deutscher Gewerkschaftsbund,* FDGB) the same principle prevailed as in the government and the

SED, that is, the principle of "democratic centralism," which established the dominance of power from the top—in this case, from the SED high command. At the same time, the FDGB was itself a participant in sovereign state power, being the manager of the social insurance system, the income and expenditure of which was part of the state budget. In the workshops the unions were in charge of supervising execution of the Plan and compliance with workers' protective legislation and of stimulating overfulfillment of norms.

Why did not the system dispense with an association of unions altogether? What may at first seem to be an unnecessary complication within the state power structure turns out to be a practical instrument for the relaxation of social tensions. The FDGB seemed to decentralize power to some extent without weakening it at the center. Within the FDGB, directed from above, the individual worker was left to find his own adjustment to the commands of the state and the Plan; the entire labor force was thus included in the framework of the centralized organization without the SED bureaucracy being expanded and diluted beyond what it could bear. Conflicts between the workers' interests and the state were to be largely ironed out within the FDGB, which combined employer and employee functions.

In 1948 the FDGB itself passed a resolution to abolish the shop councils which were still democratically elected and were attempting to exercise codetermination functions not in harmony with the plans. They were replaced by union officials in the shops who, in contrast to the members of the shop councils, were subject to the hierarchy of the FDGB. The shop union boards entered into so-called collective shop contracts, which were only secondarily concerned with improving working conditions and providing cultural facilities. Their primary function was to insure compliance with the plans. However, efforts toward achieving some measure of codetermination of the workers in the shops never ceased entirely. Even some party members, impressed by the Yugoslav experiments and the events of 1956 in Hungary and Poland, repeatedly petitioned for increased rights for the workers. The Party finally made the concession that workers' committees be formed in the state enterprises, although only in 18 selected factories, where soon they were again to disappear. In 1959, the workers received some rights of codetermination in "permanent production councils," conferences of workers' representatives who were to discuss the best methods of plan fulfillment. In doing so they only served to insure intensified work efforts. After some time spontaneous cells sprang up in various places to represent the workers' wishes, in the form of "socialist brigades," after 1958 following an example set in Soviet Russia among those employed in the same branches of production. When they tried to gain influence over the determination of work norms, on works plans, and on disciplinary practices, a most vigorous countermove from the top of the Party was exerted to stifle these first signs of Yugoslav-style workers' independence.

Also in the practice of wage determination there was at first some confusion, as it seemed necessary to refrain from abruptly breaking with traditional institutions. On principle, defining wages was a function of the state, since it was an integral element of central planning. And yet, after 1958 this task was partly transferred to the unions. A framework of collective agreements was inaugurated within the state factories, which however could only modify in a few details the directives laid down by the government and the central planning authorities.

At the Fifth Party Congress of the SED in July, 1958, the principles governing the entire economy in the Soviet Bloc countries were once more formally confirmed. It was declared that a rise in wages would always have to be conditional on a previous rise in productivity. The means for "accumulation" were always to grow faster than consumption. In the Soviet Bloc wages were not regarded, as in the West, as a source of potential savings. It seemed self-evident that they would be consumed. Since individual property existed only within narrow limits, society as a whole was to provide the saving. In fact, average wages rose only by 25 per cent in the DDR between 1955 and 1960 while productivity rose by more than 50 per cent. Thus, the share of wages in the Gross National Product declined. There is no way of ascertaining, theoretically or empirically, whether or not this constitutes exploitation of the wage earners. In West Germany the opinion had become prevalent that it was fair to raise the share of wages in the Gross National Product or at least to keep it constant. In an economy of the kind that existed in the Soviet zone no such bench mark was applicable since it was asserted that all social savings were used in the interest of all, and hence a decreasing wage quota was no cause for uneasiness.

Indeed, neither the general wage quota nor the average wage rates tell the whole story about what people in the DDR are able to consume. Here, as in the entire Soviet Bloc, not only production but also consumption was socialized, much more so than in the Federal Republic. Socialization begins with the kindergarten, continues into the youth organizations and schools, and ends with the leisure time of the adults. Following the Nationalist Socialist pattern set by the Deutsche Arbeitsfront the workers now spent their organized vacations with the institutions of the FDGB in vacation homes or, if they belonged to the activist groups, on sea voyages with the union fleet.

In earlier stages of the Socialist movement the wide discrepancies of incomes had been a principal target of the criticism leveled against capitalism. A popular slogan of the workers singled out another evil: "Piecework wages are murder" (*Akkord ist Mord*). Neither of these basic evils was ever eradicated in the DDR because the authorities realized that plans would not be fulfilled unless the workers were given individual incentives. The spread in labor incomes was on the contrary markedly increased, as had happened in the Soviet Union after 1931. Also in accordance with the Soviet pattern, piecework rates became the dominant feature in the wage system. When in May, 1953, the Council of Ministers arbitrarily raised all work norms, in effect imposing a general wage cut, this incensed the workers to such a degree that the bloody revolt of June 17, 1953, ensued.

The system of social security was radically altered. Following the Soviet pattern, the previous multiplicity of insurance schemes was replaced by one single fund. The different treatment of blue- and white-collar workers was abolished. In 1951 the unified social security system came under the management of the FDGB, which after 1956 was also placed in control of the insurance of the self-employed. Why was the insurance system preserved, and why were the unions put in charge? In itself, the social and economic system did not require a separate social insurance organization. The unified social insurance scheme had no kinship with the original idea of spreading the cost of aid for the needy over the whole working community. Since in principle all citizens are entitled to get help in case of sickness, child bearing, death in the family, disability to work, or old age the benefits could just as well have originated in the state budget. The contributions received by the fiscal offices, graduated according to income brackets, could have been replaced by a somewhat higher income tax or, alternatively, wages could have been lowered. Since the insurance fund could not impose taxes independently and the unions had no free elections of their representatives, the alleged self-government of the insurance system had no substance. However, the top authorities enjoyed the political advantage that the unions, not their own agents, were obliged to intervene in case of abuses and to take preventive measures. Thus it was up to those who received the benefits to settle any conflicts among themselves.

The official statistics of the DDR never openly reported unemployment; however, it became known in the West that up to 1954 unemployment must have been rather widespread. Afterwards, full employment like that in the Federal Republic was reported. In a system of central planning it would have been a sign of very poor performance had the existence of unemployment been admitted. It could never pose a serious problem to allocate some work to every person. The unemployment benefits provided by the still existing insurance schemes were low in order to discourage shirkers. The old age pensions too were kept down in order to motivate people to work beyond the pension age. The principle of the "duty to work"—just beyond the legal work load—was proclaimed. "Voluntary" overtime work and unpaid leisure time work was organized for many different purposes—for harvesting, for the construction of roads and community facilities, but also to overcome bottlenecks in the workers' own factories. On principle, the workers were still free to choose their jobs and professions; they could be forced to accept other work only temporarily. However, the state did not forego its right to direct manpower to the places where the Plan required it, for instance by way of the wage differentials described above, through political pressure, or by opening and shutting educational channels.

Schools and institutions of higher education were used as potent instruments to revolutionize society. In the West, too, educational facilities had increasingly become the means by which members of the younger generation were sent on their way up the social ladder, since inherited property and membership in a social class were losing their power to determine a person's life. However, this social change was a comparatively slow process because the access to schools and universities was not yet free to all gifted individuals. The bourgeois classes still enjoyed better opportunities to give their children a good education than the working classes. This was different in the DDR where the recently leading strata of society had been expropriated and their children were at a disadvantage compared to the children of workers.

From the first the regime was under compulsion to compensate for the great loss of knowledge and experience which it had inflicted on itself by excluding the upper strata of society from the society's efforts. Schools and institutes of higher education were opened wide, especially to workers' and farmers' children, who were first asked to demonstrate their political reliability and second what gifts they had to offer. Social opportunities were reserved to those who could be expected to contribute to stabilizing the new system. Old educational privileges were replaced by new ones.

Access to a leading stratum of society, even for the lowest group, should not be misunderstood as a characteristic of a freedom-loving democracy. Nor is it a feature of a classless society. In the DDR formally all the means of production were held by the state, and the state was in theory held by the workers and farmers. In reality the decisive power over the means of production was concentrated in a small elite group of the SED party which was not controlled by a majority of the people but had the entire leadership of the state in its hands. The members of this group used their power according to the dictates of a doctrine which promised mankind future bliss, and they felt entitled to sacrifice to this promise man's happiness today. In consciously using the living person to attain an unprovable purpose the leading functionaries divorced themselves from every humanitarian impulse which had originally given rise to Socialism.

APPENDIX A

GERMANY IN 1940

Preface to the First Edition of 1940, by Gustav Stolper

HISTORY NEVER ENDS. But by chance the following tale has met with an incisive conclusion. The caesura is the outbreak of what future historians may call the second world war. The economic history of modern Germany which this book narrates covers the period from the founding of the Reich to the present day. It is an economic, not a political history that is told here. The account of Germany's economic history probably reveals, however, a much closer interrelation between politics and economics than that of any other great European nation.

This book has not been written to bear out any preconceived theory, or to prove a thesis. Nevertheless, it will disclose in every chapter, up to the very end, an amazing continuity of the underlying trend: the ascendancy of the state over the economic life of the nation. Without the preparatory work of their predecessors Hitler and National Socialism would not have been possible. The totalitarian regime of the Nazis is the climax of expansionist tendencies and developments of governmental power over the destinies of the German people.

The historian must not be a prophet. I therefore refrain from an attempt to appraise the future. It would be tempting indeed to outline how far recent developments in Germany have strengthened or weakened her power of resistance in the present war. The new military technique of Germany, so surprising to the outside world, is a direct offspring of the restrictions imposed on Germany after the last war. As Germany was denied general conscription by the Versailles treaty, she was induced to devise methods by which the tiny army of one hundred thousand professional soldiers might achieve its maximum effectiveness. Emphasis was therefore laid not on maneuvering masses, but on using small units made up of men technically skilled to the limit and trained in independent action. These are the men required for *Blitzkrieg* tactics, groups of fifty to five hundred men who by their skill and daring may decide campaigns.

The German economy was no less prepared for war than was the military machine. German industry, too, had been trained for war for many years, under heavy outside restrictions before Hitler, but free of restrictions ever since the Nazis came into power. This preparation undoubtedly is a most important source of strength. All the problems of transition and adjustment from peacetime to wartime methods of production and distribution, technical and otherwise, that cause so much friction and delay to democratic nations with a free economy, do not exist for Germany. That country has been living on a war footing for several years. It was mobilized economically as well as militarily. The two so-called Four Year Plans decreed by Hitler were nothing but war plans thought out and carried out to the minutest detail. Economic considerations were thoroughly subordinated to military requirements. It will take considerable time for the Allies to catch up with this advantage. Will they have the time?

Living on a war footing had heavily taxed the nerves as well as the material resources of the German nation even before the supreme test of actual warfare started. Germany entered the war with a tired and unenthusiastic population and an industry operating at capacity, with little possibility of further expansion. This will be felt ever more intensely the longer the war lasts. All the drive of the elite shock troops and all the perfection of the German war machine cannot compensate for that weakness unless the Blitzkrieg technique succeeds. On this technique Germany has staked her very existence. On the success or the failure of this technique the fate of our world depends. If this technique succeeds, not only are the British and French empires doomed; the face of the globe will be altered beyond recognition. The security of the Western Hemisphere will be directly threatened, its liberties and institutions exposed to attacks from without and disruption from within. Even with the utmost straining of our imagination we shall hardly be able to cope with the new realities.

The time factor will determine the effectiveness of the blockade, obviously the strongest and most dangerous weapon the Allies wield against Germany.

Since the war broke out in September, 1939, both sides have changed their position somewhat with respect to the time factor. It was a widespread belief in the Allied countries, particularly in Britain, that the Allies perhaps did not need to do anything but steadily tighten the blockade in order to force Germany to her knees. After a few months public opinion began slowly to see that this thesis was neither so simple nor so sure. People began to realize that under conditions of inactive warfare consumption could be so radically curtailed that Germany, given time to organize the resources of countries still accessible to her, might be able to hold out indefinitely. On the other hand, Germany herself seemed to be more and more inclined to believe that the time factor worked in her favor. This was true in the period when she seemed to entertain unbounded hopes with respect to Russia. If Russia were sincerely willing to cooperate economically with Germany, obviously time was needed for the Hitler-Stalin alliance to work itself out, because it would take years to develop Russian resources on a scale large enough for German purposes. It seems to me that it was disbelief in Russian help that drove Hitler to invade Scandinavia, Holland, Belgium, and France. He must have understood by the spring of this year that he could not count on Russia's help on a large scale, and this realization was tantamount to the recognition that Germany could not stand a long war. Hitler's attack on the West may or may not demonstrate military superiority; it certainly betrays economic weakness.

In appraising the blockade problem it has been customary to sum up the production of foodstuffs and basic raw materials in Germany herself and the countries within her reach and to compare the results with her presumable needs. But whatever this balance may be, it leaves out the fundamental changes to which all countries concerned are subjected by the war itself. At the moment of this writing the Balkan countries are not yet engulfed by the war. It seems to me highly doubtful whether that will still be true when this book appears. Caught up in the war or not, all these countries are very poor. They are living virtually without any reserves, and the fact that their manpower has been mobilized since September, 1939, is bound to have devastating effects on their production. These countries never had any substantial surpluses. The technical methods of their production were always so backward that the result of their labor was not in proportion to their natural resources. Here, too, years of inactive warfare might have enabled Germany to bring about great changes from which she could have benefited. As things actually developed, this chance has been forfeited. The year 1940 may see the greatest famine in modern European history.

Since the war broke out in all its ferocity over western Europe, the blockade problem has assumed much greater resemblance than before to what it had been between 1914 and 1918. Up to the invasion of Scandinavia, Germany boasted that she could still trade with twenty-three countries, which up to September, 1939, supplied 44 per cent of German imports and took 56 per cent of German exports. Even before the recent events this claim could be taken only with a big grain of salt. It is certainly no longer true since the invasion of Scandinavia and the Low Countries. Now the ring of the blockade is virtually closed unless Germany can break it by military means or Russian all-out support should be forthcoming against all appearances and expectations.

How strong or weak economically is Germany within the domain her forces have occupied? First of all, contrary to widespread assumptions, the invasion of Scandinavia, Holland, Belgium, and France has weakened rather than strengthened Germany's economic position. We are accustomed to look at Denmark as a producer of large food surpluses. But Denmark is more a manufacturer than a producer of foodstuffs; that is, the export surpluses essential to the livelihood of that unhappy country were produced from imported products. From its own soil Denmark could not feed more than a fraction of its livestock. Cut off from former sources of fodder, the dairy, meat, and fat production of Denmark must fall off rapidly. Norway has always been dependent on imports of foodstuffs. It paid for them, by and large, with the income from its fisheries and its merchant marine, the fourth largest in the world. Both sources of income are no longer available to the Norwegians. Their fishing grounds are patrolled by the Allied fleets; their ships (apart from the small number caught by the Germans in Norwegian ports) are now at the disposal of the Allies. There is very little that Germany can take out of Norway. Germany will, on the other hand, now have to take care of Norway's minimum needs.

Sweden—for the moment still nonbelligerent—is in a different position. It is not occupied by German troops, and yet, because of its geographical location, it is within the German blockade zone. Sweden no longer has access to the Western world to which it sold the greater part of its products and from which it bought the greater part of its raw materials. Sweden has two precious assets, wood and iron ore. Both are much wanted by Germany. In fact, Swedish ore is the vital raw material which Germany cannot acquire from any other source unless eastern France is once more conquered. This dependence on Swedish ore is probably the most important difference between the basic conditions of the second world war blockade and those of the first. From 1914 to 1918 there was no ore problem for Germany. In possession of Lorraine, Belgium, and northern France, Germany actually had an abundance of ore. After the loss of Lorraine in 1918, Germany's steel production was virtually dependent on Swedish ore. Had the Allies not failed in their attempt to drive the Germans out of Norway, the supply of Swedish ore to Germany could have been stopped. In the absence of such a successful move by the Allies the Germans have still to face a serious transport problem through the Baltic Sea, since its northern ports are normally icebound for more than six months a year.

Less simple and more pressing appears the oil problem. There is no way of gauging with any degree of certainty German oil consumption and oil supply. Within wide ranges we depend on more or less well-reasoned guesses. The fact stands, however, that Germany's production of natural and synthetic oil (including the meager contribution of Poland) together with maximum imports of Rumanian oil must fall far short of the requirements of active warfare. German technicians might be able to enlarge Rumanian production greatly by better methods. But this again requires not only complete domination of the country but, even more essential, time—time in terms of years, not months, and certainly a longer period than Germany can be supplied with oil at the present rate of consumption.

All other shortages and weaknesses in the German war situation seem, to me, manageable for a number of years. Germany's food supply is not ample, but it is sufficient to keep her population above the starvation level, and without doubt it is far better than it was between 1916 and 1918. There is a definite shortage of fats, which in the long run will have devastating effects on the health of the German people, particularly the younger generation. But this is not an issue of immediate concern. If Germany's food supply were her only difficulty, Hitler would not be subject to the desperate pressure under which he apparently acts. There must be more compelling weaknesses in the whole economic setup on which he depends. It is beyond the scope of this book to go into that matter.

This book tells economic history and therefore refrains from taking sides in issues which appeal to emotions of our age. But it is written from a very definite viewpoint, which this writer wishes to be understood. There is no such thing as absolutely objective history. But there are some definite moral and intellectual standards by which we measure historical achievements. They are the standards of the fundamental philosophy of our Western civilization, which must not be abandoned, which indeed cannot be abandoned without jeopardizing the very notion of truth and thereby this civilization itself.

* * *

For the preparation of this book I am greatly indebted to Dr. Alfred Braunthal, without whose help it might never have come into being. I wish gratefully to acknowledge his contribution. . . .

G. S.

New York, May 12, 1940

APPENDIX B. *Foreign Exchange Rates for the Mark (German currency needed to buy one United States dollar, 1870–1966)*

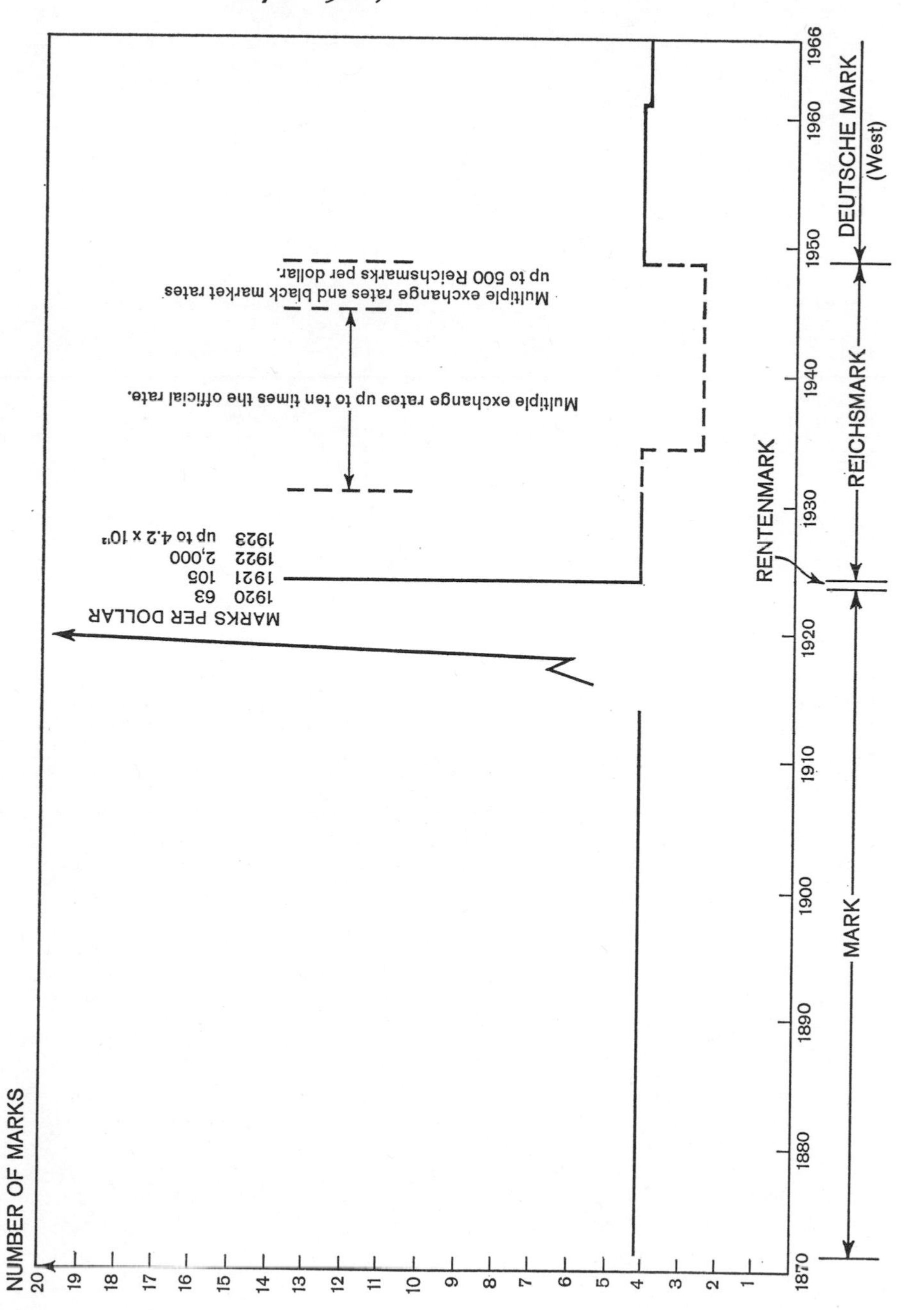

SOURCES: *Statistisches Jahrbuch für das Deutsche Reich; Statistisches Jahrbuch für die Bundesrepublik Deutschland;* for the years 1916–23, Otto Veit, *Grundrisse der Währungspolitik* (Frankfurt/Main: Fritz Knapp Verlag, 1961).

BIBLIOGRAPHY

Source Materials and Literature

FOR THE present expanded edition of *The German Economy,* the principle established in the first edition of 1940 remains unchanged: not to interrupt the text with footnotes on sources and the literature. Wherever possible, facts and figures were taken from official statistics, primarily from publications of the Statistisches Reichsamt, the Statistisches Bundesamt, the official Central Administration for Statistics in the DDR (*Staatliche Zentralverwaltung für Statistik*), the Reichsbank, the Bank deutscher Länder, the Bundesbank. The publications of all these institutions are the main sources for modern German economic history. There are supplementary materials in numerous official, semiofficial and private publications, such as, for the period before the second world war, the publications of the Institut für Konjunkturforschung in Berlin, and, for more recent times, the publications of the various institutes for economic research.

The following bibliographical notes offer some signposts to the literature, but obviously they cannot presume to be complete. References to economic facts are scattered over a large body of literature of the most varied character. The sources listed here were chosen primarily for being easily accessible to students and for offering a fairly comprehensive picture. There are no detailed references to official and semiofficial publications such as those of the Statistisches Reichsamt, to the current reports issued by the German Federal Government, to the monographs of the Institut für Konjunkturforschung, and similar sources and documents. Neither do we refer to textbooks on economics or to essays in various periodicals and articles in the encyclopedias, such as the *Handwörterbuch der Staatswissenschaften,* the *Handwörterbuch der Sozialwissenschaften,* or the *Staatslexikon der Görres-Gesellschaft.* In many of these reference books the student will find additional bibliographical guidance.

A. *Literature for the Entire Period 1870–1965*

1. GENERAL HISTORY

Brandt, Otto, Arnold Oskar Meyer, and Leo Just, eds., *Handbuch der deutschen Geschichte,* Konstanz, 1955–59, vols. III and IV.

Gebhardt, Bruno, in collaboration with Friedrich Baethgen, *et al., Handbuch der deutschen Geschichte,* 8th ed. (herausgegeben von Herbert Grundmann), Stuttgart, vol. III, *Von der französischen Revolution bis zum ersten Weltkrieg,* 1960; vol. IV, *Die Zeit der Weltkriege,* 1959.

Herzfeld, Hans, *Die moderne Welt,* 3rd ed. ("Geschichte der Neuzeit," herausgegeben von Gerhard Ritter), Braunschweig, part I, *Die Epoche der bürgerlichen Nationalstaaten 1789–1890,* 1961; part II, *Weltmächte und Weltkriege; die Geschichte unserer Epoche 1890–1945,* 1960.

Rassow, Peter, ed., *Deutsche Geschichte im Überblick,* 2nd ed.; Stuttgart, 1961.

2. GENERAL ECONOMIC HISTORY

Ashworth, William, *A Short History of the International Economy Since 1850,* 2nd ed., London, 1962.

Bechtel, Heinrich, *Wirtschaftsgeschichte Deutschlands im 19. und 20. Jahrhundert,* Munich, 1956.

Facius, Friedrich, *Wirtschaft und Staat; die Entwicklung der staatlichen Wirtschaftsverwaltung in Deutschland vom 17. Jahrhundert bis 1945* ("Schriften des Bundesarchivs," No. 6), Boppard/Rhein, 1959.

Kuczynski, Jürgen, *Die Geschichte der Lage der Arbeiter unter dem Kapitalismus* (in progress), East Berlin, 1961–66, vols. III, VI, VII parts A and B, XII, XIV, XV, and XVI.

Lütge, Friedrich, *Deutsche Sozial- und Wirtschaftsgeschichte,* 3rd ed.; Berlin, 1966.

Treue, Wilhelm, *Wirtschaftsgeschichte der Neuzeit; im Zeitalter der industriellen Revolution 1700–1960,* Stuttgart, 1962.

3. GROWTH AND BUSINESS CYCLES

Hoffmann, Walter G., in collaboration with Franz Grumbach and Helmut Hesse, *Das Wachstum der deutschen Wirtschaft seit der Mitte des 19. Jahrhunderts,* Berlin, 1965.

Hoffmann, Walter G., and Heinz J. Müller, *Das deutsche Volkseinkommen 1851–1957,* Tübingen, 1959.

Kroll, Gerhard, *Von der Weltwirtschaftskrise zur Staatskonjunktur,* Berlin, 1958.

Mendershausen, Horst, *Two Postwar Recoveries in Germany,* Amsterdam, 1955.

Schumpeter, Joseph, *Business Cycles,* 2 vols., New York, 1939.

Spiethoff, Arthur, *Die wirtschaftlichen Wechsellagen,* 2 vols., Tübingen, 1955.

4. SPECIALIZED SUBJECTS

Bry, Gerhard, *Wages in Germany, 1871–1945* (National Bureau of Economic Research), Princeton, 1960.

Haushofer, Heinz, *Die deutsche Landwirtschaft im technischen Zeitalter* ("Deutsche Agrargeschichte," herausgegeben von Günther Franz, vol. V), Stuttgart, 1957.

Reisser, Jacob, *The German Great Banks and Their Concentration in Connection with the Economic Development of Germany,* 3rd ed. (National Monetary Commission), Washington, D.C., 1911.

Schulze-Gaevernitz, Gerhart von, *Die deutschen Kreditbanken,* Tübingen, 1922.

Schwerin von Krosigk, Lutz, *Die grosse Zeit des Feuers; der Weg der deutschen Industrie,* 3 vols., Tübingen, 1957–59.

Stucken, Rudolf, *Deutsche Geld- und Kreditpolitik 1914–1963,* 3rd ed., Tübingen, 1964.

Terhalle, Fritz, *Handbuch der Finanzwissenschaft,* 2nd ed., vol. I, *Geschichte der öffentlichen Finanzwirtschaft vom Beginn des 19. Jahrhunderts bis zum Schlusse des zweiten Weltkrieges,* Tübingen, 1952.

Weber, Adolf, *Der Kampf zwischen Kapital und Arbeit,* 6th ed., Tübingen, 1954.

B. *Literature for Certain Defined Periods*

1. BEFORE 1918

Clapham, John H., *The Economic Development of France and Germany, 1815–1914,* 4th ed., New York, 1955.

Gerloff, Wilhelm, *Die Finanz- und Zollpolitik des Deutschen Reiches nebst ihren Beziehungen zu Landes- und Gemeindefinanzen,* Jena, 1913.

Helfferich, Karl, *Deutschlands Volkswohlstand 1888–1913,* 6th ed., Berlin, 1915.

Henderson, W. O., *Studies in German Colonial History,* London, 1962.

Sartorius von Waltershausen, A., *Deutsche Wirtschaftsgeschichte 1815–1914,* 2nd ed., Jena, 1923.

Shotwell, J. T., ed., *The Economic and Social History of the World War,* German Series, 12 vols., 1927–37; Austrian Series, 11 vols., 1923–32.

Sombart, Werner, *Die deutsche Volkswirtschaft im 19. Jahrhundert und im Anfang des 20. Jahrhunderts,* 5th ed., Berlin, 1921.

2. THE WEIMAR REPUBLIC

a. GENERAL HISTORY

Bracher, Karl Dietrich, *Die Auflösung der Weimarer Republik,* 3rd ed., Stuttgart and Düsseldorf, 1960.

Eyck, Erich, *Geschichte der Weimarer Republik,* 2 vols., 3rd ed., Erlenbach and Zürich, 1959, 1962.

Friedensburg, Ferdinand, *Die Weimarer Republik,* 2nd ed., Hannover and Frankfurt, 1957.

b. ECONOMIC HISTORY

Brady, A., *The Rationalization Movement in German Industry: A Study in the Evolution of Economic Planning,* Berkeley, 1953.

Bresciani-Turroni, C., *The Economics of Inflation,* London, 1937.

Clausing, Gustav, *Die wirtschaftlichen Wechsellagen von 1919 bis 1932,* Jena, 1933.

Elster, Karl, *Von der Mark zur Reichsmark. Die Geschichte der deutschen Währung in den Jahren 1914–1924,* Jena, 1928.

Fischer, Wolfram, *Die wirtschaftspolitische Situation der Weimarer Republik,* ("Schriftenreihe der niedersächsischen Landeszentrale für politische Bildung"), 1960.

Grotkopp, Wilhelm, *Die grosse Krise,* Düsseldorf, 1954.

Harms, Bernhard, *Strukturwandlungen der deutschen Volkswirtschaft,* 2 vols., Berlin, 1928.

Helbich, Wolfgang J., *Die Reparationen in der Ära Brüning,* Berlin, 1962.

Keynes, John M., *The Economic Consequences of the Peace,* London, 1919, New York, 1920.

Laursen, Karsten, and Jørgen Pedersen, *The German Inflation, 1918–1923,* Amsterdam, 1964.

Lüke, Rolf, *Von der Stabilisierung zur Krise,* Zürich, 1958.

Netzband, Karl-Bernhard, and Hans Peter Widmaier, *Währungs- und Finanzpolitik der Ära Luther 1923–1925,* Basel and Tübingen, 1964.

Predöhl, Andreas, *Das Ende der Weltwirtschaftskrise; eine Einführung in die Probleme der Weltwirtschaft,* Hamburg, 1962.

Preller, Ludwig, *Sozialpolitik in der Weimarer Republik,* Stuttgart, 1949.

Salin, Edgar, ed., *Das Reparationsproblem* (Publications of the Friedrich-List-Gesellschaft), Berlin, 1929, vol. I, *Die Konferenz von Pyrmont;* vol. II, *Die Konferenz von Berlin.*

3. THE PERIOD OF NATIONAL SOCIALISM

a. GENERAL HISTORY

Bracher, Karl Dietrich, Wolfgang Sauer, and Gerhard Schulz, *Die nationalsozialistische Machtergreifung; Studien zur Errichtung des totalitären Herrschaftssystems in Deutschland 1933–1934,* 2nd ed., Köln and Opladen, 1962.

Buchheim, Hans, *Das Dritte Reich; Grundlagen und politische Entwicklung,* Munich, 1958.

Bullock, Alan, *Hitler: A Study in Tyranny,* rev. ed., New York, 1960.

Mau, Hermann, and Helmut Krausnick, *Deutsche Geschichte der jüngsten Vergangenheit 1933–1945,* 5th ed., Stuttgart, 1961.

b. ECONOMIC HISTORY

Bettelheim, Charles, *L'économie allemande sous le nazisme,* Paris, 1946.

Birkenfeld, Wolfgang, *Der synthetische Treibstoff 1933–1945; ein Beitrag zur nationalsozialistischen Wirtschafts- und Rüstungspolitik,* Göttingen, 1964.

Erbe, René, *Die nationalsozialistische Wirtschaftspolitik 1933–1939 im Lichte der modernen Theorie,* Zürich, 1958.

Esenwein-Rothe, Ingeborg, *Die Wirtschaftsverbände von 1933–1945.* Berlin, 1965.

Federau, Fritz, *Der zweite Weltkrieg; seine Finanzierung in Deutschland,* Tübingen, 1962.

Fischer, Wolfram, *Die Wirtschaftspolitik des Nationalsozialismus* ("Schriftenreihe der niedersächsischen Landeszentrale für politische Bildung"), 1961.

Georg, Enno, *Die wirtschaftlichen Unternehmungen der SS* ("Schriftenreihe der Vierteljahreshefte für Zeitgeschichte," No. 7), Stuttgart, 1963.

Guillebaud, C. W., *The Economic Recovery of Germany from 1933–1938,* London, 1939.

Klein, Burton S., *Germany's Economic Preparations for War,* Cambridge, Mass., 1959.

Milward, Alan, *The German Economy at War,* London, 1965.

Schweitzer, Arthur, *Big Business in the Third Reich,* Bloomington, Ind., 1964.

Treue, Wilhelm, *Deutsche Wirtschaft und Politik 1933–1945,* 4th ed., Stuttgart, 1962.

U.S. Strategic Bombing Survey, *The Effects of Strategic Bombing on the German War Economy,* Overall Economic Effects Division, Washington, D.C., October 31, 1945.

Wagenführ, Rolf, *Die deutsche Industrie im Kriege 1939–1945,* 2nd ed., Berlin, 1963.

Welter, Erich, *Falsch und richtig planen: eine kritische Studie über die Wirtschaftslenkung im zweiten Weltkrieg,* Heidelberg, 1954.

4. THE PERIOD AFTER 1945

a. 1945–48

Balabkins, Nicholas, *Germany Under Direct Controls: Economic Aspects of Industrial Disarmament, 1945–1948,* New Brunswick, N.J., 1964.

Clay, Lucius D., *Decision in Germany,* Garden City, N.Y., 1950.

Die deutsche Wirtschaft zwei Jahre nach dem Zusammenbruch (herausgegeben vom Deutschen Institut für Wirtschaftsforschung), Berlin, 1947.

Möller, Hans, ed., *Zur Vorgeschichte der Deutschen Mark; die Währungsreformpläne 1945–1948, Tübingen,* 1961.

Nettl, Joseph Peter, *The Eastern Zone and Soviet Policy in Germany, 1945–1950,* London and New York, 1951.

Schlange-Schöningen, Hans, *Im Schatten des Hungers,* Hamburg and Frankfurt, 1955.

Stolper, Gustav, *German Realities,* New York, 1948.

Wirtschaftsprobleme der Besatzungszonen (herausgegeben vom Deutschen Institut für Wirtschaftsforschung), Berlin, 1948.

b. THE FEDERAL REPUBLIC OF GERMANY

Achterberg, Erich, *General Marshall machte Epoche,* Berlin, 1964.

Boarman, Patrick, *Germany's Economic Dilemma: Inflation and the Balance of Payments,* New Haven, Conn., 1964.

Ehrenberg, Herbert, *Die Erhard Saga; Analyse einer Wirtschaftspolitik, die keine war,* Stuttgart, 1965.

Erhard, Ludwig, *Germany's Comeback in the World Market,* New York, 1954.

Fünf Jahre Deutsche Mark; der Wiederaufbau der deutschen Wirtschaft seit der Währungsreform (herausgegeben vom Ifo-Institut für Wirtschaftsforschung), Berlin, 1953.

Götz, Hans Herbert, *Weil alle besser leben wollen; Portrait der deutschen Wirtschaftspolitik,* Düsseldorf, 1963.

Gutmann, G., H. J. Hochstrate, and R. Schlüter, *Die Wirtschaftsverfassung der Bundesrepublik Deutschland; Entwicklung und ordnungspolitische Grundlagen,* Stuttgart, 1964.

Lampert, Heinz, *Die Wirtschafts- und Sozialordnung der Bundesrepublik Deutschland,* Munich and Vienna, 1965.

Die finanzielle Liquidation des Krieges ("Schriftenreihe des Bundesministeriums der Finanzen," vol. 3), Bonn, 1962.

Möller, Hans, "Internationale Wirtschaftsorganisationen," in *Wirtschaftswissenschaften,* Wiesbaden, 1960.

Mötteli, Carlo, *Licht und Schatten der sozialen Marktwirtschaft,* Zürich, 1961.

Piettre, André, *L'économie allemande contemporaine 1945–1952,* Paris, 1952.

Pounds, N. J. G., *The Economic Pattern of Modern Germany,* London, 1963.

Price, Harry Bayard, *The Marshall Plan and its Meaning,* Ithaca, N.Y., 1955.

Reuss, Frederick G., *Fiscal Policy for Growth Without Inflation: The German Experiment,* Baltimore, 1963.

Roskamp, Karl W., *Capital Formation in West Germany,* Detroit, 1965.

Sachverständigenrat zur Begutachtung der gesamtwirtschaftlichen Entwicklung, *Stabiles Geld—Stetiges Wachstum; Jahresgutachten 1964–65,* Stuttgart and Mainz, 1965.

Spiro, Herbert J., *The Politics of German Codetermination,* Cambridge, Mass., 1958.

Untersuchungen zum deutschen Vertriebenen- und Flüchtlingsproblem, "Schriften des Vereins für Socialpolitik," Neue Folge, vols. VI and VII (herausgegeben von Bernhard Pfister), Berlin, 1954–62.

Die Vertriebenen in Westdeutschland (herausgegeben von Lemberg-Edding), 3 vols., Kiel, 1959.

Vogt, Winfried, *Makroökonomische Bestimmungsgründe des wirtschaftlichen Wachstums der Bundesrepublik Deutschland von 1950 bis 1960,* Tübingen, 1964.

Wallich, Henry C., *Mainsprings of the German Revival,* New Haven, Conn., 1955.

Wandlungen der Wirtschaftsstruktur in der Bundesrepublik Deutschland, "Schriften des Vereins für Socialpolitik," Neue Folge, vol. XXVI (herausgegeben von Heinz König), Berlin, 1962.

Wirtschaft ohne Wunder; volkswirtschaftliche Studien (herausgegeben von Albert Hunold), Erlenbach and Zürich, 1953.

C. SOVIET ZONE AND THE LOST TERRITORIES

Boettcher, Bodo, *Industrielle Strukturwandlungen im sowjetisch-besetzten Gebiet Deutschlands,* Berlin, 1956.

Das Finanzsystem der DDR (Authors' Collective), Berlin, 1962.

Gleitze, Bruno, *Ostdeutsche Wirtschaft,* Berlin, 1962.

———, *Die Industrie der Sowjetzone unter dem gescheiterten Siebenjahrplan,* Berlin, 1964.

Hoffmann, Emil, *Comecon; der gemeinsame Markt in Osteuropa,* Opladen, 1961.

Horn, Werner, *Die Errichtung der Grundlagen des Sozialismus in der Industrie der DDR 1951–1955,* Berlin, 1963.

Huebbenet, Georg von, *Die rote Wirtschaft wächst; Aufbau und Entwicklungsziele des Comecon,* Düsseldorf, 1960.

Köhler, Heinz, *Economic Integration in the Soviet Bloc, with an East German Case Study,* New York, 1966.

Krause, Heinz, *Economic Structure of East Germany and Its Position Within the Soviet Bloc* (Council of Economic and Industrial Research), Washington, D.C., parts I and II (forthcoming).

Ökonomik in der DDR (Authors' Collective), 2nd ed., Berlin, 1963.

Pritzel, Konstantin, *Die wirtschaftliche Integration der sowjetischen Besatzungszone Deutschlands in den Ostblock und ihre politischen Aspekte* ("Bonner Berichte aus Mittel- und Ostdeutschland"), Bonn, 1962.

Roustang, Guy, *Développement économique de l'Allemagne Orientale,* Paris, 1963.

Schenk, Fritz, *Magie der Planwirtschaft,* Köln and Berlin, 1960.

Seidel, Gerhard, ed., *Die Landwirtschaft der Deutschen Demokratischen Republik,* Berlin, 1961.

Stolper, Wolfgang F., with the assistance of Karl W. Roskamp, *The Structure of the East German Economy,* Cambridge, Mass., 1960.

Zauberman, Alfred, *Industrial Progress in Poland, Czechoslovakia, and East Germany: 1937–1962,* London and New York, 1964.

d. COMPARISON OF THE ZONES AND INTERZONAL TRADE

Bosch, Werner, *Marktwirtschaft—Befehlswirtschaft; ein Vergleich der Wirtschaftsordnungen in West- und Mitteldeutschland,* Heidelberg, 1960.

Holbik, Karel, and Henry Myers, *Postwar Trade in Divided Germany,* Baltimore, 1964.

Stolper, Wolfgang F., *Germany Between East and West* (National Planning Association), Washington, D.C., 1960.

INDEX

A 6
B 7
C 8
D 9
E 0
F 1
G 2
H 3
I 4
J 5